LAW FOR NURSE LEADERS
A COMPREHENSIVE REFERENCE

Paula DiMeo Grant, RN, BSN, MA, JD, is a nurse attorney admitted to practice law in the District of Columbia and currently is in private practice. Her experience includes litigation and mediation. Since 1991, she has served as a mediator for the Superior Court of the District of Columbia primarily mediating medical malpractice and personal injury cases. From 1998 to 2004, she served as Of Counsel to the law firm of Ross & Hardies and its successor McGuireWoods LLP. Ms. Grant, a registered nurse, received her BSN from Boston College and an MA in nursing education from New York University. She has developed legal nurse consulting programs and has lectured on nursing and the law. She has also published on the subject. She is a member of Sigma Theta Tau International and is past president of The American Association of Nurse Attorneys Foundation.

Diana C. Ballard, RN, MBA, JD, is an experienced health care executive, health care attorney, and business owner. She has served in hospital executive management as chief nursing officer, vice president, and chief compliance officer.

She is owner of a consulting firm offering services in business and program development, health care and health systems management, and customer service training. She was Of Counsel to the law firm of Susman, Duffy & Segaloff, P.C., of New Haven, CT, for 15 years, practicing in all aspects of health law. She has held adjunct faculty appointments at the University of Connecticut, Adelphi University, Yale University School of Nursing, and the University of New Haven, among others, and has taught and published extensively in health care and health law subjects. She has wide experience as a public spokesperson, keynote speaker, seminar leader, and broadcast media guest, including appearances on a televised weekly health series. She is the creator of CarePower®, a self-improvement approach to developing excelence in customer service. A Pace University Law School-educated attorney and a registered professional nurse, Ms. Ballard holds a BS degree in Psychology and an MBA.

UNIVERSITY OF BRADFORD
MAKING KNOWLEDGE WORK™

HEALTH STUDIES LIBRARY

Law for Nurse Leaders
A Comprehensive Reference

Editors

Paula DiMeo Grant, RN, BSN, MA, JD
Diana C. Ballard, RN, MBA, JD

SPRINGER PUBLISHING COMPANY
NEW YORK

Springer Publishing Company, LLC
11 West 42nd Street
New York, NY 10036
www.springerpub.com

Acquisitions Editor: Allan Graubard
Senior Production Editor: Diane Davis
Cover Design: Joseph DePinho
Composition: Newgen Imaging

ISBN: 978-0-8261-2452-4
E-book ISBN: 978-0-8261-2453-1

11 12 13 14/ 5 4 3 2 1

The author and the publisher of this Work have made every effort to use sources believed to be reliable to provide information that is accurate and compatible with the standards generally accepted at the time of publication. Because medical science is continually advancing, our knowledge base continues to expand. Therefore, as new information becomes available, changes in procedures become necessary. We recommend that the reader always consult current research and specific institutional policies before performing any clinical procedure. The author and publisher shall not be liable for any special, consequential, or exemplary damages resulting, in whole or in part, from the readers' use of, or reliance on, the information contained in this book. The publisher has no responsibility for the persistence or accuracy of URLs for external or third-party Internet Web sites referred to in this publication and does not guarantee that any content on such Web sites is, or will remain, accurate or appropriate.

Library of Congress Cataloging-in-Publication Data
Law for nurse leaders : a comprehensive reference / [edited by] Paula DiMeo Grant, RN BSN MA JD, Diana C. Ballard, RN MBA JD.
     p.
   Includes bibliographical references and index.
   ISBN 978-0-8261-2452-4 — ISBN 978-0-8261-2453-1 (e-book)
   1. Nursing—Law and legislation—United States—Outlines, syllabi, etc.
I. Grant, Paula DiMeo. II. Ballard, Diana (Nurse attorney)
   KF2915.N8L33 2011
   344.7304'14—dc22   2010052708

Printed in the United States of America by Bang Printing.

When you're a nurse you know that every day you will touch a life or a life will touch yours.

—Author Unknown

We dedicate this book to all nurses.

Contents

CONTRIBUTORS

Diana C. Ballard, RN, MBA, JD
Pompano Beach, Florida

Donna-Marie Boulay, RN, JD, MANM
Roseville, Minnesota

Edie Brous, RN, MS, MPH, Esquire
New York, New York

Valerie Burger, RN, MA, MS, OCN®
Good Samaritan Hospital Medical Center, West Islip, New York

Paula DiMeo Grant, RN, BSN, MA, JD
Washington, DC

Shellie Karno, RN, BS, JD
Lowis & Gellen, LLP, Chicago, Illinois

Pamela D. Miller, RN, BSN, JD, CPHRM
St. Vincent's Medical Center, Bridgeport, Connecticut

Michelle Mitchell-Stoddard, MS, JD
North Broward Health District, Fort Lauderdale, Florida

Liston E. Radney, III, Esquire
Boca Raton, Florida

Neil J. Reardon, Esquire
Hampstead, New Hampshire

John J. Vecchione, Esquire
Valad & Vecchione, PLLC, Fairfax, Virginia

PREFACE

It is no secret that health care has become one of the most complex areas of our society. This is true regardless of the area of health care you might be associated with. Many factors have influenced its growth and intricacy, including, among others, technology advances, pharmaceutical development, advances in medical and surgical technique, new treatment modalities, information technologies, the financial framework, and of course, the role of health care's perpetually prominent caregivers, nurses!

Complex environments often lead to the need for refined and highly discerned decision making. This usually calls for knowledge of the law in order to guide the direction of the decisions and the ability to see impacts and implications that can be legally analyzed before a decision is final. These factors improve the quality of decision making and make for more successful outcomes.

This is true for nurses as well. The practice of professional nursing continues to grow in sophistication. Whether you are a nurse practicing in a clinical area, a nurse manager or administrator, or a nurse consultant, the need for legal knowledge is vital.

All nurses are leaders. Whether leading the nursing team, leading hospital nursing care as chief nursing officers, leading the education of others in nursing and in health care, or leading hospitals as chief executive officers and chief operating officers, nurses have leadership responsibilities. Nurses in such positions are faced every day with a myriad of complex decisions and not always in a serene environment where one has time to contemplate quietly!

Therefore, all nurses and indeed many outside the nursing profession will welcome this book. The editors and authors of this text caution that the information provided does not constitute legal advice, as only retained counsel with full knowledge of any specific situation can provide such representation. However, this book takes complex topics and legal theories, explains them in no-nonsense, understandable language, and makes them relevant to the current world in which nurses practice their profession. In other words, this is knowledge and information that nurses will find practical and useful!

Nursing is such a wonderful profession, and nurses have many choices as to where their profession will take them in the world of health care. For the editors and authors of this fine text, that world has included the practice of health care law. The editors have brought together a skilled team that truly understands health care, nursing, and the law. The result is this thorough and convenient reference that nurses will find indispensable.

Paula DiMeo Grant, RN, BSN, MA, JD
Diana C. Ballard, RN, MBA, JD

ACKNOWLEDGMENTS

Many people helped to make this book a reality and we are most grateful.

We thank Springer Publishing Company for always being supportive of the nursing profession and bringing to nurses excellent material to help them do their vital work. We are proud that they are the publisher of our book.

Allan Graubard, Executive Editor at Springer, has been an invaluable resource. We have learned from him, and the excellence of his feedback has made us better authors and editors. Elizabeth Stump, Assistant Editor at Springer, has helped us to keep the project organized and on track. She was wonderful to work with and always on top of every detail. Thanks to Diane Davis, Senior Production Editor, and her team who so capably led us to the finish line!

We are deeply grateful to our contributors who worked diligently and never wavered in their commitment to this book. Thank you for your dedication and hard work.

We are indebted to our friends and colleagues, and to our families, who were always ready to assist in so many ways while this book was being written. Their support and encouragement was so deeply appreciated as we were working on this project. To our husbands who were patient and supportive beyond description. To Paula's husband, Dr. James Grant; and to Diana's husband, John Capone, a recent author himself who understood the dedication and time requirements needed to complete a book project. Ms. Grant gratefully acknowledges the contributions of Kathleen Emily Reardon, Legal Assistant, and Tanya Allen, Paralegal. Ms. Grant remembers and recognizes with love and gratitude her late parents, Samuel and Emilie DiMeo, and will be forever grateful to them for inspiring her to continually strive for achievement and excellence.

When undertaking a major project such as this, the ability of editors to work together is the foundation of the success of the task. We are indebted to each other for the mutual consideration, kindness, friendship, and respect that made it possible to bring this book to reality.

INTRODUCTION

The practice of nursing is both art and science. It requires a broad range of skills and capabilities. Nurses can choose from a number of areas and levels of practice, and the demands of the profession are matched only by the rewards. Nurses are the heart of caring in health care.

It is our belief that in practicing the profession, nurses should focus on just that—the practice of the profession of nursing. However, as highly educated and skilled professionals, nurses are faced with decisions that require the application of judgment to complex situations. We wrote this book to assist nurses in this process through the availability of this convenient and comprehensive reference that will enhance their ability to make considered decisions through the acquisition of information.

This book is, therefore, written by nurses for nurses. Each chapter is authored or coauthored by a nurse attorney. The following is an overview of what is included in the book and key information regarding the approaches and tools used throughout the book to enhance the reader's experience.

A few general notes on the use of legal cases. To the extent possible, we have tried to follow a similar format in presenting the legal cases, by noting the case citation, statement of the subject matter of the case, a fact summary or court discussion about the case, and the holding or court decision. While the formats are not identical in every case, we have tried to use this logical flow to make the cases illustrate the important points. Chapter Five contains case studies, which are fictional examples of the types of situations that arise and are drawn from an aggregate of the education and experiences of the chapter author.

Each chapter begins with a statement of objectives, which will make the reading of the chapter most meaningful. There is a Key Points feature in each chapter, pointing out, in brief statement, the essential elements that have been presented. In addition, each chapter ends with a Conclusions and Trends section, to briefly summarize the material included in the chapter and offer a forward looking perspective for nurses to consider in future planning. A chapter by chapter review follows next.

Chapter One presents an overview of law relevant to nurses' interests, including basic legal principles that underlie and form the framework for the practice of nursing. In addition, the regulatory law issues such as licensure, professional standards, the administrative law process, and insurance considerations are discussed.

Chapter Two covers the law of corporations and provides information on the types of business structures that can be used for health care business and facility operations. Nurses will find this helpful in understanding some of the corporate issues of the entities they are affiliated with, and perhaps also in how to go about selecting and establishing an entity for conducting their own business. The Doctrine of Corporate Liability, discussing a corporation's liability for health care actions, is also included.

Chapter Three addresses the relatively new and developing area of corporate compliance and the nurses' role in regard to it. Nurses will learn the history of the establishment of the Medicare program and the development of the field of corporate compliance. This is an evolving area and it is important for nurses to become familiar with the key laws and issues of compliance. Nursing documentation, for example, can assist a compliance investigation looking into the care and services provided to a patient. We believe that nursing's role in matters of corporate compliance will increase in the future.

Chapter Four provides comprehensive information on employment and employment related law. The chapter begins with Attorney John Vecchione's material on anti-discrimination law. Attorney Paula DiMeo Grant addresses issues of employment contracts, types of employment, and the employer–employee relationship. Nurses will benefit from knowing employee and employer rights and responsibilities in the workplace.

In Chapter Five, risk management and continuing quality improvement are covered—emphasizing that risk management is paramount to patient safety. Nurses will learn what the essentials of a hospital risk management program consist of, will identify the relevant legal, policy, and procedural framework of the program and how the organization's risk management activities are monitored by accreditation bodies, law, and administrative agencies.

In this chapter, case studies are used to illustrate key points and concepts. Case studies are fictional situations drawn from an aggregation of typical occurrences in the health care environment. While they are not actual cases, the situations are of the types that are actually encountered in the real world.

Chapter Six is devoted to nurses' documentation responsibilities and practice. The chapter begins with Attorney Edie Brou's presentation of the fundamentals and principles of documentation. Attorney Donna-Marie Boulay and nursing consultant Valerie Burger then discuss systems of documentation, including electronic systems. The chapter contains numerous legal cases, and as we have tried to do as much as possible throughout the book, the legal cases are presented in similar—although not identical—format, so that the reader can readily discern what the case is about and what the court discussed and decided. Documentation always has been and continues to be a key area for legal analysis.

Patient rights are the subject of Chapter Seven. The legal focus is informed consent and the patient's right of self determination—that is, to determine what shall be done to one's person. Patient rights with regard to care, decision making, and privacy issues will be covered in this chapter. With permission from "Aging with Dignity," the excellent Five Wishes Living Will is included. Nurses will benefit from becoming familiar with this tool that can assist people with end of life decision making.

Chapter Eight is about nursing malpractice and negligence. Nurses reading this chapter will learn the elements necessary to prove whether malpractice has occurred. The chapter will include the defenses to a malpractice action. Areas of high risk are identified. Case examples will be used to illustrate the legal points.

The title of Chapter Nine is "Anatomy of a Trial." The focus is on *both civil and criminal trials.* Attorney Paula DiMeo Grant explains how the civil trial process works from initiation of a law suit through discovery, trial and verdict, and appeal. Taking and defending depositions will be discussed as well as how a trial is conducted, including the role of the expert nurse witness. Attorney Neil J. Reardon presents the criminal process from investigation to trial and explains the process of a criminal trial. Felony and misdemeanor charges and plea bargaining is also included. Since most nurses now undergo criminal background checks for licensure or admission to a clinical program, the potential effects of a criminal charge against a licensed professional nurse is explained.

Chapter Ten discusses alternate methods of dispute resolution. Alternative methods included are arbitration, mediation, and negotiation, and there is explanation of each method detailing advantages and inherent problems of each. The emphasis is on negotiation and mediation, including principles and practice. This is an important and relatively new area for nurses as the process of mediation expands to the health care arena.

As nurse attorneys, we get asked a lot of questions. Some questions are asked repeatedly, and the "Ask the Nurse Attorney" feature presents some of those frequently asked questions which are then analyzed and responded to by nurse attorneys. We note that as with this entire text, the material presented in this section does not constitute legal advice, as each situation requires detailed analysis and review by counsel. However, the responses are of a general nature and will help nurses identify the key aspects to consider when contemplating the questions.

We are confident that nurses will find this reference book to be a practical, understandable, and frequently used tool.

LAW FOR NURSE LEADERS
A COMPREHENSIVE REFERENCE

CHAPTER ONE

THE NURSE AND THE LAW: A PRIMER

Paula DiMeo Grant

OBJECTIVES

- Describe Nightingale's influence on nursing education and practice.
- Discuss the purpose of the Nurse Practice Act (NPA).
- Explain the Nurse Licensure Compact (NLC).
- Describe the three branches of government and the relationship to nursing and the law.
- Identify the four primary sources of law.
- Describe the powers and duties of the Board of Nursing.
- Describe the nursing licensure disciplinary process.

INTRODUCTION

This chapter will provide an overview of nursing and the law, including important milestones. It begins with an historical perspective of nursing, including Florence Nightingale's influence on nursing education and practice. The purpose of the Nurse Practice Act (NPA) will be examined and key ethical concepts relating to nursing practice will be discussed. The Nurse Licensure Compact (NLC) was formed to facilitate nursing practice across state lines and those states belonging to the compact are identified. State boards of nursing regulatory authority and the nursing disciplinary process will also be discussed. Specific examples of statutory and case law will be utilized. An explanation of how the three branches of government relate to nursing and the law will be given, and the primary sources of law will be identified. Readers will be able to appreciate and understand the interrelatedness of law and nursing and its effects on nursing practice that are complex.

1

HISTORICAL PERSPECTIVE

Florence Nightingale Pledge

I solemnly pledge myself before God and in the presence of this assembly, to pass my life in purity and to practice my profession faithfully. I will abstain from whatever is deleterious and mischievous, and will not take or knowingly administer any harmful drug. I will do all in my powers to maintain and elevate the standard of my profession, and will hold in confidence all personal matters committed to my keeping and all family affairs coming to my knowledge in the practice of my calling. With loyalty I will endeavor to aid the physician in his work, and devote myself to the welfare of those committed to my care (Florence Nightingale Pledge, American Nurses Association [ANA], 2010).

This pledge, first written in 1893, includes many of today's legal and ethical aspects of nursing and describes the beginnings of the interrelationship between law and nursing. It was named the Florence Nightingale Pledge as a token of esteem for the founder of modern nursing.

Florence Nightingale was born in Florence, Italy, to privilege and wealth in 1810, and she died in 1910 in London, United Kingdom, leaving a lasting and impressive legacy. She overcame opposition by her family to become a nurse and care for soldiers during the Crimean War in Turkey. Following the end of the war in 1856, and largely through her efforts, the hospitals were well run and mortality rates had decreased (BBC, 2010). According to Rehmeyer (2008) as described below, it was Nightingale's later work that is far less known and saved many more lives. How she influenced health care reform is illustrated below in her presentation of statistics.

Nightingale's Coxcomb: A Campaign for Health Care Reform

Upon returning to England after the Crimean War, Nightingale began a campaign for health care reform. This was based, in part, on her concern about the number of deaths that were caused by hospital-acquired conditions. In order for sweeping changes in health care to be implemented, she had to first persuade the Queen of England.

Her evidence-based research and statistics formed the basis of a report to be presented to the queen. As part of this presentation, she used a graphic known as a "coxcomb" to illustrate the number and causes of death each month during the war. A "coxcomb" is a variation of the familiar modern pie graph (Reymeyer, 2008, p. 2).

Apparently, this presentation using the coxcomb was a major factor in convincing the queen that health care reform was necessary. Nightingale successfully and cleverly used statistics to prove her point. Indeed, the founder of nursing was also "The Passionate Statistician," as she was referred to in Rehmeyer's article. Her work in reforming health care showed Nightingale's tremendous intellect, capabilities, and her ability to persuade by critical thinking and evidence-based practice that is currently part of nursing curricula and widely practiced by professional nurses. Her work remains an important milestone in nursing's history.

Nightingale's Influence on Nursing Education and Practice

There is little or no doubt that Florence Nightingale had an enormous impact on the profession of nursing as evidenced in 1860 when she successfully formed the "Nightingale Training School for Nurses." It was the first of its kind to train individuals to become qualified nurses to teach and administer patient care in hospitals in England and around the world. Graduates of this program were highly sought after (*World History of Nursing*, 2010).

Florence Nightingale's nursing theory of disease as a reparative process and the importance of environmental basics such as pure air, clean water, proper ventilation, cleanliness, and proper nutrition are as relevant today as they were in the 1800s. She emphasized the importance of patient confidentiality and accurate patient observation (Nightingale, 1860). Although the definitions of nursing have been expanded over the years, the basic tenets of nursing, as defined by Nightingale, remain the same.

Table 1.1 presents milestones in nursing and the law, and though this list is by no means exhaustive, it shows the historical progress and development of nursing and its relationship to law. A discussion of some of these important milestones will follow.

NURSING: PAST AND PRESENT

Nursing Education

In the United States, the Bellevue Hospital School of Nursing in New York City was one of the first nursing programs developed on the basis

Table 1.1 Nursing and the Law: Milestones

1859: Nightingale's publication of Notes on Nursing: What it is and what it is not

1860: Nightingale's Training School for Nurses was founded in England

1873: Formal training for nurses begins in the United States with schools in New York, Connecticut, and Boston

1893: Formation of the American Society of Superintendents of Training Schools for Nurses now known as National League for Nurses (NLN)

1896: An association of nurses was formed that later became the American Nurses Association (ANA)

1903: The first Nurse Practice Act was passed by the state of North Carolina on March 3, with New York and Virginia following suit

1923: All 48 states have legislation regulating nursing practice

1929: First nurse attorney, Mary Eleanor McGarvah, graduated from the University of Detroit with a law degree

1931: Jurisprudence for Nurses is published: Mary Eleanor McGarvah, first nurse attorney, is one of its authors

1950: Code for Professional, a revision of the "Tentative Code" was unanimously accepted by the ANA's House of Delegates

1960: Code for Professional Nurses was revised

1968: Code for Professional Nurses was again revised

1973: ANA published its first Standards of Nursing Practice

1976: ANA published Code for Nurses with Interpretive Statements

1978: National Council of State Boards of Nursing was formed (NCSBN)

1980: ANA published Nursing: Social Policy Statement

1982: The American Association of Nurse Attorneys, Inc. (TAANA) was founded by Cynthia Ellen Northrop, RN, MS, JD

1984: *Adkins v. Annapolis Hospital*, 420 MICH. 87 (March 1984). Registered Nurses were now subject to the professional malpractice standard of 2-year statute of limitations instead of the longer one.

1987: ANA published *The Scope of Nursing Practice*

1989: American Association of Legal Nurse Consultants (AALNC) was founded

1989: TAANA's first group admission to the United States Supreme Court: Movant, TAANA past president Mary Elizabeth Kelly, RN, BSN, JD

1991: ANA published Standards of Clinical Nursing Practice

1992: AALNC adopted A Code of Ethics and Conduct with Interpretive Discussion for Legal Nurse Consultants

1995: ANA published Scope and Standards of Advanced Practice Registered Nursing

1998: TAANA's papers archived at Boston College: Nursing, Law and Ethics Collection dedicated to the memory of Cynthia Ellen Northrop, TAANA's founder

2001: ANA published Bill of Rights for Registered Nurses

(Continued)

Table 1.1 Nursing and the Law: Milestones *(Continued)*

2003: ANA published Nursing: Scope and Standards of Practice
2003: ANA published Nursing's Social Policy Statement, 2nd edition
2004: *Sullivan v. Edward Hospital* 806 N.E. 2d 654 (Ill 2004): Physician was not qualified as an expert witness to testify regarding nursing standard of care
2008: Nursing Jurisprudence Examination required for nursing licensure in Texas

Source: ANA, 2003; Northrop & Kelly, 1987; North Carolina Nurses: A Century of Caring 2010; Texas BON, 2010.

of principles of nursing established by Florence Nightingale. The 3-year diploma school operated at Bellevue Hospital from 1873 until its closure in 1969. The Johns Hopkins School of Nursing also designed its program on the basis of Florence Nightingale's concepts and opened in 1889; the program is still in operation as the Johns Hopkins University School of Nursing.

Basic nursing education in the United States has shifted from the original hospital-based 3-year diploma school programs to the college-based 2-year associate degree programs and the 4-year bachelor's degree programs for entry into the practice of nursing. There are also programs known as nursing as a second degree for graduates, the first degree in a field other than nursing. Students graduating from any of these programs are qualified to take the National Council Licensure Examination (NCLEX) to become a registered nurse (RN).

Although there has been controversy among nurse leaders as to the best program to prepare nurses for the entry level, there is consensus among nurse leaders and educators that the best preparation for entry into nursing practice is the 4-year bachelor's degree.

Nursing Defined

In 1980, the ANA, in its *Nursing: A Social Policy Statement*, defined nursing as "the diagnosis and treatment of human responses to actual or potential health problems" (ANA, 2003, p. 69).

Since the 1980s, and according to the ANA, the definitions of nursing have included essential characteristics of contemporary nursing practice. These four essential characteristics are as follows:

1. Attention to the full range of human experiences and responses to health and illness without restriction to a problem-focused orientation,

2. The integration of objective and subjective data using knowledge gained from an understanding of the patient or group's experiences,
3. Application of scientific knowledge to the processes of diagnosis and treatment, and
4. Provision of a caring relationship that facilitates health and healing (ANA, 2003, p. 69).

To meet the challenges of the health care delivery system and the progress of nursing, a broader definition of nursing was necessary. Thus, the ANA defined nursing as "the protection, promotion and optimization of health and abilities, prevention of illness and injury, alleviation of suffering through the diagnosis and treatment of human response, and advocacy in the care of individuals, families, communities and populations" (ANA, 2003, p. 6).

This broader definition of nursing is consistent with professional nursing's commitment to providing optimal health care across the life span and in a variety of settings. Nursing has a broad reach as it influences the organizational, societal, economic, legal, and political factors within the health care system with implications that affect cost, access, and quality of health care (ANA, 2003). Throughout this textbook, you will examine the legal aspects of nursing and its impact and influence on the health care delivery system beginning with the NPA.

Nurse Practice Act

In 1903, the first Nurse Practice Act (NPA) was passed by the legislature in the state of North Carolina. The NPA defines the scope of nursing practice and contains the legal parameters of practice; each state has its own NPA. The states of New York and Virginia followed North Carolina and passed laws regulating the practice of nursing. And by 1923, 48 states had legislation regulating nursing practice (N.C., 2010).

In addition to the NPAs, rules and regulations promulgated by the boards of nursing and nursing organizations also regulate nursing practice by setting forth educational and licensing requirements. The major goal of nursing licensure is to protect citizens of each state from the unlawful practice of nursing. All nurses should know and understand the NPA in the state where they practice.

It is also important for nurses to stay current on any amendments to the NPA. Courts may look to the NPA for guidance in deciding medical malpractice cases or practice issues as it did in the *Sermchief v. Gonzalez* (1983) case discussed in this chapter.

Accountability remains one of the hallmarks of nursing, and nurses will be held accountable for their actions while delivering patient care; therefore, all nurses must remain vigilant to the NPA and other laws, rules, and regulations that govern nursing practice.

Nurse Licensure Compact States: Registered Nurses and Licensed Practical Nurses

The NLC was formed as a mechanism for mutual recognition of registered nurses (RNs) and licensed practical nurses (LPNs). It facilitates the practice of nursing across state lines without additional licensure. Table 1.2 identifies those states that are part of the NLC.

This compact should not be confused with reciprocity. NLC, unlike reciprocity, does not require an additional license to practice nursing in the member states. Reciprocity does, however, require the nurse to obtain a license to practice nursing. In most states, this process is also referred to as "nursing by endorsement."

Should you have any questions regarding nursing licensure mechanisms, contact your state Board of Nursing for additional information. You may access the state boards of nursing in all 50 states and the District of Columbia and other U.S. territories by logging on to the National Council of State Boards of Nursing's (NCSBN) Website (https://www.nsbn.org/index.htm).

Advanced Practice Registered Nurse Compact

The Advanced Practice Registered Nurse Compact (APRN) was developed in 2000 by NCSBN in conjunction with the advanced practice nurses. However, it has not been implemented and there is no anticipated date of implementation at this time. The APRN Compact addresses the need to promote consistent quality of care delivered by advanced practice nurses within states and across state lines (NCSBN, 2010).

This compact is similar to the NLC in that it would allow states to mutually recognize the APRN licensed in another state. There is an important caveat: If a state decides to adopt the APRN Compact, it must have adopted the NLC. To date, only the states of Utah, Iowa, and Texas have passed laws authorizing the APRN Compact (NCSBN, 2010).

Table 1.2 Nurse Licensure Compact States

State	Date of Entry Into NLC
1. Arizona	7/01/2002
2. Arkansas	7/01/2000
3. Colorado	10/1/2007
4. Delaware	7/1/2000
5. Idaho	7/1/2001
6. Iowa	7/1/2000
7. Kentucky	6/1/2007
8. Maine	7/1/2001
9. Maryland	7/1/1999
10. Mississippi	7/1/2001
11. Nebraska	1/1/2000
12. New Hampshire	1/1/2006
13. New Mexico	1/1/2004
14. North Carolina	7/1/2000
15. North Dakota	1/1/2004
16. Rhode Island	7/1/2008
17. South Carolina	2/1/2006
18. South Dakota	1/1/2001
19. Tennessee	7/1/2003
20. Texas	1/1/2000
21. Utah	1/1/2000
22. Virginia	1/1/2005
23. Wisconsin	1/1/2000

Note. Pending: Missouri 1/20/10 (NCSBN, 2010). Reprinted with permission from the National Council of State Boards of Nursing, Inc. (NCSBN ®.)

For additional NLC information, you may contact your state Board of Nursing or the NSCBN.

Regulatory Authority for Advanced Practice Nurses

State NPAs along with the states' boards of nursing regulate and define the scope of nursing practice including the legal boundaries, for advanced practice nurses. There are also state laws and regulations that provide the parameters of practice for nurse practitioners who enter into collaborative agreements with physicians. Nurse practitioners should be cognizant of the state laws and regulations regarding their practice.

Key Concepts in Ethics and Nursing Practice

Whereas the state NPAs set forth the legal scope of nursing practice, it is the Code of Ethics for Nurses with Interpretive Statements published by the ANA (2001) that defines the ethical parameters for the practice of nursing. The key concepts in ethics are set forth below:

1. *Autonomy:* The ethical concept of individual autonomy; that is, the right of an individual to make decisions regarding his or her life and medical care is the basic principle underlying patients' rights. This principle was articulated as far back as 1914 by Justice Cardozo in the landmark case of *Schloendorff vs. Society of New York Hospital* (1914), when he said: "Every human being of adult years and sound mind has a right to determine what shall be done with his own body" (p. 94).
2. *Justice:* The ethical concept of justice is based on fairness to all people. It is expanded into "distributive justice"; the term implies equal access to health care for all regardless of race, sex, marital status, medical diagnosis, and economic and social standing.
3. *Fidelity:* The concept of fidelity is an individual's obligation to be faithful to commitments made to self and to others. In the health care setting, fidelity includes the professional's faithfulness or loyalty to agreements and responsibilities accepted as part of the profession. It also includes the concept of accountability. For example, you may be asked to work an additional weekend because of staffing problems, and you carry out that responsibility to remain faithful to your commitment.
4. *Beneficence:* The ethical concept of beneficence is your obligation to do good for patients under your care. In doing good for patients under your care you take into consideration not only the patient's personal beliefs, feelings, and wishes but also that of his or her family and significant others in his or her life. It can be a challenge to determine what is good under certain circumstances and who can best make that decision.
5. *Nonmaleficence:* The ethical concept of nonmaleficence is to do no harm either intentionally or unintentionally. It also means to protect from harm those who cannot protect themselves, such as children and the elderly. States have passed statutory laws regarding the protection of children and the elderly that give rise not only to a moral or ethical obligation but also a legal obligation.

6. *Negligence or malpractice:* Negligence or malpractice is unintentional harm caused by the commission or omission of an act. For example, in *Norton v. Argonaunt* (1964), the director of nursing unintentionally administered to an infant a wrong dose of Digoxin, and by the wrong route; this act resulted in the infant's death. In this case, even though the outcome was tragic, it does present an example of nursing negligence caused by an unintentional act. Additional information on malpractice can be found in Chapter 8.

7. *Veracity:* The ethical concept of veracity includes the patient's right to know truthful information. Health care providers are not to deceive or mislead patients. There may, however, be limitations if it is determined that the information revealed may distress or harm the patient. An ethical dilemma, such as this, is best addressed by the patient's family, health care providers, and other team members. The process of mediation is sometimes used for the resolution of these dilemmas. For more information on mediation, please refer to the Chapter 10.

8. *Best interests:* This ethical concept takes into consideration what the individual has expressed: either formally in a living will, durable power of attorney, or informally to family members or significant others about the care they wish to receive in the event they are unable to make the determination for themselves. We have witnessed the difficulties presented in the notable right-to-life cases, including the following: Karen Ann Quinlan, Nancy Cruzan, and Terri Schiavo matters. Additional information on these cases is provided in Chapter 7. Nurses play a pivotal role in collaboration with other health care professionals when end-of-life decisions are made for the patients and ethical dilemmas are presented. The Code of Ethics for Nurses, along with a recent ANA publication titled *Guide to the Code of Ethics for Nurses: Interpretation and Application* (2008), addresses the application of ethical principles that form the framework for nurses responding to ethical dilemmas.

Nurses' Obligations

Inherent in the key concepts of ethics as described previously is the nurses' obligation in the application of those concepts to specific situations. An obligation as defined by *Black's Law Dictionary* (1979) is derived from the Latin substantive "obligatio," a term that has wide and varied meanings depending on the context in which it is used. In other words, it refers to an act that a person is bound to do or not to do. Obligations fall into two categories: legal and moral.

1. Legal obligations are those obligations that have become formal statements of law and are enforceable by law, and
2. Moral obligations are those obligations that are based on moral or ethical principles but are not enforceable under the law.

The ANA adopted a Code of Ethics for Nurses with Interpretive Statements for Nurses in 2001. Accordingly, the Code of Ethics serves the following purposes:

1. It is a statement of ethical obligations of nurses in carrying out their duties,
2. Those obligations are nonnegotiable, and
3. It expresses nursing's commitment to society as a whole (ANA, 2005).

Today's nurse is confronted with the ever-changing landscape of the health care delivery system and the challenges faced in delivering optimum health care. Although in many instances the code is in harmony with the law, often times it does exceed the law. The Code of Ethics nine provisions are listed below:

ANA Code of Ethics for Nurses: Nine Provisions

1. The nurse, in all professional relationships, practices with compassion and respect for the inherent dignity worth, and uniqueness of every individual, unrestricted by considerations of social or economic status, personal attributes, or the nature of health problems.
2. The nurse's primary commitment is to the patient, whether an individual, family, group, or community.
3. The nurse promotes, advocates for, and strives to protect the health, safety, and rights of the patient.
4. The nurse is responsible and accountable for individual nursing practice and determines the appropriate delegation of tasks consistent with the nurse's obligation to provide optimum patient care.
5. The nurse owes the same duties to self as to others, including the responsibility to preserve integrity and safety, maintain competence, and continue personal and professional growth.

6. The nurse participates in establishing, maintaining, and improving health care environments and conditions of employment conducive to the provision of quality health care and consistent with the values of the profession through individual and collective action.
7. The nurse participates in the advancement of the profession through contributions to practice, education, administration, and knowledge development.
8. The nurse collaborates with other health professionals and the public in promoting community, national, and international-level efforts to meet health needs.
9. The profession of nursing, as represented by associations and their members, is responsible for articulating nursing values, maintaining the integrity of the profession and its practice, and shaping social policy (ANA, 2001). (© 2001 By American Nurses Association. Reprinted with Permission. All rights reserved.)

Challenges Nurses Face

Nursing Shortage

The American Association of Colleges of Nursing (AACN) *Fact Sheet* (2010) states that the "U.S. is in the midst of a shortage of RNs that is expected to intensify as baby boomers age and the need for health care grows." This shortage is expected to grow to "260,000 RNs by 2025" (p. 1). Age is another contributing factor to the projected increase in the nursing shortage; for example, the average age of RNs as of 2004 was 46.8 years, which is expected to rise to 50 years or more in 2012 (AACN, 2009).

According to the AACN in 2008, nursing has turned away 49,948 qualified applicants from baccalaureate and graduate nursing programs, which is due not only to the insufficient number of nursing faculty but also to other shortcomings such as inadequate clinical sites, classroom space, clinical preceptors, and budgetary problems.

The U.S. Bureau of Labor Statistics (2009) further reports that the health care sector of the economy continues to grow despite the significant job losses in many of the other major industries.

Although the need for nurses continues to rise steadily, the number of RNs is growing at a rate slower than that seen in previous years. A national sample survey of RNs in 2004 reported that during the period 2000–2004 there was a total of 2,909,357 RNs—an increase of only 7.4% from the previous survey that was conducted during the period 1992–1996 that showed a 14.2% increase.

A high turnover of nurses in the workplace remains problematic. As cited in the AACN *Fact Sheet* (2010), Dr. Christine T. Kovner and colleagues found that 13% of newly licensed RNs had changed principal jobs after 1 year and 37% reported that they were ready to change jobs. This study was published in the *American Journal of Nursing* in an article titled "Newly Licensed RNs Characteristics, Work Attitudes and Intentions to Work." The nursing shortage remains an imperative that requires attention and specific strategies focusing on the delivery of safe patient care. This article may be found at http:www.ajnonline.com.

A 2007 report released by the PricewaterhouseCoopers' Health Research Institute found that the average voluntary turnover for first-year nurses was 27.1% (AACN, 2009). The nursing shortage continues to remain an impediment requiring attention and specific strategies for the delivery of safe patient care.

Delivery of Safe Patient Care

The delivery of safe patient is paramount, more so because the nursing shortage can adversely affect good treatment outcomes. Many recent studies point to the connection between adequacy (or lack thereof) in the number of RNs required and safe patient care (AACN, 2010, p. 4).

The *Fact Sheet* further explains that, according to Dr. Peter Buerhaus and associates, the majority of RNs (79%) and Chief Nursing Officers (68%) believe the nursing shortage is affecting the overall quality of patient care in hospitals and other settings, including long-term care facilities, ambulatory settings, and student health centers (see http://www.medscape.com/viewarticle/52560). Nursing leaders are very concerned and aware of the challenges to the delivery of optimum health care as the rapid changes in health care take place.

According to Sieg (2009), "Current conditions have created a critical time for nurse leaders to not only know what they know, but to know what they don't know" (p. 2).

Nurse leaders are working diligently to bring about the necessary changes to meet the critical demands of the present and the future. As a result of the changes in the health care, it has become increasingly important for nurses to understand the law and how it affects nursing practice. Significant change takes place with the passage of legislation affecting health care; consequently, it is important for nurses to have a working knowledge of the legislative process that will be discussed later in this chapter.

Understanding the legal framework regarding professional practice is vital to nursing practice. This knowledge is essential as the role of the nurse continues to evolve in the current health care environment, which seems to be in a constant state of flux.

LAW AND NURSING PRACTICE

What Is Law?

Law, according to *Black's Law Dictionary* (1979), is "that which is laid down, ordained, or established; a rule or method according to which phenomena or actions co-exist or follow each other. Law, in its generic sense, is a body of rules of action or conduct prescribed by controlling authority, and having binding legal force" (p. 795).

All citizens are subject to the law, and it must be obeyed and followed. If the law is not obeyed and followed, citizens will be subject to sanctions or legal consequences. "The term is also used in opposition to 'fact'. Thus, questions of law are to be decided by the court, while it is the province of the jury to resolve questions of fact" (*Black's Law Dictionary*, 1979, p. 796). Law falls into two major categories: civil law and criminal law.

Civil law is the body of law affecting the rights of the citizens of a state, whereas criminal law deals with crimes committed against the person or property with intent to harm. Each category will be referred to throughout this textbook.

Three Branches of Government

To have a better understanding of the legal process, it is necessary to review the three branches of government because each has a distinct role in forming the four sources of law that impacts nursing licensure and practice. The three branches of government consist of the legislative, executive, and judicial, and they are often referred to as the tripartite system of government.

Parallel systems exist on both the state and federal levels. The purpose of the tripartite system is the creation of checks and balances, giving each branch distinct powers and functions while guarding against overstepping of boundaries by any or all of these branches. This doctrine is known as the separation of powers. Nurses are probably most familiar with the legislative branch of government, the branch that is responsible for the NPAs that define and regulate nursing practice.

The Legislative Branch

The U.S. Constitution grants all legislative powers to Congress that consists of the Senate the House of Representatives. Some of the powers vested with the Senate are as follows: providing for the general welfare of the United States, establishing tribunals or courts that are inferior to the Supreme Court, and making all laws that are necessary and appropriate to execute the powers enumerated. The Constitution also imposes certain restrictions and limitations on Congressional powers. For example, the rights guaranteed to individuals under the Constitution also serve as limitations restricting the federal and state governments from taking certain actions against individuals. In particular, some of the best-known limitations include those enumerated in the Bill of Rights (the first 10 Amendments of the U.S. Constitution) that encompasses such rights as:

- freedom of speech,
- free exercise of religion,
- freedom of unreasonable search and seizures, and
- the right not to be deprived of life, liberty or property without due process of the law.

The legislative branch of the government requires a bill or resolution to be brought forth and passed by Congress. Certain legislation does have an impact on the delivery of health care and nursing practice; therefore, knowledge of the legislative process is an important aspect of nursing practice. The following is a synopsis of the legislative process.

The Legislative Process

Original Bill or Resolution

1. An original bill or resolution is studied by a specific committee of the Senate or House of Representatives, then either
   a. the bill or resolution dies without further action, or
   b. the bill or resolution is reported in original form or with recommended amendments, and the committee indicates approval or disapproval.

2. House of Representatives and Senate vote whether to pass and
   a. if it does not pass either the Senate or the House of Representatives, the bill or resolution dies in committee, or
   b. if it passes both the Senate and House of Representatives, the bill or resolution is submitted to the President of the United States.
3. President considers bill or resolution and either
   a. signs the bill or resolution, and it becomes law, or
   b. in the alternative, the president vetoes the bill or resolution.
4. The House of Representatives and Senate vote to override the vetoed bill or resolution and
   a. if bill or resolution fails to pass or override by a two-thirds vote, the bill or resolution does not become law.
   b. if bill or resolution passes by two-thirds vote of the Senate and the House of Representatives, the bill or resolution becomes law (Northrop & Kelly, 1987, p. 10).

Whereas the above example refers to the federal legislative process, the states have a similar process with the governor exercising veto power or signing the bill or resolution into law. An example of a recent federal statute passed by Congress and signed into law by President Barack Obama is "The Health Care and Education Affordability Reconciliation Act of 2010." The ANA in an effort to assist nurses to have a better understanding of the new act is providing nurses with online Health Care Reform Legislative Guides that will explain the provisions of the law with the effective dates (ANA, 2010).

The Executive Branch

The U.S. Constitution states that "the executive power shall be vested in a President of the United States of America. He shall hold his office during the term of four years." The president, before assuming the duties of the presidency takes the following oath of office: "I do solemnly swear (or affirm) that I will faithfully execute the office of President of the United States, and will to the best of my ability, preserve protect and defend the Constitution of the United States." The president also issues executive orders for the purpose of interpretation and implementation or giving effect to the Constitution or of some other law. The orders are published in the Federal Register.

Governors are granted similar powers on the state level. In exercising executive power, the governor of a state appoints members to the

Board of Nursing, to serve terms of office. The composition of the members of the board is set forth in the statute of each state. In addition to RNs, the board may include advance practice nurses, LPNs, licensed nursing assistants, and lay persons. The Board of Nursing sets forth the educational and licensure requirement for nurses and also monitors the practice of nursing through its powers to conduct hearings and take disciplinary action against nurses when warranted.

The Judicial Branch

In accordance with the U.S. Constitution, the judicial power is vested in one Supreme Court and lower courts. The judicial branch is responsible for the adjudication of cases and controversies by interpreting the law and applying the law to the specific facts of each case. The court system consists of state and federal trial courts, appellate courts, and supreme courts as illustrated in Figure 1.1:

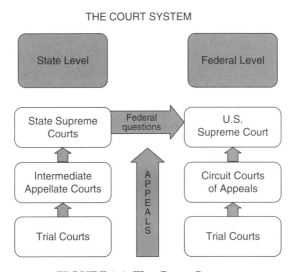

FIGURE 1.1 The Court System.

Note. Depending on the state, intermediate appellate courts may be called Superior Court, Circuit Court, Appellate Division, or Court of Appeals. Cases are appealed from a lower to a higher court. The Circuit Court of Appeals at the federal level may also decide some federal questions from state supreme courts. Decisions made by administrative agencies are generally appealed to a lower court.

affords a nurse or other party who has expe-
.ecision at the lower-court level or by a hearing
ıgher-court level. Each of the states, the District
: federal government have their own set of rules,
nd court structure. Throughout this text book, case
.rses and nursing practice will be cited. It is, however,
ı. ᴧember that the profession of nursing determines the
stanɑ. re for the practice of nursing. The judicial process, based
on the eviᴄ ce presented, determines whether or not those standards of
care have been breached and what the appropriate remedies should be.
The following sources of law will further illustrate the interrelatedness of
law and nursing.

Four Primary Sources of Law

1. Constitutional Law
2. Common Law
3. Statutory Law
4. Administrative Law

Constitutional Law

The preamble to the U.S. Constitution, written by our founding fathers,
is as follows:

> We the people of the United States, in order to form a more per-
> fect union, establish justice, insure domestic tranquility, pro-
> vide for the common defense, promote the general welfare, and
> secure the blessings of liberty to ourselves and our posterity, do
> ordain and establish this Constitution for the United States of
> America.

According to *Black's Law Dictionary* (1979), Constitutional Law is

(1) That branch of the public law of a state which deals with the
organization and frame of government, the organs and powers of
sovereignty, the distribution of political and governmental authorities and functions, the fundamental principles which are to regulate
the relations of government and subject, and which prescribes generally the plan and method according to which the public affairs of
the state are to be administered (p. 282).

Case Examples

In order for a court to have jurisdiction to hear certain matters, there are basic principles of law that apply. Two of those principles are justicability and standing. Justicability means that the matter brought before the court is appropriate for court review. Standing in this context means "standing to sue." In other words, the party bringing the action has a sufficient stake in the outcome. The purpose of standing is to have the court avoid situations where there is no real controversy.

The court addresses justicability and standing in the cases of *Commonwealth of Massachusetts v. Mellon* (1923) and *Frothingham v. Mellon* (1923). These cases are used as examples to demonstrate basic concepts in the law.

The two cases arose as a result of a challenge to the constitutionality of the Maternity Act of 1921. The Act is a federal statute that provided funds to states undertaking programs to reduce maternal and infant mortality. Both cases were dismissed because the court lacked jurisdiction. The following synopsis of the cases will illustrate the principles of justicability and standing.

CASE EXAMPLES:

The Commonwealth of Massachusetts v. Mellon (1923)

Issue: Is the matter brought before the court justicable or appropriate for court review?

In the *Commonwealth of Massachusetts v. Mellon* (1923), Massachusetts contends that the Maternity Act was beyond congressional power because it invaded the power of self-government reserved to the states by the Tenth Amendment. It further believed that the state had an unconstitutional option to yield to the federal government or lose its share of the moneys allotted. The court disagreed. The court's rationale was based on the fact that the Maternity Act imposed no obligation; rather it extends an option for the state to accept or reject. The court's analysis included its power as granted by Article III of the Constitution and that power granted to the court extends only to proceedings "of justicable character . . . "

COURT'S DECISION: In the final analysis, the court held that Congress had not usurped its power when passing the Maternity Act because nothing had been done to Massachusetts State and nothing is to be done without its consent. Therefore, the question presented was one that is political in character, and not one for the exercise of judicial power.

The court went on to say that they were called upon to adjudicate "abstract questions of political power, of a sovereignty, of government." Therefore, the matter was not justicable and subsequently not acted upon by the court.

Frothingham v. Mellon (1923)

Issue: Did Ms. Frothingham have sufficient stake in the outcome, that is, standing to bring suit?

Frothingham v. Mellon (1923) is about a federal taxpayer by the name of Frothingham who contended that the Maternity Act exceeded the power of Congress. She further believed that there would be an increase in the burden of future taxation and, thereby, her property would be taken without due process of the law. The court held that a suit of this nature cannot be maintained for the following reason.

COURT'S DECISION: A person asking the court to hold a federal act unconstitutional "must be able to show not only that the statute is invalid, but that he has sustained or is immediately in danger of sustaining some direct injury as the result of its enforcement, and not merely that he suffers in some indefinite way in common with other people generally" (p. 52). The court went on to say: "To do so, would be, not to decide a judicial controversy, but to assume position of authority over the governmental acts of another and coequal department, an authority which plainly we do not possess" (p. 52).

The aforementioned cases illustrate two basic legal principles necessary in bringing a law suit. The following case example tests the constitutionality of a state statute.

Griswold v. Connecticut (1965)

Issues: (1) Whether or not the Connecticut statute violated the right to marital privacy?, and (2) Whether or not the statute is constitutional?

In 1879, the Connecticut legislature passed a statute prohibiting the distribution of contraceptives. This statute was rarely, if ever, enforced until a birth-control clinic in New Haven, Connecticut, was opened in 1961.

At the time, Estelle Griswold was executive director of Planned Parenthood, League of Connecticut, and Dr. C. Lee Buxton was a physician and professor at the Yale School of Medicine. They opened the birth-control clinic in New Haven. Shortly following the opening of the clinic, they were both arrested.

LOWER COURT'S DECISION: They were tried and found guilty of violations of the Connecticut statute prohibiting the distribution of contraceptives. They were each fined US$100.00. The convictions were appealed and upheld by the highest court in the state of Connecticut. Griswold then appealed her conviction to the Supreme Court of the United States, the highest court in the land.

Griswold based her appeal on the 14th Amendment of the U.S. Constitution that provides that "No state shall make or enforce any law which shall abridge the privileges or immunities of citizens of the United States; nor shall any state deprive any person of life, liberty, or property, without due process of the law; nor deny to any person within its jurisdiction equal protection of the laws."

SUPREME COURT'S DECISION: The U.S. Supreme Court in a landmark decision, by a vote of 7–2, held that the Connecticut statute was unconstitutional on the grounds that it violated the "right to marital privacy."

An important aspect of the Griswold case, as it relates to nursing and medical practice, is that the statute in question was a criminal statute. Criminal actions are serious in nature and may subject the nurse to fines, prison, and license revocation if found guilty of a criminal act. Additional information on criminal actions may be found in Chapter 9. The above-referenced cases give nurses the basic foundation to better understand Constitutional Law. For the U.S. Supreme Court oral argument recordings of major constitutional cases with multimedia resources, see the Oyez Project at http:www.oyez.org.

Common Law

Common Law is defined by *Black's Law Dictionary* (1979) "as distinguished from law created by the enactment of legislatures; the common law comprises the body of those principles and rules of action relating to the government and security of persons and property which derive their authority solely from usages and customs . . . , or from the judgments and decrees of the courts recognizing, affirming, and enforcing such usages and customs. . . . " "The common law is all the statutory and case law background of England and the American colonies before the American revolution" (p. 251). Common Law is grounded in the concept of *stare decisis*, which is Latin for "to abide by, or adhere" (p. 1261).

The principle of precedent or *stare decisis* is following what has been previously decided by the court; it gives predictability to future outcomes. Strict applications of the doctrine can lead to narrow and rigid decisions that may not be in the best interest of the parties, whereas too much flexibility gives rise to uncertainty.

Common Law is often referred to as judge-made law or case law. Tort Law (negligence and malpractice) and Contract Law have developed from Common Law and are further discussed in this text. The states have developed their own body of Common Law based on the court decisions of their respective states, with Louisiana being the exception as it is considered a "civilian law" state, and it depends heavily on scholarly research and written codes of law passed by the legislature, such as the French Civil Code (Code Napoleon). Louisiana judges, unlike their counterparts, are not bound by judicial precedent. Common-Law judges adhere to the doctrine of *stare decisis* that requires that outcome of a lawsuit be governed by precedent (Louisiana Law, 2010).

It is possible for Congress and state legislatures to overrule or incorporate Common-Law principles by enacting a statute. Many states have enacted statutes in the areas of tort, contract, and property laws, though a large body of Common Law in these areas still exists in many jurisdictions. In the event that a statute is passed that overrules or modifies existing Common Law, the courts are bound to follow the statute provided that it does not violate or conflict with the U.S. Constitution or the state's constitution (Northrop & Kelly, 1987).

The expanded practice of nurses is one example of how judicial precedent is developed in this area. The following case example illustrates this dynamic.

CASE EXAMPLE:

Sermchief v. Gonzales, 660 S.W. 2d 683 (Mo. Banc 1983)

Issue: Whether or not the nurse practitioners were practicing the unauthorized practice of medicine?

In *Sermchief,* nurses and physicians brought a petition for a declaratory judgment (which asks the court to establish the rights of parties or express an opinion of the court) and an injunction (which is a court order to stop a person from performing a specific act under certain circumstances) that the practices of nurses were authorized by the NPA and did not constitute the unauthorized practice of medicine. The petition further requested that the Medical Board be enjoined from taking any steps, either civil or criminal, to enforce the unauthorized practice of medicine against these parties.

The facts of the case are mainly undisputed. Appellant Nurses Solari and Burgess are RNs with postgraduate training in obstetrics and gynecology licensed to practice in Missouri. They are employed by an agency that provides medical services to the general public in the fields of family planning, obstetrics, and gynecology.

The appellant physicians are also employed by the same agency and licensed to practice medicine (the healing arts) pursuant to Missouri statutes. They joined this action because they were charged with aiding and abetting the unauthorized practice of medicine by the nurses.

The respondents, meaning the parties answering the complaint, are the members and executive secretary of the Missouri State Board of Registration for the Healing Arts (Medical Board) and are charged with the responsibility of enforcing, implementing, and administering the rules and regulations of the Medical Board.

The services provided by the nurses and complained of by the Medical Board included, but are not limited to history taking, breast and pelvic examinations, Papanicolaou (PAP) smears, gonorrhea cultures, blood serology, information about birth control, and the dispensing of certain medications.

The nurses were following written standing orders and protocols that were signed by the appellant physicians and specifically written for the Nurses Solari and Burgess. No act by the nurses is alleged to have caused injury or harm to any person.

LOWER COURT'S DECISION: The lower court denied the petition, and the case was appealed to the Missouri Supreme Court that reversed the decision and held that services routinely provided by nurses and complained of by Board of Registration for the Healing Arts fell within the legislative standard of "professional nursing."

APPELLATE COURT'S DECISION: The Supreme Court in reversing the decision and remanding, that is, sending it back to the Lower

Court, stated:

> The Nursing Practice Act of 1975 substantially revised the law affecting nursing profession by redefining the term "professional nursing" to expand the scope of authorized nursing practices permitting Nurses to assume responsibilities heretofore not considered to be within field so long as those responsibilities were consistent with nurse's specialized education, judgment and skill.

In 1975, the Missouri legislature made a substantive change in the NPA, which had a positive outcome for this case. The court went on to say, "professional nursing standard provided in the amended statute did not constitute the unlawful practice of medicine, where nurses' diagnoses were within the limits of nurses' respective knowledge and nurses referred patients to physicians upon reaching limits of their knowledge" (p. 683).

The court also said, "the hallmark of the professional is knowing the limits of one's professional knowledge" (p. 690). In this matter, the nurses made the proper referrals to the physicians in accordance to the written protocols. In reversing the Lower Court's decision, this case is significant in that it represents the broadening of the scope of nursing practice that was authorized by the legislature and recognized by the Appellate Court.

This case is an example of both the legislative and judicial branches of government and its effect on nursing practice. *Sermchief* is an illustration of Nursing Law and how the scope of nursing practice was substantially changed by the NPA and how that law was applied by the court.

According to nurse attorney scholar Kjervik, Nursing Law delineates and clarifies the relationship between legal view points and nursing theory and practice. She further states that "nursing jurisprudence describes the law affecting nursing care, explains legal understanding of the concepts, and makes predictions for improvement based upon proposed changes in the law or nursing practice" (Kjervik ,1995, p. 40).

Statutory Law

Statutory Laws are enacted by the legislatures on the both the federal and state levels. *Black's Law Dictionary* (1979) defines a statute as "an act of the legislature declaring, commanding, or prohibiting something; a particular law enacted and established by the will of the legislative department of the government ... " (pp. 1264–1265). There are numerous statutory laws that are enacted by federal and state legislatures, examples of which will be illustrated in this book.

There are broad powers given to the states and to the federal government to legislate for the general welfare of the people. As it pertains to health care, those powers are exercised in a variety of ways. The state's role is this regard is known as "parens patriae, literally parents of the country" (*Black's Law Dictionary*, 1975, p. 1003). It refers to the role of state as a guardian; for example, the licensing of health care providers, including nurses, is administered by a state to protect the general welfare of its citizens.

Statutory Law is primarily the vehicle responsible for the educational, licensing, and regulation of nursing practice. Each state sets forth the conditions for education, licensing, and regulation of nursing. Upon passing the examination to become an RN, the regulation of practice is mainly accomplished by state boards of nursing. These boards consist of members appointed by the governors of each state, and each state has set forth the necessary requirements for appointment. The following include examples of the Board of Nursing composition and its power and duties in the state of Vermont.

STATE BOARDS OF NURSING

Statutory Law: Boards of Nursing

At the state level, an example of statutory law is the creation of the Board of Nursing (26 V.S.A. Section 1573) as given below:

(a) There is hereby created a Vermont state Board of Nursing consisting of five registered nurses, including at least one endorsed as an advanced practice registered nurse, two practical nurses, nursing assistant, and two public members. Board members shall be appointed by the governor in accordance with statutory law. (see 26 V.S.A., Section 1573)

(b) Appointments of registered and licensed practice nurse members shall be made in a manner designed to be representative of the various types of nursing education programs and nursing services.

(c) Each member of the board shall be a citizen of the United States, and a resident of this state.

    (1) The registered nurse members shall

        (A) hold a license to practice registered nursing in Vermont and

        (B) have at least 5 years' experience in the practice of registered nursing. Three of these 5 years shall have been immediately preceding appointment.

    (2) The licensed practical nurse members shall
        (A) hold a license to practice practical nursing in Vermont, and
        (B) have a least 5 years' experience in the practice of practical nursing. Three of these 5 years shall have been immediately preceding appointment.
    (3) The public members shall not be members of any other health-related licensing boards, licensees of any health occupation boards, or employees of any health agencies or facilities, and shall not derive primary livelihood from the provision of health services at any level of responsibility.
(d) Any vacancy occurring on the board shall be filled for the unexpired term by appointment to be made by the governor (amendments to this provision were made in 1993, 2005, and 2007) (26 V.S.A. Section 1573).

Powers and Duties of the Board of Nursing

The board shall:

(1) Hold annual meetings at which it shall elect a chair, a vice chair, and a secretary from its members, and hold such other meetings as may be deemed necessary to transact its business;
(2) Conduct business at any meeting only if five members are present to constitute a quorum and keep a record of its proceedings that shall be a public record;
(3) Prescribe standards for educational programs and approve such nursing education programs in Vermont as meets the requirements of this chapter and board rules;
(4) Establish standards for registration and licensure of individuals for the practice of nursing, including the endorsement of advanced practice registered nurses and practical nurses, and those in special areas of nursing practice that require additional education and experience;
(5) Examine, register, license, and renew the licenses of duly qualified applicants and keep a record of all persons registered by this state, all persons currently licensed as registered nurses and practical nurses, and all persons meeting standards that may be established in defined special areas of nursing practice;
(6) Provide standards for and approve education programs for the benefit of nurses who are reentering practice following a lapse of 5 or more years;
(7) Investigate complaints and charges of unauthorized practice, unprofessional conduct, or incompetency against any person and take proper action under Sections 1582 or 1584 of this title, as the case may be;

(8) Compel the attendance of witnesses and the furnishing of evidentiary material in connection with a hearing by subpoenas issued by the executive officer of the board with the approval of the board; and

(9) Adopt rules necessary to perform its duties under this subchapter (26, V.S.A., Section 1574; amendments to this provision were made in 1979, 2005, and 2007).

Regulatory Authority of Board of Nursing (26. V.S.A. Section 1582)

(a) The board may deny an application for registration, licensure, or relicensure; revoke or suspend any license to practice nursing issued by it; discipline or in other ways condition the practice of a registrant or licensee upon due notice and opportunity for hearing in compliance with the provisions of the law should a person engage in certain conduct or the conduct set forth in Title 3, Section 129 (a).

The conduct may include the following:

(1) Has made or caused to be made a false, fraudulent, or forged statement or representation in procuring or attempting to procure registration or renew a license to practice nursing;

(2) Whether or not committed in this state, has been convicted of a crime related to the practice of nursing or a felony that evinces an unfitness to practice nursing;

(3) Is unable to practice nursing competently by reason of any cause;

(4) Has willfully or repeatedly violated any of the provisions of this chapter;

(5) Is habitually intemperate or is addicted to the use of habit-forming drugs;

(6) Has a mental, emotional, or physical disability, the nature of which interferes with the ability to practice nursing competently; or

(7) Engages in conduct of a character likely to deceive, defraud or harm the public (28 V.S.A., Section 1582).

Unprofessional conduct is further described in 3 V.S.A. Section 129a that includes the following.

(a) In addition to any other provision of the law, the following conduct by a licensee constitutes unprofessional conduct. When that conduct is by an applicant or person who later becomes an applicant, it may constitute grounds for denial of a license or other disciplinary action.

Any one of the following items, or any combination of items, whether or not the conduct at issue was committed within or outside the state, shall constitute unprofessional conduct:

(1) Fraudulent or deceptive procurement or use of a license.

(2) Advertising that is intended or has a tendency to deceive.

(3) Failing to comply with provisions of federal or state statutes or rules governing the practice of the profession.

(4) Failing to comply with an order of the board or violating any term or condition of a license restricted by the board.

(5) Practicing the profession when medically or psychologically unfit to do so.

(6) Delegating professional responsibilities to a person whom the licensed professional knows, or has reason to know is not qualified by training, experience, education, or licensing credentials to perform them.

(7) Willfully making or filing false reports or records in the practice of the profession and willfully impeding or obstructing the proper making or filing or reports or records or willfully failing to file the proper reports or records.

(8) Failing to make available promptly to a person using professional health care services, that person's representative, succeeding health care professionals or institutions, upon written request and direction of the person using professional health care services, copies of that person's records in the possession or under the control of the licensed practitioner.

(9) Failing to retain client records for a period of 7 years, unless laws specific to the profession allow for shorter retention period. When other laws or agency rules require retention for a longer period of time, the longer retention period shall apply.

(10) Conviction of a crime related to the practice of the profession or conviction of a felony, whether or not related to the practice of the profession.

(11) Failing to report to the office a conviction of any felony or any offense related to the practice of the profession in a Vermont district court, a Vermont superior court, a federal court, or a court outside Vermont within 30 days.

(12) Exercising undue influence on or taking improper advantage of a person using professional services or promoting the sale of services or goods in a manner that exploits a person for the financial gain of the practitioner or a third party.

(13) Performing treatments or providing services that the licensee is not qualified to perform or that are beyond the scope of the licensee's education, training, capabilities, experience, or scope of practice.
(14) Failing to report to the office within 30 days a change of name or address.
(15) Failing to exercise independent professional judgment in the performance of licensed activities when that judgment is necessary to avoid action repugnant to the obligations of the profession.
  (b) Failure to practice competently by reason of any cause on a single occasion or on multiple occasions may constitute unprofessional conduct, whether actual injury to a client, patient, or customer has occurred. Failure to practice competently includes:
    (1) Performance of unsafe or unacceptable patient or client care, or
    (2) Failure to conform to the essential standards of acceptable and prevailing practice.
  (c) The burden of proof in a disciplinary action shall be on the state to show by preponderance of the evidence that the person engaged in unprofessional conduct (3 V.S.A. Section 129a 1–15, b1, 2c).

In summary, the powers and duties of the Board of Nursing, as a regulatory authority, include establishing standards for the education of nurses, licensing and licensing renewal, and disciplining up to and including license revocation. This process will be discussed in this chapter. Although the reasons for discipline may vary from state to state, the nurse will be afforded due process and an opportunity to be heard.

As evidenced by the Vermont statute pertaining to the Board of Nursing, broad powers are given to the boards of nursing to carry out their functions in accordance with the law. The primary function is to safeguard the public from unlawful and unsafe practice of nursing.

It is important for the nurse to understand the broad reach of what is deemed "unprofessional conduct." It is recommended that nurses become familiar with the statutory language regarding unprofessional conduct in the state of licensure.

The disciplinary process is established by the Administrative Procedure Act of each state that also allows any person adversely affected by board action to appeal the decision to a court of law.

Administrative Law

Administrative Law is formed by rules, regulations, orders, and decisions made by administrative agencies. Rules and regulations and other actions taken by the boards of nursing fall into this area of the law. Administrative agencies are charged with the administration and implementation of various legislation on both the state and federal levels.

The Administrative Procedure Act was passed in 1946 and governs proceedings brought before federal agencies for adjudication. The states have also enacted similar legislation governing proceedings or hearings brought before state agencies.

Presiding at these hearings are Administrative Law Judges (ALJ) or hearing officers. In accordance with the Administrative Procedure Act, the ALJ has the power to adjudicate disputes and issue final dispositions in all matters brought before the agency. The dispositions by the ALJ may be appealed to a court of law. ALJs decide nursing disciplinary matters brought before them by the Board of Nursing. Those decisions become part of the body of Administrative Law for the state.

Nursing licensure. The state boards of nursing regulate nursing licensure and relicensure. In 1978, the NCSBN was created as an organization to collaborate with state boards of nursing on common matters affecting the public health, safety, and welfare, including the licensure of RNs.

The NCSBN introduced the National Council Licensing Examination for RNs and LPNs known as NCLEX that covers five major nursing areas. Since 1994, NCLEX is administered by computerized examination, with interactive participation, at designated testing centers in each state. The candidates receive the results within 1 week to 10 days following the examination that is scored on a pass/fail basis. The nurse may then be eligible to practice across state lines without obtaining an additional license, only if the state of licensure and the other state of interest are members of the NLC as previously discussed.

The nurse who passes the examination is required to practice nursing in conformity to the NPA and in accordance with all the laws, rules, and regulations that are promulgated by the profession. Should a violation of the NPA, rules, regulations, or ANA Ethical Code of Conduct occur, a nurse may be brought before the Board of Nursing for disciplinary action more fully described in this section.

Criminal background checks for licensure. To ensure the general welfare and safety of the public, there have been an increasing number of states requiring criminal background checks for nursing licensure or relicensure. To date, approximately 37 states have passed legislation requiring criminal background checks. Whereas some states require self-disclosure about criminal convictions, there are other states that do not require either self-disclosure or criminal background checks (NCSBN, 2010).

As of 2010, the District of Columbia, in accordance with the District of Columbia Official Code, has implemented legislation that requires criminal background checks for nurses and other health care providers. According to the law, new applicants seeking licensure are required to be fingerprinted by the District of Columbia Metropolitan Police Department, or, if applying from out of state, they are required to have their finger prints taken at a designated local state agency or police department. The criminal background check will be completed by the Federal Bureau of Investigation (FBI; a federal administrative agency) within 24 hours. Any adverse information will be reviewed by the Board of Nursing along with all other pertinent information. The board decides whether an applicant should be licensed to practice nursing. Any criminal offense may have a serious impact on licensure. All questions regarding this subject should be directed to competent counsel in the state of licensure.

Nursing Disciplinary Process

Complaint filing: board of nursing. The disciplinary process begins with a complaint to the Board of Nursing alleging certain violations of practice by the nurse. The individual filing the complaint against the nurse is called the complainant.

Generally, there are certain criteria that must be met for a complaint to be accepted and investigated. For example, the professional activity requires the individual to be licensed, and in most instances, the unprofessional conduct alleged is based on the laws and rules related to the profession. If the basic criteria are met, a case is opened against the nurse and a case number is assigned. In the event that the criteria are not met, a case will not be opened and the complainant will be notified.

The complaint contains the name, address, and telephone number of the individual who is being complained about, as well as the name, address, and telephone number of the facility or business involved, if any. In some situations, there will names of witnesses with factual knowledge of the events leading up to the complaint. A description of the allegations with the type of services rendered and dates will also be included. The statement of complaint is signed by the complainant and sent to the Office of Professional Responsibility or to the appropriate party as designated by state statute.

Disciplinary case opened and reviewed. In the state of Vermont, for example, once a disciplinary case against a nurse is opened, a letter of notification is sent to the complainant (person filing the complaint) by the Office of Professional Regulation. A letter is also sent to the nurse or respondent stating that a complaint was received and that a case has been opened for investigation. A copy of the complaint information will be included.

At this juncture, it is advisable for the nurse to remain calm and seek experienced legal counsel for consultation and possible representation if charges are filed. In the event the nurse is covered by an individual malpractice insurance policy, notification to the carrier should be made as some carriers provide coverage for this type of action against the nurse.

The Office of Professional Regulation then assigns the case to an investigative team. The team may include a unit administrator, a staff investigator, a board member or advisor, and a prosecuting attorney. Both the complainant and the respondent nurse (respondent is the party who answers or responds to the complaint) will be contacted by an investigator along with witnesses or others having knowledge of the complaint.

Investigation. The investigation usually begins when the investigator or designated person obtains copies of written documentation and any relevant records pertaining to the complaint. The investigator may request a statement from the nurse describing the incident. In addition, specific questions may be asked by the investigator to be answered by the nurse in writing. After a review of the records and the documentation submitted, the investigator will report the findings to the team with a recommendation to pursue or not to pursue formal charges against the nurse. If the decision is made not to pursue formal charges, the case will be closed without disciplinary action and the matter will remain confidential.

If the recommendation is to pursue formal charges, the prosecuting attorney prepares the formal charges against the nurse. In some jurisdictions the formal charges are described as "notice of intent to take disciplinary action."

Depending on the complexity of the matter, the investigation can take 6 to 9 months or longer to complete. This investigatory period can be a very stressful time for the nurse. And in some instances, the nurse may be unaware that an investigation is going on until the formal charges are filed. Once formal charges are filed, the investigatory phase is no longer confidential. The investigatory process may vary depending on the circumstances and the state's procedure for investigation of these claims.

Formal charges filed against the nurse. If formal charges are filed against the nurse, the prosecuting attorney drafts the charges in the form of allegations that are made in the complaint and confirmed by the investigatory process. Each charge or allegation is listed separately with a description of the unprofessional conduct and or breach of the NPA, rules, and/or regulations, which are the basis for the Board of Nursing to take the proposed action pursuant to the statutory requirement of the state where the charges are filed.

The Complaint Against the Nurse

For example, a nurse may be charged in the complaint as follows:

Charge I. You demonstrated a willful or careless disregard for the health, welfare, or safety of a patient in violation of the specific statute.

It may state, "On or about June 4, 2003, you failed to timely notify the physician that Mr. Jones' temperature had risen to 104 degrees. Mr. Jones expired the next morning."

Answer to Charge I: In accordance with the hospital's policy and procedure, Nurse Smith called the supervisor on duty to report the elevated temperature and she did not call the physician because she followed the hospital's written policy and procedure.

The charges (allegations) if there are others, Charges II and III, will continue in this manner and will include the statute that gives the board the authority and then a brief description of the charge. The complaint is signed and dated by the prosecuting attorney. At this juncture, the respondent nurse is served the complaint with the allegations of the wrongdoing in a manner consistent with the Administrative Procedure Act of that particular state.

If the nurse has not contacted counsel, it is imperative to do so before answering the complaint. Upon receipt of the complaint outlining the formal charges against the nurse, action must be taken because there are only a certain number of days to respond to the charges. If responses to the allegations are not made within the proscribed time, a default judgment against the nurse may be taken.

The responses, by the nurse or respondent, to the charges generally take three forms:

1. An admission,
2. An admission with an explanation, or
3. A denial.

The allegations and the answers to the allegations will form the foundation for the hearing before the ALJ. The nurse will be afforded a hearing and due process in accordance with the law.

Hearing procedures.   Hearings are conducted in accordance with the procedures detailed in the states' Administrative Procedure Act before an Administrative Law Judge (ALJ). Specific procedural rules of the court will generally be followed.

The ALJ will set forth submission requirements with his or her required deadlines in accordance with those rules or other authority for managing and adjudicating the case. Hearsay may be admissible in this type of hearing. *Hearsay,* as defined by *Black's Law Dictionary* (1979), is: "A statement, other than one made by the declarant while testifying at the trial or the hearing offered in evidence to prove the truth of the matter asserted" (p. 649). The trial phase of the hearing is the nurse's opportunity to refute the evidence and to call witnesses to testify on his or her behalf.

The prosecuting attorney has the burden to prove, by a preponderance of evidence, all of the allegations against the nurse, in order for the ALJ to find that the nurse is guilty of the charges presented. The ALJ will issue a final order based on the testimony and evidence presented at the hearing and either party may appeal the final order to a court of law.

In the alternative, a "consent agreement," which is a settlement between the Board of Nursing and the nurse, may be entered into to avoid the uncertainty of the decision of the ALJ following the hearing. The attorney representing the nurse will provide guidance, support, and legal analysis throughout the process in answering the complaint and in preparation for the hearing, or in negotiating a consent agreement.

Consent agreement and orders.   A consent agreement sometimes referred to as a consent order or a stipulation may be entered into by the government (prosecuting attorney), respondent (nurse) and Board of Nursing. Following the investigatory stage, an agreement may be reached prior to the hearing. If there is more than one respondent, an agreement may be reached by one respondent and not the other. The hearing will go forward for the remaining respondent or respondents.

It is important for the nurse to understand the ramifications of entering into a consent agreement. Negotiating a consent order does give the nurse some control of the outcome; however, the nurse will waive the right to contest the matter at a hearing and/or appeal the decision made at the hearing should it be unfavorable. The decision to enter into a consent agreement is one that is thoughtfully made by the nurse with the advice of counsel.

The consent agreement may contain certain provisions as follows:

Example of a Consent Agreement

1. The Board of Nursing has jurisdiction to investigate the complaints against the nurse and also had the power to approve a consent order;
2. It will state that the nurse is licensed in a certain state;
3. Name of employer of the nurse;
4. Specify the facts of the situation such as violating provisions of the NPA and so on, and where the action took place;
5. Respondent Nurse admits to such violation(s);
6. The Respondent Nurse accepts the conclusions of the Board of Nursing;
7. The Respondent Nurse voluntarily enters into the agreement after consultation with counsel and is not coerced into signing agreement;
8. Respondent Nurse waives the right to charges and a contested hearing before the Board of Nursing;
9. Respondent Nurse agrees that the Board of Nursing may enter the order. The order will set forth the terms and conditions for the agreement or stipulation;
10. A recitation of the grounds for discipline;
11. A license reprimand, suspension, or revocation, with the number of years specified, and the licensee may also have conditional privileges;
12. The order may have mandatory conditions such as supervision and/ or educational courses and probation;
13. Notification provision to the Board of Nursing of current employers;
14. If conditional privileges are granted, the respondent may have to report the current employer report to the Board of Nursing;
15. There may be prohibited duties outlined;
16. If there is a violation of the stipulation and consent order, further disciplinary action may take place;
17. Following a completion of the terms and conditions as set forth in the order, the Board of Nursing in its discretion can reinstate and renew the nurse's license.
18. The Consent Agreement will contain the date and signatures of the parties.

The stipulation and consent orders become a matter of public record and may be reported to other licensing authorities in accordance with state statutes. It usually remains part of the respondent's permanent licensing file and may be used for the purposes of determining sanctions in future disciplinary matters.

The consent agreement will contain the terms and conditions based on the facts of a particular case, and it may not have all the provisions as outlined previously. In the event that an agreement is not reached, the matter will proceed to a hearing as previously described.

According to Karno (2005), as a result of the severe consequences that may occur from the disciplinary process, nurses are strongly advised to exercise the right to counsel. "Legal representation should ensure full protection of nurses' rights and will optimize the nurse's bargaining power when negotiating a consent order" (p. 215).

The following case is an illustration of a nurse who appealed an unfavorable decision regarding licensure to a court of law. Here, the nurse is referred to as the "petitioner" (the one bringing the action or appeal).

Administrative Law

CASE EXAMPLE:

Husher v. Commissioner of Education of the State of New York, et al. (1992); Case Appealed

Issue: Whether or not the nurse abandoned patients by failing to work a second shift?

This case arose in the state of New York when the nurse (petitioner, in this case, an RN and LPN) was charged with two instances of professional misconduct:

(1) Abandoning her professional employment with the hospital, and
(2) Practicing the profession with gross negligence.

The facts reveal and are undisputed that the petitioner nurse worked as an RN on an assigned unit in the hospital from 7:00 A.M. to 3:00 P.M. and that the petitioner was previously advised by her supervisor that due to a staff shortage on the 3:00 P.M. to 11:00 P.M. shift, one of the day-shift nurses would have to remain on duty for an additional 8-hour shift.

Petitioner had the least seniority, and in accordance with the hospital's mandatory overtime policy, was obligated to stay on duty until relieved. She informed the supervisor that she would remain on duty for several hours until properly relieved. Shortly after the second shift began at 3:00 P.M., petitioner left the unit and went to the supervisor's office. She told the staff on the unit to page her in the event of an emergency. After meeting with the supervisor, petitioner left the hospital without returning to the unit or without notifying the staff covering the unit.

HEARING PANEL'S DECISION: The panel found that the hospital had a bona fide overtime policy, of which the petitioner was aware. The policy required the nurse with the least seniority to remain on duty during an emergency situation. The panel found that an emergency situation did in fact exist on the day in question.

Furthermore, the petitioner nurse had knowledge of the emergency and was advised by her supervisor that she would have to remain on duty. She did not remain on duty and left the unit approximately 45 minutes after the shift began, leaving the unit unattended by an RN. Respondent, Board of Regents, accepted these findings and concluded that petitioner was guilty of professional misconduct and ordered that her licenses to practice as an RN and LPN be suspended for 1 year and run concurrently.

The execution of the suspensions was stayed, which means that although the petitioner was disciplined, she could still practice nursing. Petitioner appealed the decision.

THE NEW YORK SUPREME COURT APPELLATE DIVISION'S DECISION: The decision of the Hearing Panel was affirmed by the New York Supreme Court, Appellate Division. The court found that there was uncontroverted evidence to meet the necessary requirements to support a finding of misconduct under 8 NYCRR 29.2(a)(1), namely,

(1) abandonment of professional employment,
(2) without reasonable notice, and
(3) under circumstances that seriously impaired the delivery of professional care to patients.

The court concluded that petitioner's conduct seriously impaired the delivery of professional care to patients and that a review of the record sufficiently supports the conclusion that petitioner's actions constituted gross negligence.

In this case, the nurse exercised her right to appeal the decision of the Hearing Panel to the New York Supreme Court, Appellate Division. Although the outcome did not change on appeal, the issue of mandatory overtime has been known to spark controversy.

Mandatory Overtime: An Opposing View

Mandatory overtime is viewed by some to present patient safety issues because it is believed that an overworked and tired nurse is more likely to make errors in judgment causing harm to patients. Although there may be situations that warrant mandatory overtime, the employer has an obligation to ensure appropriate staffing so that nurses can deliver safe nursing care to patients at all times.

Over the years, the issue of mandatory overtime has presented opposing views. For example, in the state of Vermont, there is legislation pending to ban mandatory overtime except in unforeseeable emergency situations. The Bill H. 268: An Act Relating to Prohibiting Mandatory Overtime for Health Care Employees was submitted in the 2009–2010 Legislative Session. Passage of the bill would prohibit any mandatory overtime provision in a contract, or agreement of understanding as unenforceable and void as against public policy. An employee may agree to extend work hours.

Tracking Nursing Disciplinary Cases

In an effort to reduce nursing errors, and to track disciplinary cases regarding patient care brought before boards of nursing, the NCSBN has developed an instrument called TERCAP® (registered trademark). TERCAP stands for:

(1) Taxonomy of Error,
(2) Root-Cause Analysis, and
(3) Practice Responsibility.

Four Practice Areas

TERCAP covers four practice areas:

(1) Safe medication administration: The nurse administers the right dose of the right medication, via the right route to the right patient at the right time and for the right reason.

(2) Documentation: The nurse ensures complete, accurate and timely documentation.
(3) Attentiveness: The nurse is knowledgeable about the patient's care and maintains vigilance as to what is occurring with patient and staff. The nurse observes the patient's clinical condition and responses to therapy, as well as potential hazards or errors in treatment.
(4) Clinical reasoning: The nurse demonstrates appropriate decision making, critical thinking, and sound clinical judgment. Clinicians use science and technology as well in making decisions (NCSBN, 2010).

These four important practice areas along with various legal examples will be more fully described in the remaining chapters of this book. TERCAP is another example of the regulatory authority of the state Board of Nursing. This evaluation tool will provide a mechanism to assist the profession in the reduction of nursing errors

Reporting Requirements for Nursing Disciplinary Actions

As reported by the NCSBN, the National Practitioner Data Bank (NPDB) and the Healthcare Integrity and Protection Data Bank (HIPDB) are two federal data banks created to serve as repositories of information about health care providers in the United States. Federal law requires that adverse actions taken against a health care professional's license be reported to these data banks. Information about nursing disciplinary actions is reported to the HIPDB by the board taking the action. All information included in these banks is not available to the general public. They are, however, available to employers and state and federal governmental agencies, hospitals, professional societies, health plans, health care providers, and through self-query (NCSBN, 2010).

According to Blatt and Vorabhauda, on March 1, 2010, the Social Security Act (SSA) expanded the types of state licensure actions reportable to the NPDB by implementing Section 1921 of the Act. As a result of this expansion, state licensing authorities must now report all adverse actions taken against all health care practitioners, not just physicians and dentists, as well as those actions taken against health care entities. State licensing authorities are further mandated by law to report "all adverse license actions not just those based on professional competence" (p. 12).

NPDB reportable actions. In accordance with the SSA, Section 1921 (2010), state licensure actions taken as a result of formal proceedings are reportable to the NPDB. These actions include the following:

- Any adverse action, including revocation or suspension of a license, reprimand, censure, or probation;
- Any dismissal or closure of the proceedings by reason of the practitioner or entity surrendering the license or leaving the State or jurisdiction;
- Any other loss of the license, whether by operation of law, voluntary surrender (excluding those due to nonpayment of licensure renewal fees, retirement, or change to inactive status, or otherwise); and
- Any negative action or finding that is publicly available information (Blatt & Vorabhanda, 2010, p. 14).

HIPDB reportable actions. Federal or state licensing and certification actions that are reportable to HIPDB include the following:

- Formal or official actions, such as revocation, suspension, or probation of a license, or reprimand or censure;
- Any other loss of, or the loss of the right to apply for or renew a license, certification agreement, or contract for participation in government health care programs, whether by operation of law, voluntary surrender, or nonrenewal (excluding nonrenewals due to nonpayment of fees, retirement, or change to inactive status), or otherwise;
- Any other negative action or finding that is publicly available information (Blatt & Vorabhanda, 2010, p. 20).

It is important to note that each state should interpret the reporting requirements based on its own laws, regulations, and rules concerning the above-listed actions.

CONCLUSIONS AND TRENDS

There is little doubt that the changing landscape of health care in this country will present new and exciting opportunities for nurses. It is, therefore, incumbent on the profession of nursing to exert its power and to maintain autonomy and control of nursing practice.

TERCAP, as discussed previously, is just one example of how to accomplish those goals. Nurses need to be fully aware of the changes in educational requirements, licensure, and relicensure matters, as well as how current case law affects nursing practice. The need for this information is evidenced by the fact that there are more nursing and the law courses being offered at the undergraduate and graduate levels of nursing education. Moreover, the Texas legislature recently passed a law requiring that RNs take a Nursing Jurisprudence Examination for licensure.

The trend is to fully recognize nurses as expert witnesses as evidenced by recent court decisions. In the past, for example, it was common for physicians to testify as expert witnesses as to the standard of nursing practice. As nurses gain autonomy and accountability that custom is being eroded as illustrated by the *Sullivan v. Edward Hospital* (2004) case that held that a physician was not competent to testify as an expert witness as to the standard of nursing care (see Chapter 9).

We have also witnessed the role of the nurse practitioner expand. The need for those services is expected to increase in the future as health care reform takes effect and primary physicians remain in short supply.

To facilitate nursing practice across state lines, the NLC was formed. Although there are only 24 member states member in the compact to date, that number is expected to grow. There is further indication that nurse practitioners may also be included in an advanced nursing compact at a later date.

Nurses will remain at the center of the delivery of health care in various settings across the country. The challenges they face will be many. Those challenges will enable nurses to draw upon their knowledge, skills, and expertise in not only providing optimal care but also in advocating for their patients' best interest. The law provides an important mechanism for accomplishing many of nursing's goals.

KEY POINTS

- The Nurse Practice Act (NPA) defines the scope of nursing practice and contains the legal parameters of practice; each state has its own NPA.
- The Nursing Licensure Compact (NLC) was formed as a mechanism for mutual recognition of registered nurses (RNs) and licensed practical nurses (LPNs). It facilitates the practice of nursing across state lines without additional licensure. To date, there are 24 member states.
- Accountability remains one of the hallmarks of nursing, and nurses will be held accountable for their actions while delivering patient care;

therefore, all nurses must remain vigilant to the NPA and other laws, rules, and regulations that govern nursing practice.
- Understanding the legal framework regarding nursing is a vital component of nursing practice.
- The Board of Nursing in each state has broad powers to regulate the educational and licensing requirements for RNs, which includes all disciplinary matters as well.
- It is reported that the shortage of RNs is expected to grow as the "baby boomers" age and the need for health care grows.

REFERENCES

American Association of Colleges Nursing. (2009). *Nursing shortage fact sheet* (PDF Document). Retrieved February 17, 2010, from http:www.aacn.nche.edu/media/shortageresource.htm

American Nurses Association. (2001). *Code of ethics with interpretive statements.* Washington, DC: Author.

American Nurses Association. (2003). *Nursing: A social policy statement* (2nd ed.). Washington, DC: Author.

American Nurses Association. (2010). *Florence Nightingale pledge.* Retrieved February 17, 2010, from http://www.nursingworld.org/Functional menu categories/About ANA/Wherewecomefro

An act prohibiting mandatory overtime for health care employees. H. 268, (2009–2010). Vt. Leg. session. Retrieved March 29, 2010, from http://www.leg.state.vt.us/database/status/summary.cfm

BBC-history-historic figures: Florence Nightingale (1820–1910). (n.d.). Retrieved April 14, 2010, from http://www.bbc.co.uk/history/historic_figures/nightingale_florence.shtml

Black's law dictionary. (1979, 5th ed.). St. Paul, MN: West Publishing Company.

Blatt, D., & Vorabhanda, S. (2010). *Reporting to the data banks: Information and guidance for state licensing authorities.* Retrieved May 31, 2010, from http.//www.npdb-hipdb.hrsa.gov/servlet/stateboardsservel?token=8000

Executive. 3 V.S.A., Section 129a.1–15, (b) 1, 2 (c). Unprofessional conduct. Retrieved February 3, 2010, from http://www.leg.state vt.us/statutes/fullsection.cfm?Title=03 & Chapter=005& Section=00129A.

Fowler, D. M. (Ed.). (2008). *Guide to the code of ethics for nurses: Interpretation and application.* College Park, MD: American Nurses Association.

Frothingham v. Mellon 262 U.S. 447 (1923).

Griswold v. Connecticut 381 U.S. 479 (1965).

Husher v. Commission of Education of State of New York 591 N.Y. 2d 99, 188 A.D. 2d 739 (1992).

Karno, S. (2005). Defending your license. *Journal of Nursing Law, 10*(4), 214–215.

Kjervik, D. K. (1995). The hermeneutics of nursing law research. *Journal of Nursing Law, 55,* 39–45.

Louisiana law: A short history and the Code Napoleon. (n.d.). Retrieved June 5, 2010, from htpp://www.La-legal.com/history_louisiana_law.htm

National Council of State Boards of Nursing. (2009). *APRN compact.* Retrieved February 14, 2010, from https://www.ncsbn.org/917.htm

National Council of State Boards of Nursing. (n.d.). *History 1.* Retrieved February 28, 2010, from http://www.ncsbn.org/181.htm

National Council of State Boards of Nursing. (n.d.). *Nursing licensure compact (NLC).* Retrieved February 28, 2010, from https://www.ncsbn.org/nlc.htm

National Council of State Boards of Nursing. (2009, October). *Participating states in the NLC.* Retrieved February14, 2010, from https://www.ncsbn.or/158.htm

National Council of State Boards of Nursing. (n.d.). *TERCAP.* Retrieved February 14, 2010, from https://www.ncsbn.org/441htm

National League for Nursing. (n.d.). *About the NLN.* Retrieved February 28, 2010, from http://www.nln.org.about nln/index.htm

Nightingale, F. (1860). *Notes on nursing: What it is and what it is not* (First American Edition). New York: D. Appleton & Company. Retrieved February 18, 2010, from http://digital library.Upenn.edu/women/nightingale/nursing.html

North Carolina nurses: A century of caring. Nursing then and now, 1–4. (n.d.). Retrieved February 17, 2010, from http://www.unctv.org/ncnursing/thenand-now.html.

Northrop, C. E., & Kelly, M. E. (1987). *Legal issues in nursing.* St. Louis, MO: C.V. Mosby Company.

Norton v. Argonaut Insurance Company, 144 So. 2d 249 (1962).

Professions and occupations, 26 V.S.A., sections 1571–1601. Retrieved February 3, 2010, from http: www.Leg.state vt.us/statutes/full chapter.cfm? Title=26 & Chapter 028

Rehmeyer, J. (2008). Florence Nightingale: The passionate statistician. *Science News.* Retrieved February 17, 2010, from http://www.sciencenews.org/view/generic/id/38937/title/Florence_Nightingale_The passion . . .

Schloendorff v. Society of New York Hospital, 211 N.Y. 125, 105 N.E. 92 (1914).

Seig, D. (2009). *What* nursing *leaders know: Seven truths from top health care professionals. Reflection on nursing leadership* (Vol. 35, No. 3). Retrieved February 17, 2010, from http:// www.reflections on nursing leadership.com/Pages/Vol 35_3_Sieg_Nursing Leaders.aspx

Sermchief v. Gonsalves, 660 S. W. 2d 683 (Mo. banc 1983).

The Constitution of the United States of America. (n.d). Washington, DC: The Supreme Court Historical Society, and Supreme Court of the United States.

World history of nursing: The history of nursing. (n.d.). Retrieved February 17, 2010, from https://www.gonursingschools.com/The_History_of_Nursing.htm

ADDITIONAL READINGS

American Association for the History of Nursing. (1996–2008). *AAHN nursing history centers, museums and archives*. Retrieved February 17, 2010, from http://www.aahn.org/resources/centers.html

American Nurses Association. (2004). *Nursing scope and standards of practice.* Washington, DC: Author.

Kjervik, D., & Brous, E. A. (2010). *Law and ethics for advanced practice nursing.* New York: Springer Publishing Company.

Nursing library collection. (2009). Retrieved February 17, 2010, from http://www. bc.edu/schools/son/research/resources/library.html

The American Association of Nurse Attorneys. (2005). *Business and legal guidebook for nurse practitioners.* Columbus, OH: Author.

CHAPTER TWO

CORPORATE LAW

*Diana C. Ballard, Michelle Mitchell-Stoddard, and
Liston E. Radney, III*

OBJECTIVES

- Identify the types of entities that can be formed for the purpose of conducting business.
- Identify the major differences among C corporations, S corporations, professional corporations, partnerships, and limited liability type entities.
- Understand the extent of personal liability for owners associated with the major business entity types.
- Be informed of the key areas of responsibility of hospital corporations and identify the articulated duties owed to patients.
- Understand the differences in purposes for existence and disposition of earnings between for-profit and not-for-profit corporations.
- Understand the meaning and the implications of a fiduciary duty and the duties of care and loyalty.

INTRODUCTION

In its broadest sense, corporate law encompasses the legal entities that may be formed to conduct business and describes the attributes of the various structures. Nurses and nurse leaders can benefit from familiarity with this area of the law, not only to understand the nature of the operation of the legal entity they may be associated with but also in the event they may wish to start their own business. If the latter is the case, it is necessary to understand the legal methods of obtaining or filing required documents and whether an official charter, Articles of Incorporation, or other legal filings or approvals may be needed to operate a particular business entity.

There are a number of entities a nurse can choose to operate, and knowledge of the attributes of each will assist in making an informed and appropriate choice. Nurses contemplating formation of an entity for the purpose of conducting business should seek advice of competent counsel and other professional advisors to explore the full range of entity types available and to assure its proper formation.

Corporations may be organized as a for-profit business, for the practice of a profession such as a law office or medical practice, or as a nonprofit entity, which operates for charitable, social, religious, civic, or other public service purposes. Corporations are governed by state corporation laws and local laws and are also affected by Internal Revenue Service (IRS) tax laws and regulations.

The most common forms of businesses are the C corporation, the S corporation, sole proprietorship, partnership, limited liability company, and a number of variations of these entity types (http://www.irs.gov).

Each entity provides for differences in management, governance, taxation, and nature of the business to be conducted. Although a review of every type of business entity is beyond the scope of this chapter, an overview of the major different types of entities to consider and some of their key traits is presented.

Finally, under the Doctrine of Corporate Liability, a hospital has duties owed to its patients. Courts have identified these duties, and it is vital that they are recognized and understood.

CORPORATIONS

Definition and Types

A corporation is the most common form of business organization. A corporation is broadly defined as a legal entity or structure created under the authority of the laws of a state, consisting of a person or group of persons who become shareholders. A corporation's existence is considered separate and distinct from that of its members, and the corporation has certain rights separate from its owners.

Incorporation is the process of forming or becoming a corporation. Incorporation gives the company separate legal standing from its owners and protects those owners from being personally liable in the event that the company is sued (a condition known as limited liability). Incorporation also provides companies with a more flexible way to manage their ownership structure. In addition, there are different tax implications for corporations, which include the difference between a C corporation and an S corporation, and a tax-exempt versus a taxable corporation. More discussion of these points follows (http://www.investorwords.com).

Because a corporation is an entity considered separate and distinct from its members, a corporation itself can enter into contracts, sue and be sued, pays taxes separately from its owners, and can carry out actions necessary to conduct business. A corporation is also liable for its own debts and obligations. As a result, providing that corporate formalities are followed, the corporation's owners (the shareholders) enjoy limited liability and are legally shielded from the corporation's liabilities and debts.

The existence of a corporation is not dependent upon who the owners or investors are at any particular point in time. Once formed, a corporation continues to exist as a separate entity, even when shareholders die or sell their shares. A corporation continues to exist until the shareholders decide to dissolve it, merge it with another business, or the state government dissolves the entity for administrative reasons.

Corporations are subject to the laws of the state where they are incorporated and to the laws of any other state in which the corporations conduct business. As such, corporations may be subject to the laws of more than one state. Every state has corporation statutes that set forth the ground rules as to how corporations are formed, maintained, and operated (http://www.allbusiness.com).

Some key characteristics of a corporation are as follows:

- Limited liability of its owners, because the law views a corporation as a legal entity, separate from its owners, and
- Issuance of ownership in the corporation through shares of stock that can be easily transferred from one owner to another unless restricted by the bylaws.

C Corporations

C corporations are corporations that are taxed separately from the shareholders, which means that the corporation itself pays taxes on net taxable income. Unlike the S corporation described in the following section, the C corporation does not pass on business losses to the shareholders. The C corporation pays taxes on its taxable income before making dividend distributions to stockholders.

S Corporations

S corporations are corporations that elect to pass corporate income, losses, deductions, and credit through to their shareholders for federal income tax purposes. This permits shareholders of S corporations to report their share of corporate income and losses on their personal tax returns. Accordingly, they are assessed tax at their individual income tax rates. This allows S corporations to avoid double taxation, which would be tax assessed on the corporate entity as well as tax paid on the income of the individual.

To qualify for S corporation status, a corporation must meet certain requirements, some of which are listed in the following:

- The corporation must be a domestic corporation, that is, formed in the state in which the shareholder resides and not in another state.
- The corporation must have only allowable shareholders, which includes individuals, and certain trusts and estates, but may not include partnerships, corporations, or nonresident alien shareholders.
- The corporation cannot have more than 100 shareholders.
- The corporation can have only one class of stock.
- The corporation must be a type of corporation that is eligible to be formed as an S corporation. Ineligible corporations are certain financial institutions, insurance companies, and domestic international sales corporations.

For-Profit and Not-for-Profit Corporations

For-Profit Corporations

For-profit corporations' primary goal is to earn a profit and distribute such profit to shareholders. They can be privately held or publicly owned. Public companies trade on public markets and shares of the company can be purchased so that the purchasers or shareholders share in the profits or losses of the company. Most for-profit hospitals are investor owned, and thus one of the goals is to secure a profit for shareholders.

The profit of a corporation is taxed to the corporation when earned, and then is taxed to the shareholders when distributed as dividends. This creates a double tax. The corporation does not get a tax deduction when it distributes dividends to shareholders. Shareholders cannot deduct any loss of the corporation on an individual basis.

Nonprofit Corporations

A nonprofit corporation (also referred to as not-for-profit) entity is a corporation that is formed and exists to carry out educational, charitable, or religious purposes. It is an organization incorporated under state laws and generally approved by both the state's Secretary of State and its taxing authority. Based on the type of nonprofit corporation and the purpose for which it is created, application may also be made to the IRS for income tax exemption and other beneficial tax treatment. Note that state tax treatment and federal (IRS) tax treatment are distinct tax concerns, are applied for separately, and approval of one does not necessarily confer approval from the other.

The history behind the decision to allow not for profits is based on the fact that the hospital is organized and operated exclusively for religious, charitable, scientific, or educational purposes. What this purpose translates to is that ultimately the community is to receive a benefit in return for the government's decision to allow the hospital to receive preferential tax treatment. Nonprofit hospitals are not precluded from paying employees, managers, physicians, or others for their services; however, they are under more scrutiny to ensure that payment for those services is not detrimental to the community. In fact, the incorporators, officers, or trustees of such an entity do not receive any financial benefits. Rather, any earnings from a not-for-profit entity are used to further the goals of its educational, charitable, or religious purpose.

A nonprofit corporation is formed by incorporators and has a board of directors and officers, but no shareholders. These incorporators, directors, and officers may not receive a distribution of (any money from) profits, but officers and management may be paid reasonable salaries for services to the corporation.

Upon dissolution, which is disbanding or ceasing the existence of a nonprofit corporation, its assets must be distributed to an organization existing for similar purposes under the "*cy pres* doctrine." The French words *cy pres*, literally translated, mean "as close as possible," therefore, the assets of a dissolved nonprofit entity must be distributed to an organization operating for similar, or "as close as possible" purposes.

In order for contributions to a nonprofit corporation to be deductible to the donor as charitable gifts on federal income taxes, the corporation must submit a detailed application (with a substantial fee) for an IRS ruling confirming that the corporation is established for one of the specific nonprofit purposes spelled out in the Internal Revenue Code. Not every tax-exempt entity will fit this requirement, so a donor must verify the specifics enabling a deduction for certain contributions.

Nonprofit corporations also must file informational tax returns annually with the IRS and the state taxing body. In addition, a state's Attorney General generally has oversight powers to determine if the corporation is abiding by state laws by limiting its activities to its approved nonprofit purposes (http://legal-dictionary.thefreedictionary.com).

Nonprofit hospitals are usually organized under section 501(c)(3) of the Internal Revenue Code. Not-for-profit hospitals organized in this manner are exempt from federal income taxes. Exemption from state taxes is not automatic, and a not-for-profit corporation must request exemption from state taxes according to the laws of the state.

Professional Corporations

A professional corporation (PC) is a corporation formed specifically for the purpose of conducting a profession that requires licensure to practice, such as physicians, nurses, attorneys, dentists, certified public accountants, architects, and real estate brokers. Most states provide for such PCs under special statutes that allow the corporation to operate under the direction of professionals in the discipline for which the corporation is formed. Nurses (and many members of licensed professional disciplines) should be sure to check the laws governing PCs in their state. State laws vary, and it is necessary to know which disciplines are eligible for this type of entity. In addition, there may be specific provisions governing whether a nurse can form a PC with another professional discipline, such as a physician. As such, the nurse should consult with competent counsel, and other professional advisors before moving forward with these decisions.

In addition, unlike other corporations where the corporation itself can provide protection from some individual liability, the professional organization does not provide a shield for liability for any professional negligence (malpractice) by the licensed professionals. This means that the professional practitioner still will be personally liable for any negligent acts occurring in the practice of their profession despite the fact that they have incorporated (http://legal-dictionary.thefreedictionary.com).

Essential Requirements to Create a Corporation

State laws will identify the requirements for incorporation in the particular state, and these laws must be reviewed when considering the establishment of a corporation. This section identifies and lists the essential elements required for incorporation in most states.

Articles of Incorporation

The Articles of Incorporation (sometimes also referred to as the Certificate of Incorporation or Corporate Charter) are the primary rules governing the management of a corporation in the United States and are filed with the appropriate state agency. A corporation's Articles of Incorporation generally provide information such as the following:

- The corporation's name, which has to be unique from any other corporation in that jurisdiction. As part of the corporation's name, certain words such as "incorporated" or "corporation" or some equivalent are often included in the name to indicate to persons doing business that the organization is an incorporated entity.
- The name of the person(s) organizing the corporation.
- Whether the corporation is a stock corporation or nonstock corporation. This means that it must be specified whether the corporation has owners who are represented by shares of stock.
- Whether the corporation's existence is permanent or limited for a specific period of time. Generally, a corporation's existence is forever or until (1) it stops paying the state's corporate renewal fees or otherwise fails to do something required to continue its existence or (2) it files a request to wind up and dissolve.
- In some states, a corporation must declare the purpose for which it was formed. Some jurisdictions permit a general statement such as for any lawful purpose, but some require explicit specifications and this should be done as required under the specific state law.
- Whether the corporation is for profit or not for profit.
- If a stock corporation, the number of shares the corporation is authorized to issue, or the maximum amount in a specific currency of stock that the board may issue.
- The number and names of the corporation's initial board of directors.
- The identity and location of the corporation's registered or statutory agent. This is the person or business designated to receive notice when the corporation is a party in a legal action such as a lawsuit.

Most states permit a corporation to be formed by one person; in other cases, such as with nonprofit corporations, the law may require three or more people to form the corporation. Articles of Incorporation vary widely from corporation to corporation and from jurisdiction to jurisdiction but generally do not go into great detail about a corporation's operations. The details of the businesses operation are usually spelled out in more detail in a company's bylaws.

Bylaws

Corporate bylaws regulate how a corporation is run on a day-to-day basis. Bylaws often cover such topics as follows:

- Location of the business and registered agents and offices;
- The place, time, notice provisions, and rules for shareholders' meetings;
- Rules regarding shareholder voting rights;
- Actions that can be taken by shareholders without convening a meeting;
- The functions, qualifications, compensation, number, election and term, removal of directors, quorum and voting requirements, and actions board of directors can take without a meeting;
- How to deal with director conflicts of interest;
- Duties of officers, removal of officers, vacancies, and compensation of officers;
- Authorized issuance of stock certificates, form of stocks, transfer of stocks, how to deal with lost, stolen, or destroyed certificates;
- How books and records of the corporation are maintained and shareholders inspection rights with regard to such books and records;
- Distributions to shareholders from corporate profits; and
- Indemnification of directors, officers, and employees. Indemnification means to compensate another party to a contract for any loss that such other party may suffer during the performance of the contract. With regard to corporate directors, officers, and employees, it means that persons in these roles will be protected from harm and compensated by the corporation (often through insurance coverage) for losses that may result in the course of performance of their duties to the corporation.

SOLE PROPRIETORSHIP, PARTNERSHIP, GENERAL PARTNERSHIP, LIMITED LIABILITY PARTNERSHIP, AND LIMITED LIABILITY COMPANIES

Sole Proprietorship

The sole proprietorship is the simplest business form for an individual to utilize. As the name indicates, a sole proprietor is someone who owns an unincorporated business by himself or herself. An owner can generally begin to operate a sole proprietorship quickly without the necessity of filing any documents with the state where the proprietorship operates. Under a sole proprietorship, an owner can combine assets, using one checking account for personal and business purposes and one account for taxes owed on his or her personal tax returns. However, an individual who does business as a sole proprietor will also be personally liable for all debts of the business. If a sole proprietor should decide to share the responsibilities of his or her business with another person or party, the sole proprietorship will immediately and automatically be viewed legally as another entity, such as a partnership, regardless of the intent of the parties (Kopf, 2005).

It should be noted that even though one operates as a sole proprietor, there may be other required filings and approvals to consider based on the nature of the business to be carried out, such as health care licensing or approvals for health care services to be delivered.

Partnership

A partnership is the relationship existing between two or more persons who join together to carry on a trade or business. Each partner contributes money, property, labor, or skill, and expects to share in the profits and losses of the business. Partnerships are created under the laws of the state where the business is to be carried out.

A partnership must file an annual IRS information return to report the income, deductions, gains, losses, and so on from its operations, but it does not pay income tax. Instead, it "passes through" any profits or losses to its partners. Each partner includes his or her share of the partnership's income or loss on his or her tax return. Partners are not employees and should not be issued IRS Form W-2 Wage and Tax Statement. The partnership annually files a Return of Partnership Income Form 1065, and must furnish copies of Schedule K-1 from this return to the partners, which details each partners share of taxable income and tax deductions.

There are also specific types of partnerships, and some of these are presented in the following sections.

General Partnership

Under a general partnership, two or more individuals are operating in a fashion where losses and profits are shared. General partnerships are typically the easiest entity to form under state law and they enjoy tax advantages, such as passing through earnings to the owners without paying taxes as an entity.

A general partnership is the default business form in most states when two or more individuals operate as a business without filing documents with the state where the partnership operates. As was noted previously, not all states require filing of partnership formation documents when a partnership is created.

Under the laws governing general partnerships, each general partner is generally responsible for all of the debts of the business. If a partner to the arrangement dies, the partnership is automatically dissolved.

Limited Partnership

A limited partnership (LP) is a partnership where there are two tiers of partners—general partners and limited partners. LPs are created according to the law governing such entities in the state in which they are formed. All partners share in the profits and losses of the entity, but there must be at least one general partner. The general partners retain the same liabilities as a partner in a general partnership and are personally liable for the debts of the business. However, limited partners have limited exposure to liability; specifically, they are liable for obligations only to the extent of their capital contributions, plus any distributions made by the partnership to the limited partners.

An LP receives the same tax advantages of a general partnership. Most states require a certificate to be filed with the respective Secretary of State in order to be able to legally operate.

Limited Liability Partnership

A limited liability partnership (LLP) is essentially a general partnership but with limited liability for all members. Unlike a general partnership, the LLP is created by following formal statutory requirements. Similar to a general partnership, the LLP is not taxed as a separate entity and, therefore, all members are subject to flow-through taxation at the state and federal level.

The LLP format was formed to protect innocent partners from liability due to misconduct of other partners. The limited liability of all members is one important way in which the LLP differs from the general partnership. Unlike limited partners, LLP nonmanaging partners are liable only when participating in or supervising particular conduct or partners. In addition to misconduct, LLP members are not individually liable for all of the debts of the business. LLPs are subject to more stringent registration requirements, name restrictions, and insurance requirements. Failure to comply with statutory requisites can cause an entity to be deemed a general partnership (as compared to an LP that fails to comply with the statute will generally retain LP status).

Continuity of existence in partnerships. The death or withdrawal of a general partner, or the expiration of the term of the general partnership, will dissolve the partnership. Continuation of the partnership following such events can be contemplated in advance in a partnership agreement. Because a partnership is generally a voluntary association, any general partner who no longer desires to be associated with the partnership may withdraw and force dissolution. Dissolution of a partnership, as a general rule, requires winding up of its affairs and a liquidation of the partnership assets.

The relationship between the general partner and limited partner in an LP is different from that of a general partnership. If there is at least one general partner, the death or withdrawal of another general partner will not result in termination of the partnership. Moreover, limited partners, similar to a passive investor like a shareholder of a corporation, will not affect the continuity of the partnership they withdraw from.

Limited Liability Company

A limited liability company (LLC) is a flexible business structure that blends characteristics of partnerships and corporations. LLCs provide greater protection for members to manage the business and shield themselves from personal liability for the debts and obligations of the business. They are allowed by state statute, although the statutes governing their existence vary by state. LLCs are popular because, similar to a corporation, owners have limited personal liability for the debts and actions of the LLC. Other features of LLCs are more like a partnership, providing management flexibility and the benefit of pass-through taxation.

Owners of an LLC are called members. Because most states do not restrict ownership, members may include individuals, corporations, other LLCs, and foreign (out of state) entities. There is no maximum number of members. Most states also permit "single member" LLCs, which have only one owner.

This business structure is not available to all types of businesses. Generally, banks and insurance companies cannot operate as LLCs. It is necessary to check the various states' statutes and the federal tax regulations for further information when starting a business with this structure.

As was noted previously, LLCs share some of the characteristics of both partnerships and corporations. Similar to corporations, a filing is required to be filed with the state upon formation of the entity. Like partnerships, an LLC can be member managed. In most states, members may manage an LLC directly or delegate management responsibility to one or more managers. Managers of an LLC are usually elected or appointed by the members. A manager owes a duty of loyalty and care to the LLC. Unless the members consent, a manager may not use LLC property for personal benefit and may not compete with the LLC's business. In addition, a manager may not engage in self-dealing or usurp an LLC's business opportunities (see further discussion of this under fiduciary duties in this chapter).

Nearly every LLC maintains a separate written operating agreement, which is an agreement between the members that governs the affairs and operation of the LLC. The operating agreement typically provides the procedures for admitting new members, outlines the status of the LLC upon a member's withdrawal, and outlines the procedure for the dissolution of the LLC. Unless state law restricts the contents of an operating agreement, members of an LLC are generally free to develop the operating agreement as they see fit.

A member of an LLC possesses a membership interest, which is usually only an economic interest. A membership interest is considered personal property and may be freely transferred to nonmembers or members as provided in the operating agreement or under state law, although it does not include the right to participate in the management of the LLC. Accordingly, if a member assigns or sells a membership interest to another person, that other person typically receives only the right to the assigning member's share of profits in the LLC.

Members of an LLC contribute capital to the LLC in exchange for the membership interest. The default rule is that the total amount of a member's capital contribution to an LLC determines the member's voting and financial rights in the LLC. Distributions of profits or assets to members are usually governed by an LLC's operating agreement. Most state LLC laws do not require distributions to members other than when a member withdraws or terminates membership. Members vote to determine all aspects of distributions to members, including amount and timing. Because a member's share of any distribution or loss depends on a member's share of all capital contributions to an LLC, the LLC maintains records of each member's capital contribution.

State LLC statutes provide that members of an LLC are not personally liable for the LLC's debts and obligations, which is similar to the protections afforded shareholders in a corporation. An individual member is generally personally liable for his or her own torts (civil wrongdoings) and for any contractual obligations entered into on behalf of the member and not on behalf of an LLC. In addition, a member is personally liable to a third person if the member personally guarantees a debt or obligation to the third person. A person who incurs debts and obligations on behalf of the LLC prior to the LLC's formation is jointly and severally liable with the LLC for those debts and obligations.

Members may also become personally liable in some states under a "piercing the corporate veil" theory. As was stated earlier in this chapter, corporations exist in part to shield the personal assets of shareholders from personal liability for the debts or actions of a corporation. Because the corporation is a legal entity separate from its owners, the protection it affords is referred to as the "corporate veil." The "piercing the corporate veil" doctrine imposes personal liability upon corporate shareholders where it is determined that the corporation was not operated in compliance with applicable laws. In such a situation, the personal protection from corporate liability is "pierced," and an individual may be held liable. It is essential that the formation and operation of the corporation be carried out according to the law to avoid the imposition of this doctrine in a dispute or legal proceeding.

LLCs are permitted under the IRS regulations to elect whether to be treated as a corporation or partnership for taxation purposes. The regulations, known as "check the box" regulations have allowed LLC owners to determine their tax treatment, that is, whether to be taxed as a corporation or as a partnership. Therefore, LLCs can enjoy the best of both worlds by centralized corporate ownership like a corporation, but with pass-through partnership tax status.

FIDUCIARY DUTIES: DUTIES OF CARE AND LOYALTY

A fiduciary duty is an obligation to act in the best interest of another party. In this discussion, the party to whom the fiduciary duty is owed is called the client. The client can be another person or an entity such as a corporation, among other things. When one person agrees to act for another in a fiduciary relationship, the law forbids the fiduciary from acting in any manner adverse or contrary to the interests of the client, or from acting for his own benefit in relation to the subject matter. Clients are entitled to the best efforts of the fiduciary on their behalf and the fiduciaries must exercise all of the skill, care, and diligence at their disposal when acting on behalf of clients. A person acting in a fiduciary capacity is held to a high standard of honesty and full disclosure in regard to the client and must not obtain a personal benefit at the expense of the client (http://www.definitions.uslegal.com).

For instance, a corporation's board member has a fiduciary duty to the shareholders; a trustee has a fiduciary duty to the trust's beneficiaries; and an attorney has a fiduciary duty to a client. Fiduciary duties fall into two broad categories—the duty of loyalty and the duty of care.

A fiduciary obligation exists whenever the relationship with the corporation, client, or other entity involves a special trust, confidence, and reliance on the fiduciary to exercise their discretion or expertise in acting for the other party. The fiduciary must knowingly accept that trust and confidence to exercise their expertise and discretion to act on the other party's behalf.

In the discussion in the following sections on duty of care and duty of loyalty, the duties described apply in any situation where a fiduciary obligation or duty exists. The use of the word "corporation" should not be interpreted to mean that the information applies only to a corporation. The use of the word "corporation" in this discussion is intended to encompass any structure or entity where the duty arises.

Duty of Care

The duty of care is a standard of behavior that requires a board member to exercise the same reasonable care that an ordinary, prudent person would exercise in a like position under similar circumstances. For example, a publicly traded company's board of directors has a duty of care to its shareholders.

Reasonable care has two elements: (1) the board must be acting in good faith for the benefit of the company and must believe that the actions they are taking are in the best interests of the company and (2) that the actions taken are in the best interests of the company based on a reasonable investigation of the options available. In other words, they must carefully consider the available options within the time and financial constraints presented before they make a decision or take a particular action on behalf of the company. Board members should attend board meetings and be sure they are informed about the activities of the organization in order to be able to make informed and independent decisions when voting.

Duty of Loyalty

The duty of loyalty is a standard that requires board members to act in good faith, be faithful to the company, and pursue the company's best interests. In other words, board members must be dedicated to the organization's mission and put the interests of the organization above self-interest. The duty of loyalty is the duty of constant and unqualified fidelity.

Self-Dealing

A breach of the duty of loyalty would be self-dealing, which means taking a corporate opportunity and using it to benefit oneself instead of the corporation. In order to help eliminate the problem of self-dealing, directors are advised to provide full disclosure of any issues that could cause a potential conflict of interest. A conflict of interest in any situation arises where an individual has an interest or relationship that either does, or has the potential to, make it difficult or impossible to act completely in the best interest of the organization. If potential conflicts of interest occur, the affected board members generally should disclose the conflict, should not attempt to unduly influence the rest of the board, and should recuse — that is remove — themselves from voting on the matter.

Over the years, exceptions to self-interested transactions have been carved out to make the rule more workable and potentially advantageous to companies. In some states, self-interested transactions may be upheld if the decision was ratified by a fully informed and disinterested majority of the board or if a majority of shareholders approves the deal, or if the transaction was fully fair to the company.

Corporate Opportunities

If a corporate officer or director is presented with a business opportunity that the corporation is financially able to undertake and it is (1) in the line of the corporation's business and is of practical advantage to it, (2) is one in which the corporation has an interest or reasonable expectancy, and (3) by embracing the opportunity, the self-interest of the officer or director will be brought into conflict with that of the corporation, the law will not permit officers or directors to seize the opportunity for themselves. Some of the factors that a court may weigh when testing whether an officer or director took control of a corporate opportunity are as follows:

- Whether there were prior negotiations with the company regarding the opportunity;
- Whether the director concealed the opportunity from the company;
- Whether the director used company funds to pursue the opportunity;
- Whether the opportunity will create competition for the company; and
- Whether the company has nonmoney resources, such as human resources and technology sufficient to capture the opportunity.

CORPORATE DIRECTORS LIABILITY ISSUES

Corporate directors and officers increasingly face the possibility of liability for their actions with respect to their companies. Directors' and officers' personal assets can be at risk from lawsuits that contain allegations such as fraud, antitrust claims, unfair trade practices, and breach of contract in connection with their corporate duties.

Liability can stem from a variety of sources in the corporate structure, such as the following:

- *Employees*—Allegations arising from employees against directors and officers have been increasing over the past years. Largely, the increase has been related to employment allegations such as wrongful termination, discrimination, and harassment. Directors and officers are often able to purchase, or have purchased for them, Directors and Officers Liability Insurance policies, such as an Employment Practices Liability Insurance policy, which can provide protection against these types of allegations.
- *Shareholders*—Shareholders lawsuits are increasingly placing the spotlight on officers and directors for their actions in such situations as stock offerings, the amount of debt carried by the company, the types of investments made by the company, and mergers and acquisitions.
- *Strategic partners*—Directors and officers may face claims by any party with which the corporation contracts or even discusses a

contractual relationship. Claims of unfair business practices can arise and sometimes directors and officers find themselves in the middle of disputes.

Intellectual property—Claims may be made against directors and officers for copyright, patent, and trademark infringement. Increasingly, allegations of wrongdoing against directors and officers involve the hiring of competitors' key personnel and the proprietary technology or information that comes with the person hired.

Government agencies—Especially in today's era of increased government interaction in the health care field, directors and officers are seeing lawsuits and government actions that involve violations of regulatory acts, monopolistic behavior, and numerous other charges that can create additional liability for the company, and directors and officers as individuals.

Potential transactions and allegations that directors and officers should pay special attention to are the following:

- Compensation arrangements,
- Corporate gifts or contributions,
- Dissemination of false or misleading information,
- Excessive compensation to directors and officers,
- Failure to require withholding in connection with social security taxes,
- Fraudulent conduct,
- Conflicts of interest,
- Disclosure of material facts,
- Failure to examine reports or documents before signing,
- Failure to detect or stop embezzlement,
- Failure to supervise the activities of others in a proper manner,
- Improper repurchases of stock,
- Inducing the company to commit breach of contract,
- Insufficient administration resulting in financial loss,
- Neglect of proper management with regard to corporate debt,
- Permitting the company to engage in activities prohibited by statute,
- Transactions between corporations having common directors,
- Violation of specific Articles of Incorporation or bylaws,
- Wasting of corporate assets,
- Discrimination,
- Inducing or abetting willful wrongdoing by the company,
- Loans by company to directors and officers,

- Permitting the company to libel or slander,
- Purchase or sale of shares to regain management control,
- Sale of corporate assets for unreasonably low price, and
- Wrongful termination.

Indemnification

Indemnity provisions are often one of the methods by which companies will attempt to alleviate the concerns of officers and directors regarding their personal exposure to liability and thus their financial well-being. Indemnity is where the company, either directly or via insurance coverage, provides assurances against personal loss resulting from liability in connection with their duties to the company. However, indemnification is not available in all circumstances. Indemnification can be limited by the financial solvency or condition of the company. Indemnification in some situations may be prohibited by law, or by being contrary to public policy or statutory limitations. It is critical that directors and officers of companies understand their potential personal exposure to liability.

HOSPITAL CORPORATE LIABILITY: DUTIES OWED TO PATIENTS

In the early days of health care, hospitals were typically charitable institutions. Because of this, the courts protected charities from suits for negligence under a theory known as charitable immunity (Blumenreich, 2005, p. 253). Under the theory, the hospital as a charitable organization was immune from liability for negligent acts. The underlying purpose was to protect the ability of the charitable organization to raise money and thus preserve the availability of services. However, it also made it difficult, if not impossible, for a harmed patient to pursue a claim. The grant of immunity also meant that those causing any harm to a patient were unlikely to face any consequences of their actions (Blumenreich, 2005).

Over time, the courts considered other theories to allow a harmed patient to recover for their injuries. Theories such as "the captain of the ship" and "borrowed servant" imposed liability on the surgeon or hospital for the wrongdoing, based at least in part upon a belief that the surgeon or hospital had the means to pay the claim and that surgeons, particularly in the operating room, had some control over the hospital's employees. Under this theory, there was a way to award some compensation to a harmed patient (Blumenreich, 2005).

These theories too became obsolete as the courts began to develop a better understanding of the modern business of healthcare. (Blumenreich, 2005).

It was recognized that there were many activities that take place in the hospital that had nothing to do with the surgeon or the operating room and that there were others who could or should be held liable for negligence resulting in harm to patients.

Another factor influencing the development of thought on the issue of corporate liability was the availability of insurance purchased by hospitals to cover the costs of its liability. Once this became a more prevalent practice, the courts did not have to be as concerned about where they could find the money to compensate patients who had been harmed.

The prevailing theory now is based on the Doctrine of Corporate Liability. This doctrine seeks to impose liability on hospitals for the negligence of physicians and other health practitioners, particularly when these persons are not employees. A key question in this theory is whether a hospital is liable for the negligent acts of a physician or other practitioner who is not an employee of the hospital.

As discussed in Chapter 4 of this book, we know that the hospital or health care organization as employer can be held liable for the actions of its employees and agents under the vicarious liability doctrine of respondeat superior. Because employers typically exercise some degree of control and supervision over their employees, they could be held liable if those employees were negligent. However, physicians have traditionally been independent contractors and not subject to the same controls with respect to their work; therefore, under traditional legal theories a hospital was not liable for their acts.

However, courts have recognized that patients generally do not have control over certain medical services they receive from physicians who may work at the hospital as independent contractors. Anesthesiologists, radiologists, and pathologists are often examples of such services provided to patients without a patient's input or control. Hospitals' medical staff generally approves policies of certain medical and professional practitioners. Furthermore, patients rely on the reputation of the hospital in choosing where to go for their health needs and services. Therefore, the courts have expanded hospital liability for negligent acts committed on its premises under what is referred to as the legal theory of "ostensible or apparent agency." Ostensible or apparent agency is the condition that arises where the patient believes that a physician is acting under the authority of the hospital (in this case called the principal) when that authority has not in reality been granted through a relationship such as employment.

The Doctrine of Corporate liability for hospitals was first applied in the following case.

CASE EXAMPLE:

Darling v. Charleston Community Hospital (1965)

Issue: Whether hospital administrators had a duty to supervise and evaluate care delivered by physicians within the tospital.

This case was brought on behalf of a minor patient who was being treated for a leg injury. Plaintiff alleged negligent care on the part of the hospital that resulted in amputation of the patient's leg.

The hospital argued that it could not be held responsible since a hospital does not practice medicine and that the only duty it owed to its patients was limited to using reasonable care in selecting medical doctors for its staff.

COURT'S DECISION: In reaching a decision on this case, the court drew on JCAHO standards, the hospitals own bylaws and other documents in outlining the extent of the hospital's responsibility, and the court held that the hospital owed an independent duty of care to the patient (*Darling v. Charleston Hospital*, 1965).

Later cases refined the concept of corporate negligence, outlining the sources of standards that the plaintiff could offer as to hospital negligence and have identified the duties of the hospital as follows:

1. The duty to use reasonable care in the maintenance of safe and adequate facilities and equipment
2. The duty to select and retain only competent physicians
3. Duties to oversee all medical care
4. The duty to formulate, adopt, and enforce adequate rules to ensure quality care for the patients (Nathanson, 1993).

At least 33 states have adopted or recognized corporate liability, imposing these or similar duties upon its hospitals (Weinstock & Chopko, 2008).

CONCLUSIONS AND TRENDS

Whether seeking to be informed as to the business entity structure of a health care provider, or determining which structure should be selected to start one's own business, it is essential to be informed as to the entity choices available and the key attributes of each entity. There are many choices and aspects to consider, such as cost of formation, management and control, liability, and taxation, which are some of the factors that will influence the decisions made.

Corporations and other business structures are primarily controlled by state laws in terms of their formation and operation. Newer entity types, such as the LLPs and LLCs, are popular and offer flexibility in key areas of management, exposure to liability, and tax treatment.

It is essential that competent counsel be sought to assist with entity choice, formation, tax treatment, and other aspects. All legal requirements must be met, in order to assure that the desired entity type and other aspects of operation are in fact achieved.

Fiduciary duties are legal obligations that require anyone in a position of trust as to a company to act in the company's best interest. When serving in a fiduciary capacity, one must be fully informed in rendering the best decisions and being alert to any limitations they may have in this regard, such as conflicts of interest. Fiduciaries must also be aware of the potential areas of liability exposure that they may encounter in their area of responsibility.

Under the Doctrine of Corporate Liability, hospitals have an independent duty of care to the patients they serve. In responding to this duty, the nurse leader should be aware of relevant hospital policies and procedures, be sure that they are followed, and maintain alertness to the quality of care rendered to patients in their organizations.

KEY POINTS

- There are many types of business entities, with each having certain key characteristics that affect the type of business and its operation, such as management, tax effects, and exposure to liability. Nurses and nurse leaders should have a general knowledge of these elements whether it is to gain an understanding of the nature of the organization they are associated with or plan to start their own business.
- Most corporations and other business entity types are governed primarily by state law, which differs from state to state. Federal laws also have an effect, particularly in the area of income tax treatments.

◦ Businesses must also be aware of the laws of any state in which they do business as there may be relevant laws affecting the business operations.

◦ For health care businesses, state and federal laws and regulations may affect the manner in which the business is structured and operated.

◦ Where one sits in a position of trust to another person or entity, they undertake a role as fiduciary and are bound by the duties of care and loyalty. These obligations have the force of law and fiduciaries must know when they may have a self-interest that should be disclosed and addressed if there is any possibility that their objectivity toward the organization they serve is affected.

◦ Hospitals, in particular, owe specific duties to the patients they care for under the Doctrine of Corporate Liability. It is important to know what these duties are and for nurses and nurse leaders to continue in an advocacy role with respect to the care the patients receive.

REFERENCES

Blumenreich, G. A. (2005). Legal Briefs: The Doctrine of Corporate Liability. *AANA Journal, 73*(4), 253–257. Retrieved August 23, 2010, http://www.aana.com/Resources.aspx?id=4559

Darling v. Charleston Hospital, 33 Ill.2d 326, 211 N.E. 2d 253 (1965).

http://www.allbusiness.com/legal/contracts-agreements-incorporation/529–1.html

http://definitions.uslegal.com/b/breach-of-fiduciary-duty

http://www.investorwords.com/1140/corporation.html#ixzz10RgXVLkj

http://www.irs.gov/businesses/small/article/0,,id=98359,00.html

http://legal-dictionary.thefreedictionary.com/cy+pres+doctrine

http://legal-dictionary.thefreedictionary.com/Not-for-profit+corporation

http://legal-dictionary.thefreedictionary.com/professional+corporation

Kopf, R. (Ed.). (2005). *Business and legal guide book for nurse practitioners* (pp. 5–11). Columbus, OH: The American Association of Nurse Attorneys Health Law, Legislation and Compliance Section.

Nathanson, M. J. (1993). Hospital corporate negligence: Enforcing the hospital's role of administrator. *Tort and Insurance Law Journal, 28*, 575–595.

Weinstock, D. S., & Chopko, C. M. (2008). Developing and supporting theories of hospital liability in catastrophic injury cases. *Feldman Shepherd Wohlgelernter Tanner Weinstock & Dodig.* Retrieved August 20, 2010, from http:www.feldmanshepherd.com

CHAPTER THREE

CORPORATE COMPLIANCE

Diana C. Ballard

OBJECTIVES

- Understand the concept of corporate compliance and become familiar with the framework of law and regulation that governs compliance.
- Have a comprehensive understanding of what is meant by fraud and abuse.
- Be able to articulate why federal and state governments devote considerable resources to identify the cause, incidence, and prevention of fraud and abuse among health care providers.
- Understand the key elements, benefits, and requirements of an effective corporate compliance program.
- Recognize the role of nurses with regard to corporate compliance, including the impact on its practice and responsibilities.
- Understand how agencies and organizations can be prepared and respond effectively to government inquiries, audits, and surveys.

INTRODUCTION

Compliance is being in conformance with the requirements of laws, regulations, policies, procedures, and conduct. One should not be misled by the brevity or seeming simplicity of this statement. The state of being in conformance is multifaceted. The laws and regulations governing compliance are numerous and complex. In fact, it is one of the most complicated areas of law.

The business aspects and actual delivery of health care services consist of multiple complex activities and processes that must comply with various laws, regulation, and policy. There are, literally, hundreds of thousands of constantly changing Medicare program rules, regulations, interpretations, and various advisories and directives to comply with. One can only imagine the tens of thousands of hours and number of personnel health care organizations must devote to assuring that their business practices and policies are in compliance with these program requirements. Therefore, it is rather easy to see that the business and delivery of health care is greatly affected by the voluminous and complex requirements of compliance. It is also understandable that the more knowledgeable key health care professionals are with respect to compliance requirements, the more likely the organization is to have a successful compliance program.

Compliance requirements also apply to the numerous business and service arrangements among and between hospitals, physicians, free-standing surgery centers, skilled nursing facilities, and other health care facilities and entities. Every contract, every arrangement, every relationship must conform to specific laws, regulations, or policies.

As you will see in this chapter, the penalties for noncompliance can be severe. In some cases the relevant laws are criminal statutes, and penalties can include imprisonment. In both civil and criminal cases, penalties can include significant monetary penalties and even exclusion from participation in any government health care program. Exclusion from participation in a governmental health program means that a provider may not provide health care services to any person where his or her care would be reimbursed by any governmental payment source.

One might ask, "What are the implications for nurses and for nursing practice?" The answer is that nurses play an important role in assuring compliance—both directly and indirectly.

Much of the enforcement of the rules as noted previously is based on documentation that appears in patient records. This documentation serves to justify that the services provided were medically necessary and delivered in accordance with Medicare requirements.

If services are determined by Medicare as not to have been provided in compliance with the regulations, then the provider may not be reimbursed for the services even though they have already been delivered. Reimbursement payment decisions by the Medicare program to pay providers for the provision of health care services often rises or falls on the basis of the quality of medical documentation in the patient record. Nursing documentation can help to explain and lend support to the medical documentation even though, in most cases, nursing documentation alone cannot be used by Medicare for reimbursement decisions.

There is one area, however, where nursing documentation can serve directly as the basis for reimbursement by Medicare. Medicare can look to the nursing documentation, for example, to determining the stage of a pressure ulcer at the time of a patient's admission to the hospital. This is significant because Medicare will not pay the full reimbursement for the hospital stay where a patient develops a pressure ulcer during the hospitalization. You will read more about this in this chapter and in the chapter on nursing negligence in the discussion of "significant adverse events" (which were formerly referred to by Medicare as "never events") and "hospital-acquired conditions" (HACs).

Indirectly, as stated earlier in this section, nursing documentation in the record can support the medical documentation that Medicare might review when making reimbursement determination. This underscores the always-present need for precision, completeness, and specificity in nursing documentation.

Origins of Corporate Compliance

The federal government began focusing on health care fraud and abuse in the 1990s due to concerns over the amount of money that was being spent to support the Medicare program (Michael, 2003).

Corporate compliance has as its legal basis the Federal Sentencing Guidelines that came into force in 1991 and imposed stiff penalties and sanctions for corporations convicted of wrongdoing.

> In recent years, health care replaced the defense industry as the number-one fraud enforcement priority of the U.S. federal government. It is estimated that fraud, waste, and abuse make up between 3% and 10% of this country's US$1-trillion annual health care expenditures. During the fiscal year 1997 alone, the Medicare program reported that US$20.3 billion—11% of all Medicare fee-for-service payments—was due to fraud and abuse (Fowler, 1999, p. 50).

In the fiscal year 2009, it is estimated that US$54 billion was spent on improper Medicare payments. Medicare expenditures are expected to increase at a rate of 7.1% in 2010, and the rate of improper payments is expected to increase similarly (Simmons, 2009).

"Enacted piecemeal over the past 20 years, the fraud and abuse laws are a patchwork collection of statutes, regulations, cases, and official rulings that govern financial dealings and arrangements between health care providers and public or private payers" (Bolin & Clark, 2004, p. 546).

The only mitigating factors that can significantly reduce sanctions and penalties for violations of compliance requirements are those associated with an effective program to prevent violations of law, to encourage self-reporting of violations, and to cooperate with authorities in investigations. Corporate compliance programs (CCPs) that include these elements can facilitate risk reduction in areas of civil and criminal liability (Fowler, 1999).

The CCP is an organization-wide program comprised of a code of conduct and written policies, internal monitoring and auditing standards, employee training, feedback mechanisms and other features, all designed to prevent and detect violations of governmental laws, regulations, and policies (U.S. Sentencing Commission Guidelines, 2007). It is a system or method of ensuring that employees understand and will comply with laws that apply to what they do every day (Fowler, 1999).

"In 1995 the government launched a multidistrict, multigovernment agency initiative called Operation Restore Trust (ORT), a collaborative program with a focus on ferreting out fraud and abuse on a large scale" (Fowler, 1999, p. 50).

According to published reports, the enforcement efforts associated with these laws have paid off. Although the return on investment estimates vary and can be calculated any number of ways, the federal government believes that it is recovering approximately US$22.00 in fines and penalties from providers for every dollar that it spends in enforcement activities (Michael, 2003).

All health care providers have been the focus of investigation, including hospitals, home health agencies, hospices, physicians, long-term care facilities, and individuals. We can expect that these activities will continue and will be expanded into the future, making any provider of health services who receives payment from governmental programs a potential target of review (Michael, 2003).

Given the fact that expansion of such investigations and potential recovery of money to the Medicare program are indeed growing, in November 2009, the president of the United States issued an executive order focusing on reducing improper payments made by the Medicare program. That order focused on boosting transparency, holding agencies accountable, and creating strong incentives for compliance.

Building on the November 2009 order, in March 2010, President Obama signed a presidential memorandum that directed all federal departments and agencies to expand and intensify their use of payment recapture audits under the authority they currently have. In announcing this initiative, the president noted that the federal government expects to recapture at least US$2 billion over the next 3 years (The White House, Office of the Press Secretary, 2010). It is clear that the need for effective compliance efforts are as vital as ever!

Compliance Enforcement Produces Results

In its Annual Performance Report for Fiscal Year 2008, the Department of Health and Human Services (HHS) Office of the Inspector General (OIG) reported that

- US$2.35 billion in HHS receivables were returned to the Medicare Trust Fund via court orders or agreements to be paid through civil settlements that resulted from cases developed by OIG investigators,
- OIG audits identified US$1.33 billion in potential recoveries that were agreed to be pursued by HHS program managers, and
- the return on investment measuring the efficiency of the OIG's health care oversight efforts continued its trend of increasing returns and reached US$17 for every dollar spent in enforcement efforts for the reporting period (Message from the Inspector General, 2008).

History of the Medicare Program

Given that health care corporate compliance origins are associated with the Medicare program, it is useful to review the history and development of this federal medical insurance program. The Medicare program marked the beginning of governmental control and influence of a major entitlement program affecting millions of Americans and, ultimately, imposing significant authority over the providers that deliver health care services. These factors affect the way services are delivered and affect the professionals who deliver them.

President Lyndon B. Johnson signed the Social Security Act on July 20, 1965, establishing both Medicare and Medicaid. American citizens and permanent residents qualify for Medicare if they fulfill any (or all) of the following criteria: citizens aged 65 years or more and/or are entitled to Social Security or Railroad Retirement disability cash benefits for at least 24 months, citizens having end-stage renal disease (ESRD), or citizens in a category of certain otherwise noncovered aged persons who elect to pay a premium for Medicare coverage (Bissey, 2006).

Today, the government exerts significant control over health care markets. Medicare dramatically influenced this transformation, making the federal government the biggest purchaser of health care services and a primary determinant of the type, quality, and cost of health care services in major segments of the U.S. health care market (Twight, 1997).

Medicare was a responsibility of the Social Security Administration (SSA), whereas federal assistance to the State Medicaid programs was administered by the Social and Rehabilitation Service (SRS). Both agencies, SSA and SRS, were organized under what was then known as the Department of Health, Education, and Welfare (HEW).

In 1977, the Health Care Financing Administration (HCFA) was created under HEW to effectively coordinate Medicare and Medicaid. In 1980 HEW was divided into the Department of Education and the HHS. HCFA became an agency under HHS.

On June 14, 2001, the Bush administration announced that the agency that runs Medicare and Medicaid was getting a new name—the Centers for Medicare and Medicaid Services (CMS). According to Tommy Thompson, then secretary of Health and Human Services, the name change was to reflect a "new culture of responsiveness" at the agency (Pear, 2001). The CMS is the name currently used to identify the agency. Those in the health care field will have to judge whether or not this name change met its objective.

Medicare Conditions of Participation

Organizations that participate as providers of services in the Medicare program must meet specific standards set forth by CMS in the Conditions of Participation (CoP). CoP are identified by CMS as minimum health and safety standards that are the foundation for improving quality and protecting the health and safety of beneficiaries (CMS, 2009). Organizations must know the CoP that are relevant to the type of services they provide.

Any provider entity that participates in the Medicare program must meet the statutory—or legal—definition of the entity, as published in the Medicare Act. For example, in order for a hospital to participate in the Medicare program, it must meet the statutory definition of a "hospital" as found in Section 1395x(e) of the Medicare Act.

The secretary of HHS may refuse to enter into an agreement or may terminate an agreement after determining that a hospital fails to substantially meet this definition, thus removing a provider's eligibility to participate as a provider in the Medicare program (42 U.S.C. Section 1395x[e]).

As an example, provided in what follows is a part of the federal statute cited earlier that specifies the legal definition of a hospital for purposes of Medicare participation:

(e) Hospital
The term "hospital" (except for purposes of Sections 1395f (d), 1395f (f), and 1395n (b) of this title, subsection (a)(2) of this section,

paragraph (7) of this subsection, and subsection (i) of this section) means an institution which —

(1) is primarily engaged in providing, by or under the supervision of physicians, to inpatients

(A) diagnostic services and therapeutic services for medical diagnosis, treatment, and care of injured, disabled, or sick persons, or

(B) rehabilitation services for the rehabilitation of injured, disabled, or sick persons;

(2) maintains clinical records on all patients;

(3) has bylaws in effect with respect to its staff of physicians;

(4) has a requirement that every patient with respect to whom payment may be made under this subchapter must be under the care of a physician, except that a patient receiving qualified psychologist services (as defined in subsection (ii) of this section) may be under the care of a clinical psychologist with respect to such services to the extent permitted under State law;

(5) provides 24-hour nursing service rendered or supervised by a registered professional nurse, and has a licensed practical nurse or registered professional nurse on duty at all times; except that until January 1, 1979, the Secretary is authorized to waive the requirement of this paragraph for any one-year period with respect to any institution, insofar as such requirement relates to the provision of twenty-four-hour nursing service rendered or supervised by a registered professional nurse (except that in any event a registered professional nurse must be present on the premises to render or supervise the nursing service provided, during at least the regular daytime shift), where immediately preceding such one-year period he finds that....

CASE EXAMPLE:

BASED ON MEDICARE CoP

ANA v. Leavitt (2009)

As has already been noted, an entity must be in compliance with the requirements of the CoP in order to participate and receive reimbursement under the Medicare program.

SUMMARY OF CASE: In an interesting use of this law, the following case questioned whether the level of nurse staffing in a hospital was in compliance with the CoP as required. Plaintiffs in this case were American Nurses Association, who sought to address the issue of adequacy of nurse staffing in hospitals by challenging whether the staffing level met the Medicare CoP. They further alleged that by "deeming" hospitals to be in compliance on the basis of their Joint Commission accreditation, that the secretary had improperly delegated the enforcement of the staffing requirements to the Joint Commission.

CASE HOLDING (RESULT): Plaintiffs did not prevail in this case, and HHS won a motion to dismiss. HHS won because the court found that the secretary did not, lawfully or unlawfully, delegate to the Joint Commission the enforcement of staffing requirements as articulated in the act.

Rather, the court stated that the secretary delegates to the Joint Commission only a finding of fact, that is, whether or not the institution meets the requirements for Joint Commission accreditation. Therefore, the court said that the plaintiffs have not presented a cause of action upon which relief can be granted.

What this means is that the information and facts presented to the court were not sufficient to support the claims alleged in the suit. Therefore, the court could not act on the request and dismissed the suit.

PLAINTIFFS SOUGHT A DECLARATORY RULING: The court challenge in this matter was a special type of case in that Plaintiffs were seeking a declaratory judgment. In seeking a declaratory judgment, the parties bringing the court action are asking *the court to clarify an issue or provision of a law.*

It is not brought on behalf of any specific hospital or facility. Rather, it is brought on behalf of any facility that might be covered by the law as it is written and would, therefore, benefit from a court determination that would explain and clarify the meaning of the law. In this case, the court is asked to determine whether a hospital's nurse staffing levels meet the requirements specified in the CoP.

The reason that plaintiffs might do this is so that the ruling of the court, via the declaratory ruling, would then potentially affect staffing in other hospitals and facilities. In effect, if plaintiffs had been successful and received a ruling from the court that said the secretary was not enforcing staffing levels as required by law, then they could use that as a basis for seeking higher staffing levels in any number of facilities that would be subject to the CoP.

Staffing requirements as required in the CoP: CoP for hospitals require that a hospital " . . . provides 24-hour nursing service rendered or supervised by a registered professional nurse, and has a licensed practical nurse or registered professional nurse on duty at all times; . . . " (42 U.S.C. 1395x[e][5]).

HHS promulgated a regulation interpreting this Section 1395x(e) with respect to nursing requirements (see 42 C.F.R., Section 482.23). The interpreting regulation, with respect to nursing staffing, states

> The nursing service must have adequate numbers of licensed registered nurses, licensed practical (vocational) nurses, and other personnel to provide care to all patients as needed. There must be supervisory and staff personnel for each department or nursing unit to ensure, when needed, the immediate availability of a registered nurse for bedside care of any patient.

This interpretation was called into question and further clarified in this as a result of this court challenge. The plaintiffs (or parties bringing the suit) were the American Nurses Association, and two of its constituents, the New York State Nurses Association and the Washington State Nurses Association. The action was brought against Michael O. Leavitt, secretary of HHS, and Mark McClellan, administrator of the CMS (collectively, "HHS" or the "Secretary") seeking a declaratory judgment. To reiterate, a declaratory judgment means that the parties bringing the suit want the court to explain or further interpret a question or point of law to resolve an uncertainty so that it can avoid serious legal trouble in the future. In this case, we can see that plaintiffs were challenging hospital staffing levels and seeking to apply the CoP as a measure to ensure adequate staffing.

Plaintiffs claimed that HHS has unlawfully permitted inadequate staffing of registered nurses at hospitals that participate in the Medicare program. They argue that the Medicare Act, and regulations promulgated by HHS pursuant to it, requires HHS to ensure "the immediate availability of a registered nurse for bedside care of any patient."

An additional point of this legal challenge involved HHS deeming hospitals to be in compliance with the staffing requirements of the CoP if they are accredited by the Joint Commission. Since the Joint Commission is a private organization, plaintiffs contended that HHS unlawfully failed to ensure compliance with the staffing requirement and unlawfully delegated its authority to a private party.

By way of background, the Medicare Act permits an institution to be "deemed" to meet the requirements of Section 1395x(e) of the regulations if it has been accredited by the Joint Commission. The two requirements are that the accrediting organization's standards are at least equivalent to those promulgated in the regulations by the secretary of HHS and that the institution has not been found by the secretary to have significant deficiencies (Medicare Act, Sections 1395BB[a] and [d]).

To pursue a cause of action, or proceed to have a complaint heard by a court, the allegations must include what legal wrong has been committed and what remedy is available from the court to correct it. If the facts are not adequate to show a legal wrong, then there can be no case and, of course, no remedy, since it is already judged not to be sufficient to show a violation of the law. This point is further illustrated in Chapter 8 in the discussion of elements of negligence.

OIG Compliance Guidance for Hospitals

In 1996, Congress passed the Healthcare Insurance Portability and Accountability Act (HIPAA), which granted the federal government new weapons in its investigative arsenal, by, among other things, creating a new federal crime called "health fraud" and by expanding the criminal and civil penalties for health care fraud and abuse (HIPAA of 1996, Public Law 104–191; the Balanced Budget Act [BBA] of 1997, Public Law 105–133).

To assist in these efforts and help establish practices that will lead to effective compliance programs, the HHS' OIG encourages health care facilities to develop CCPs and publishes model guidance to assist in the structuring and effective performance of such programs. Guidance documents can be found on the OIG Web site (visit http://www.oig.hhs.gov/). OIG guidance documents are available for a number of organization and business types, including but not limited to:

- ambulance suppliers,
- clinical laboratories,
- DMEPOS (Durable Medical Equipment, Prosthetics, Orthotics, and Supplies) industry,
- individual and small-group physician practices,
- home health agencies,
- hospices, and
- hospitals.

The OIG is the primary source of direction and information about the requirements and conduct of health care CCPs.

The OIG prepares and publishes its "work plan" annually. The OIG work plan is an important tool for determining what priorities of investigation, review, or analysis will be of interest to the OIG for the upcoming year. Compliance departments use this as one of the sources of information that serves as a basis for the development of their organization's annual compliance work plan.

COMPLIANCE PROGRAM GUIDANCE FOR HOSPITALS

The OIG has issued original and supplemental guidance documents that together offer a set of guidelines that hospitals would be well advised to become familiar with when developing and implementing a new compliance program or evaluating an existing one (Medicare Act Sections 1395BB[a] and [d]). In fact, all providers should be familiar with the documents relevant to their type of entity and use them as a guide in establishing their compliance programs.

In issuing its supplemental hospital guidance document, the OIG outlines the following benefits of a CCP:

A successful compliance program addresses the public and private sectors' mutual goals of reducing fraud and abuse, enhancing health care providers' operations, improving the quality of health care services, and reducing the overall cost of health care services.

Attaining these goals benefits the hospital industry, the government, and patients alike. Compliance programs help hospitals fulfill their legal duty to refrain from submitting false or inaccurate claims or cost information to the federal health care programs or engaging in other illegal practices. A hospital may gain important additional benefits by voluntarily implementing a compliance program, including the following:

- Demonstrating the hospital's commitment to honest and responsible corporate conduct;
- Increasing the likelihood of preventing, identifying, and correcting unlawful and unethical behavior at an early stage;
- Encouraging employees to report potential problems to allow for appropriate internal inquiry and corrective action; and
- Through early detection and reporting, minimizing any financial loss to government and taxpayers, as well as any corresponding financial loss to the hospital.

An effective compliance program demonstrates a hospital's good-faith effort to comply with applicable statutes, regulations, and other federal health care program requirements and may significantly reduce the risk of unlawful conduct and corresponding sanctions. Organizations should recognize that Compliance Program Guidance is not intended to be a model for all organizations to strictly model their program after. Rather, it should be used by organizations as suggestions to use in developing their own programs. Every setting has its own characteristics and needs. They need to do risk assessments to identify their areas of greatest focus, evaluate the resources they have available for the program, and determine what other elements of their unique environment will help to shape the compliance program to best serve their needs (Federal Register, 2005).

Compliance program policies and procedures ensure that you know what to do, for example, if a government request for payment comes in or when an employee brings a compliance concern forward. Compliance procedures should be included in departmental policies so that employees in work areas have information that will improve their compliance-related performance in the conduct of their everyday duties; thus, it is important to have an effective compliance program that translates into an effective compliance culture. Accordingly, the compliance program must have *systems* in place that will lead to the realization of the program's key goals.

In its initial compliance program guidance, the OIG identified the following seven elements that should, at a minimum, be included in a comprehensive compliance program for hospitals. They are as follows:

1. The development and distribution of *written standards* of conduct as well as written policies and procedures that promote the hospital's commitment to compliance (e.g., by including adherence to compliance as an element in evaluating managers and employees) and address specific areas of potential fraud, such as claims development and submission processes, code gaming, and financial relationships with physicians and other health care professionals;
2. The designation of a chief compliance officer and other appropriate bodies, for example, a corporate compliance committee, charged with the responsibility of operating and monitoring the compliance program and who report directly to the CEO and the governing body;
3. The development and implementation of regular, effective education and training programs for all affected employees;

4. The maintenance of a process, such as a hotline, to receive complaints, and the adoption of procedures to protect the anonymity of complainants and to protect whistleblowers from retaliation;
5. The development of a system to respond to allegations of improper/ illegal activities and the enforcement of appropriate disciplinary action against employees who have violated internal compliance policies, applicable statutes, regulations, or federal health care program requirements;
6. The use of audits and/or other evaluation techniques to monitor compliance and assist in the reduction of identified problem areas; and
7. The investigation and remediation of identified systemic problems and the development of policies addressing the nonemployment or retention of sanctioned individuals (Federal Register, 1998).

LEGAL FRAMEWORK: LAWS THAT FORM THE LEGAL BASIS FOR COMPLIANCE

The Civil False Claims Act

The Civil False Claims Act (FCA; 31 U.S.C. S3729–33) *is the primary federal* statute that defines how the government can determine whether a person may be held responsible or may have liability for making a false claim. The FCA states that liability can exist if:

(a) the person "knowingly" presents or causes to be presented a false or fraudulent claim for payment or approval (31 U.S.C. s.3729[a][1]);
(b) "knowingly" makes, uses, or causes to be made or used a false record or statement to get a false or fraudulent claim paid or approved (31 U.S.C. s.3729[a][2]);
(c) conspires to defraud the government by getting a false or fraudulent claim allowed or paid (31 U.S.C. s.3729[a][3]);
(d) "knowingly" makes, uses, or causes to be made or used a false record or statement to conceal, avoid, or decrease an obligation to pay or transmit money or property to the United States (31 U.S.C. s.3729[a][7]).

For purposes of interpreting this statute, "knowing" means that a person has actual knowledge of the information or acts in deliberate ignorance of the falsity or truth of the information or acts in reckless disregard of the veracity of the information.

The False Claims Act (FCA) was signed into law at the close of the Civil War by President Lincoln after reports of rampant abuse by suppliers to the Union Army who sold shoddy or broken war equipment, sickly horses and mules, and rotten food. It was not until the mid-1990s that fraud and abuse became one of the top priorities of the Clinton administration and resulted in the government substantially increasing its efforts to stem such activity (Bolin & Clark, 2004, p. 547).

The FCA was amended in 1986 to expand the types of claims that could be prosecuted and to lower the level of proof necessary to recover payments (Smith, 1999). This changed the nature of medical billing and coding inaccuracies in that they can be a basis for exclusion in addition to heavy fines and penalties.

The Antikickback Statute

The antikickback statute (42 U.S.C. s1320a-7b[b]) is a criminal statute that prohibits a person from "knowingly and willfully" giving or offering to give "remuneration" if that payment is intended to constitute an "inducement" that will influence the recipient to:

- "refer" an individual to a person for the furnishing of any item or service for which payment may be made, in whole or in part, under a federal health care program (a covered item or service);
- "purchase," "order," or "lease" any covered item or service;
- "arrange for" the purchase, order, or lease of any covered item or service; or
- "recommend" the purchase, order, or lease of any covered item or service.

The antikickback statute also prohibits the solicitation or receipt of remuneration for any of these purposes.

The antikickback statute is so broad that it covers a number of various common and nonabusive arrangements. There are many statutory exceptions and safe harbors to this law.

A "safe harbor" means that an arrangement is structured in such a way that it fits perfectly into the legal description of the safe harbor. In such a case, the arrangement will be immune from prosecution under the antikickback statute. Of course, an arrangement must fit precisely within the safe harbor description to be immune.

Stark II Act 42 U.S.C. 1395nn

According to CMS, the Stark Law serves to curb overutilization of services, prevent limitations on a patient's choice of services based on financial considerations, and avoids restricting competition. The Stark Law, often referred to as the antireferral law, prohibits a physician from making a referral:

- to a health care entity,
- for the furnishing of a Designated Health Service (DHS),
- for which payment may be made under Medicare or Medicaid, and
- if the physician or an immediate family member has a financial relationship with the entity.

But in general, for Stark Law's purposes, a financial relationship is interpreted more broadly and includes ownership interests, and almost any form of compensation arrangement, direct or indirect. To name a few, these can be medicolegal agreements for administrative services, personal services contracts, or lease arrangements.

DHS is explicitly named and published by Current Procedural Terminology (CPT) code annually. The DHS categories included in the list of codes are as follows:

- Clinical laboratory services,
- Physical therapy services (including speech-language pathology services),
- Occupational therapy services,
- Radiology and certain other imaging services, and
- Radiation therapy services and supplies.

The following DHS categories are not defined by CPT codes but are considered DHS: durable medical equipment and supplies; parenteral and enteral nutrients, equipment, and supplies; prosthetics, orthotics, and prosthetic devices and supplies; home health services; outpatient prescription drugs; and inpatient and outpatient hospital services (for information regarding DHS that are not defined by codes, refer to 42 CFR Ch. IV [10–1-02 Edition §411.351]).

If a financial relationship as defined under Stark Law exists and patients are referred for a DHS, then the activity must either comply with an exception or the activity is illegal.

The compensation arrangements that constitute an exception under Stark Law include, among other things, bona fide employment arrangements, rental of office space or equipment, and physician recruitment.

Again, the activities should be carefully analyzed by counsel fully informed of the specifics of the arrangement to ensure that the arrangement is structured as required in order to be considered an exception. The Stark Law is one of the most complex laws in the health care arena.

The Stark Law is a civil law, and thus proof of intent is not required to find wrongdoing. Penalties for Stark Law violations include payment denial from the governmental health program, civil monetary penalties, and exclusions from federal and state programs.

Table 3.1 provides a side-by-side comparison of the key elements of the Stark Law and antikickback statue.

Table 3.1 A Comparison Between Stark and Antikickback Laws

	Stark	**Antikickback**
Scope of law	Pertains only to Medicare and Medicaid services and only to clinicians who are considered physicians under the Medicare program (MDs and DOs, dentists, podiatrists, chiropractors but not nurse practitioners, physician assistants, clinical psychologists, clinical social workers, nurse midwives, or clinical nurses specialists.	Applies to all federal healthcare programs (except Federal Employee Health Benefits Program) and to any type of health care or non–health care organization who may conduct business within federal health care programs
Prohibited actions	Prohibits a physician or immediate family member from referring a Medicare of Medicaid patient for certain type of health services (DHS) to an entity with which they have a financial relationship, unless the transaction fits into an exception. "Designated Health Services" are enumerated in the current list published by CMS.	Prohibits giving or offering to give payment to another if the payment is intended to induce referrals or induce the ordering, providing, leasing, furnishing, recommending, or arranging for a service, item, or any goods payable by a federal health care program. Provides for "safe harbors" that describe transactions that tend to induce referrals but will not be considered to violate the statute. Any actions that do not fit precisely within a safe harbor will be analyzed according to the facts and circumstances of the specific actions under review.

(Continued)

Table 3.1 A Comparison Between Stark and Antikickback Laws
(*Continued*)

	Stark	Antikickback
Civil versus criminal	Stark is a civil statute and does not have criminal penalties,but it does include civil and administrative sanctions, exclusion from the Medicare program, and imposition of civil monetary penalties for violations.	Is a criminal statute, has both civil and criminal penalties, including fines and jail, and exclusion from federal programs.
Intent	Strict Liability law, meaning that the law may be violated by actions that are not intentional.	Has a "state of mind" requirement in that the defendant must have acted "knowingly and willfully."

THE EMERGENCY MEDICAL TREATMENT AND LABOR ACT (EMTALA)

EMTALA (42 USCA, Section 1395dd) was enacted in 1986 to prohibit the practice of "patient dumping." Patient dumping, as referred to in the statute, means a hospital's refusal to provide basic emergency care, usually based on the individual's insurance status or inability to pay.

Originally referred to as the "antidumping" law, it requires hospitals to provide appropriate medical screening to any person who comes to the hospital emergency department and requests treatment or an examination for a medical condition.

The law arose from several high-profile reports of patients who were "sent away from" or not treated in hospital emergency rooms because they did not have insurance or could not afford to pay. In those widely reported examples, the consequences of an unstable patient being "dumped" without having received life-saving treatment resulted in serious medical consequences, and is some cases, death.

Patient deaths in the ED waiting room, before evaluation by the physician, are frequently reported in the news. For example a 58-year-old man died in a Texas ED waiting area after waiting for 19 hours to see a doctor for abdominal pains. A 49-year-old woman collapsed and died on the waiting room floor of a New York City psychiatric hospital and lay there ignored for more than an hour. She had been waiting nearly 24 hours for treatment before expiring (ED Legal Letter, 2009).

There have been numerous cases of EMTALA violations. In its 2001 report entitled "Questionable Hospitals," the Public Citizen Health Resource Group confirmed 527 such violations by hospitals in 46 states. Two examples are provided on the following pages.

Consider the case of *Burditt V. U.S. HHS* (1991). This was the first case in which a physician was sanctioned, or penalized, for an EMTALA violation.

CASE EXAMPLE:

Burditt V. U.S. HHS (1991)

Issue: Whether physicians can be held liable for an EMTALA violation.

SUMMARY OF CASE: The case involved a woman who arrived at the emergency room of DeTar Hospital in Victoria, Texas, at approximately 4:00 P.M. on the afternoon of December 5, 1986. She was pregnant with her sixth child and was at or near term. She was experiencing contractions every 3 minutes, and her membranes had ruptured. She was examined by two obstetrical nurses, who found indicia of labor and dangerously high blood pressure of 210/130.

The patient had received no prenatal care and did not have a regular doctor, nor did she have the means to pay for treatment. Dr. Burditt was on call according to the hospitals' rotating list and was notified. According to the court record, he told the nurse that he "did not want to take care of this lady" and asked that she be prepared for transfer to John Sealy Hospital in Galveston, Texas, which was 170 miles away.

Officials at DeTar Hospital advised Dr. Burditt that both he and the hospital had an obligation for the care of this patient. However, Dr. Burditt ordered the patient transferred to the hospital in Galveston. A nurse accompanied the patient in the ambulance for the transfer, and the patient delivered a healthy baby in the ambulance approximately 40 miles into the 170-mile trip. The nurse directed the ambulance to drive to nearby Ganado hospital so she could obtain Pitocin to control the patient's bleeding. While there, the nurse telephoned Dr. Burditt back at DeTar Hospital, and the physician ordered her to continue to Galveston despite the birth.

However, the patient insisted that they return to DeTar. A DeTar official then persuaded Dr. Burditt to permit another physician to take over the patient's care, and after a 3-day hospital stay under the care of the new physician, the patient was discharged in good condition.

In mid-1988, the Inspector General of the United States held a hearing into the conduct of Dr. Burditt in this case. The OIG found that the physician knowingly violated EMTALA and fined him US$20,000.00. The doctor appealed, but the decision of the OIG was upheld. Among the violations found by the OIG were that the physician failed to properly treat the patient's hypertension that put her at high risk of complications; that the physician ordered the transfer to another hospital even though the evidence showed that there was insufficient time, due to her condition, to do so safely; and that the physician transferred the patient without stabilizing her conditions as required.

DECISION: The OIG found that the physician's violations were "knowing," meaning that he was fully aware of his obligations to the patient but did not fulfill them even though he knew he was legally required to do so. The court made this determination by the facts of the case, including that hospital officials advised him of the EMTALA obligations and information provided to him by the nurses about the patient's condition.

In another EMTALA case against St. Joseph's Medical Center in Stockton, California, the judge found the hospital's failures "shocking" and characterized the treatment of a patient as "constituting a complete collapse of the system of care it purported to offer emergency patients."

The case involved the hospital's failure to provide care to an 88-year-old man who came to the emergency room for treatment. The OIG determined that the hospital failed to provide the required medical screening examination (MSE). The patient remained in the waiting room for nearly 3 hours, while the family pleaded unsuccessfully for help. The patient went into cardiopulmonary arrest and died without receiving treatment (Blalock & Wolfe, 2001).

Congress enacted EMTALA, which applies to any facility that participates in Medicare and has an emergency department, including military and Veterans' Administration facilities (Assid, 2007). Virtually all hospitals in the United States participate in Medicare.

Under the EMTALA rules, patients who go to a covered provider seeking care for an emergency condition, must be given an MSE. The purpose of the MSE is to determine whether or not an emergency medical condition exists or whether a patient is in active labor. *It is important to note that triage does not meet the requirements of the MSE.*

The person carrying out the MSE must be properly trained and qualified to do this examination and must be credentialed under the organization's bylaws and governing documents. Proper training under EMTALA means that the person has had specific training in conducting the MSE to determine whether or not an emergency medical condition exists. Note the discussion later in this section regarding nurse triage: Triage does not constitute an EMS exam unless the nurse carrying out the triage has had specialized training to conduct the MSE and is specifically credentialed through the hospital's medical staff–credentialing process.

For pregnant patients, the practice of conducting triage in the emergency department and sending them to the hospitals labor and delivery suite for the MSE is acceptable.

EMTALA does not prohibit asking a patient about their method of payment for the ED visit (Assid, 2007). Federal law permits the obtaining of information in the routine registration process, but the MSE or stabilizing treatment cannot be delayed because such information is not available or obtaining of such information is underway. In addition, EMTALA does not permit such information to be obtained "under duress." For patients presenting at an emergency room, this becomes a crucial factor because the experience of going to or being in an emergency room can be stressful. Accordingly, many hospital emergency departments do not initiate inquiries into insurance coverage or payment arrangements at least until the MSE has been completed, including consideration of the patient's condition at the time.

Hospitals must take care that such inquiries do not result in any delay in screening, stabilization, or treatment obligations under EMTALA.

If the examination reveals an emergency condition or active labor, the hospital must stabilize the condition or, if appropriate, transfer the person to another medical facility for care. This law applies to all hospitals, including critical-access hospitals that offer emergency services and participate in the Medicare program. EMTALA covers all individuals treated at those hospitals, not just those who receive Medicare benefits.

In a July 13, 2006, memo from CMS, the agency clarified that a hospital has an EMTALA obligation at the time a person "presents" at a hospital's dedicated emergency room or on hospital property other than the emergency room and requests treatment or examination for an emergency medical condition. This memo resulted from reports of "parking" patients. CMS described "parking" as a hospital's practice of preventing the transfer of patients from the EMS stretcher to the hospital bed or stretcher (CMS Memorandum, Ref: S&C-06–21, July 13, 2006).

Hospitals mistakenly believed that until they actually took responsibility for the patient, they were not obligated to provide care or accommodate the patient. CMS pointed out in the memo that such practices may be a violation of EMTALA and that the EMTALA obligation is triggered at the time the patient "presents" as discussed previously.

Hospitals and physicians can be assessed penalties if they negligently fail to provide stabilizing treatment to a person with an emergency medical condition or transfer an individual in an inappropriate manner. Violations of the law can result in fines up to US$50,000 and exclusion from the Medicare program.

A key to this law is to understand what constitutes an MSE. Nurses should know that emergency department triage does not generally constitute medical screening—unless the triage nurse has had specific training and has been credentialed by the hospital to perform this function. Triage is determining priorities for seeing patients in the emergency room. The MSE must be adequate to determine whether or not an emergency condition exists and must be carried out by a person with the knowledge and qualification to do this and be credentialed within the organization's relevant procedures.

The key to triggering EMTALA is whether the patient requests treatment for an emergency condition. Thus, a person can appear in an area of your hospital campus other than the emergency room, and if he or she requests emergency care, the EMTALA requirements can apply.

As with any legal analysis, care should be taken to seek opinion of counsel who is skilled in the area of your inquiry. In addition, state laws should be consulted, as there are often specific state enactments that are relevant to these questions.

Health Insurance Portability and Accountability Act

This law includes a comprehensive set of antifraud provisions and established four new enforcement programs:

- The Fraud and Abuse Control Program
- The Medicare Integrity Program
- The Beneficiary Incentive Program
- The Health Care Fraud and Abuse Data Collection Program

HIPAA also increased the funding for the fraud enforcement programs and gave the government more tools in the fight against fraud by creating new criminal offenses specifically for health care providers.

HIPAA also made changes to the Civil Monetary Penalties Law (CMPL; 42 U.S.C. Section 13201–7a) These changes included prohibitions on such acts as patterns of upcoding or wrongfully claiming medical necessity. Upcoding is when the standard procedure or CPT code that is used for billing purposes indicates a higher level of care than was actually provided as evidenced by documentation in the record. HIPAA also increased the penalties that can be levied against health care organizations or providers (Michael, 2003).

HIPAA provided even more motivation for all health care providers and organizations to establish CCPs, as it increased the criminal, civil, and administrative penalties applicable to health care providers that violate federal health care program provisions. Known as the "Kassebaum/ Kennedy Act," it amended and strengthened the federal health care fraud and abuse laws and increased authority and resources available to enforce them (Smith, 1999).

THE BALANCED BUDGET ACT OF 1997

The BBA addressed fraud and abuse by adding several new provisions that included permanent exclusion from the Medicare program for repeat offenders. In addition, the BBA required the OIG to maintain a toll-free hotline for Medicare beneficiaries to report Medicare waste, fraud, and abuse.

Sanctioned Persons and Exclusion List

The U.S. Congress seeks to protect the health and welfare of the nation's aged adults and those living in poverty, by implementing legislation to prevent certain individuals and businesses from participating in federally funded health care programs. As mandated by Congress, the OIG established a program to exclude individuals and entities that may have been banned from participation in the programs due to certain types of misconduct. The OIG imposes such exclusions under the authority of Sections 1128 and 1156 of the Social Security Act.

The federal government will not reimburse for Medicare or Medicaid services that are furnished or prescribed by an individual or entity that has been excluded. Those currently excluded parties are identified on the List of Excluded Individuals/Entities. Persons or entities listed on the federal OIG exclusion database must receive reinstatement through the OIG to be eligible for reimbursement through Medicare and Medicaid if and when the circumstances leading to their exclusion are resolved.

If a health care provider arranges or contracts (by employment or otherwise) with an individual or entity that is excluded by the OIG from program participation for the provision of items or services reimbursable under such a federal program, the provider may be subject to civil monetary penalty (CMP) liability if it renders services that are reimbursed, directly or indirectly, by such a program.

CMPs of up to US$10,000 for each item or service furnished by the excluded individual or entity and listed on a claim submitted for federal program reimbursement, as well as an assessment of up to three times the amount claimed and program exclusion, may be imposed.

For liability to be imposed, the statute requires that the provider submitting the claims for health care items or services furnished to an excluded individual or entity "knows or should know" that that person (or entity) was excluded from participation in the federal health care programs (Section 1128A(a)(6) SSA; 42 CFR 1003.102[a][2]).

Providers and contracting entities have an affirmative duty to check the program exclusion status of individuals and entities prior to entering into employment or contractual relationships, as failing to do so involves the risk of CMP liability. Providers must check the OIG List of Excluded Individuals and Entities on the OIG Web site (see http://oig.hhs.gov/fraud/exclusions.asp).

"A high percentage of nurses and nurses aides are listed on the OIG list of sanctioned providers, accounting for nearly 50% (more than 10,000 individuals) of those prosecuted for health care fraud" (Bolin & Clark, 2004, p. 546).

Bases for exclusion include convictions for program-related fraud and patient abuse, licensing board actions, and default on Health Education Assistance Loans.

CASE EXAMPLE:

PROVIDERS REQUIRED TO CHECK MEDICARE EXCLUSION LIST

DOJ v. Silver Hill Hospital (2009)

Issue: Whether Silver Hill Hospital violated the FCA by submitting claims to Medicare for services performed by a nurse who was on the exclusion list.

The Department of Justice (DOJ) brought charges against Silver Hill Hospital in New Canaan, Connecticut, for employing a nurse who was on the OIG list of sanctioned providers (DOJ, 2009). The allegations involved claims submitted to federal health care programs for services performed at the hospital by a nurse who was excluded from Medicare and Medicaid.

In September, 1999, HHS-OIG advised health care providers in an advisory bulletin that they must check the List of Excluded Individuals/Entities on the HHS-OIG Web site as part of their responsibility to perform appropriate due diligence to ensure that payments were not being made for services provided by an excluded individual or entity.

The hospital in this case, Silver Hill Hospital, employed a registered nurse who had been excluded from Medicare and Medicaid after her nursing license in the state of Connecticut was revoked. Although the Connecticut Board of Examiners for Nursing later reinstated her nursing license, the nurse did not apply for reinstatement to Medicare and the state's health care programs.

Silver Hills Hospital hired the nurse and failed to check the HHS-OIG online exclusion database as required. The nurse worked at the hospital for 4 years, after which the hospital terminated her when it learned that she was listed in the exclusion database.

DECISION: Because the hospital had submitted claims for services that were performed by this nurse who was excluded from Medicare, they were liable under the FCA. In addition to the monetary penalty, the hospital was required to establish policies and procedures to check both prospective and current employees to make sure they have not been excluded from federal health care programs.

As a result of the case, the DOJ imposed a civil monetary penalty of US$60,338.49 against the hospital to settle allegations under the FCA (DOJ, 2009).

Health care providers must have procedures in place so that every new employee is properly screened to be sure he or she is not on any excluded or sanctioned persons list. Failure to do so can result in imposition of penalties.

Whistleblower Cases (Qui Tam)

Qui tam is the name given to any type of action that an individual brings when he or she reports suspected fraud and abuse to the government. The person who brings the *qui tam* suit is called the "relator," and the relator files a claim to the DOJ. *Qui tam* relators, also referred to as *whistleblowers*, relay to the government potential violations under the FCA.

Whistleblowers can share in the proceeds of a suit. They are entitled to 15% and can recover up to 25% of any award (30% if the government doesn't intervene) rendered against an organization (31 United States Code, Section 3730).

In a *qui tam* case, the relator's claim is "under seal," which means that the complaint does not become public knowledge. The government has 60 days to investigate the allegations and decide whether to "intervene," which means they will take up the case and litigate with the relator. They can also decline to take up the case, and, in that case, the relator may "proceed" or litigate the case on his or her own (Michael, 2003).

Fraud and Abuse

Fraud is an intentional deception or misrepresentation with the intention of receiving some unauthorized benefit. Among the many types of fraud are billing for services not provided or improperly or incorrectly billing for services that were rendered (*Medicare Carriers Manual*, Section 11,102).

Abuse is a practice (usually a pattern of errors) that results in financial loss to the Medicare or Medicaid program. Abuse goes a step beyond fraud or inappropriate billing in that it questions whether a service was medically necessary for the patient. It further expands to the issue of whether the service that was provided met the standard of clinical care and whether it met the appropriate level of quality (*Medicare Carriers Manual*, Section 11,102).

The following are types of actions or behaviors that may constitute a fraudulent or abusive act and possibly be subject to prosecution:

- Obstruction of a federal audit;
- Making false statements in conjunction with Medicare or state health care programs;
- Making false statements with respect to conditions or operations of health care organizations or agencies;
- Accepting kickbacks, rebates, and bribes;
- Receiving discounts or other reductions in price obtained by a provider who does not properly disclose the fact that the discounts have been given;
- Presenting false, fictitious, or fraudulent claims;
- Conspiracy to defraud the government; and
- Making any false statement to the government.

Medicare Modernization Act of 2003

In the Medicare Modernization Act (MMA, 2003), Section 306, HHS was directed to demonstrate the use of Recovery Audit Contractors (RAC) to identify under- and over-payments and recoup payments in the Medicare program. RACs are companies engaged by CMS to perform the actual work of reviewing, auditing, and identifying improper Medicare payments. The 3-year demonstration project began in California, Florida, and New York and expanded to Massachusetts and South Carolina (MMA, 2003).

The RACs reviewed Medicare claims data to see whether the claim was paid correctly. The RAC entities are contractors who were paid on a contingency-fee basis during the demonstration project; that is, they were paid on the basis of the amount of overpayments collected. The contingency fee payment arrangement, and other elements of the RAC program will be modified when the program becomes permanent.

The demonstration project concluded in March 2008, and under the legislation became permanent, and will be expanded to all states by 2010.

CERT (Comprehensive Error-Rate Testing)

This program was developed by the CMS to determine national and contractor-specific claims payment–error rates. The purpose of the program is to measure and improve the accuracy of Medicare claims submission, processing, and payment.

The major focus is the paid-claims-error rate, determining if and when Medicare is paying claims that meet the benefit requirements, are reasonable and necessary, are coded correctly, and meet all other program policies and requirements. CMS reports the error rate each year and seeks to reduce the error rate to meet CMS accuracy targets.

Continued Movement Toward Quality

Compliance and quality go hand in hand. Both have a strong focus on process improvement. Failure to provide quality care can result in a violation of the FCA. The reason for this is that Medicare has made it known that delivery of services of poor quality does not meet the requirements for reimbursement consistent with the CoP and other quality measures. The case of the Ivy Ridge personal care center illustrates this point.

In a first-of-its-kind case, a settlement was announced involving the owners of personal care homes (DOJ, 2008). Under the settlement, the Ivy

Ridge Personal Care Center, Inc. (Ivy Ridge) would cease operating facilities in Philadelphia.

Ivy Ridge operated four personal care facilities in Pennsylvania. An investigation revealed that many residents at the owner's personal care homes received disability and social security payments. The federal government alleged that during these periods the entities and their owners failed to provide the level of service required by federal law. Specifically, the federal government found that the residents were subjected to grossly inadequate, dangerous housing and care, such as unsafe housing, inadequate security, insufficient food and nutrition, unsanitary conditions, and limited and irregular personal care, including inadequate oversight of administration of medications and unclean clothing and bedding.

The owners were also alleged to have diverted the disability and social security payments from use for the care of the residents to the owners' own use and benefit.

The settlement included a monetary penalty of US$700,000 from the owners. The owners also agreed to never again participate in a federally funded health care program or to ever again own, co-own, or operate any facility for which care is provided—whether federally funded or self-pay (DOJ, 2008).

In a statement, U.S. Attorney Patrick L. Meehan said,

> Care providers are trusted to carry out the duties that ensure a certain quality of life especially if funds, like social security, are involved. When the criteria set by the government are not met or are ignored, it is incumbent upon us to defend those who cannot defend themselves over those shortfalls (DOJ, 2008).

It is logical that as compliance efforts seek to include more quality and performance data that they will look to the level and quality of nursing care provided. Most hospitals and other provider entities recognize that most of the work is done by nurses. Medicare is proposing to add measures of nursing care to federal initiatives that ties pay to going public with performance measures on HHS' Web site, http://hospitalcompare.hhs.gov. The four measures are failure to rescue, pressure ulcers, falls, and falls with injuries (Evans, 2008).

As mentioned elsewhere in this chapter in the discussion of present on admission (POA), as of October 2008 adjustments in Medicare reimbursement will be made for patient care when the patient experiences a so-called preventable condition while in the hospital. You will note that many of these avoidable conditions are nurse-sensitive measures.

As the world of compliance moves to include patient care–quality issues it is important that nurses become more informed about the ways nursing performance relates to the organization's compliance program. I would suggest that a nursing compliance officer might become as common in some organizations as the corporate compliance officer is at this time.

Never Events

The National Quality Forum (NQF), a nonprofit national coalition of physicians, hospitals, businesses, and policy makers, has identified 28 events as occurrences that should never happen in a hospital and can be prevented (Leapfrog Group, 2008). Because they are considered preventable, and as stated earlier, should never happen in a hospital, they are also referred to as "never events" or "serious reportable events."

The NQF list encompasses 28 serious reportable events:

- Artificial insemination with the wrong-donor sperm or donor egg;
- Unintended retention of a foreign object in a patient after surgery or other procedure;
- Patient death or serious disability associated with patient elopement (disappearance);
- Patient death or serious disability associated with a medication error (e.g., errors involving the wrong drug, wrong dose, wrong patient, wrong time, wrong rate, wrong preparation, or wrong route of administration);
- Patient death or serious disability associated with a hemolytic reaction due to the administration of ABO/HLA-incompatible blood or blood products;
- Patient death or serious disability associated with an electric shock or elective cardioversion while being cared for in a health care facility;
- Patient death or serious disability associated with a fall while being cared for in a health care facility;
- Surgery performed on the wrong body part;
- Surgery performed on the wrong patient;
- Wrong surgical procedure performed on a patient;
- Intraoperative or immediately postoperative death in an ASA Class I patient;
- Patient death or serious disability associated with the use of contaminated drugs, devices, or biologics provided by the health care facility;
- Patient death or serious disability associated with the use or function of a device in patient care, in which the device is used or functions other than as intended;

- Patient death or serious disability associated with intravascular air embolism that occurs while being cared for in a health care facility;
- Infant discharged to the wrong person;
- Patient suicide, or attempted suicide resulting in serious disability, while being cared for in a health care facility;
- Maternal death or serious disability associated with labor or delivery in a low-risk pregnancy while being cared for in a health care facility;
- Patient death or serious disability associated with hypoglycemia, the onset of which occurs while the patient is being cared for in a health care facility;
- Death or serious disability (kernicterus) associated with failure to identify and treat hyperbilirubinemia in neonates;
- Stage 3 or 4 pressure ulcers acquired after admission to a health care facility;
- Patient death or serious disability due to spinal manipulative therapy;
- Any incident in which a line designated for oxygen or other gas to be delivered to a patient contains the wrong gas or is contaminated by toxic substances;
- Patient death or serious disability associated with a burn incurred from any source while being cared for in a health care facility;
- Patient death or serious disability associated with the use of restraints or bedrails while being cared for in a health care facility;
- Any instance of care ordered by or provided by someone impersonating a physician, nurse, pharmacist, or other licensed health care provider;
- Abduction of a patient of any age;
- Sexual assault on a patient within or on the grounds of the health care facility; and
- Death or significant injury of a patient or staff member resulting from a physical assault (i.e., battery) that occurs within or on the grounds of the health care facility.

Voluntary Safety Initiatives: The Leapfrog Group

The Leapfrog Group is an initiative driven by member organizations who are working to initiate breakthrough improvements in the safety, quality, and affordability of health care for Americans. With support by its members, Leapfrog aims at mobilizing employer purchasing power to alert America's health industry that big leaps in health care safety, quality, and customer value will be recognized and rewarded (Leapfrog, 2008).

Leapfrog has issued a policy asking hospitals to commit to four actions if a "Never Event" occurs within their facility. The four actions are as follows:

1. Apologize to the patient,
2. Report the event,
3. Perform a root cause analysis, and
4. Waive costs directly related to the event (Leapfrog Group, 2008).

There is some difference of opinion with regard to patient apologies. Some attorneys do not recommend this, as they believe it does or may amount to an admission of wrongdoing. Some states have enacted so-called sorry laws, which prohibit an apology from being admissible as evidence in a civil action. A section of the relevant Florida Statute is presented below as an example.

> Florida Evidence Code Section 90.4026:
> (2) The portion of statements, writings, or benevolent gestures expressing sympathy or a general sense of benevolence relating to the pain, suffering, or death of a person involved in an accident and made to that person or to the family of that person shall be inadmissible as evidence in a civil action. A statement of fault, however, which is part of, or in addition to, any of the above shall be admissible pursuant to this section.

Nurses should inquire as to the policy in their facilities and should participate in discussions in formulation of such policy. This author believes that a properly delivered and sincere apology is appropriate for the patient or family in such situations and can also contribute to reduced incidence of litigation.

Present on Admission

Medicare has noted that those conditions identified as "never events" result in increased costs to the program and that payment for such occurrences would not be consistent with the goals of Medicare reforms that would adjust payments to providers on the basis of quality and efficiency of care.

Therefore, starting October 1, 2007, hospitals were required to identify certain secondary diagnoses that are POA. If the condition was *not*

POA but, rather, was developed during the hospitalization, it is considered an HAC. An HAC is considered a condition acquired during a hospital stay that is reasonably preventable. HAC is subject to reduced payment from Medicare.

These POA diagnoses are drawn from those conditions identified by the NQF and identified as "never events" or serious reportable events. The purpose of the POA indicator is to differentiate between conditions present at admission and conditions that develop during an inpatient admission (AHIMA, 2007).

The Deficit Reduction Act of 2005 (DRA) requires a "quality adjustment" in Medicare Diagnosis–Related Group (DRG) payments for certain HACs, meaning that providers will not be paid at the highest allowable level for certain conditions acquired during a hospital stay, as such conditions are considered preventable (Murer, 2008).

The following conditions are subject to the Medicare POA reporting and payment reduction initiative as of October 1, 2008:

1. Object left in surgery (Serious Preventable Error [SPE] or "Never Event");
2. Air embolism (SPE);
3. Blood incompatibility (SPE);
4. Vascular catheter–associated infection;
5. Surgical site infection—mediastinitis after coronary artery bypass graft (CABG) surgery;
6. Catheter-associated urinary tract infections;
7. Pressure ulcers (decubitus ulcers), Stages 3 and 4;
8. Hospital-acquired injuries, such as fractures, dislocations, intracranial injury, crushing injury, burns, and other unspecified effects of external cause;
9. Surgical site infections, following orthopedic and bariatric surgery for obesity;
10. Poor glycemic control associated with certain conditions; and
11. Deep vein thrombosis or pulmonary embolism, following total knee and hip replacement.

NURSING'S ROLE IN COMPLIANCE

Although this chapter focuses predominantly on hospitals, findings discussed in the chapter highlight the point that every health care facility should have a program to ensure compliance with law, regulation, policy, procedure, and conduct. The breadth and complexity of compliance laws are vast; thus, it is beyond the scope of this chapter to review them in more detail.

As stated earlier, compliance guidance has been issued for numerous health care entity types. These guidance documents are an excellent blueprint for the development of compliance programs.

There are numerous benefits to having a well-established and comprehensive compliance program.

In the event of a government inquiry, there may be significant reductions in criminal and civil penalties for providers with an effective compliance program. The sentencing guidelines include a reduction in fines for effective plans as well as further reduction for self-reporting and cooperation.

You may be able to avoid imposition of a corporate integrity agreement (CIA) if there is an effective compliance program in place. CIA's are costly and cumbersome and include lengthy government oversight. CIA's are also costly to implement due to the programs, plans, and resources they may require you to put into place.

A compliance program includes education of the workforce, as a knowledgeable workforce is more alert to errors and other compliance issues. This will help in addressing problems early, before they become more serious and potentially widespread.

An effective compliance program that includes education can enhance the knowledge of billing personnel and thus help to avoid billing errors. Billing errors can result in under- as well as over-billing.

The patient information documented in the record by nurses and others becomes the basis for identifying many of the services for which a provider can submit a bill to Medicare or to another payer. While the medical documentation in the record must be present for proper billing determinations, proper nursing documentation can help to verify the appropriateness of billing. Any mismatch between the billing information and the documentation would lead to delays in payouts (Michael, 2003). It is wrong, of course, to ask a nurse to match documentation to billing. Rather, the billing should match the documentation, and nurses should document completely and accurately to assure that the record is complete. Any nurse who falsely documents care jeopardizes his or her career by putting his or her license at risk and makes himself or herself vulnerable to state or federal prosecution.

Nurses should be active participants in the organization's CCP. They should know who the corporate compliance officer is and should take advantage of all required and optional compliance training. They must maintain current knowledge of compliance-related materials that are disseminated from time to time either by the organization or through professional associations, journals, and publications.

Nurses should know how compliance concerns are reported in their organization and immediately report any activities they suspect may be inappropriate or appear to be violations of any state or federal statute or regulation.

Internal audits and monitoring activities are important ongoing tools of a compliance program. Therefore, employees involved in internal audits or procedure reviews should be fully cooperative.

Nurses can also assist with compliance-related policy and procedure implementation efforts and participate in the enforcement of compliance standards. Take steps to inform your workers about the compliance policies and procedures relevant to their area of work (Michael, 2003).

An effective compliance program can result in improved communication with the work force, which may then be more likely to bring issues and concerns to the attention of management. In addition to earlier intervention that helps to limit the scope of a problem, the enhanced communication can also encourage your employees to bring their concerns to the attention of management in the organization rather than to the press or to the government.

Indeed a compliance program may require significant commitment, including investing time and resources. However, superficial efforts or programs that are hastily constructed and implemented without a long-term commitment to a culture of compliance likely will be ineffective and may expose a facility to greater liability than if it had no program at all (Federal Register, March 16, 2000).

CONCLUSIONS AND TRENDS

As the population ages and the need for health care for the older adults grows, efforts of the federal government to control costs of care will increase. We can expect that programs designed to identify errors in billing and claim submission will grow, and of particular importance to nurses, the trend toward focus on quality will continue.

Nurses need to be alert to the need for precise and complete documentation because their inputs to the patient record will support the need for medical care and services rendered. In addition, we may see an increase in actions such as we now see in the POA rules with regard to pressure ulcers, that is, that nurse's notes may be relied upon while determining the progression of a disease/condition through various stages, for example, different stages of pressure ulcers, as discussed earlier. This is a significant change and may have an influence on other aspects of care as well.

CCPs will continue to be a crucial component of the health care organization and can serve to reduce liability if they are effective and include the necessary key elements as outlined in the OIG guidance documents. Nursing will, and must, take a more prominent role, and perhaps we will see nursing compliance evolving as a specialist area in the future, given the complexity of the work involved. I suggest that some elements may already be in place, given the current role of case management and nurse documentation specialists, who play a key role in assessing the nature and quality of patient-record documentation.

Nurses are among the largest health care worker group on the OIG's exclusion list. As you can see by the *Silver Hill* case in this chapter, nursing departments must be sure to ascertain that all nurses and health care assistants are screened with respect to being named on the OIG's exclusion list prior to employment. As in the *Silver Hill* case, the hospital paid a hefty penalty for failure to follow this law.

EMTALA is a very important law and relevant to nurses, as they are often the first contacts with patients coming to the emergency room. Nurses must be sure to understand the difference between triage and the MSE, as well as the qualifications and authority needed to perform the MSE. As we saw in the Burditt case, a physician as well as the hospital can be liable for failure to comply with EMTALA. Can nursing be far behind?

Nursing's key role in the provision of quality services to patients has always been important, and that focus will only continue to expand. Knowledge of what compliance is and how nursing can participate in assuring that all actions are proper and legal will enhance the health care experience for patients and permit the nurse to continue to serve as a key advocate for the provision of quality health care in the future.

KEY POINTS

- Federal government began focusing on health care fraud and abuse in the 1990s over concerns about the cost of the Medicare program. Only recently health care replaced the defense industry as the number-one fraud enforcement priority of the U.S. federal government.

Corporate compliance programs (CCPs) that are operated effectively, and include prevention, self-reporting, and cooperation with investigations, are the only factors that can help reduce penalties if violations are found.

Health care facilities that participate in federal programs must screen employees and business associates to be sure that they are not on the OIG list of excluded providers or persons, or face penalties.

EMTALA is a very important law that requires that hospitals conduct medical screening examination (MSE) in all patients requesting emergency treatment—whether they are covered by Medicare or not. The MSE must be adequate to determine whether an emergency medical condition or active labor exists, and the treatment cannot be delayed if a patient does not have the means to pay for the services.

As compliance efforts move toward focus on quality the responsibility of nurses increases. Nursing documentation is expected to occupy an increasingly important role in compliance with respect to determining the quality of services provided.

REFERENCES

AHIMA Clinical Terminology and Classification Practice Council. (2007). Planning for present on admission. *Journal of AHIMA, 10,* 73–77.

American Nurses Association v. Leavitt (D.C. 1–13-2009); Civil Action 06–01087 (HHK).

Assid, P. A. (2007). Emergency medical treatment and active labor act: What you need to know. *Journal of Emergency Nursing, 33*(4), 324–326.

Balanced Budget Act of 1997 (Public Law 105–133).

Bissey, B. S. (2006). *The compliance officer's handbook.* Danvers, MA: HCPro, Inc.

Blalock, K. R. N., & Wolfe, S. (2001, July). *"Questionable hospitals: 527 hospitals that violated the Emergency Medical Treatment and Labor Act: A detailed look at "patient dumping".* Washington, DC: Public Citizen Health Research Group.

Bolin, J. N., & Clark, L. S. (2004). Avoiding charges of fraud and abuse: Developing and implementing an effective compliance program. *Journal of Nursing Administration, 34*(12), 546–550.

Burditt V. U.S. HHS, 934 F.2d 1362 (CTA 5th 1991).

Centers for Medicare & Medicaid Services. (2006, July 13). *Memorandum Ref: S&C-06–21, "Parking of Emergency Medical Patient in Hospital."* Baltimore, MD: Author.

Centers for Medicare & Medicaid Services. (n.d.). Available from http://www.cms.hhs.gov/CFCsAndCOPs/

Civil Actions For False Claims, 31 United States Code Section 3730.

Civil False Claims Act (FCA) (31 U.S.C. S3729–33)

42 CFR Ch. IV (10–1-02 Edition §411.351

Corporate compliance: Get ready for health care quality's new frontier. (2000, November). *Hospital Peer Review, 25*(11), 145–147.

Department of Health and Human Services. *Medicare Carriers Manual* (Section 11,102). Washington, DC: Author.

Department of Justice. (2009, January 8). Silver hill hospital pays $60,338.49 to settle allegations under the False Claims Act. *United States attorney's office district of Connecticut press release.* Available from http://www.usdoj.gov/usao/ct/Press2009/20090108–1.html

Department of Justice. (2008, June 10). U.S. attorney announces first settlement involving personal care homes. *United States attorney eastern district of Pennsylvania.* Available from http://www.usdoj.gov/usao/ct/Press2009/20090108–1.html

Emergency department triage—the new hotbed of litigation? (2009). *ED Legal Letter.* Retrieved March 19, 2010, from http://www.highbeam.com/doc/1G1–204358108.html

Evans, M. (2008, April 21). Nursing great expectations. *Modern Healthcare,* 28–30.

Federal Register, January 31, 2005, p. 4859.

65 Fed. Reg. 14289, March 16, 2000

Fla. Stat. § 90.4026 Statements expressing sympathy; admissibility; definitions.

Fowler, N. (1999). Corporate compliance: Framework and implementation. *Radiology Management, 21*(1), 50–53.

HIPAA of 1996 (Public Law 104–191)

Leapfrog Group. (2008, March). *Factsheet—"Never Events."* Washington, DC: Author.

Medicare Act, Sections 1395BB(a) and (d).

Medicare Modernization Act of 2003, P.L. 108–173.

Michael, J. (2003). What home healthcare nurses should know about fraud and abuse. *Home Healthcare Nurse, 21*(8), 522–530.

Murer, C. G. (2008, August-September). Present on admission overview. *Rehab Management.* Retrieved January 24, 2009, from http://www.rehabpub.com September /issues/articles/2008–08_13.asp

Office of the Inspector General. (1999). The effect of exclusion from participation in federal health care programs. *Special Advisory Bulletin.* Available from http://oig.hhs.gov/fraud/alerts/effect_of_exclusion.asp#f3)

Office of the Inspector General. (2009). *Annual performance report for fiscal year 2008.* Retrieved January 23, 2009, from http://oig.hhs.gov/publications/docs/budget/FY2008_APR.pdf

Office of the Inspector General's compliance program guidance for hospitals. (1998, February 23). *Federal Register, 63*(243), 8987.

Office of the Inspector General. (2009, February 17). *OIG news: Administrative law judge upholds HHS—OIG's $50,000 civil monetary penalty against St. Joseph's Medical Center for violating EMTALA.* Washington, DC: Author.

Office of the Inspector General's supplemental compliance program guidance for hospitals. (2005). *Federal Register, 70*(19), 4859.

Practice brief. Seven steps to corporate compliance: The HIM role. (1999). *Journal of the American Health Information Management Association, 70*(9), 84–84.

Simmons, J. (2009, November 18). HealthLeaders Media. CBO: Physician Payment Bill Would Cost Medicare Beneficiaries. http://www.healthleadersmedia.com/content/PHY-232345/CBO-Physiciam-Payment-Bill-Would-Cost-Medicare-Beneficiaries. Accessed 16 January 2011.

Smith, R. K. (1999). *Corporate compliance in healthcare: A marketing framework.* Retrieved January 12, 2009, from http://sbaer.uca.edu/Research/sma/1999/27.pdf

Social Security Act Sec. 1128A(a)(6). [42 CFR 1003.102(a)(2)] Civil Monetary Penalties.

Social Security Act Sec. 1867. [42 U.S.C. 1395] Examination and Treatment for Emergency Medical Conditions and Women in Labor.

Twight, C. (1997). Medicare's origin: The economics and politics of dependency. *The Cato Journal, 16*(3), 309–338.

United States Code (42 USCA Sec. 1395dd).

United States Code (42 U.S.C. 1395x(e).

United States Code (42 U.S.C. 1395x(e)(5).

United States Sentencing Commission Guidelines. (2007). In *Federal Sentencing Guidelines Manual* (Chapter 8). Washington, DC: Author.

The White House, Office of the Press Secretary. (2010, March 10). *President Obama announces new effort to crack down on waste and fraud.* Washington, DC: Author.

ADDITIONAL READINGS

Gosfield, A. G. (2004, January/February). Ten myths about the Stark statute debunked. *Journal of Medical Practice Management*, 200–203.

Head, B. (2000). Corporate compliance and the hospice nurse. *Home Healthcare Nurse, 18*(5), 290–301.

Mintz, et al. (2003) Health law advisory: CMS final rule clarifies hospital responsibilities under EMTALA. Retrieved January 9, 2009, from http://www.Mintz.com/publications/1143/Health_Advisory_CMS_Final_Rule_Clarifies_Hospital_Responsibilities_Under_EMTALA. Accessed 16 January 2011.

Ortquist, S., & Vacca, S. (2004). Evaluating compliance program effectiveness. *Journal of the American Health Information Management Association, 75*(1), 74–75.

Pear, R. (2001, June 15). Medicare agency changes name in an effort to emphasize service. *New York Times.* From http://www.nytimes.com/2001/06/15/us/medi-care-agency-changes-name-in-an-effort-to-emphasize-service.html. Accessed 16 January 2011.

Schaffer, C. L. (1999). What corporate compliance means to a practicing nurse. *Home Healthcare Nurse, 17*(6), 395–396.

Siegel, S. (2004, February). Why nursing homes' next QI initiative should be build-
    ing an effective compliance program. *Health Care Law Monthly*, 3–14.
Vernaglia, L. W. (2000). Demystifying healthcare corporate compliance programs.
    JONA's Healthcare Law, Ethics, and Regulation, 2(3), 73–75.
Whitson, F. (2006, January) When Medicare asks for medical records or requests
    money back: What do you do [Electronic Version]. Florida Orthopaedic Society
    Quarterly Newsletter Winter 2006. http://www.fos-society.com/Winter2006.
    pdf. Accessed 15 January 2011.

CHAPTER FOUR

LAWS GOVERNING THE WORKPLACE

Paula DiMeo Grant and John J. Vecchione

OBJECTIVES

- Identify three federal antidiscrimination laws.
- Describe the types of discrimination that Title VII of the Civil Rights Act of 1964 prohibits.
- Become familiar with the Age Discrimination in Employment Act (ADEA), the Americans with Disabilities Act (ADA), and the Family and Medical Leave Act (FMLA).
- Explain the function of the Equal Employment Opportunity Commission (EEOC).
- Identify the three essential elements of an employment contract.
- Discuss the purpose of the National Labor Relations Act and the function of the National Labor Relations Board (NLRB).
- Discuss the nurse's ethical obligations in the workplace.
- Describe the purpose of Occupational Safety and Health Act (OSH Act) and the function of the Occupational Health and Safety Administration.

INTRODUCTION

Laws governing the workplace include a vast array of state and federal laws. The chapter begins with an overview of the major federal antidiscrimination laws and the types of discrimination prohibited by these laws. The purpose of the Equal Employment Opportunity Commission (EEOC) is discussed along with the procedure for bringing a claim before that Agency. An explanation of antidiscrimination laws on the state level is also included.

The chapter then presents the elements of an employment contract and explains the "employment-at-will doctrine." Exceptions to this doctrine are explored. Employee and employer rights and obligations in the workplace are discussed. Case examples are used to illustrate salient points.

Nurses will benefit from knowledge of this important area of the law, both in terms of improving their management of human resources in the workplace and enhancing their level of understanding of employer and employee rights and responsibilities.

OVERVIEW OF FEDERAL ANTIDISCRIMINATION LAWS

The federal laws and regulations governing the workplace are many and varied. The principal laws dealing with employee's rights, however, address equality, fairness, and discrimination claims. The three oldest and most traditional are:

1. The Civil Rights Act of 1866 ("Section 1981"),
2. The Civil Rights Act of 1871 ("Section 1983"), and
3. Title VII of the Civil Rights Act of 1964 ("Title VII"; 42 U.S.C. Sections 1981, 1983 and 2000 [e] *et seq.*).

Sections 1981 and 1983 of the Civil Rights Act were passed just after the Civil War. They were written primarily to address racial discrimination in various contexts, though Section 1983 protects against many constitutional violations beyond race discrimination. Title VII was initially passed during the civil rights' revolution of the 1960s and, as we shall see, prevents many other forms of discrimination. These three acts constitute the "trinity" of discrimination claims and are often brought together when racial discrimination is involved.

Joining these three laws are the following:

1. The Age Discrimination in Employment Act ("ADEA"), 29 U.S.C. Section 621;
2. The Americans with Disabilities Act ("ADA"), 42 U.S.C. Section 1201; and
3. The Family and Medical Leave Act ("FMLA"), 29 U.S.C. Section 2601.

Each of these important laws provides the American worker with protections from discrimination on the basis of age or disability and provides certain rights to those with family obligations.

Not all of these laws apply to all employers in the United States. For instance, Section 1983 of the Civil Rights Act is to provide remedy to those whose constitutional rights have been violated by someone acting under state or federal authority (a government actor). Title VII affects only employers with at least 15 employees, whereas the ADA requires a minimum of 20 employees. Taken as a whole, however, these laws apply to most large health care employers in the United States. In each case, employers can violate them not only by engaging in prohibited discrimination or activity, but also by taking retaliatory action against an employee for asserting his or her constitutional rights.

These laws affect every activity associated with employment, and no activity can be engaged in by the employer that does not meet the limits and requirements of the laws. Each protects against separate wrongs, though there is often overlap depending on the nature of the claim and the class protected.

Civil Rights Act of 1866 (Section 1981)

Section 1981 of the Civil Rights Act of 1866 is the oldest of the widely known civil rights statutes, though it has been amended since its inception. It broadly protects against all forms of racial (and national origin) discrimination in the making and enforcing of contracts. It provides that:

> All persons within the jurisdiction of the United States shall have the same right in every State and Territory to make and enforce contracts, to sue, be parties, give evidence, and to the full and equal benefit of all laws and proceedings for the security of persons and property as is enjoyed by white citizens, and shall be subject to like punishment, pains, penalties, taxes, licenses, and exactions of every kind, and to no other (Section, 1981 [a]).

The statute now defines "make and enforce contracts" broadly to encompass all aspects of the employment relationship. The term is defined as follows:

> For purposes of this section, the term "make and enforce contracts" includes the making, performance, modification, and termination of contracts, and the enjoyment of all benefits, privileges, terms, and conditions of the contractual relationship (Section, 1981 [b]).

Finally, it makes clear that, unlike some other protections, Section 1981 extends to private impairment of these rights, as well as those done by the government or those bodies under its authority, stating, "The rights protected by this section are protected against impairment by nongovernmental discrimination and impairment under color of State law" (Section 1981, [c]). This means that private entities, such as nongovernmental employers, are held to the requirements of this law if they are serving a function or acting under the authority of the government. This is often called "acting under color of law."

In many ways Section 1981 is the broadest of the civil rights statutes. It prevents private employers from discriminating on the basis of race, and given that it would also apply to health care contracts, its purview extends to private contracts as well, preventing the possibility of any racial discrimination in such contracts. There is no limit as to who is prevented from taking such discriminatory action. It covers governmental as well as private parties or entities; furthermore, the private parties or entities need not have a minimum number of employees, as is the case with some other federal statutes. Individuals can also be sued and held liable under Section 1981, not just employers or companies. In other ways it is very narrow. Section 1981 does not protect against sex or religious discrimination or cover any other protected class beyond that of race.

Civil Rights Act of 1871 (Section 1983)

Section 1983 of the Civil Rights Act of 1871 protects against not only racial discrimination, but any violation of constitutional rights. It states:

> Every person who, under color of any statute, ordinance, regulation, custom, or usage, of any State or Territory or the District of Columbia, subjects, or causes to be subjected, any citizen of the United States or other person within the jurisdiction thereof to the deprivation of any rights, privileges, or immunities secured by the Constitution and laws, shall be liable to the party injured in an action at law, suit in equity, or other proper proceeding for redress, except that in any action brought against a judicial officer for an act or omission taken in such officer's judicial capacity, injunctive relief shall not be granted unless a declaratory decree was violated or declaratory relief was unavailable. For the purposes of this section, any Act of Congress applicable exclusively to the District of Columbia shall be considered to be a statute of the District of Columbia.

It is vital to understand that Section 1983 of the Civil Rights Act of 1871; though broad in its scope, it applies only to state (government) officials or those acting under color of law. Private discrimination will not be deemed inequality under the law, unless there is a clear link or evidence of manipulation of the law or its agencies to give sanction or encouragement to a private party or entity for doing so.

CASE EXAMPLES:

A Pennsylvania court in the case of *Weyandt v. Mason's Stores, Inc.* (1968), decided that there was no Section 1983 claim against store manager or detective for a wrongful shoplifting arrest. The law allowed a store manager to detain a person for shoplifting until the police arrived, but that did not mean he was acting under the color of state law. He was not acting as an officer himself. Similarly, just because the state issued detective licenses to security employees it does not mean they were not acting "under color of law"; they were not acting on behalf of the state.

A state-owned or state-run hospital or health care facility might violate Section 1983 by failing to provide due process before making an employment decision or discriminating on the basis of sex or race, but it would not apply to a private hospital. This is so even if the hospital receives Medicaid or Medicare payments and, therefore, is required to comply with state regulations of those programs. For example in *Carter v. Norfolk Community Hospital Association, Inc.* (1985), the court held that there was no Section 1983 violation for termination of physician's professional privileges.

In the case of *Wong v. Stripling* (1989), the court decided that revocation of hospital privileges is not "state action" even when state legislation authorized revocation and made courts available for review of procedural fairness of revocation. Therefore, there was no section 1983 violation. In *Sarin v. Samaritan Health Care Center* (1987), the revocation of privileges was not state action even when the hospital was licensed and regulated by the state, and the court decided in favor of the Health Care Center. In each of the above cases, the facts did not support a finding of a violation of the statute.

Nonetheless, Section 1983 does apply to those working for state or federal hospital systems (*Nieto v. Kappoor*, 2001). This was a case of harassment by medical director of public hospital and was thus found to be covered by Section 1983, as the public hospital was a state actor. It covers a much broader range of activities than Section 1981, including both racial and sex discrimination.

Furthermore, procedural failures to provide due process can also trigger claims under Section 1983. However, this law is limited to the government and those who act under its auspices, so it does not reach the vast majority of employment situations in the United States.

Title VII of the Civil Rights Act of 1964 (Title VII)

The premier antidiscrimination statute of the federal government is Title VII. It bars certain practices by employers. It states in pertinent part (42 U.S.C. Section [e-2]):

> It shall be an unlawful employment practice for an employer—
>
> (1) to fail or refuse to hire or to discharge any individual, or otherwise to discriminate against any individual with respect to his compensation, terms, conditions, or privileges of employment, because of such individual's race, color, religion, sex, or national origin; or
>
> (2) to limit, segregate, or classify his employees or applicants for employment in any way which would deprive or tend to deprive any individual of employment opportunities or otherwise adversely affect his status as an employee, because of such individual's race, color, religion, sex, or national origin (42 U.S.C. Section 2000(e)-2[a]).

Title VII also prohibits such activity on the part of Employment Agencies or Labor Unions (42 U.S.C. Section 2000 [b] [c]). Title VII makes explicit that any practice that has a "disparate impact" on one of its listed protected classes (race, color, religion, sex, or national origin) can be the basis for a claim of unlawful discrimination in certain circumstances. Disparate impact means that the practice, though not intended to be discriminatory, disproportionately affects individuals having a disability or belonging to a particular group based on their age, ethnicity, race, or sex. As a result, even a neutral rule or regulation can be a basis of legal action if the plaintiff can plead and prove:

> (1)(A) An unlawful employment practice based on disparate impact is established under this subchapter only if—
>
> (i) a complaining party demonstrates that a respondent uses a particular employment practice that causes a disparate impact on the basis of race, color, religion, sex, or national origin and the respondent fails to demonstrate that the challenged practice is job related for the position in question and consistent with business necessity; or

(ii) the complaining party makes the demonstration described in subparagraph (C) with respect to an alternative employment practice and the respondent refuses to adopt such alternative employment practice.

(B)(i) With respect to demonstrating that a particular employment practice causes a disparate impact as described in subparagraph (A)(i), the complaining party shall demonstrate that each particular challenged employment practice causes a disparate impact, except that if the complaining party can demonstrate to the court that the elements of a respondent's decision making process are not capable of separation for analysis, the decision making process may be analyzed as one employment practice.

(ii) If the respondent demonstrates that a specific employment practice does not cause the disparate impact, the respondent shall not be required to demonstrate that such practice is required by business necessity (42 U.S.C. Section 2000 [e]-2[k]).

What this means is that once a practice is demonstrated to disproportionately affect one protected group the employer must demonstrate it is necessary to its business. Title VII is unlike Sections 1981 and 1983 because it requires a plaintiff to first take their complaint to the EEOC and get a "right to sue letter." This procedure is discussed later in the chapter.

Title VII Actions: Employee Versus Employer

Title VII does not apply to everyone. Under Title VII an employee sues the employer. Supervisors are not liable, even though they may have been responsible for the prohibited conduct as exemplified in the case of *Sherez v. State of Hawai'i Dept. of Education* (2005). The court held that the vice-principal of a school is not liable under Title VII. The court, relying on precedent and the language of the statute, noted that the statute's definition of "employer" did not include supervisors. An employer must take affirmative steps to monitor and remove discrimination (*Dunn v. Washington County Hospital*, 2005). In that case a doctor was alleged to be discriminating against female staff. Even though he was an independent contractor, if the hospital knew of the sexual discrimination, it had to act or would be held liable. Independent contractors in contrast to employees are discussed later in this chapter.

Sexual discrimination is forbidden by Title VII, and this includes creating a sexually harassing environment or discriminating on the basis of sex. To prevail in a case of sexual discrimination, a plaintiff must plead and prove that (a) she or he belongs to a protected class, (b) she or he was subjected to unwelcome sexual harassment, and (c) the harassment was based on sex (*Ackel v. National Communications, Inc.*, 2003). As a general rule, employers provide sexual harassment prevention training to supervisors and other personnel. The requirements of the training may vary from state to state. Employers are encouraged to have policies and procedures in place pertaining to sexual harassment in the workplace. Should a lawsuit be brought with allegations of sexual harassment, sexual harassment educational training of employees as well as policies and procedures will be scrutinized by the court.

Age Discrimination in Employment Act

The ADEA, which became effective in 1967, prohibits discrimination on the basis of age. In practice this means persons aged 40 years or older are protected. Discrimination against younger persons is not a basis for action under the statute. The law makes it unlawful for an employer

1. to fail or refuse to hire or to discharge any individual or otherwise discriminate against any individual with respect to his compensation, terms, conditions, or privileges of employment because of such individual's age;
2. to limit, segregate, or classify his employees in any way that would deprive or tend to deprive any individual of employment opportunities or otherwise adversely affect his status as an employee, because of such individual's age; or
3. to reduce the wage rate of any employee in order to comply with this chapter (29 U.S.C. Section 623).

It places similar restrictions on employment agencies and labor organizations (29 U.S.C. Sections 623 [b] [c]).

The ADEA exempts many companies and individuals from its protections. For example, independent contractors are not covered as the court held in *Hayden v. LA-Z Boy Chair Co.* (1993).

The ADEA also exempts firefighters and police from its protections if a locality wants to enact a mandatory retirement age, as in the case of *Correa-Ruiz v. Fortuno* (2009). The ADEA also exempts employers who have fewer than 20 employees, and it does not apply to the federal government (29 U.S.C. Section 630[b]). Moreover, bona fide seniority systems and pension funds are not prohibited by the act. Just as in Title VII, it is possible to create a hostile environment on age discrimination by statements, acts, and policies that are hostile to older workers.

It is important to note that there is no employer prohibition on terminating someone based on their ability to do the job. If age and infirmity have made the person no longer capable of performing the legitimate, bona fide duties of employment, the ADEA does not require that he or she be retained. However, this can be a point of contention in litigation.

Americans With Disabilities Act

The ADA (42 U.S.C. Section 12101 *et seq*) became effective in 1992; the act was designed to ensure that the disabled had full access to the American employment market. Its basic premise is that all jobs that can be done by a person with a disability should be open to them. Disability is defined broadly as any person with

(A) a physical or mental impairment that substantially limits one or more major life activities of such individual;
(B) a record of such an impairment; or
(C) being regarded as having such an impairment (42 U.S.C. Section 12102).

The last point, item C, is important. Even if one is not disabled, the ADA forbids discrimination against those *regarded by others* as having such a disability (*Eshelman v. Agere Systems, Inc.*, 2009).

Major life activities under the ADA are also broadly defined to include, but are not limited to caring for oneself, performing manual tasks, seeing, hearing, eating, sleeping, walking, standing, lifting, bending, speaking, breathing, learning, reading, concentrating, thinking, communicating, and working (*Eshelman v. Agere Systems, Inc.*, 2009). The ADA excludes any temporary disabilities (those not likely to last more than half a year).

Whether one has a disability or not is determined without regard to ameliorative medicine or devices that may correct the problem, except in the case of ordinary glasses or contact lenses.

The ADA requires an employer to make a reasonable accommodation to the employee with the disability. A reasonable accommodation is a modification or adjustment to the job or work environment that enables a worker or applicant to perform essential job functions. However, in no case does the law tolerate a direct threat to the health or safety of others that cannot be eliminated with reasonable accommodation.

The ADA applies to businesses employing more than 15 people. The federal government is not subject to the ADA.

Family and Medical Leave Act

The FMLA (1993) requires employers to grant up to 12 weeks of unpaid leave to employees suffering various family emergencies, after which they must be reinstated. This law applies to private employers with 50 or more employees as well as to public sector employees (*Nevada Department of Human Resources v. Hibbs*, 2003).

There is a requirement that the employee must have worked at least 1,250 hours, or a minimum of 1 year, to be eligible for the benefits conferred by the FMLA. The circumstances that are triggered by the FMLA are as follows:

1. The birth or adoption of a child, or to care for a child;
2. A serious health condition that makes the employee unable to perform his or her duties; and
3. The serious medical condition of a spouse, child, or parent requiring care.

It is important for employers to have policies and procedures regarding the implementation of this law as well as others. Exhibit 4.1 is a compilation of the federal antidiscrimination statutes discussed in this chapter.

Exhibit 4.1 Federal Antidiscrimination Laws

1. The Civil Rights Act of 1866, Section 1981
2. The Civil Rights Act of 1871, Section 1983
3. VII of the Civil Rights Act of 1964
4. Age Discrimination in Employment Act (ADEA)
5. Americans with Disabilities Act (ADA)
6. Family and Medical Leave Act (FMLA)

OVERVIEW OF STATE EMPLOYMENT LAWS

State laws in the employment area may cover many more protected classes. They may protect sexual preference, family structure, or even personal appearance discrimination as in the case of *Ivey v. District of Columbia*

(2008), which adjudged personal appearance discrimination (in this case obesity) actionable. Each state determines the statute of limitations on such claims. Some states make age discrimination against anyone over the age of 18 actionable. Many states have passed laws prohibiting discrimination in employment on the basis of sexual orientation or marital status. These laws and other types of prohibited discrimination along with compliance requirements, complaints, and procedures for filing complaints are found in each state's Human Rights Act.

Perhaps the most comprehensive discrimination statute in the country is the District of Columbia Human Rights Act (DCHRA). This act prohibits discrimination on the basis of "race, color, religion, national origin, sex, age, marital status, personal appearance, sexual orientation, gender identity or expression, family responsibilities, genetic information, disability, matriculation, or political affiliation" (D.C. Code Section 2–1402.11).

State and local statutes may require employees to bring their claim to an independent agency such as the EEOC before filing suit or before allowing the direct access to the courts for redress of the their discrimination claims.

FILING A CLAIM OF DISCRIMINATION WITH THE EEOC

The EEOC is the federal agency charged with the investigation of certain discrimination charges. The EEOC also has the authority to issue "Right to Sue" letters to claimants bringing charges against employers. A "Right to Sue" letter means that a claimant is allowed to file a lawsuit in court. There are times when the EEOC will also institute litigation or mediation for the resolution of claims. For a general description of the mediation process, refer to the Chapter 10.

EEOC offices are located throughout the country. According to the EEOC, in order for a valid charge of discrimination to be investigated by the EEOC, a charge must be filed with that agency within 180 days from the date of the alleged violation. That deadline may be extended to 300 days if the charge is also covered by state or local antidiscrimination laws.

Charges brought to the EEOC may include any complaint of discrimination based on race, color, national origin, religion, sex, and/or disability. To bring charges against an employer, in most instances, the employer charged must have a minimum of 15 employees. For an age claim, however, the minimum number of employees is 20. In the event that there are charges against employers with less than the requisite number of employees as required by this federal statute, charges may be filed with the appropriate state or local agency within the time limits as set forth by that particular state's statute. Federal employees or applicants for federal employment are covered under the Federal Sector Equal Employment Opportunity Complaint Processing Regulations (29 CFR Part 1614).

Any employee who believes that his or her employment rights have been violated as described by any of the federal laws that fall under the EEOC's purview may file a claim of discrimination. Questions should be addressed to competent counsel and/or the EEOC. For additional information on filing a charge with the EEOC, see the Web site: http://www. eeoc.gov/charge/overview_charge_filing.html.

THE EMPLOYMENT RELATIONSHIP: EMPLOYER/EMPLOYEE WORKPLACE RIGHTS AND RESPONSIBILITIES

The development of modern employment law can be seen as a shift from the master–servant relationship to one based on status. The employment relationship between employer and employee gives rise to certain rights and responsibilities as well as remedies for breach of contract. Many believe that in order for a contract to be valid, it must be in writing. Case law indicates otherwise, as will be illustrated in this chapter. Collective bargaining and oral and written agreements give rise to an employment relationship.

The Employment Contract

A valid contract consists of three essential elements: an offer made by the employer, acceptance of the offer by the employee, and consideration. Consideration is what has been promised or given by the employer. Generally speaking, work promised by the nurse employee will be adequate consideration for the nurse's employer's promise of compensation. The offer can be accepted or rejected by the employee, or the employer could withdraw the offer before it is accepted. Once the offer is accepted by the employee, a valid contract exists. The formation of the contract also requires that there is mutual understanding or mutual assent to the terms and conditions of employment. This is also referred to as a "meeting of the minds." Contract elements are not always easy to determine, and it becomes more complex when there is an implied contract of employment (one that is not in writing) established by an employee handbook or manual.

Employee Handbook/Manuals

Many employers publish and distribute employee handbooks or manuals to its employees. These manuals contain employment policies and procedures as well as standards for employers to follow. They also help to promote uniform supervisory administration and give the employee a sense of fairness in employment matters (Bakaly & Grossman, 1992).

Historically, the law provided that the manual was a unilateral statement of conditions of employment made by the employer. Therefore, it was discretionary as to whether or not the employer followed the terms and conditions of employment as outlined. In recent years, however, case law indicates that in many instances the courts have determined that the employer is bound by the terms as set forth in manual distributed to its employees. The leading case illustrating this principle was decided in *Toussaint v. Blue Cross & Blue Shield* (1980) and will be discussed later in this chapter.

In other cases, the decisions of the courts will turn on the language in the handbooks, for example, in such instances as terminating an employee for "just cause" only. Another central question is whether or not the parties intended the provisions of the manual to be binding. Most courts recognize that an employer can avoid being bound by the terms and conditions of the manual if the manual contains an express or written disclaimer. When a claim is suspected based on a violation of a provision of an employment manual, a careful analysis of the issues presented should be performed by an experienced employment attorney.

Managerial Registered Nurses, Nurse Practitioners, and Employment Contracts

The employment contract governs performance and conduct in the workplace. It is especially important for nurses in management and other executive roles as well as nurse practitioners to have a clear understanding of the employment relationship. This can be accomplished with a written contract. Written contracts allow the parties to negotiate the terms and conditions of employment and have a better understanding of their rights and responsibilities in the workplace. Just cause for termination and noncompete clauses may also be included in these types of employment contracts. When negotiating the contract, there needs to be a discussion of the compensation and benefits package that may include a bonus and/or profit-sharing provision.

Insurance Considerations

Professional liability insurance types and amount of coverage should also be carefully reviewed, especially for the nurse who is an independent contractor. Independent contractors are usually excluded from an employer's insurance policy unless they are added as an additional insured. The determination of the independent contractor status is discussed later in this chapter.

Among the professional liability insurance considerations to be examined are "claims made" and "occurrence" types of policies. "Claims made" policies will only cover claims reported while the policy is in effect unless there is also "prior acts" coverage. In the event of a malpractice claim predating the current policy's effective date, "prior acts coverage will date back to a specific date agreed upon in the current insurance policy. Coverage for prior acts can be purchased with what is called "tail" coverage (Kopf, 2005). "Occurrence" type insurance policies provide coverage for all acts and omissions that occur during the policy period irrespective of when the claims are reported. A careful and complete analysis of the type of coverage necessary for your particular practice should be made in consultation with knowledgeable individuals.

Collaborative Agreements

In some situations, collaborative agreements between nurse practitioners and physicians are required by state law where the health care services are delivered. These agreements may also be required for certain reimbursement for services rendered. Collaborative agreements should clearly delineate the physician and nurse practitioner's responsibilities, including prescriptive authority. In the absence of state law governing collaboration, and according to the American College of Nurse Practitioners (2008), collaboration is a process in which a nurse practitioner has a relationship with one or more physicians to deliver health care services. Such collaboration is to be evidenced by nurse practitioners documenting the nurse practitioners' scope of practice and indicating the relationships that they have with physicians to deal with issues outside their scope of practice. Nurse practitioners must document this collaborative process with physicians.

Contract Formation

Although there are many factors to consider when accepting employment, as discussed previously, the most fundamental are as follows:

1. Do I fully understand and agree to the terms and conditions of employment?
2. Was there a meeting of the minds or mutual assent between employee and employer?

In addition to the three essential contract elements of offer, acceptance, and consideration, a valid contract requires the above questions to be answered in the affirmative.

Breach of Employment Contract

Once a valid contract is formed, it may be breached by either party. A breach of contract occurs when the terms and/or conditions of employment have been violated. Careful drafting of employment contracts may reduce breach-of-contract claims but do not necessarily prevent them. The majority of breach-of-contract claims is instituted by the employees for wrongful discharge. A discussion of wrongful-discharge claims based on federal discrimination actions was discussed earlier in this chapter. A sampling of wrongful-discharge claims and breach-of-contract claims will be illustrated in this part of the chapter.

Breach-of-contract claims can also occur in the workplace when an employer constructively discharges an employee. Constructive discharge arises when the employer has created intolerable working conditions and refuses to remedy the situation that results in resignation by the employee. Some examples of constructive discharge include the employer decreasing the employee's salary without justification, decreasing the employee's workload, requiring the employee to complete menial tasks, or, in the alternative, increasing the workload to a point where it is impossible to achieve the goal within the specified time frame allotted.

It is common to have a "just cause" clause for termination and remedies for breach of contract in written agreements. Arbitration clauses to settle disputes may also be included. Those kinds of provisions further acknowledge the rights and responsibilities of the parties. Remedies for breach-of-contract claims vary from case to case and may include monetary damages and reinstatement of employment.

Three Categories of Employment

There are three main categories of employment: employment at will, fixed or specified term, and independent contractors. An employee will generally fall into one of those categories.

Employment at Will

The employment-at-will doctrine was well documented in the Treatise on the Law of Master and Servant in 1877 by Professor Horace Wood. This traditional doctrine gave the employer the absolute right to terminate the employee for any or no reason absent statutory or contractual restrictions. An employee at will is one who does not have a contract that states the duration of the employment relationship. Therefore, either party may terminate the relationship at anytime for any reason or no reason in the absence of federal or state laws prohibiting such. Although the employment-at-will doctrine has been slowly eroded by statutory and case laws, employers have historically used it to terminate employees without liability. There are exceptions to this doctrine that are fully discussed later in this chapter.

Fixed- or Specified-Term Employment

Fixed- or a specified-term employment is one that usually provides the employee with a written or express contract for a fixed term or specified length of time for employment. There is a legal doctrine called the statute of frauds that, as the name suggests, is in place to prevent fraud. It requires that certain contracts be in writing. In the employment context, the statute of frauds requires that contracts that cannot be performed within 1 year be reduced to writing and signed in order to be enforceable (Contract Law Cases, 2008). For example, if one is offered a job for 2 years, the statute of frauds requires that it be in writing in order to be valid. This law varies from state to state.

Independent Contractor

According to *Black's Law Dictionary* (2010), an independent contractor is "one who is entrusted to undertake a specific project but who is left free to do the assigned work and to choose the method for accomplishing it" (p. 659).

Whether the employment relationship is defined as one of independent contractor or employee depends on certain factors as set forth by the law; these include the following:

1. The employer's right to control,
2. The job skills required for the job,
3. The length of service of the employee,
4. The method of payment used, and
5. The intent of the parties.

The Internal Revenue Service (IRS) monitors the classification of independent contractors. There are specific rules that govern this category of employment. Generally, the IRS will look to three main areas in determining who is an independent contractor. The three main areas are behavioral control, financial control, and the relationship of the parties. A written contract can help determine whether or not there was intent to establish an independent contractor relationship or an employee–employer relationship when it is difficult to distinguish between the two.

It is imperative for all nurses, especially nurse practitioners, to have a clear understanding of the independent contractor status for professional liability purposes as well as for the occurrence of work-related injuries; both these areas more fully discussed later in this chapter.

Collective Bargaining

In addition to oral and written agreements, collective bargaining gives rise to an employment relationship between parties. Over the years, the issue of unionization for registered nurses (RNs) has been met with controversy by opponents and proponents. Many staff nurses throughout the country are members of collective bargaining units.

The National Labor Relations Act (NLRA) is the statutory law that provides the right of employees to engage in collective bargaining activities, including the formation of, and/or joining, a labor organization. It also provides the right to collectively bargain for adequate wages, benefits, scheduled assignments, promotions, disciplinary procedures, and other terms and conditions of employment. The National Labor Relations Board (NLRB) is the federal agency responsible for enforcement of these laws.

The duties of the NLRB include the conducting of elections for union formation, the determination of what constitutes an appropriate bargaining unit, and the resolution of labor management disputes. According to Numerof and Abrams (1984), following the passage of the amendments to the Taft Hartley Act in 1974, collective bargaining agreements between voluntary, nonprofit hospitals and their nursing staffs increased by 25%, with compensation being one of the major factors for unionization.

In 1987, the NLRB issued rules permitting eight bargaining units for acute care hospitals. Those units are as follows:

1. RNs in nonsupervisory positions,
2. Physicians,
3. Professionals other than RNs and physicians,
4. Skilled maintenance employees,
5. Business office clerical employees,
6. Technical employees,
7. Guards, and
8. All other unprofessional employees (*Nurses Legal Handbook*, p. 270).

Collective Bargaining Agreements

A collective bargaining agreement is "a contract between an employer and a labor union regulating employment conditions, wages, benefits and grievances" (*Black's Law Dictionary*, 2010, p. 240). It is necessary that all nurses who are covered by collective bargaining agreements, and managers who supervise them, know and understand the terms and conditions of employment that are outlined in the provisions of the agreement. The rights and responsibilities of the employer and employees have been negotiated and agreed upon before the contract is accepted and ratified by the employees. Thus, the collective bargaining agreement establishes the legal framework for the employment relationship, as a breach of the agreement by either party can result in legal consequences.

Progressive Discipline

It is common for collective bargaining agreements to have provisions for progressive discipline unless the act committed by the employee warrants immediate discharge or termination as specified by the contract. Progressive discipline gives the employee an opportunity to correct the unsatisfactory job performance without termination. For example, if the agreement states that an employee can be dismissed after receiving three warnings for absenteeism, the employee may not be dismissed after receiving only two warnings for this infraction.

It is also important for both the employee and employer to closely follow the contract's procedures for progressive discipline for unsatisfactory job performance and for any other reason indicated up to and including termination. Once the employee is disciplined, there are specific deadlines for filing a grievance and for management to respond to the grievance. If the grievance is not resolved at an early stage, it may be necessary to have the case heard by an impartial arbitrator. There are also specific time limitations as outlined in the agreement for filing appeals. The goal is to afford the employee due process rights and a fair hearing. For additional information on the process of arbitration, refer to Chapter 10, Dispute Resolution for Nurses.

CASE EXAMPLE:

NLRB v. Weingarten, Inc., 420 U.S. 251(1975)

Issue: Whether or not the employer's denial to an employee's request to have a union representative present at an investigatory interview was unlawful?

The U.S. Supreme Court decided this important case in 1975. It is instructive to management and nonmanagement nurses alike. The facts of this case reveal that the employee of Weingarten worked in a retail store with food counters, owned and operated as a one of a chain of 100 retail stores. She was a member of a collective bargaining unit and worked at a food counter at one of the retail stores.

She was suspected of theft by the employer, which she denied. In this matter, the company's Loss Prevention Specialists spent 2 days observing the employee prior to the interview in question. The observation by the specialists turned up no evidence to support the allegations of theft. Nevertheless, the employee was summoned to an interview with the Company's Loss Prevention Specialist and store manager to discuss the matter. An interrogation took place, and an accusation of theft was made by the company's representative.

The employee reasonably believed that this investigation might lead to disciplinary action; therefore, she made several requests that the manager call a union representative to be present at the investigatory interview. The requests were repeatedly denied. Following the interview, the union, on behalf of the employee, filed for an unfair labor practice claim against the employer with the NLRB.

NLRB'S DECISION: The NLRB issued a ruling in favor the employee. It held that the employer's denial of the employee's request to have a union representative present at an investigatory interview was unlawful because the employee reasonably believed that the investigation might result in disciplinary action. Thus, the action by the employer constituted an unfair labor practice in violation of the NLRA, as amended. The NLRB ruled that the employer cease and desist from the requirement that an employee take part in an investigatory interview without a union representative present provided that the employee requests one and reasonably fears disciplinary action. The employer appealed the decision to the Court of Appeals.

FIFTH CIRCUIT COURT OF APPEALS' DECISION: The Court of Appeals disagreed with the NLRB's ruling and refused to enforce its order citing a long line of previous cases that held a union representative need not be present at an investigatory hearing. The NLRB appealed the decision to the U.S. Supreme Court, the highest court in the land.

U.S. SUPREME COURT'S DECISION: The U.S. Supreme Court reversed the decision by the Court of Appeals and found in favor of the NLRB. Its rationale was based in part on the fact that the NLRB's decision was a permissible construction of the NLRA and that the NLRB was charged by Congress with enforcement of the act. The court further justified its decision by giving deference to the NLRB because of its competence in the field.

This case has become known as the "Weingarten Rights" and exemplifies the rights of employees and responsibilities of employers. It is also a good example of the different levels of the appeals process.

EMPLOYER/EMPLOYEE WORKPLACE RIGHTS AND RESPONSIBILITIES

Exceptions to the Employment-At-Will Doctrine

According to Bakaly and Grossman (1992), the employer will generally be prohibited from terminating an employee for any or no reason if one of the following exceptions to the at-will doctrine applies. These exceptions vary from state to state and include the following legal theories:

1. Public policy,
2. Promissory estoppel,

3. Breach of the covenant of good faith and fair dealing, and
4. Implied contract.

Public Policy Exception

The public policy exception to the employment-at-will rule is based on the principle of what is in the best interests of the general public. Many states have enacted whistleblower statutes to protect employees from retaliatory actions should an employee report a violation of the law or a state or federal rule or regulation. In addition, whistle-blower statutes further protect employees who report wasteful expenditures of tax money or activities that threaten the public health or safety of the citizens (Standler, 2000). For a discussion of whistleblowers refer to Chapter 3.

There are, however, important questions to be answered regarding the public policy exception to the employment-at-will rule, including the following:

1. Was the employee terminated because he or she was requested by the employer to perform an act prohibited by law?
2. Was the employee terminated because of performing a civic duty, or because of filing a workers' compensation claim or a claim for discrimination?

If the answers to any of the above questions are yes, the public policy exception to the employment-at-will rule may apply.

Promissory Estoppel Exception

The promissory estoppel exception to the employment-at-will rule is based on the employee's reliance on the employer's promise that caused the employee to suffer a loss. This exception is not recognized in all states. The questions, in this instance, are as follows:

1. Did the employer make a promise to the employee that the employer failed to honor?
2. Did the employee reasonably rely on the promise by the employer? For example, if the employee resigned from his or her present employment and moved to the city of promised employment or made plans

to move to the new city, and then learned that there was no job offer. These are examples of reasonable reliance.

3. And lastly, as a result of the reasonable reliance, did the employee suffer a loss? In the example above, if the employee lost income by terminating employment and also suffered other monetary losses involved in the move or plan to move, the employee may prevail on the theory of promissory estoppel.

Covenant of Good Faith and Fair Dealing Exception

The covenant of good faith and fair dealing is a contract principle of law that is recognized in some states as an exception to the employment-at-will rule. A breach of this covenant has been recognized by courts to place limits on the employment-at-will doctrine. There is an implied covenant of good faith and fair dealing that employers will treat employees in good faith and fairly when addressing contractual rights in the workplace. This covenant may have been breached if the following actions have occurred:

1. Has the employer decreased the salary of the employee without justification?
2. Has the employer decreased the responsibilities of the employee or required the employee to complete menial tasks?

Unwarranted actions such as these may give rise to a breach-of-employment-contract claim. In some instances, employees find the work environment intolerable and resign. This is known as "constructive discharge" by the employer as previously discussed in this chapter.

Implied Contract Exception

An implied contract is one that is not explicitly written or stated. It is the opposite of the written or "express" contract outlining the terms and conditions of employment. An implied contract is considered by many courts to be an exception to the employment-at-will rule. There are certain inferences made from an implied contract that give rise to employee expectations. For example, if an employer issues an employee handbook, and it contains a progressive discipline provision or a "just cause" for termination of employment, the employee has the right of expectation that the policy and procedure will be followed by the employer. Some courts have held that there is an exception to the employment-at-will rule if there is an implied contract as illustrated in the following case example.

CASE EXAMPLES:

WRONGFUL TERMINATION CLAIMS

Toussaint v. Blue Cross & Blue Shield (1980)

Issue: Whether or not the language in the employment manual was deemed to form an implied contract of employment?

Plaintiff Toussaint was employed for a period of 5 years as a middle management employee before his termination. His employer, Blue Cross & Blue Shield, considered him an "at-will" employee, which it believed gave it the right to terminate him for any or no reason. Following termination, the plaintiff brought this wrongful-discharge claim against his employer. The facts reveal that at the time of hiring, Toussaint was given an employment manual that, among other provisions, contained a "just cause" for termination clause. The manual also provided for disciplinary procedures for termination that apparently were not followed in this matter. Toussaint also claimed to have been given job security assurances by a Blue Cross representative at the time of hiring. The Michigan Supreme Court found in Toussaint's favor under the theory of implied contract, based on the language in the employment manual.

COURT'S DECISION: The court based its rationale on the fact that an employer will be denied its right to terminate an at-will employee for any reason whatsoever if the employer chooses to publish an employee handbook with a "just cause" for termination. The employee manual, in this case, was deemed to form an implied contract for employment. At the time, this landmark decision became a national trend. Since this case was decided, Michigan has clarified and modified the employment-at-will doctrine. Today, the doctrine varies from state to state as illustrated in the following Delaware case example.

EMPLOYMENT MANUAL: SPECIFIED TERM

Garcia v. Aetna Finance Co. (1984)

Issue: Whether or not the termination of employment was in violation of the employment manual?

Plaintiff Garcia brought this action against his employer Aetna Finance Company for wrongful discharge, on the basis of his belief that he was an employee with a specified term or fixed term of employment because of annual appraisals and language in the employee manual/handbook. An important aspect of this case and the deciding factor was the deposition testimony given by Garcia. In the deposition, he admitted that he had not bargained for the policy established in the handbook regarding fixed-term employees.

COURT'S RATIONALE: The court found for the employer and based its rationale on the fact that the employee had not bargained for the policy that was established in the employment handbook or manual. Thus, a valid contract between employee and employer did not exist. Rather, the policy had been unilaterally adopted by the employer. The "mutual assent" or "meeting of the minds" element to establish a valid contract was absent as evidenced by Garcia's deposition testimony. Garcia appealed the decision and the Court of Appeals affirmed the lower court's decision.

This handbook case is clearly distinguished from the Toussaint case previously illustrated whereby the employee prevailed. Here, the case turned on a missing component to a valid contract, the "mutual assent" requirement.

Ethical Obligations and Wrongful Discharge

The American Nurses Association (ANA) Code of Ethics for Nurses (2001) "is a succinct statement of the ethical obligations and duties of every individual who enters the nursing profession." The Code further states that it is the "profession's non-negotiable ethical standard" (p. 5). At times, workplace situations between employee and employer present ethical dilemmas for professional employees, and these situations may conflict with ethical codes of conduct

The public policy exceptions and the whistler blower statutes provide additional protection to employees from the employment-at-will doctrine when the action taken by the employee is for the public good. The language used in the following New Jersey case illustrates this principle; however, it does not guarantee the employee will have a favorable outcome when terminated, as demonstrated by the Pierce case below.

CASE EXAMPLES:

DOCTOR REFUSES TO WORK ON NEW DRUG FOR ETHICAL REASONS

Pierce v. Ortho Pharmaceuticals (N.J. 1980)

Issue: Whether Dr. Pierce was wrongfully terminated from employment for refusing an assignment because of an ethical belief?

Dr. Pierce was an employee of Ortho Pharmaceuticals in New Jersey. She was assigned to work on a new drug product by her employer. Dr. Pierce refused the assignment for ethical reasons because she believed that a safer drug that would be more beneficial to the public could soon be developed. She was terminated by her employer for refusing the assignment. She brought a lawsuit for wrongful termination.

COURT'S DECISION: The court found in favor of the employer, Ortho Pharmaceuticals. However, the court also recognized that employees owe a special duty to abide by not only federal and state laws but also by the recognized codes of ethics promulgated by their professions. In this case that "special duty" wasn't deemed by the court to fall into the category of the public policy exception to the at-will rule.

Clearly, this situation presented an ethical dilemma for the employee that the court recognized, yet it ended unfavorably for the employee.

Since the Pierce case was decided, the New Jersey legislature has enacted a whistle blower statute and the Conscientious Employee Protection Act of 1986 (CEPA; Standler, 2000). Although there are no guarantees of outcome when a lawsuit is filed, this case may have had a different outcome if these laws were in place at the time of the suit.

NURSE QUESTIONS CONSENT FORM

Kraus v. New Rochelle Hospital (N.Y. 1995)

Issue: Whether a nurse was wrongfully discharged for questioning informed-consent forms?

This lawsuit was brought by a vice-president of nursing against her employer for wrongful-discharge and other claims. The facts reveal that the plaintiff identified problems with informed-consent forms that were obtained by a physician. She presented her concerns regarding the informed-consent forms to the hospital's administrator. The hospital's medical board was notified about the complaint made by the vice-president of nursing. A meeting with the hospital's medical board was subsequently held to discuss the issue. The outcome of the meeting was a "vote of no confidence" for the vice-president of nursing by the medical board. As a result of the board's vote, the nurse's employment was terminated even though she had above-average performance evaluations. A wrongful termination suit was commenced, and there was a trial by jury.

COURTS' DECISIONS: The jury found in favor of Nurse Kraus and awarded her damages of US$703,250 for loss of income and fringe benefits. In addition, she was awarded US$587,200 in legal fees and expenses for her wrongful-discharge suit. The employer appealed the decision. The Court of Appeals reduced the award and also ordered that she be reinstated to her former position as vice-president of nursing.

NURSE REFUSES TO FLOAT

Winkleman v. Beloit Memorial Hospital (Wisc. 1992)

Issue: Whether or not the nurse was wrongfully discharged for her refusal to float to an area where she felt unqualified?

Nurse Winkleman had 40 years of experience in maternity and neonatal care and was employed by Beloit Memorial Hospital. As a result of short staffing, she was ordered by the hospital to "float" and provide nursing care to postoperative and geriatric patients. She refused to "float" on the grounds that she was not qualified to work in those areas of nursing because her expertise was in maternity and neonatal care. The hospital interpreted her refusal to "float" as a voluntary resignation from employment. Winkleman filed suit for wrongful discharge. She had a trial by jury.

COURTS' DECISIONS: A jury in Wisconsin found that the nurse had been wrongfully discharged for her refusal to float to an area of the hospital where she did not feel competent. She was awarded US$39,344 in lost earnings. The employer appealed the decision to the Supreme Court of Wisconsin that affirmed the decision of the lower court.

Although this decision was favorable for the nurse, each case will be decided on its own set of facts and the law applied to those facts. Another nurse, in a similar situation, cannot be guaranteed the same outcome.

Issues in Wrongful-Discharge Cases

It is common to have a combination of contract and tort theories or charges of discrimination in wrongful-discharge cases. In general, these tort actions may include fraud, intentional or negligent infliction of emotional distress, defamation (which includes libel and slander), and negligence. For example, in an action for infliction of emotional distress, the burden is on the plaintiff to prove that the conduct by the employer was extreme and outrageous. In defamation actions, the employer usually has a "qualified privilege" to discuss employee performance and reasons for the termination as long as the employer acts in good faith and is not motivated by malice.

There are many issues present in wrongful-discharge cases that require a careful analysis by competent counsel. Some of these issues are as follows: What constitutes "just cause" or "good reason" for termination from employment? Is the discharge based on the employment-at-will doctrine? Do any exceptions to the at-will doctrine apply? Is there a breach of the employment agreement? Are there tort theories that apply? What state or federal laws apply? Is the employee covered by a collective bargaining agreement? What are the remedies, including monetary damages available for redress? Finally, is there a requirement to exhaust internal remedies before bringing a legal action in court? An internal remedy may include filing a claim with the EEOC before filing suit for an alleged discrimination action.

The employment arena gives rise to certain employee/employer rights and responsibilities in the workplace as demonstrated in this chapter. Collective bargaining agreements, employee manuals/handbooks and case law form the basis for those rights and responsibilities. There are also guidelines promulgated by professional organizations as demonstrated below.

Exhivbit 4.2 is a list of Workplace Tools for Nurses that can provide guidance and assist nurses in clarifying issues that may arise in the workplace.

Exhibit 4.2 Workplace Tools for Nurses

1. Nurse Practice Acts
2. Employment contracts
3. Collective bargaining agreements
4. Employment manuals or handbooks
5. Employment policies and procedures
6. Standards of nursing practice
7. ANA Code of Ethics for Nurses with Interpretive Statements
8. ANA Bill of Rights for Nurses
9. ANA Workplace Position Statements
10. Nursing Specialty Organizations Position Statements

Professional Organizations Guidelines

ANA: Bill of Rights for Registered Nurses

The ANA adopted the Bill of Rights for Registered Nurses in 2001. This bill is a statement of professional rights, and, though not legally binding on its own, it can be used as a guide in the development of organizational policies and procedures. It can also serve to form the basis for employment contracts and collective bargaining agreements. The purpose of the bill is to support nurses in various workplace situations, including unsafe staffing, mandatory overtime, health and safety issues such as needle-stick injuries, and workplace violence.

According to the ANA (2001), to maximize the contribution that nurses make to society, it is necessary to protect the dignity and autonomy of nurses in the workplace. To that end, the following rights must be afforded without restriction in regard to social or economic status, these rights include:

1. Nurses have the right to practice in a manner that fulfills their obligations to society and to those receiving nursing care.
2. Nurses have the right to practice in environments that allow them to act in accordance with professional standards and legally authorized scopes of practice.
3. Nurses have the right to a work environment that supports and facilitates ethical practice, in accordance with the Code for Nurses With Interpretive Statements.
4. Nurses have the right to freely and openly advocate for themselves and their patients, without fear of retribution.

5. Nurses have the right to fair compensation for their work, consistent with their knowledge, experience, and professional responsibilities.
6. Nurses have the right to a work environment that is safe for themselves and their patients.
7. Nurses have the right to negotiate the conditions of their employment, either as individuals or collectively, in all practice settings (ANA, 2001). (© 2001 By American Nurses Association. Reprinted with permission. All rights reserved.)

It is important to note that the ANA's Bill of Rights contains policy statements and does not necessarily reflect rights embodied in state and federal law. This Bill of Rights lends itself to interpretation and guidance on the nursing profession.

Delegation of Nursing Tasks

The delegation of nursing tasks in the workplace has generated much concern and discussion. Moreover, some delegation decisions have also ended up in a court of law. In an effort to assist the RN with practice strategies when delegating patient care to nursing assistive personnel (NAP) and others, the American Association of Nurses has published *Principles for Delegation* (2005). This information is relevant to the practice of RNs in most states and U.S. territories. However, it is advisable to ascertain any regulations or directives as promulgated by the State Board of Nursing and/or the Nurse Practice Act of the state of licensure and practice. "Thus, the framework for clinical practice including delegation is determined by individual state statutes, state regulations and policy statements and by generally accepted professional nursing standards" (ANA, p. 3).

As emphasized throughout this textbook, RNs are accountable to the public for providing safe patient care. In addition, RNs are also accountable for supervising those individuals to whom they have delegated nursing tasks. The RN is not only accountable for the decision to delegate but also for the adequacy of the care given by the delegatee. It is vital that the RN use critical thinking skills before delegating any nursing tasks. First, the RN must ascertain whether or not the task is one that can be delegated, and second, whether the person to whom the RN is delegating the task is properly trained, as illustrated in a case example later in this chapter.

According to the ANA, nursing-related principles of delegation include, but are not limited to, the following:

1. RN may delegate elements of care, but does not delegate the nursing process itself.
2. RN maintains the duty to answer for personal actions relating the nursing process.
3. RN takes into account the knowledge and skills of any individual to whom the RN may delegate elements of care.
4. The RN delegates only those tasks for which she or he believes the other health care worker has the knowledge and skill to perform, taking into consideration training, cultural competence, experience, and facility/agency policies and procedures (ANA, 2005, p. 6).

Delegation and Responsibilities of Chief Nursing Officers and Organizations

The ANA (2005) further states that "Chief nursing officers are accountable for establishing systems to assess, monitor, verify and communicate ongoing competence requirements in areas related to delegation both for RNs and delegatee" (p. 7). The ANA has also identified the following organization-related principles as they relate to delegation:

1. The organization is accountable for delegation through the allocation of resources to ensure sufficient staffing so that the RN can delegate appropriately.
2. The organization is accountable for documenting competencies for all staff providing direct patient care and ensuring that the RN has access to competency information for staff to whom the RN is delegating care.
3. Organizational policies on delegation are developed with the active participation of all nurses (staff, managers, and administrators).
4. The organization ensures that the educational needs of nursing assistive personnel are met through the implementation of a system that allows for nurse input.
5. Organizations have policies in place that allow input from nurses indicating that delegation is a professional right and responsibility. (© 2005 By American Nurses Association. Reprinted with Permission. All Rights Reserved.)

The process of delegation requires a collaboration of effort among nurses and organizations in workplace settings. "All decisions related to delegation and assignment are based on the fundamental principles of protection of the health, safety and welfare of the public" (ANA, Principles of Delegation, 2005, p. 5).

Case Example:

Delegation of Nursing Tasks

Singleton v. AAA Home Health, Inc. (2000)

Issue: Whether or not the nurse was negligent in delegating a nursing task?

Plaintiff Singleton brought suit against AAA Home Health, Inc. as a result of prolonged healing process of a hip decubitus that was sustained in a hospital. It was alleged that healing was delayed by 1 year as a result of old gauze embedded at the site. Old gauze was found when a surgical procedure was performed on the decubitus. The record reflects that the physician wrote an order for the home health nurses to repack the hip decubitus wound with antiseptic gauze. Apparently, the nurses delegated the responsibility to home health aides to repack the wound by showing them how to repack and then leaving them on their own to complete the task.

At the trial, the nursing agency defended the lawsuit by claiming that the nurses had shown the nurse's aides how to repack the wound with sterile gauze and change the outer bandage, to prove that the standard of care was not breached by the nurses.

TRIAL COURT'S DECISION: The jury found in favor of the defendant, Home Health Agency and, as a result, did not find the nurses negligent. The plaintiff, in presenting the facts, insisted that her physician had ordered skilled nursing care to perform the task and she was entitled to it. The plaintiff's expert nurse witnesses testified regarding the standard of care. The expert's testimony revealed that the nurses do not have the option to modify or change physician's orders. The judge accepted the testimony of the expert nurse as to the standard of care and overturned the jury's verdict. The process used by the judge is called *judgment non-obtantante veredicto* (JNOV). This process essentially overrules the jury. The judge makes the independent determination, notwithstanding the jury's verdict.

This process is used at the complete discretion of the judge and is not taken lightly.

JUDGE'S RATIONALE FOR JNOV: According to the court, since the physician ordered specific skilled nursing care, it means that those functions are to be performed by skilled nurses or by nonlicensed persons with direct supervision by the nurse. It was further noted that there was no documentation that the licensed nurses performed the repacking procedure or observed the nonlicensed persons completing the procedure. The aides had apparently signed off that they had completed the procedure, but there was no documentation of exactly what they did. The judge's interpretation, on the basis of lack of documentation, was that only the outer dressing was changed and that was inadequate care. The plaintiff was awarded more than US$100,000 from the Home Health Agency. The case was appealed by the Home Health Agency.

COURT OF APPEALS' DECISION: The Court of Appeals of Louisiana upheld the judge's decision to disregard the jury and award the plaintiff damages against the nursing agency notwithstanding the jury's verdict.

Exhibit 4.3 Delegation Tips for Registered Nurses

Careful observation and assessment: Observe and assess the patient before delegation of nursing tasks. Be sure that task is delegable.

Assignment: To appropriate individual, in accordance with current policies and procedure; ascertain whether or not the individual is qualified for the task.

Resources: Provide resources as necessary; resources may include education and/or medical supplies as needed.

Evaluation: Following completion of task; be certain that task was carried out with the appropriate standard of care.

Documentation: Proper documentation; documentation should be in accordance with policies and procedures.

Workers' Compensation for Work-Related Injuries

Workers' compensation claims are governed by state law and provide employees certain rights should a workplace injury occur. Employers have the responsibility to maintain such coverage for those injuries. Should a nurse suffer a work-related injury that arises out of or during employment, the nurse may be eligible for workers' compensation. Workers' compensation laws were passed by states to protect both the employee and the employer. As a general rule, workers' compensation insurance is purchased by employers to cover the expenses associated with workers' compensation claims. The specifics are outlined in the state statutes covering workers' compensation claims.

Think of workers' compensation as a "no-fault coverage plan." Generally, it is the exclusive remedy for work-related injuries in the absence of the injury being caused by a third party or by wanton and dangerous conduct by an employer that causes the employee to suffer harm. For example, if the injury was caused by a defective product used in the workplace that was manufactured by a third party, the employee or the employer may have the right to bring an action against the third party. The employee would still be eligible for workers 'compensation; however, if the employee were successful against the third party, reimbursement of workers' compensation benefits would be required.

Determination of a Workers' Compensation Claim: Four Essential Components

Usually, in order for a workers' compensation claim to be valid and compensable, there are four essential components that must be present.

1. *A valid employer–employee relationship must exist*: Independent contractor or volunteer status will not give rise to a compensable workers' compensation claim.
2. *Injury requiring medical treatment and lost time from work*: Depending on state law, this requirement may vary in certain situations.
3. *Was the injury caused or aggravated by work?* This element is analyzed to satisfy the claim that an injury was caused "in the course of employment or aggravated by work requirement" (21V.S.A. Section 618 [a] [1]).
4. *Timely notice*: The employee is required to give the employer reasonable notice after sustaining a work-related injury. Notice provisions are mandated by state statutes and, as a general rule, followed strictly.

In the event a nurse sustains a work-related injury, the employer's policy and procedures for filing a claim should be followed. It is also recommended to consult with competent counsel for advice especially in complicated cases.

Employers Key Defenses to a Workers' Compensation Claim

If there are unresolved questions regarding a valid workers' compensation claim, the employee is afforded a hearing before an administrative law judge, and the following are key defenses used by employers to deny a claim for workers' compensation:

1. Employee is not covered under the insurance policy,
2. Injury is not causally related to employment, or
3. There is fault basis by the employee such as
   a. intoxication,
   b. intentional injury sustained by employee, and
   c. failure to use safety device (21 V.S.A. Section 649).

     Employers will use the above defenses to a workers' compensation claim when an employment relationship could not be established or is difficult to establish. It is important from the onset of employment to be certain what the relationship is. An employment contract that is in writing helps in the determination of the relationship. In the second example, if an employee is injured and the injury sustained is not causally related to employment and it can be proven as such, a workers' compensation claim will be denied. In the third example, if the injury sustained is based on fault of the employee, such as injury occurring as a result of drinking alcoholic beverages on the job or any intentional act, a claim may be denied. Furthermore, if the employee assumes the risk by failing to use a safety device as a precautionary measure to prevent an injury from occurring, a workers' compensation claim may be denied. Employees are responsible to act in a prudent manner while in the workplace.

Employee Workers' Compensation Benefits

If a claim is deemed compensable, the injured employee may be eligible for the following benefits:

1. Medical and pharmaceutical expenses;
2. Assistive devices and certain modifications to vehicles and in some instances residences may be covered;
3. Reimbursement for travel and meals to meetings and/or hearings;
4. Payment for independent medical examination. An independent medical examination is usually requested by the employer and is performed

by the nontreating physician approved by the Workers' Compensation Board;

5. Vocational rehabilitation in the event the employee cannot return to original employment; and

6. Monetary reimbursement consisting of temporary disability benefits based on salary and formula indicated by the state statute (Phillips, 2009, p. 91).

Monetary benefits are generally paid until the employee reaches the end medical result or, in the alternative, successfully returns to work. End medical result is defined as "the point at which a person has reached substantial plateau in the medical recovery process, such that significant further improvement is not expected regardless of treatment" (Phillips, 2009, p. 92). In some jurisdictions, end medical result is referred to as maximum medical improvement. When that event occurs, if the employee sustained a permanent or partial permanent injury, a disability rating is performed by a competent specialist. The employee may be eligible for a monetary settlement based on the percentage of permanent injury according to medical guidelines. The amount of compensation awarded is provided in the state's workers' compensation statute and may vary from state to state.

Nurses should not hesitate to seek the advice of competent counsel prior to any settlement for partial or permanent disability resulting from a workers' compensation claim.

Occupational Safety and Health Act

Employees have a right to a safe workplace. According the U.S. Department of Labor (2010), "the Occupational Safety and Health Act (OSH Act) was passed to prevent workers from being killed or seriously harmed at work" (p. 1.). The law, which was enacted in 1970, requires that employers provide their employees with working conditions that are free from known dangers. Employers may be faced with fines and/or sanctions for known dangerous working conditions. The U.S. Department of Labor (2010), states that "employers must provide their employees with a workplace that does not have serious hazards and follow all OSHA safety and health standards" (p. 2).

To enforce the provisions of the OSH Act, the Occupational Safety and Health Administration (OSHA) was formed. OSHA establishes and enforces health standards and workplace safety measures. It also provides information and training to both employers and employees. Employees may request an inspection from OSHA if they believe that the employer is not complying with the OSHA standards or if there are serious hazards in the workplace.

Employers' responsibilities also include the following OSHA safety and health standards:

1. Informing employees about hazards through training, labels, alarms and color-coded systems, chemical information sheets, and other methods;
2. Keeping accurate records of work-related injuries and illnesses;
3. Performing tests in the workplace, such as air sampling required by OSHA standards;
4. Providing hearing exams or other medical tests required by OSHA standards;
5. Posting OSHA citations, injury and illness data, and the OSHA poster in the workplace where workers will see them;
6. Notifying OSHA within 8 hours of a workplace incident as a result of which there is death or three or more workers go to a hospital; and
7. Not discriminating or retaliating against an employee for using his or her rights under the law (U.S. Department of Labor, 2010, pp. 1, 2).

Blood-Borne Pathogens in the Workplace

All health care providers, and nurses in particular, are exposed to blood-borne pathogens in the workplace. OSHA (2010) defines blood-borne pathogens as "infectious materials in blood that can cause disease in humans, including hepatitis B and C and human immunodeficiency virus, or HIV. Workers exposed to these pathogens risk serious illness or death" (p. 1). The full text of OSHA's Blood-Borne Pathogens Standard is published in Title 29 of the Code of Federal Regulations (CFR) 1919.1030.

Employers are required to protect workers in the manner described in the following Summary of the Blood-Borne Pathogens Standards listed below:

1. *Establish an exposure control plan:* This requires a written plan with updates annually to reflect technological changes that help eliminate or reduce exposure to blood-borne pathogens. Input should be solicited from frontline employees.

2. *Use engineering controls:* These are devices that isolate or remove the blood-borne pathogen hazard from the workplace. Included are sharps disposal containers and self-sheathing needles and other safer medical devices to protect the worker.

3. *Enforce work practice controls:* These are practices that reduce the likelihood of exposure by changing the way a task is performed. They include appropriate procedures for hand washing, sharps disposing, lab specimen packaging, laundry, and contaminated material cleaning.

4. *Provide personal protective equipment:* This equipment includes gloves, gowns, and masks. Employers must clean, repair, and replace this equipment as needed.

5. *Make available Hepatitis B vaccinations:* All employees with occupational exposure to blood-borne pathogens should have Hepatitis B vaccinations within 10 days of assignment.

6. *Provide postexposure follow-up to any worker at no cost to the worker:* This includes but is not limited to conducting laboratory tests, providing confidential medical evaluation, and identifying and testing the source of the individual. If feasible, test the exposed employee's blood with his or her consent and offer counseling. All diagnoses must remain confidential.

7. *Use labels and signs to communicate hazards:* Warning labels should be affixed to containers of regulated waste, refrigerators and freezers, and other containers used to store or transplant blood or other potentially infectious materials. Facilities may use red bags or containers instead of labels. Employers must also post signs to identify restricted areas.

8. *Provide information and training to employees:* Employers must ensure that their workers receive regular training that covers the dangers of blood-borne pathogens, preventive practices, and postexposure procedures. Employers must offer this training on initial assignment, then at least annually. Laboratory and production facility workers must receive specialized training.

9. *Maintain employee medical and training records:* The employer must maintain a Sharps Injury Log unless it is an exempt industry under OSHA's standard on Recording and Reporting Occupational Injuries and Illnesses (*OSHA Fact Sheet on Bloodborne Pathogens,* 2002).

For more information about blood-borne pathogens and needlesticks see http://www.osha.gov/STLC/bloodbornepathogens; http://www.osha.gov/needlesticks and http://www.osha.gov/STLC/needlestick.

OSHA Enforcement and Penalties

OSHA's broad reach includes more than 100 million workplaces in the United States (Justia, n.d.). Employees in the private sector and state, local, and federal sectors are under OSHA's jurisdiction or authority (U.S. Department of Labor, 2010).

Most employees in this country fall under the authority or jurisdiction of OSHA, either through Federal OSHA or an OSHA state-approved program (U.S. Department of Labor, 2010). The main goal of the OSH Act is to provide workers in the private, federal, state, and local sectors with a safe and healthy environment in which to work. OSHA sets forth standards and guidelines for employers to adhere to.

OSHA primarily enforces its standards by conducting unannounced workplace inspections. If violations are found to exist, citations may be issued that may result in fines and/or criminal sanctions. For example, if an employee believes that a workplace hazard exists, the employee or the employee's representative may file a complaint with OSHA and request an inspection. The employee is protected from retaliatory action by the OSH Act. The employer is prohibited from firing, demoting, transferring, or discriminating in any way against the employee.

In the event that the OSHA compliance officer finds an immediate danger during an inspection, the employer will be obligated to end the danger. If the employer fails to end the danger, an injunction will be sought in court to shut down the site (Justia, 2010). An injunction is a court proceeding to seek a judgment to do or to stop doing a certain act or acts.

There are strict notification rules that employers must adhere to when there is a workplace accident that causes death, or when there is hospitalization of three or more employees. Employers are required to inform OSHA within 8 hours if either of the above situations occurs. OSHA will then proceed with an investigation. If the death of an employee resulted from a willful violation of an OSHA standard, the employer may be subject to criminal penalties. The penalty is a misdemeanor (a lesser crime than a felony) with a maximum jail sentence of 6 months (Justia, n.d.).

Nurse leaders should be fully informed of the OSHA standards and regulations in the particular setting where they are employed. It is essential that they oversee the education of the staff regarding OSHA standards and regulations. It is also important that nurse leaders stay abreast to all current OSHA changes and modify the policies and procedures accordingly.

CONCLUSIONS AND TRENDS

A vast array of federal and state laws protects job applicants and workers from varying types of discrimination. Employers must be aware of the requirements of law in their locations and should take steps to identify, remove, and prevent discrimination from occurring in their workplaces.

Antidiscrimination laws have increasingly been more inclusive of protected classes and have broadened the definition of persons covered. This tendency is likely to continue. In many instances antidiscrimination claims are brought in conjunction with breach of contract claims.

The laws governing the workplace are vast in number on the federal and state levels. Furthermore, there are numerous rules and regulations promulgated and enforced by federal and state agencies. This chapter is just a small sampling of those laws, rules, and regulations.

Employer rights and responsibilities in the workplace, as discussed in this chapter, provide the parties with an overview of the expectations. Union contracts, employment contracts, employment policies and procedures, and employee handbooks or manuals provide further guidance in the area of workplace rights and responsibilities.

Employers will be encouraged to use creative strategies for attracting and retaining nursing personnel as the need for nurses continues. According to Wood (2010), in order to maintain the retention of nurses some hospitals are turning to nurse residency programs when hiring new graduates. It is expected that these programs will serve to enhance and improve the working environment for nurses.

The role of the advanced practice nurse is a trend that is expected to continue given the shortage of primary care physicians and the demands of health care reform. Nurse leaders are well aware of the current and future need for highly skilled and well-educated nurses in the workplace. Nurses will meet the challenges and seize the new opportunities presented while remaining agents of advocacy for patients.

KEY POINTS

- The principal laws dealing with employee rights address equality, fairness, and discrimination claims.
- The premier antidiscrimination statute of the federal government is Title VII of the Civil Rights Act of 1991. It prohibits an employer from

discrimination against an individual due to a person's race, color, religion, sex, or national origin. It does not apply to all employers.

- The Equal Employment Opportunity Commission (EEOC) is the federal agency responsible for investigating certain discriminatory charges. There are specific time limits to filing a complaint with the EEOC.
- States Human Rights Acts protect employees from certain discriminatory actions. There are specific guidelines for compliance and administrative procedures for filing complaints.
- Employers have a duty to prevent sexual harassment in the workplace.
- The Age Discrimination in Employment Act (ADEA) prohibits discrimination in the workplace for persons 40 years of age or older; the act became effective in 1967.
- The Family Medical Leave Act of 1993 (FMLA) requires employers with 50 or more employees to grant up to 12 weeks of unpaid leaves of absence for employees experiencing various family emergencies.
- Americans with Disabilities Act (ADA) became effective in 1992, and its purpose is to protect the disabled from discrimination in the workplace.
- The employment relationship between employer and employee gives rise to certain rights and responsibilities as well as remedies for breach of contract. It is important for nurses in management and other executive roles to have a clear understanding of the employment relationship, and this can be accomplished with a written contract.
- Written employment contracts allow the parties to negotiate the terms and conditions of employment and have a better understanding of their rights and responsibilities in the workplace.
- Once a valid contract is formed, it may be breached by either party. A breach occurs when the terms and conditions of the contract have been violated. The majority of breach-of-contract claims are brought by the employee for wrongful termination of employment.
- The three main categories of employment are employee at will, a fixed- or specified-term employee, and independent contractor.
- The National Labor Relations Act (NLRA) is the statutory law that provides the right of employees to engage in collective bargaining activities. The National Labor Relations Board (NLRB) is the federal agency responsible for enforcing these laws.
- The American Nurses Association adopted the Bill of Rights for Registered Nurses in 2001. Although on its own it is not legally

binding, it can serve as a guide in the development of organizational policies and procedures in the workplace.

Registered Nurses (RNs) are accountable for supervising those individuals to whom they have delegated nursing tasks. The RN remains accountable for the decision to delegate and also for the adequacy of care given by the delegatee.

Should a nurse suffer a work-related injury that arises out of or during employment, the nurse may be eligible for workers' compensation benefits. Workers' compensation benefits are governed by state law.

The Occupational Safety and Health Act (OSH Act) was passed in 1970, and it requires employers to provide their employees with a workplace free from dangerous working conditions. Employers are also required to follow health standards and workplace safety measures established and enforced by Occupational Safety and Health Administration (OSHA).

REFERENCES

Ackel v. National Communications, Inc., 339 F.3d 376 (5th Cir. 2003).

ADA questions and answers by the U.S. Equal Employment Opportunity Commission and the U.S. Department of Justice (n.d.). Retrieved August 16, 2010, from http://www.ada.gov/employmt.htm

Age Discrimination in Employment Act (ADEA) 29 U.S.C. Section 621 *et seq.*

American Nurses Association. (2001). *Bill of rights for registered nurses.* Washington, DC: Author

American Nurses Association. (2001). *Code of ethics for nurses with interpretive statements.* Washington, DC: Author.

American Nurses Association. (2005). *Principles for delegation.* Silver Spring, MD: Author. Retrieved, July 26, 2010, from htpp://www.healthsystem.virginia.edu./internet/e-learning principles delegation.pdf

Americans with Disabilities Act (ADA) 42 U.S.C. Section 1201 *et seq.*

Bakaly, G., Jr., & Grossman, J. M. (1983). Historical overview of employment relationship. In *Modern law of employment contracts: Formation operation and remedies for breach* (pp. 1–11). New York: Law & Business, Inc./Harcourt Brace Joavanovich.

Carter v. Norfolk Community Hospital Association, Inc., 761 F. 2d 970 (4th Cir. 1985).

Civil Rights Act of 1866 42 U.S.C. Section 1981.

Civil Rights Act of 1871 42 U.S.C. Section 1983.

Correa-Ruiz v. Fortuno, 573 F. 3d 1 (1st Cir.). Correa-Ruiz v. Fortuno, 573 F. 3d 1—Court of Appeals, 1st Circuit 2009 CORREA-RUIZ v. FORTUNO, 130 S. Ct. 640—Supreme Court 2009.

District of Columbia Human Rights Act (DCHRA) D.C. Code Section 2–1402.11 (2006 as amended).

Dunn v. Washington County Hospital, 429 F. 3d 689 (7th Cir. 2005).

Eshelman v. Agere Systems, Inc., 554 F. 3d 426 (3d Cir. 2009).

Family and Medical Leave Act (FMLA) 29 U.S.C. Section 2601 *et seq.*

Federal Sector Equal Employment Opportunity 29 CFR Part 1614.

Garcia v. Aetna Finance Company, 752 F. 2d 488 (10th Cir.1984).

Hayden v. LA-Z Boy Chair Co., 9 F. 3d. 617 (7th Cir.1993), certiorari denied 114 S. Ct. 1371, 511 U.S. 1004, 128 L. Ed. 2d 47.

Ivey v. District of Columbia, 949 A. 2d 607 (D.C. App. 2008).

Justia. (n.d.). *OSHA compliance overview* (pp. 1–4). Retrieved July 12, 2010, from http://www.justia.com/employment/osha-compliance/

Kopf, R. (Ed.). (2009). *Business and legal guide book for nurse practitioners.* Columbus, OH: The America Association of Nurse Attorneys Health Law (Legislation and Compliance Section).

Kraus v. New Rochelle Hospital, 628 N.Y.S. 2d 361 (NY App., 1995).

National Labor Relations Act, 29 U.S.C. Sections 151–169. Retrieved July 31, 2010, from http://www.nlrb.gov/about_us/overview/national_labor_relations_act.aspx

Nevada Department of Human Resources v. Hibbs, 538 U.S. 721, S. Ct. 1972 (2003).

Nieto v. Kappoor, 268 F. 3d 1208 (10th Cir. 2001).

N.L.R.B. v. Weingarten, Inc. 420 U.S. 251 (1975).

Nurses rights as employees. (1992). In *Nurses legal handbook of law and ethics* (p. 267). Springhouse, PA: Springhouse Corporation.

OSHA Fact Sheet. (2002). Washington, DC: U.S. Department of Labor, Occupation Safety and Health Administrator.

Phillips, P. (2009). *The basics of workers' compensation.* Proceedings from Vermont Department of Labor's Workers' Compensation Adjusters' Conference. Burlington , VT, pp. 84–95.

Pierce v. Ortho Pharmaceutical Corporation 417 A. 2d 505 (N.J. 1980).

Sarin v. Samaritan Health Care Center, 813 F.2d 755 (6th Cir. 1978).

Sherez v. State of Hawai'i Department of Education, 396 F. Supp. 2d 1138 (D. Hawaii 2005).

Singleton v. AAA Home Health, Inc. 772 So. 2d 346 (La. App. 2000).

Standler, R. B. (2000). *Professional ethics & wrongful discharge* (pp. 1–24). Retrieved, June 25, 2010, from http://www. Rbs2.com/ethics.htm

Title VII of the Civil Rights Act of 1964, 42 U.S.C. Sections 2000 (e) *et seq.*

Toussaint v. Blue Cross & Blue Shield 292 N.W. 2d. (Mich. 1980).

U.S. Department of Labor. (2009). *Safety and health topics: Bloodborne pathogens and needlestick prevention* (pp. 1–6). Retrieved July 11, 2010, from htpp://www.osha.gov/STLC/bloobornepathogens/index.html/

U.S. Department of Labor. (2010). Occupational Safety and Health Administration. Retrieved July 11, 2010, from http://www.osha.gov/workers.html

21 V.S.A. Section 618 (a)(1).

21 V.S.A. Section 649.

Weyandt v. Mason's Stores, Inc., 279 F. Supp. 283 (W.D. Pa. 1968).

Wong v. Stripling, 881 F. 2d 200 (5th Cir. 1989).

Wood, D. (2010). Nursing leaders reveal top trends impacting nurses in 2010. *Nurse Zone*, pp. 1–4. Retrieved July 19, 2010, from htpp://www.nursezone. com/Nursing-News-Events/more-news/Nursing –Leaders-Reveal-To . . .

Woodland v. Viacom, Inc., 569 F. Supp. 83 (D.D.C. 2008).

CHAPTER FIVE

RISK MANAGEMENT

Pamela D. Miller

OBJECTIVES

- Acquaint the nurse leader with the basics of a risk management plan and program.
- Provide the information resources needed to design and implement or finalize a risk management plan to fit the clinical setting.
- Identify high-risk practice areas for health care organizations.
- Identify high-risk practice areas for nurses.
- Discuss methods to reduce risks.

INTRODUCTION

Nurses play a vital role in ensuring a safe patient care environment and in reducing risk to individuals and health care organizations. These two components contribute to what is formally known as *health care risk management*.

Health care risk management is defined by The Joint Commission (TJC) and the American Society of Health Care Risk Management (ASHRM) as a process that involves "clinical and administrative activities undertaken to identify, evaluate, and reduce the risk of injury to patients, staff, and visitors, and the risk of loss to the organization itself" (Carroll, Volume I, 2006, p. 1). The nurse leader is an essential partner in the design and implementation of an effective risk management plan.

Nurse leaders may need to design a risk management program or work within the framework of an existing program of a health care organization. This chapter will acquaint nurse leaders with the basics of a risk management plan and provide the resources needed to finalize a plan to fit the clinical setting.

The case studies presented in this chapter are fictional and are based on the author's education and experience in the field of law and risk management. They represent realistic facts and situations from which important lessons can be learned.

The Risk Management Program

An effective risk management program requires the consistent application of several key elements:

1. The program must be adequately integrated into the operations of the health care organization.
2. There must be open lines of communication and ready sharing of information and access to data.
3. There must be accountability that, though organization wide, has certain elements that may be within the purview of clinical leadership to complete.
4. There must be authority so that the person charged with being accountable for the plan has the authority to implement the plan.

As a clinical leader it is important to think of the risk management plan as a shared responsibility. In smaller organizations, risk management responsibility often lies with a clinical leader as a defined subset of his or her responsibilities. A nurse leader charged with running a risk management program on a part time basis "might find it difficult to acquire the wide range of expertise necessary to adequately fulfill his or her risk management obligations and to stay abreast of rapidly changing and often complex legal and regulatory developments affecting the field" (Carroll, 2006, p. 89).

In a large complex organization, many hands are required to administer a complete risk management program. Patient care issues may be handled by a patient safety officer or quality manager. A safety officer or engineer may handle environmental risks. Workers' compensation claims and employee complaints may be handled or coordinated by human resource professionals. The most effective risk management program is one that coordinates the activities of the respective disciplines, to promote the most efficient use of resources and prioritize the organization's risks for timely improvements.

The Comprehensive Risk Management Plan

The successful risk management plan fosters trust and credibility and does not sit in isolation from the day-to-day operations of a health care organization. Rather, "risk managers" should be in a position where they are actively involved in the functions of the clinical nurse leaders. An effective risk management program should reflect the ease with which nurse leaders and their staff approach the risk manager directly with concerns.

Help with Formalizing the Risk Management Plan

Professional organizations like ASHRM offer formalized tools for broad-based risk assessment. Risk assessment tools are also available for more focused areas by ECRI, formerly known as the Emergency Care Research Institute. A comprehensive risk management plan should contain a process for cooperating with investigations by state and local authorities, including proper record retention and preservation of evidence.

Risk management staff and qualifications. Health care organizations with effective risk management programs have full-time staff dedicated to risk management and patient safety functions. The risk manager will develop a comprehensive risk assessment plan to identify opportunities for improvement and reduction of liabilities.

A combination of state and federal regulations and accreditation requirements govern health care organizations. Therefore, a risk manager must be familiar with the regulatory framework and reporting requirements for the location or jurisdiction of the organization and have a system for complying in a timely manner with reporting deadlines.

Risk identification. How do you best identify risk in an organization? The ASHRM states incident, also known are occurrence reports are the 'cornerstone' of a health care risk management program. Incident reporting is "an early warning system intended to identify risk situations or adverse events in a timely manner to trigger prompt investigation from a claims management perspective as well as corrective action to prevent similar future events" (Carroll, Volume I, 2006, p. 552).

The incident report was traditionally a standard paper organizational form that a staff member completed after witnessing an unusual event or untoward outcome, such as a patient fall or medication error. These forms may still be in use or, in some instances, have been replaced by electronic entry systems. Regardless of the form used, the process constitutes the primary communication tool for occurrence-reporting systems.

Completing these reports at or around the time of the event when the incident is fresh in the minds of the reporter ensures the accuracy of the information and gives the risk manager a starting point for investigation. In addition, the report should be completed objectively, and include only the facts, as the information contained in these reports may ultimately be seen by others outside the organization including in a court of law.

However, occurrence-reporting systems will not be effective unless the reports are easy to use and staff knows when to use them and what to report. Nonetheless, a structured incident or occurrence-reporting system is vital to initiate an investigation, make timely reports to regulatory authorities, and track trends. Incident-reporting systems and chain of command in reporting should be designed to ensure confidentiality of protected health information and peer-review protected data. Many commercial forms are available, both paper and electronic.

Electronic reporting systems are advantageous in that many of the programs are web based and allow for access throughout multisite facilities, with immediate e-mail notification to clinical management and access by risk management. Examples of such proprietary systems commonly used in health care organizations include Patient Safety Net (PSN) or Peminic Event Reporting System.

Without regard to the particular system an organization chooses to use, it is vital that the focus of reporting be on preparing a timely report that transmits information in a way that results in effective communication based on your staffing and organizational structure. A focus on merely completing the report should not take the place of timely reporting in a way that is most effective based on your staffing and organizational structure. An effective response to the situation is the primary purpose of any reporting system.

Incident reports are not tools to measure and evaluate individual performance and should not be used in a punitive manner. Clinical staff often "self-report" their errors, so asking a staff member to complete a report to only to have it used as a basis for employee discipline is counterproductive, will reduce the likelihood of accurate and timely reporting of events, and can delay or prevent corrective action needed to prevent further injury to the subject patient or others.

Other modalities to assess risk include patient safety hotlines, e-mail notification, or direct reports. Proactive rounding in clinical areas and facility grounds can also identify risks. Additional information concerning risks can be gleaned from reviewing medical record requests, results of patient surveys, and review of diagnostic codes upon discharge.

As clinical leaders, nurses may be asked to participate in a risk management assessment of their respective area of responsibility. Instead of perceiving this as a threat, it should be viewed as an opportunity. Nurses should work with risk management proactively and provide as much information as possible to complete the assessment. Members of your staff may be interviewed and your policies may be reviewed. A physical inspection of the unit may be conducted. Investment in a risk assessment will help reduce the likelihood of an adverse event and substantial liability claim.

The Elements of Organizational Risk Management

Clinical care and patient safety. As a nurse leader, patient safety and injury are usually considered first when thinking of risk management. It is important to recognize that there are other risks to consider in addition to patient injury. However, patient care risks are a logical place to start and are the largest component of your risk management plan. The report, To Err Is Human, published by the Institute of Medicine in 2000, drew needed attention to the concern of medical errors in health care in the United States (Kohn, Corrigan, & Donaldson, 2000).

A formal patient safety movement was initiated, led by organizations like the National Patient Safety Foundation (http://www.npsf.org), an independent nonprofit agency established in 1997 for the improvement of the safety of the health care system, and the Institute for Health Care Improvement (http://www.ihi.org) an international nonprofit organization established in 1991. The Federal Agency for Health Care Research and Quality (http://www.ahrq.gov), the research arm of the Department of Health and Human Services, provides grant opportunities and publishes clinical practice guidelines for the improvement of health care. TJC publishes National Patient Safety Goals every year and provides guidance and toolkits on selected issues like surgical site identification. All of these agencies offer programs, tools, and education to clinicians and administrators in health care.

The interest in patient safety, coupled with the rise in the cost of resolving medical malpractice claims and a reduction of insurance availability, forms the base of support for loss prevention activities in clinical care. The nurse leader should be familiar with the work of those agencies and the resources available. Participation by you or your staff on an organizational patient safety committee can be an enriching experience that helps spread a culture of safety throughout your organization.

Claims management.   In the legal and insurance worlds, a claim is a written demand for payment. Malpractice claims may begin with a letter from a patient or, on behalf of a patient, from an executor of an estate, family member, or attorney. Claims may also be initiated by the formal filing of a lawsuit.

A periodic review of claims by a risk manager can help guide the institution in setting priorities for loss prevention activities and education, targeting clinical areas and issues that present as recurring themes in malpractice allegations.

A review of commonly filed malpractice claims should confirm the need to have in place the following adequate processes, procedures, or protocols:

a. Proper patient identification to prevent wrong-sided or wrong patient treatment errors,
b. Rapid response and treatment for patients who have changes in condition or who become medically unstable,
c. Adequate informed consent where consent is required,
d. Proper and timely communication among members of the health care team, and
e. A means of communicating effectively with patients and families when treatment fails or when a medical error occurs.

How the clinical leadership reacts to an adverse event or medical error is often as important to the patient and family as the adverse event itself. A total of 34 states have the so-called apology or sorry laws, which prevent the care provider's apology from being used against them in a medical malpractice suit (see Chapter 3 for additional discussion on this subject).

Resources on how to apologize to a patient or family and to perform service recovery are available from the SorryWorks coalition and in publications by Michael Woods (2007) or Gerald Hickson (2006), experts on apology and improving patient satisfaction in adverse events.

Dr. Woods describes the five "Rs" of an effective dialogue of apology:

1. Recognition of an adverse outcome;
2. Regret by offering empathy;
3. Responsibility—taking responsibility where needed and explaining how the event happened;

4. Remedy—explaining what happens next in the plan of care and offering some plan for services or compensation if appropriate; and
5. Remain engaged—staying in touch with the patient and family even when discharged from care (Woods, 2007).

According to Dr. Gerald Hickson, the founding director of the Vanderbilt University Center for Patient and Professional Advocacy, "The single biggest predictor of a physician's risk of being sued are complaints by the patient and the patient's family that the physician does not seem interested or concerned about the patient" (Hickson, 2006, p. 7).

There is a natural temptation for a caregiver to avoid the patient or family after an adverse outcome. Patients and families may feel abandoned and confused by this behavior. The lessons learned from Dr. Hickson's research and Dr. Wood's work can be applied by organizational leadership or nurse leaders in coordinating a response to the patient and family following an adverse event or outcome.

Litigation management. Litigation is the process of deciding the outcome of a dispute in court or through the administrative process. As a nurse, you may be asked to participate in the litigation process with regard to either a patient care event or an employee claim. A potential witness or person with information important to a legal case can be required to appear in court to testify as to what he or she knows. This is referred to as compulsory process. Your legal counsel will advise you when legal procedures require your response. Accordingly, it is vital that you keep the lawyers representing your organization on any matter informed of any communication you may receive with regard to a case.

Requests from an attorney or court can compel your participation in a case, and these are typically issued as "subpoenas."

A subpoena is a document in a particular case issued by an attorney, a court, or other authority such as a notary or licensing agency. The subpoena is used to require your presence at a trial, hearing, or deposition (testimony under oath).

The *subpoena duces tecum* (with documents) requires that you bring certain documents with you that are in your possession. Depending on your jurisdiction, the suit papers may be called by different names, such as a summons and complaint, a writ, or other terms. The subpoena and lawsuit papers have time-sensitive deadlines for responding.

If you are served with a subpoena, summons, or other request for testimony or writing, or one is left for you at your office or home, you should immediately notify your risk manager and legal counsel. Even a simple request by a party for a letter may cause you to be brought into a dispute. Since subpoenas, summons, or other legal requests are part of a legal process, you should never ignore any correspondence or letter stating a claim or threatening suit. Doing so may place your insurance coverage at risk and may subject you to legal consequences. In addition, any anxiety you may have over receiving such correspondence can be alleviated by your risk manager and legal counsel, who are there to assist in these activities.

Your organization may assign a matter to a trial attorney to represent it in actual or anticipated litigation or the legal process associated with a dispute. If this is the case, your organization will want this carried out as soon as possible when the need for special counsel with specific expertise is determined. This is important to preserve all of your legal rights with respect to the matter. For example, if it is a potential medical malpractice issue, you will want to assign counsel with the appropriate capabilities and experience in this area.

Risk managers are often charged with selecting counsel. The responsibilities associated with this may also include monitoring of legal bills and attorney performance. In addition, it is usually a good idea to have several firms from which to select the firm that will be used. This is important, since in a geographic region a firm you consider may already be representing another party with an interest in the same. This is referred to as a "conflict of interest," and law firms review such issues before accepting representation of a client. Therefore, if there is more than one firm that you have prescreened, you will be able to proceed expeditiously in finding the best law firm to handle the situation at hand.

Health care organizations are very diverse and highly regulated environments. Accordingly, it is expected that lawyers from various specialties may be needed to assist on matters requiring special expertise, such as Environmental Law, Corporate Law, and Labor Law. The risk manager and organization's general counsel will assist in advising on these aspects.

Personnel risks. A risk assessment should include an evaluation of how your organization hires, trains, and evaluates staff. Nurse leaders are typically directly involved in the hiring, training, retention, and termination of employees. It is important to work closely with human resource professionals to properly evaluate candidates and their qualifications and also with staff education professionals to determine the competencies and training required for your employees to deliver safe patient care.

As previously stated, the health care workplace is a highly regulated area and the nurse leader will need guidance to comply with the laws of the workplace. Financial loss to an organization can result from human resources–related claims such as workplace discrimination and workers' compensation claims. The following case study provides an example of workplace discrimination.

CASE STUDY:

EQUAL EMPLOYMENT OPPORTUNITY COMMISSION COMPLAINT

Andrew is a nurse manager of a busy orthopedic unit in an acute care hospital. He has two assistant nurse managers, Ken and Trudy. Ken, who has an associate's degree, has been a nurse for several years, having worked before as a technician in a manufacturing company. The other assistant manager is Trudy, a nurse for 30 years. Trudy is six credits short of her master's degree and had worked as a supervisor years ago before reducing her hours to raise a family.

Andrew is asked to eliminate one of the two assistant nurse manager positions as part of a reduction in work force. Other nurses on the unit tell Andrew that Trudy "is slowing down" and "can't keep up" with the pace of the unit. The nurses threaten to transfer out if Ken is laid off and Trudy stays on.

Andrew does not consult with human resources department for advice and terminates Trudy. Trudy then files a complaint with the Equal Employment Opportunity Commission (EEOC) as administered through in her state. The EEOC agency makes a determination that age-related discrimination occurred.

Trudy then files a lawsuit seeking money damages. The human resources director and the risk manager meet with Andrew and advise him that he should have reviewed the specific requirements of the job, including the particular physical requirements, and evaluated each candidate objectively.

Trudy's case proceeds to trial, where she testified that she recently completed her third New York Marathon. The jury decides in favor of Trudy and awards compensation for lost pay and money damages for emotional distress.

In this fictional EEOC case study, you can see that if Andrew had sought advice from human resources or risk management, he would have been aware of the need to conduct an objective process to determine the proper way to move forward with elimination of the position. In doing so, he could have avoided the resulting legal actions and losses to the organization that occurred. The following chart provides tips to avoid the major risks associated with human resources issues.

Exhibit 5.1 Tips to Manage Major Risks Associated with Human Resources and Personnel Management

- Consult human resources department for advice and counsel on terminations and reduction in workforce;
- Consult legal counsel whenever you have a question or there is uncertainty with an organization-related activity;
- Be sure the workers' compensation (WC) program is structured to comply with all legal requirements in your state;
- Have a reliable method for performing criminal background checks on employees, volunteers, medical staff, and clergy;
- Assess organization's compliance with federal Occupational Health and Safety Administration (OHSA) and state workplace safety regulations;
- Invest in safe, reliable lifting programs and needleless systems to reduce risk of injury to workers and to reduce WC program costs;
- Design a light duty and return to work program to reduce WC program costs

The following fictional case study involves a nurse executive's decision to change a product and enter into an agreement with a new vendor which had a deleterious effect on an employee. This case study presents another example of legal exposure where the risk can be due to issues associated with entering into a contract.

CASE STUDY:

WORKERS' COMPENSATION

Cheryl is the director of nursing at a home care infusion agency. She is encouraged to cut costs. Dissatisfied with the price of intravenous catheters quoted by the medical supply vendor her company uses, she accesses an online medical supplier that guarantees a 75% discount off the competitors if you buy in bulk. She purchases 500 catheters.

She notices that the catheters don't look exactly like the catheters they are currently using but feels that the staff will get used to them after using them a few times. Shortly after they begin using the new intravenous catheters Cheryl gets a call from Lynne, one of her nurses who had been stuck with the needle in the catheter used to start an IV. Lynne tells Cheryl that the protective sheath did not deploy as usual.

Cheryl checks the patient's chart and notices that the patient has a history of Hepatitis C. Lynne later contracts Hepatitis C, suffers liver failure, and ultimately fails Interferon therapy and is placed on the liver transplant list.

The infusion agency has a self-funded worker's compensation plan, which means that it fund its own workers compensation costs. Since Lynne's illness was confirmed as occupational, the agency must cover the costs of Lynne's care. Due to the enormous costs, the infusion agency is unable to pay its bills or cover its operating expenses and files for bankruptcy.

This infusion agency case points out a worst-case scenario resulting from good intentions but poor process. It also points out that any company should have policies for introducing new products or equipment into practice and assure that they are followed. Although this case may seem an unlikely occurrence, the fact is that such events can and do occur. Here, reasonable contract review as well as consideration given to the practical implications of changing a product without adequate input or education of staff who will use the equipment can result in substantial loss to an organization and potential harm to individuals (for more information on Worker's Compensation, see Chapter 4).

Risks associated with entering into contracts. As a nurse leader, you may have occasion to purchase goods such as clinical equipment, training materials, consulting services, software management programs, or cleaning services. Careful review and understanding of contractual provisions is essential before entering into any written agreement.

When a person is responsible for executing contracts, he or she may unknowingly enter into agreements that unduly transfer risk and its associated costs to his or her organization or may leave the organization little recourse if the goods or services fail. Nurse leaders should know what resources for contract review are available in their organization and should call upon those resources when considering any contractual relationship.

Key contract considerations that should be included in an agreement are as follows:

- An accurate description of the goods and services to be provided;
- Indemnification provisions that compensate for loss, and insurance provisions;
- Breach of contract clause so that it is clear what actions cause a breach and what remedies are available;
- Termination of contract clause.

Limitations of liability that spell out what the parties to the contract are— and are not—responsible for, and liquidated damages clauses (a statement of what payment is due if the contract provisions are not met), must be reviewed carefully, and generally are not favorable to health care organizations.

Elements such as provisions on interest payments and automatic renewals (contracts that renew automatically without any actions by the parties) are traps for the unwary that can expose you and your organization to undue financial risk and can undermine your business efforts to bring valuable services and goods to the bedside. The following fictional case study on the subject of "contractual risk" offers such an example.

CASE STUDY:

CONTRACTUAL RISK

Nan, nursing director of a long-term care facility, is asked by her chief financial officer to reduce costs associated with use of incontinence pads.

Nan favors a 1-year contract with a new company that guarantees a discount after the first 6 months if she signs the contract by the end of the month.

Vivian, the company representative, promises that the pressure ulcer rate will decrease with the use of the pads. Vivian also promises that the company will pay for nurses travel expenses to a national skin symposium as "her guests."

Vivian gives Nan a written agreement, and says, "This is just something my boss wants you to sign—just a standard contract. You and I have an agreement so don't worry about it."

Nan does not understand the provisions of the contract but does not consult with risk management or legal counsel and signs the contract. Three months after the pads are delivered she notices that the pressure ulcer rate is up.

Nurses have complained that the pads do not "breathe," stick to the patient's skin, and don't protect the linen. Nan calls the company and asks for Vivian as she wants to cancel the contract and go with another vendor's product.

Mike, Vivian's manager, tells Nan that Vivian no longer works there. He also states that they have a 5-year contract and that she had 3 days after receipt of the pads to object to the quality of the goods, which she waived because she did not make any complaint during that time period.

Nan buys another vendor's products and stops paying the first vendor. The first vendor, through Mike's attorney, serves her with a court notice commencing collection proceedings against the facility.

Nan attends the hearing alone and presents no physical evidence of the poor quality and no witnesses other than herself. To her surprise, the judge orders that her facility is in breach of contract, orders judgment in favor of the vendor, and further grants the vendor the remedies outlined in the contract, which include a security interest in the facility's expected revenue (receivables). The judge further orders garnishment (attachment) of the receivables in order to pay and satisfy the contract price over 5 years. The facility's chief financial officer receives notice of the garnishment and terminates Nan's employment.

This fictitious case certainly raises questions as to how Nan was in a position to sign a contract on behalf of the facility, seemingly without authorization. In any event, in this case Nan's actions placed contractual obligations and risks on the facility. Nan did not rely on the language of the contract but rather on the promises of the company representative. Proper legal review would likely have prevented the losses incurred in this case.

The following points, when followed, can prevent the type of situation illustrated in the case study:

Managers should consult with counsel and/or risk management early when negotiating and prior to finalizing an agreement and certainly before signing any contract.

▪ Oral representations and promises do not count. The final written contract determines the responsibilities and rights consistent with the agreement. If there are oral promises of any type made outside of the contract, any resulting dispute will be a subject of negotiation or decision by a court.

▪ If a contract is to be terminated, it should be done in writing and in accordance with any terms for contract termination that may be written into the contract. Such terms can dictate when a contract can be terminated and provide for the "notice" requirements, which determine how much notice must be given when the agreement is to be ended. If there is a claim that one party to the agreement has not performed as required, then you should be prepared to provide evidence in support of your claim that the other party has breached its duties.

Property. Issues associated with property must be addressed in the risk management plan, in order to reduce risk and prevent loss. There are two classes of property: personal property and real property.

Personal property: Personal property, or moveable goods, may belong to your patient, an employee, or to the organization. As a nurse leader, you should be sure that policies and procedures address the safeguarding of patient's property.

Generally, health care organizations prefer that unnecessary personal property be sent home with a family member or secured in a safe or locked area. Appropriate documentation describing the nature and location of personal property is required to avoid a dispute about the disposition of the property upon the patient's discharge or in the event the patient dies.

Patients have the right to keep certain valuables for their personal use available, but a health care organization can place reasonable restrictions on that property if needed to ensure the safety of the patient and others. The degree to which restrictions can be placed varies based on the care setting.

For example, property such as eyeglasses and hearing aids may be all that is allowed in a hospital intensive care room. On other units, patient-owned equipment might be allowed under some circumstances if approved by the hospital's policies and clinical caregivers and engineering staff.

In contrast, patients in a rehabilitation or long-term care environment are often encouraged to surround themselves with familiar items from home, ranging from family photos and keepsakes to furniture.

For nurses who see patients in the home setting, they must evaluate the home for any unsafe condition with regard to the use of property and should ensure that staff under their supervision understands when permission is required before removing any items and under what circumstances permission is not necessary.

Real property: Real property is property that includes land and buildings and anything affixed to the land. In health care facilities the land and buildings can have a significant impact on patient safety.

To help create and maintain a safe patient environment, nurses working in a health care facility should be consulted when engineering, safety staff, and others design patient care areas, as design features have safety implications. It is also vital that the use of fixtures and chemicals do not pose a safety hazard.

Items that are seemingly innocuous, such as holiday decorations or alcohol hand rubs, can pose significant fire hazards; thus, their use should be reviewed to maintain safety and compliance with the National Fire Protection Association (NFPA) standards for health care facilities. The NFPA is an international nonprofit organization, established in 1896, whose mission is to reduce the worldwide burden of fire and other hazards on the quality of life by providing and advocating consensus codes and standards, research, training, and education (NFPA, 2010).

If your organization rents any part of its facility property for outside use (an activity room or park-like grounds), care should be taken to enter into a contract for such use. The agreement should include adequate provisions for insurance coverage and restrictions where necessary, such as the prohibition of alcohol or dangerous activities.

Behavioral health settings may have special needs to prevent risks of suicide by hanging, choking, or ingestion of poisonous substances, or other means. In these cases, a thorough assessment of the environment and daily rounds should be carried out to avoid or minimize such risks.

Criminal and Administrative Penalties, Sanctions, and Fines

Nursing errors or lapses in judgment can sometimes lead to more than a lawsuit. The risks and events discussed previously may result in claims for civil damages where the alleged injured party sues for money damages. However, the nurse leader should be concerned about much more.

Nurses have been charged with violations of their state Nurse Practice Act. Actions such as these can result in licensure proceedings and can lead to a public reprimand, fines, probation, suspension, or revocation of licensure. Even contesting or challenging such charges is a public affair, as hearings by the state Boards of Nursing are generally public (see more discussion on this subject in Chapter 1).

State Departments of Public Health and the Center for Medicare and Medicaid Services (CMS) can also assess fines and penalties against your health care institution for violation of state laws or Medicare Conditions of Participation, either in follow-up to an adverse event or upon routine inspection (see Chapter 3). Instances such as exceeding the nurses' scope of practice or acts that violate hospital policies can result in monetary fines or penalties against one's license affecting the nurses' ability to practice.

Finally, nurse leaders and their staff can be charged with a criminal offense (see Chapter 9 for discussion of criminal offenses). Although rare, nurses who have committed a medical error or who were involved in an adverse event have been charged with manslaughter.

Criminal charges require a higher level of proof and criminal process and offenses are, therefore, brought by criminal prosecutors. There are cases brought where either the conduct was intentional or the conduct was so reckless as to show an extreme indifference to life. Nurses who alter medical records or destroy evidence can also be charged with obstruction of justice since falsifying records can interfere with the legal process of investigating a claim (see Chapter 6).

Responding to Adverse Events

When the nurse encounters an adverse event or medical error that results in harm to a patient, the response must be carried out carefully and appropriately depending on the circumstances and the extent of harm that has resulted.

An adverse event has been historically defined as an injury caused by medical management rather than by the underlying disease or condition of the patient (Institute of Medicine, 1999). This definition has been expanded in recent years to include an event that involves the patient but does not necessarily result in actual injury to the patient.

If the Patient has Been Adversely Affected

If the patient has been injured or suffered adverse ill effects, the nurse should first stabilize the patient and secure the best resources needed to help the patient transition to the next level of care. This is the time to activate your facility chain of command and to assist so that the patient receives the resources he or she needs.

Bills for services to the patient should be put on hold until it can be determined what services may have been required due to the medical error. Expenses necessitated by medical error should not be borne by the patient. In fact, Medicare may deny payment if the event is one of the "never events" now referred to as "serious adverse events" that CMS determines could have been reasonably prevented (see Chapter 3 and Chapter 8 for more information on never or serious adverse events)

Appropriate senior administration personnel should be advised promptly of any adverse event so that they can assist as needed with approval of resources and services.

Take Steps to Secure All Relevant Evidence

Make sure that medical records are secured and retained, including monitoring strips, requisitions, and other medical records. Medical devices and pathology specimens should also be retained in a secure environment. By maintaining security of such records, it is intended that the records be secured or sequestered to assure that the record as it existed at the time of the incident is not altered in any way.

You may also be asked to participate in a sentinel event determination meeting or root-cause analysis. A sentinel event is defined by TJC as an unexpected occurrence involving death or serious physical or psychological injury, or the risk thereof. TJC reviews sentinel events during its evaluation of health care organizations and evaluates the organizational response to such events. An appropriate response includes the following:

- Conducting a timely, thorough, and credible root cause analysis investigation;
- Developing an action plan designed to implement improvements to reduce risk;
- Implementing the improvements; and
- Monitoring the effectiveness of those improvements.

Root-cause analysis is a process for identifying the basic or causal factors that underlie variation in performance, including the occurrence or possible occurrence of a sentinel event (Carroll, Volume II, p. 588). A root-cause analysis focuses primarily on what systems and processes might have contributed to a medical error, not on individual performance.

In such a process described earlier, the nurse may feel as if he or she is under the microscope and may resist requests for information. However, it is important to realize that the investigation is for the improvement of all patient care, and sharing information with the root-cause analysis team is vital to help identify where improvements are needed. Be sure to voice your opinion on how proposed changes may be implemented and come prepared with suggestions of your own.

Depending on the laws of the state where you are located, the sentinel event and root-cause analysis process is usually considered peer review under state law and, therefore, may be kept confidential. Peer review is a process used for checking the work performed by one's equals (peers) to ensure it meets specific criteria. Peer review, medical peer review, and performance improvement activities have been given confidential status in many states to encourage thorough and critical review of events by health care providers who would otherwise feel vulnerable if those proceedings were capable of being made public. Nurses should be familiar with the peer review and quality improvement privileges for their state and comply with organizational policies and instructions on confidentiality that will help in assuring that the full benefit of such laws can be achieved.

Determine What Regulatory Reporting May be Required and What Agencies May be Involved

States may require prompt or immediate notification of adverse events. Currently 26 states require some form of reporting of certain defined adverse events. Other regulatory agencies may require notification, such as the Food and Drug Administration (FDA), for issues involving pharmaceuticals and medical devices, and Medicare, for patient deaths where the use of restraints was involved. Nurses should review their organization's policies and seek assistance from risk management or legal services for guidance on any reporting requirements. Where reporting is required, the manner and language used to file the report are key. Proper guidance will assure that it is done correctly.

Prepare to Inform the Patient

Risk management can and should provide you with information and preparation for disclosure discussions. You must be aware of the organization's policies for disclosure. Ultimately, it is the organizational and clinical leadership that should provide the disclosure to the family. Provide support and information as required to the next of kin.

Once you have reliable information about the event available (you do not want to delay speaking with the patient), and as guided by your organization's policies, take steps to see that the patient is advised of the event and provide the patient reasonable expectations as to next steps.

If you are not sure what caused or contributed to the adverse event, provide the patient emotional support and empathy for any change in condition and reassure him or her that you will do all you can to learn what happened and why it happened.

Care for the Caregivers

Your staff and others involved in an adverse event are often the second victims. Be sure to allow your staff to communicate in confidence their feelings surrounding the event and provide emotional support where needed. Referrals may need to be made to employee assistance programs, and time off may be recommended. In a catastrophic event, a formal debriefing may be necessary to help expedite caregiver healing and to facilitate discussion, while ensuring confidentiality and avoiding the "rumor mill."

Common Claims Against Nursing Personnel

Often it is the most basic tasks performed in a complex and busy system with a great deal of distraction that result in errors. Basic skills such as patient identification, patient medication rights, time-outs, and marking correct operative site are examples of how education can make a difference.

Lack of proper documentation presents risks in several ways; first and foremost, it can deprive other caregivers of an accurate recitation of an assessment or treatment rendered. It also fails to provide support for medical necessity needed for Medicare billing or upon regulatory inspection. Finally, it fails to support the care you or your staff gave in the event you are faced with a claim for injury.

The most effective way to improve nursing documentation is by having your documentation undergo detailed review and attending more conscientiously to your documentation (see more on documentation in Chapter 6).

There is no question that having been through a litigation experience at least once, either through deposition or courtroom testimony, raises consciousness. Short of that, nurses can improve documentation through scrutiny by their peers via periodic chart audits.

Licensure authorities pay special attention to documentation of assessments of risks, interventions, and where indicated based on significant findings or symptoms, timely notification of physicians, and Licensed Independent Professionals (LIPs). Licensed Independent Professionals include physician assistants, nurse practitioners, licensed nurse anesthetists and nurse midwives.

In addition, licensure authorities commonly inspect documentation for compliance with restraint regulations. Of particular interest are the time of restraint implementation, documentation of the physician order, periodic release of restraints, and alternatives offered in lieu of restraints.

Other areas of documentation review include the administration of pain medication, including the rationale for the use of the drug, patient response to medication, and documentation of its effectiveness. Documentation is expected to reflect not just what the nurse did, but how the nurse met the patients' needs and rights. Failure to take this responsibility seriously will leave questions on the table for regulators, patients, and their legal counsel. A complete and well documented chart will serve as a reliable record of the patient's total experience.

Policies and Procedures

Clinical leaders are called upon to draft policies to communicate procedures to staff, accreditation surveyors, or regulatory inspectors. What they may not realize is the extent to which polices can be used against them. Therefore, it is vital to exercise diligence and caution when writing policies.

Once your organization has well written policies, it is critical to follow them. Failure of an institution to follow its own policies can result in regulatory agencies finding a failure of care delivery within standards or regulations, and this finding can result in formal disciplinary action or fines. This is because your policy actually sets the standard of performance. If the policy is not followed, then the standard of performance that has been established is likely not reached.

In the case of a lawsuit, failure to follow your own policies can make it relatively easy for a court or an agency to reach a finding of negligence against the institution.

When writing policies, the language used, however well meaning, can compromise your organization and staff. Terms such as "must" and "shall" create a mandate for which you will be held accountable even where lack of resources prevent staff from following the policy as drafted. Sometimes available resources require nurse leaders to use their best judgment and deviate from policy. A policy should allow enough room for staff to exercise this judgment and deviate from the policy when safety to patients or others is at risk.

Policies should reflect your mission and provide guidance for your staff in their day-to-day functions. They should be clear, unambiguous, and readily available to staff for reference as needed.

Written policies should be "road-tested" so that the organization is confident of its ability to be effectively implemented. Policies should be based on currently accepted national standards of care, unless the practice is controlled by federal or local law or regulation. Research of medical literature and guidelines set forth by professional societies can provide the right support for enacting a policy. Policies should be reviewed periodically to ensure that their application is practical and up to date.

Retain all of your old policies as indicated by your organization's record retention guidelines. In the event there is litigation or any inquiry, policies applicable to the events in question will be requested, in order to also determine what policies were in effect during the time frame in which the event occurred. As it may take several years for a suit to be filed, and additional time for policies to be requested, it is important to set aside a copy of your policies related to an event in your investigation file so they are readily available when the request is presented.

Peer-Review Protection and Attorney–Client Privilege

Peer review is an important process and presents a unique opportunity to learn from an event or practice and to implement improvements to process. Peer review works best when participants and reviewers are not hampered by the specter of having to produce their impressions and opinions during the process of discovery in a lawsuit.

Discovery is a part of the litigation process where there is an open exchange of information among the parties to the suit in order to uncover the truth regarding the facts at issue. The process of discovery is governed by court, state, and federal rules and laws. Where appropriate, there can be protection from discovery, meaning that certain information may not have to be exchanged during the discovery process. In such cases, this legal protection is provided by state law and federal statutes such as the Health Care Quality Improvement Act (HCQIA) of 1986.

Nursing Malpractice

When one hears of medical malpractice it is usually related to an allegation that a physician failed to reach a correct diagnosis, provide timely treatment, or that he or she caused an adverse outcome.

Cases against an individual nurse for nursing negligence or malpractice in the past were rare. However, cases of negligence or malpractice or negligence against nurses have become more common. Often times, the institution is targeted, and the nurse is sued under the theory of *respondeat superior* (refer to Chapter 8 for a discussion of *respondeat superior*). This may be because the employer institution is viewed as, or is legally, the responsible entity and also because the institution is viewed as having more money—the so-called deep pocket.

Typical allegations against the nurse include failure to monitor and failure to detect and communicate to a physician changes in condition that could have made a difference to a patient's outcome. In the outpatient setting, the nurse may be charged with abandonment for failing to provide or arrange for continuous care.

A risk management program that seeks to reduce the number of claims filed due to nursing negligence should focus on the following:

- Safe medication practice through education and adherence to the seven medication rights, including the right reason and right documentation, in addition to right patient, right method, right time, right dose, and right medication;
- Education on critical thinking skills;
- Team building and simulation drills of response to emergency events;
- Providing a supportive environment for the reporting of adverse events and errors;
- Education on specific topics of clinical care with high failure and frequency rates, so-called high-risk areas; and
- Education and support on how to escalate the chain of command within the structure of the environment to mobilize the resources the patient needs. For example, accurate and complete documentation of a patient's change in condition with notification to a physician may not meet appropriate standards if the patient is not attended to or given timely assessment and life-saving intervention to treat his or her condition (see the following fictional case study).

CASE STUDY:

Pat is the registered nurse (RN) caring for a 60-year-old woman admitted for treatment of acute diverticulitis. She is receiving intravenous fluids, antibiotics, and clear liquids. On midnight rounds, the nurse finds that the patient's blood pressure is 90/60, with a heart rate of 110. Her temperature is 100.6. The nurse calls the covering physician, who assures her that the patient is probably dehydrated, and orders a bolus of 500 cc of normal saline. Pat checks her again after 2 hours and finds that the patient's blood pressure is now 80/50, with a heart rate of 120. The patient tells her that she feels "weak." Pat calls the physician again to tell him about the change in vital signs, who responds, "Didn't I just hear from you," and tells her to maintain the IV fluid at 200 cc an hour, let the patient get some rest and that he would see the patient "first thing in the morning." Pat sees the patient again at 6 A.M. When she enters the room, she notes the patient's shallow breathing. The patient is unresponsive with a blood pressure of 60 palpable. She calls out for help, but within seconds the patient stops breathing and a Code is called. The patient does not survive.

An autopsy reveals a perforated viscous, infectious peritonitis with free air in the abdomen, and positive blood cultures. Two years later, Pat is served with a lawsuit, naming her as a defendant along with the hospital and the physician. The allegations against Pat include failure to appropriately monitor and assess the patient, failure to rescue the patient when she was in danger, failure to follow the organizational chain of command, and abandonment.

CASE LESSON: In this case, consider what actions the nurse could have taken to prevent this patient outcome. Were there policies that could have guided her actions? Was there a chain of command in place that could have provided a means of summoning help for this patient? What other issues do you see in this case?

High-Risk Clinical Areas

Since there are often limited resources available, nurse leaders should focus on those areas that have historically proven to present the greatest risk to their practice or organization.

Obstetrical services, the emergency department (ED), surgical services, and anesthesia services are areas where treatment can produce adverse events that result in the greatest severity, permanent injury, or loss of life. The majority of serious claims filed in these categories allege permanent injury.

For example, obstetrical service failures may present claims of perinatal asphyxia for alleged failure to recognize fetal distress. The second most serious claim is failure to predict and properly treat shoulder dystocia, leading to Erb's palsy injury. An effective risk management program includes strategies to minimize risks, such as shoulder dystocia drills and team training on electronic fetal monitoring, whereby physicians and nurses are trained on the same national standards of interpretation.

ED claims include delays in treatment and misdiagnosis. ED overcrowding is a problem throughout the United States. Some of the most common missed diagnoses include myocardial infarction, stroke, and dissecting abdominal aneurysm.

Effective risk management strategies include the use of mandatory educational modules for physicians and computerized online documentation that supports and prompts critical decision making.

Other settings can produce unique risks. Home health services can present nonclinical risks such as the safety and security of staff entering and seeing a patient in an uncontrolled environment. Long-term facilities carry the risk of falls, pressure ulcers, and patient elopement, in an environment that favors patient rights. The behavioral health setting carries risks of suicide, injuries to others, property damage, and patient elopement.

The clinical nurse leader will need to be aware of the many regulations that govern clinical care, including the reporting of adverse events, the patient's right to be free from seclusion and restraint, and his or her right to receive mail and visitors and participate in directing his or her own care.

The clinical nurse leader should have at least a basic knowledge of the variety of regulations and work with the compliance officer in designing systems that will reduce the likelihood of a breach in regulations.

Nurse leaders should not construe general advice as good for all. Application of broad principles is a place to start, but the nurse should always verify what his or her own state requires. Every patient care situation is different, so a particular factual scenario may trigger another way of responding.

CONCLUSIONS AND TRENDS

Historically, suits for malpractice against nurses have been rare. However, this has changed and nurses have been named individually or as part of a suit against their employer under the doctrine of *respondeat superior.* The trend is to hold nurses accountable for their actions.

Policies and procedures are key tools; they act as a guide/reference not only in determining the correct practices to be carried out during the nursing process and related organizational procedures but also in communicating the expected conduct in a situation. It is vital that nurse leaders are familiar with such policies and procedures and that they seek opportunities to participate in their development.

Nurse leaders occupy increasingly responsible roles in health care management in organizations. This also means that they are responsible for decision making at higher levels that can include contract responsibility which obligates an organization and has the potential to increase risk. Thus, nurses need to be aware of the pitfalls associated with this type of decision making and also what resources are available to them to assist when needed as they carry out these processes.

The trend, along with the increased responsibility that nurse leaders are undertaking, is higher-level management responsibility for operations in high-risk areas. Knowledge of strategies to reduce risk associated with these areas will help the nurse leader to manage more effectively and reduce patient risk and enhance patient safety.

KEY POINTS

- A focus on completing a variance report should not take the place of timely reporting in the manner that is most effective based on staffing and organizational structure. Completing these reports at or around the time of the event when the incident is fresh in the minds of the reporter ensures the accuracy of the information and gives the risk manager a starting point for investigation. In addition, the report should be completed objectively and include only the facts, as the information contained in these reports may ultimately be seen by others outside the organization, including in a court of law.
- Incident reports are not an individual performance evaluation tool and should not be used in a punitive manner. To do so could inhibit the necessary open and honest communication that leads to process improvement.

■ Participation by nurse leaders and their staff on an organizational patient safety committee can be an enriching experience that helps spread a culture of safety throughout your organization.

■ How the clinical leadership reacts to an adverse event or medical error is often as important to the patient and family as the adverse event itself.

■ Policies should be written avoiding use of such terms as "must" and "shall." These words create a mandate for which you will be held accountable, even where lack of resources prevents staff from following the policy as drafted.

■ A policy should allow enough room for staff to exercise sound judgment and deviate from the policy when safety to patients or others is at risk.

REFERENCES

Agency for Healthcare Research and Quality (AHRQ). (n.d.). Retrieved April 29, 2010, from htpp://www.ahrq.gov

Carroll, R. (Ed.). (2006). *Risk management handbook for healthcare organizations* (Vol. I–II, 5th ed.). San Francisco: Jossey-Bass.

Health Care Quality Improvement Act of 1986 (HCQIA). 42 U.S.C. Sections 11101–11152.

Hickson, G. (2006). Organization works with physicians to reduce patient complaints and risk. HcPro Medical Staff Briefing. March, 2006. Vol. 16., No. 3

Institute for Healthcare Improvement (IHI). (n.d.). Retrieved April 29, 2010, from htpp://www.ihi.org

Kohn, L. T., Corrigan, J. M., & Donaldson, M. S. (Eds.). (2000). *To err is human: Building a safer health system* (A Report by Committee on Quality of Health Care in America, Institute of Medicine). Washington, DC: National Academy Press.

National Fire Protection Association (NFPA). (n.d.). Retrieved April 29, 2010, from htpp://www.nfpa.org

Woods, M. S. (2007). *Healing words: The power of an apology in medicine* (2nd ed.). Chicago: The Joint Commission Resources.

CHAPTER SIX

THE NURSE AND DOCUMENTATION

Edie Brous, Donna-Marie Boulay, and Valerie Burger

OBJECTIVES

- Review the purposes and uses of the medical record.
- Become familiar with common pitfalls to avoid in recordkeeping and documentation and learn best practices for reducing liability exposure.
- Prepare for the transition to electronic medical records (EMR) and electronic health records (EHR).
- Gain an overview of the evolution of systems of nursing documentation, and the key characteristics, benefits, and cautions associated with major systems of nursing documentation.
- Identify legislative changes and their effect on acceleration of development of EHR and recognize the major challenges for nurse leaders associated with development, implementation, and use of computerized documentation systems.
- Gain familiarity with specialized documentation systems such as OASIS (outcome and assessment information sheet) and medication-dispensing systems.

INTRODUCTION

Medical records are the legal documents reflecting clinical practice. A patient's medical record may provide the best, or even the only, evidence with which to pursue a malpractice claim against a provider. Conversely, it may be the only defense a health services provider has against charges of negligence, malpractice, professional misconduct, or criminal deeds. As such, the nurse's documentation must indicate that the care provided to a patient was within acceptable standards of practice and in accordance with regulatory mandates.

This chapter reviews the uses of the medical record, common pitfalls to avoid, best practices for reducing liability exposure, and special attention to the use of electronic medical records (EMR) and electronic health records (EHR).

The chapter also provides an overview of the evolution of various types of nursing documentation systems to the present-day computerized medical record. Readers will be familiarized with the benefits and cautions of these types of systems. There is a discussion of the legislative changes and the acceleration of the development of EHR. Laws affecting these changes will be explained along with the incentives being offered.

In addition, a review of the compliance issues as well as other major challenges with the development, implementation, and use of the computerized documentation systems will be given. Included are federal and state reimbursement laws and the implications for nursing documentation. Case examples are used for illustration of legal concepts.

DOCUMENTATION: PRINCIPLES AND PRACTICE

Purpose and Function of the Medical Record

Records of patient care are maintained for a number of reasons:

- Communication and continuity of care among providers,
- Clinical research and performance improvement,
- Reimbursement for provided services and justification for billing,
- Regulatory compliance,
- Memorializing the care provided to a patient, and
- Litigation evidence.

In all cases, the written record of patient care provides evidence of the care and services a patient received. Did the nurses communicate their clinical concerns in a timely manner and to the appropriate people? Is there an evidence basis for current practices? How much can insurance companies pay providers for rendered services? Are the provider and the institution in which he or she works functioning in accordance with local, state, and federal mandates? What medications did the patient receive and at what time? Were acceptable standards of practice followed? Although eye witness testimony may also provide critical information, it is ultimately the medical record that answers all of these questions for patients, providers, attorneys, juries, regulators, third-party payers, and researchers.

Chronology and Sequence of Events

The most important information in the medical record may be the actual sequence of events. The precise times at which medications were given, vital signs were obtained, physicians were notified, or interventions occurred provide critical information as to the chronology of care.

Every entry must indicate the complete date and time the note is being written, as well as the date and time of the event or observation being documented, and must be signed. Late entries must be identified as such. When charting after the occurrence of an event or observation, or when adding information to a previously written entry, the note should clearly indicate that it is being written as an addendum or late entry. This allows for an accurate reconstruction of events and adds credibility to a late entry by explaining the reason for it.

Handwritten notes that are continued from one page to another must be identified as continuation notes. At the end of the first page, the entry should say, "Continued," then be signed. The next page should indicate, "Continued from" with the date and time of the entry being completed. It also must be signed. This allows an accurate chronology and assures that notes can be read in their entirety. Records that do not accurately reflect the sequence of events present problems in the defense against negligence or malpractice claims. This is illustrated in the following case.

CASE EXAMPLE:

Masters v. Khuri (2004)

In this case 37-year-old chiropractor, Dr. Mathew Masters, (the plaintiff) was brought by ambulance to the emergency department (ED) experiencing an acute asthma attack. The medical records indicated that he arrived 10:53 P.M. or at 10:56 P.M. Despite being intubated he suffered a respiratory arrest, followed by pulseless electrical activity (PEA). This resulted in severe brain damage with subsequent incontinence and an inability to perform the activities of daily living.

Issue: Whether there was a delay in intubation of Dr. Masters, and if so, whether the emergency department physician was liable for the injuries resulting from the delay in treatment.

SUMMARY OF FACTS: Dr. Masters brought a malpractice action against the emergency department physician, Dr. Fadlo Raja Khuri (the defendant) claiming a delay in intubation. The critical issue in the case was the time of intubation. Some hospital records indicated that he was intubated at 11:00 P.M. (within the acceptable standard of practice). Other hospital records indicated that he was intubated 10 to 15 minutes after that time (a departure from the acceptable standard of practice.)

Dr. Masters claimed that he was intubated at the later time. He alleged that the 10- to 15-minute delay in his intubation represented a departure from the standards of practice and was a substantial contributing factor in his injury. Plaintiff's expert witnesses opined that Dr. Masters was not intubated in a timely enough fashion to prevent the cardiorespiratory arrest. The expert's opinions were based on the charted epinephrine administration times of 11:15 and 11:20 P.M. The PEA was documented at 11:15 P.M. — immediately after intubation.

Defense expert witnesses opined that the intubation occurred at 11:00 P.M. because the medical record reflected that Dr. Masters had received medications for the PEA by 11:05 P.M., prior to the epinephrine doses the plaintiff's experts referenced.

LOWER COURT'S DECISION: The jury found Dr. Khuri not negligent and Dr. Masters appealed. In his appeal, Dr. Masters argued that the trial-court judge had erred because he allowed the defense experts to testify that the charted blood gas times represented the time the results were received, not the time the blood was obtained. This was inconsistent with the recording nurse's testimony. The medical records were irregular and conflicting. They indicated that cardiopulmonary resuscitation (CPR) was started at 11:00 P.M. and intubation occurred at that time. The PEA occurred immediately after intubation. The blood gas log, however, demonstrated that blood was drawn at 11:05 P.M. — an impossibility if CPR and intubation had occurred earlier.

The ED nurse testified that Dr. Masters was intubated at 11:00 P.M. and blood gas results were documented at 11:06 P.M. She also testified that she was not certain of the accuracy of the timed events, as some of the recording was after the fact. Based on the medications given at 11:15 P.M., the medical record was determined to inaccurately reflect the time of intubation.

APPEALS COURT'S DECISION: The appeals court held that the conflicting times and the conflicting sequence of events allowed the judge to determine that the blood gas times documented represented the time the results were obtained, not the time the blood was drawn, as noted in the court record below:

The emergency room records state that the intubation procedure was performed at 11:00 P.M. However, in view of the immediate need to treat the plaintiff, record keeping was secondary. There was thus a question as to when the time was recorded and whether as recorded it was accurate. A blood gas test was ordered on the plaintiff's arrival, but the time at which blood was drawn was disputed. Since the plaintiff was wearing an oxygen mask at the time blood was drawn, the experts agreed that intubation would have then been impossible. Thus, if the blood was not drawn until 11:06 P.M as some records showed, intubation must have occurred thereafter. (p. 474)

Important lessons that can be learned from this case are that:

- during time-sensitive situations, one person should be designated to record contemporaneously with events rather than having providers attempt to reconstruct events after the fact;
- every entry must have a complete date and time, including A.M. or P.M. unless using military time;
- the recording person must use the same timepiece for each entry; and
- documentation regarding laboratory tests must clearly distinguish the time the specimens were obtained from the time the results were received.

Complete and Accurate Records

Medical records must be complete and accurate. Incomplete, missing, altered, or destroyed medical records may give rise to claims of spoliation of evidence, noncompliance with regulatory standards, violation of organization policies, and departures from the standards of practice. In addition, when critical portions of the medical record cannot be produced in response to a litigation demand, allegations may include fraud. This is evidenced in the case example below.

CASE EXAMPLE:

Chace v. Curran (2008)

Andrew Chace was born on September 22, 1995. The delivery was complicated by a prolapsed cord for which the attending physician Dr. Curran performed a Caesarian section. The infant was resuscitated upon delivery, but almost 9 years later the parents filed a complaint alleging that Andrew suffered permanent severe physical and mental disabilities from a negligent delivery.

Issue: Whether Andrew's injuries were caused by a negligent delivery and whether there was evidence of fraudulent concealment of records.

A nurse testified at her deposition that the medical records prepared by Dr. Curran and another nurse (Nurse Taylor) were inaccurate and incomplete, as they did not document that the infant had been deprived of oxygen for several minutes during the resuscitation. The lawsuit also claimed intentional fraudulent concealment, intentional misrepresentation, and fraud against Dr. Curran and Nurse Taylor.

Because the statute of limitations had expired on the malpractice claims, the trial court dismissed that part of the suit. (Statutes of limitations limits the time frame within which a suit may be brought for an alleged wrongdoing and vary depending on the type of claim and by individual state law.) The remaining claims were allowed to proceed.

The plaintiffs were allowed to amend their fraudulent concealment and intentional misrepresentation claims. They then filed amended complaints alleging that Dr. Curran and Nurse Taylor made intentional omissions and false and misleading statements in the medical record regarding the events surrounding Andrew's resuscitation. Both providers failed to document a failed intubation attempt or that he was not receiving oxygen for several minutes. The plaintiffs claimed that the medical record was written to lead the reader to conclude that resuscitation efforts were without incident. In addition, Dr. Curran and Nurse Taylor were alleged to have made the false statements and omissions knowing that a medical malpractice lawsuit could ensue and with the intent to conceal their lack of due care during the resuscitation.

Although the defendants continued to argue that the case should be dismissed because the statute of limitations for malpractice had expired, the court disagreed. The question was whether or not the defendants engaged in activity designed to hide from the plaintiffs the precise nature of the treatment they provided so that the plaintiffs would not have the knowledge they needed to sue them for it. The court found that there was evidence that, if true, might show such fraudulent concealment, and the case was allowed to proceed to trial.

Important lessons that can be learned from this case are that:

- all pertinent information must be entered into the patient's medical record,
- failing to document critical information regarding an adverse event may create the appearance of a cover-up,
- charting in a misleading manner can compromise the defense in a lawsuit, and
- falsifying a medical or business record is criminal activity and may also be considered professional misconduct by a nursing board.

Communication

The issue of reporting changes in a patient's condition is critical. Allegations such as a nurses failure to monitor for changes, failure to recognize changes in condition, failure to report changes to the physicians, and failure to intervene on behalf of the patient in a timely manner, can only be adequately refuted when the relevant information is present in the medical record. Courts have held that nurses are responsible for communicating their findings to physicians and may be held liable when failing to do so. A classic early case as well as subsequent later cases that follow illustrate this.

CASE EXAMPLES:

Darling v. Charleston Hospital (1965)

Issue: Whether nurses were negligent in failing to recognize progressive gangrene to the plaintiff's leg and failing to report the finding to the physician.

On November 5, 1960, 18-year-old Dorrence Darling II broke his leg while playing college football. He was taken to the emergency room where the leg was placed in traction and casted. Shortly after the plaster cast was applied, he complained of great pain. His toes became swollen and dark, then cold and insensitive. The cast was notched the following day. On November 8, the cast was split whereupon blood and seepage were noted, accompanied by a stench. Dorrence was transferred to another hospital on November 19. An orthopedist found a considerable amount of dead tissue caused by cast constriction. Several procedures were performed to save the leg, but Dorrence ultimately underwent a below-the-knee amputation.

In the subsequent lawsuit, Dorrence claimed that it was the nurse's duty to observe his toes for color, temperature, movement, and circulation every 10 to 20 minutes. The evidence indicated that such checks were only performed a few times a day. He further claimed that the nurses were derelict in reporting their observations to an administrator or physician.

COURT'S DECISION: The court found that the nurse's failure to recognize progressive gangrene and to inform the physician constituted a departure from acceptable standards of practice. The jury returned a US$150,000 verdict against the hospital. (This amount was reduced to US$110,000 after subtracting $40,000, the amount of the settlement received from the doctor.) The verdict was affirmed on appeal.

Nurses Must Have and Activate a Problem-Solving Procedure That Can Be Employed to Avoid Danger to the Patient (Motion to Dismiss)

Livingston v. Montgomery (2009) (Motion to Dismiss)

Issue: Were the nurses negligent in failing to notify the nursing chain of command of a situation where there were complications during birth.

In this case, the parents of Travis Colter brought a lawsuit against several physicians and nurses, claiming that Travis suffered severe neurological injuries caused by malpractice during labor and delivery. Specifically, with regard to nursing malpractice, the parents claimed the nurses failed to adequately or properly monitor fetal well-being, failed to intervene in the face of fetal distress or nonreassuring fetal heart rate patterns, failed to summon a resuscitation team in a timely manner, failed to discontinue the Oxytocin, and delayed resuscitation to a distressed newborn without a respiratory rate.

The plaintiff's expert witness testified that:

Although a nurse is not the treating physician, he or she is an integral part of the "team" effort necessary to render the standard of such combined care. He or she has an obligation to act as his or her patient's advocate. The standard of care in situations such as Ms. Montgomery's called for nurses to recognize the presence of non-reassuring fetal heart rates, especially when complicated by meconium, institute resuscitative measures, and discontinue oxytocin. They have the added obligation to notify the nursing chain of command when such danger, as with Ms. Montgomery's unborn child, continues without being effectively addressed, i.e., discontinuing the augmentation orders contraindicated by the above conditions, or without effective remedy, i.e., Cesarean rescue.

COURT'S DECISION: The defendants were unsuccessful in their motion to have this case dismissed.

Important lessons that be learned from this case are

- nursing documentation must clearly reflect that nurses are monitoring for foreseeable complications, recognizing them in a timely fashion, and identifying those concerns to a physician;
- such entries must specifically identify *which* physician was advised of the worrisome findings and at what time (avoid entries such as, "MD aware" or "GYN paged repeatedly");
- flow sheets that demonstrate frequent assessments may refute claims that nurses did not adequately monitor a patient; and
- nursing documentation must indicate that the nursing staff pursued concerns to resolution. This may include climbing a clinical ladder and notifying management.

CASE EXAMPLE:

PHYSICIAN CAN BE HELD ACCOUNTABLE FOR FAILING TO READ NURSES NOTES

Ploch v. Hamai (2006)

Physicians may be held accountable for failing to read notes written by other providers, as illustrated in *Ploch v. Hamai*, (2006). Juli Ploch underwent a laparoscopic vaginal hysterectomy performed by Dr. Kenneth Hamai. Postoperatively she complained to the nursing staff that she was experiencing pain at a level of 5 to 7 on a 1 to 10 scale. The nursing staff documented the complaints and medicated her for the pain. Nursing records also noted that there was no pain at the time of her discharge from the hospital. Dr. Hamai examined the plaintiff before discharging her but did not read the nurses notes that reflected her postoperative pain. Six months later, Ms. Ploch developed flank pain and was treated by a urologist for an obstructed ureter. One of her kidneys stopped functioning. She subsequently brought a suit against Dr. Hamai. The urologist and other experts testified that an errant suture or staple from the hysterectomy may have injured the ureter.

At trial, one of the expert witnesses testified that Dr. Hamai had departed from acceptable standards of care in failing to read the nurse's notes. Had he done so and noted the postoperative pain, diagnostic testing may have revealed the obstruction. The experts also testified that additional surgery within 72 hours of the obstruction would have prevented the kidney damage.

LOWER COURT'S DECISION: The jury returned a verdict in favor of the defendant physicians, and Ms. Ploch appealed.

APPEALS COURT'S DECISION: On appeal, it was determined that Dr. Hamai's failure to read the nurse's notes was the cause of Ms. Ploch's injury. The judgment in favor of Dr. Hamai was reversed, and the case was sent back to the lower court for further proceedings.

General Principles

Each page of the medical record must identify the patient by at least two identifiers such as name, date of birth, or medical record number. Handwritten entries must be legible, unambiguous, and written in black or blue indelible ink. Every entry must have a complete date and time that permits an accurate reconstruction of the sequence of events. A complete date and time on all entries is also required by regulatory and accrediting bodies. Each entry must be signed by the provider. Nurses must sign entries with their last name as it appears on their nursing license. Signatures should also indicate status such as RN, LPN, or CRNA. Avoid duplicate and triplicate charting, that is, charting the same information in more than one place. Such practice allows for potential inconsistency in the record and consumes valuable patient surveillance time. With hand-generated records, do not leave empty spaces because this provides the opportunity for the notes to be altered by another person or for another person to inadvertently make entries in the empty space.

Abbreviations

Any abbreviations, symbols, acronyms, or dose designations must be approved for use by the institution and/or an organizational policy. A list must be compiled and updated regularly to reflect those that are acceptable for use in the medical record. Using unapproved abbreviations may present a patient safety problem, as they can be misinterpreted. Providers unfamiliar with abbreviations, symbols, acronyms, or dose designations that they come across must be able to look them up on the approved list. Abbreviations not on the list must be avoided, even if in common use by a clinical specialty, until they are added to the list.

The Institute for Safe Medication Practices (ISMP) provides information about error-prone abbreviations, symbols, and dose designations (ISMP, 2010), and The Joint Commission (TJC) has required that organizations have a "DO NOT USE" list as part of accreditation standards since 2004 (TJC, 2010). Nurses must avoid using abbreviations on the organization's DO NOT USE list. In addition, the organizational policy should we widely circulated among all practitioners and every effort should be made to gain consistency in use of the policy.

Corrections, Alterations, and Deletions

Corrections must be performed in accordance with organizational policies and in a manner that leaves the original entry readable. With handwritten entries, a single line should be drawn through the error so the writing under the line can still be read. The provider's initials should be above the line, with the words such as "incorrect entry" or "wrong data" or "error" or whatever the institution's policy dictates.

Electronic record corrections must be performed as the organizational policy dictates. The use of pencils, scribbles, correction fluid, multiple lines, or other techniques with handwritten entries may create an impression that the provider is hiding information, altering or falsifying the record.

CASE EXAMPLES:

ALTERATIONS IN MEDICAL RECORD MAY UNDERMINE CREDIBILITY
OF DEFENSE

*Medical Review Panel of Hedda Neville, et al. v. Charity Hospital
(2008)*

In a suit against a hospital on behalf of herself and her brain-damaged son, a mother was awarded US$8 million in general damages (later reduced under the state's statutory damage cap); US$1.1 million for future lost wages; US$25 million for future rehabilitation and residential care; US$45,000 for past medical expenses; court costs; expert witness fees; and judicial interest from the original filing of her request for a medical review panel. The hospital appealed, but the judgment was upheld.

APPELLATE COURT'S DECISION: The appeals court found that the defendant hospital had not been credible due to documentation and medical-record irregularities.

The defense theory of the case could have been demonstrated with exculpatory fetal monitoring strips, and though those strips were required to be part of the medical record, they were never produced. The court considered the fact that the strips were missing as well as other issues raised by the chart itself. The medical record did not reflect an accurate sequence of events, as her membranes broke in the morning, but the charting did not note meconium in the amniotic fluid until 4:00 P.M. Fetal heart rates (FHR) were noted to be in the 170s at 11:00 P.M., but there were no further entries until midnight, when the FHR dropped into the 60s and 70s. The court noted, "Anything not recorded in the medical records would be speculation" (p. 9).

The fetal bradycardia was sustained for 3 to 4 minutes. The infant was delivered by Cesarean section, and the physician testified that she immediately suctioned moderately thick meconium from the throat and then performed resuscitative efforts. According to her testimony, the baby was not stimulated to take his first breath until after intubation. This conflicted with the medical record, which indicated that stimulation preceded intubation. The testimony and the medical record were also in conflict regarding whether the infant was placed on oxygen during the resuscitation efforts.

An entry had been changed from "O_2 noted not to be *connected* to ambu bag while resuscitation being performed" to "O_2 noted not to be *disconnected* to ambu bag while resuscitation being performed" (p. 11).

In noting the altered entries, the Court stated,

This is ominous and inexcusable no matter what the ultimate significance of the sentence may have been. Other entries are scratched out and changed. There are clear contradictions between the events as described by the obstetrical residents and as described by the pediatric residents. Finally, the chest x-rays, central to the defense theory of causation, were also missing. (p. 4)

The judgment against the hospital was upheld.

Illegible or Ambiguous Entries

Entries that are illegible or ambiguous may contribute to clinical error and adverse events. In addition, illegible and ambiguous notes compromise the defense in a malpractice action or licensing board investigation. Alterations or deletions can lead to claims of spoliation or intentional altering of evidence, fraudulent concealment, or document falsification that may also result in criminal charges. Such alteration of evidence may also allow for punitive damages in a civil claim. Punitive damages are awarded by courts to punish the wrongdoer and deter future misconduct. These problems are illustrated in the following case.

CASE EXAMPLE:

ALTERATION OF MEDICAL RECORDS LEADS TO CHARGE OF FRAUDULENT CONCEALMENT

Rosenblit v. Zimmerman (2001)

Erin Rosenblit underwent a series of chiropractic treatments for mid-back pain performed by Dr. Zimmerman. After a few visits, she identified to Dr. Zimmerman that she was experiencing neck pain, headaches, nausea, and ringing in her ears. Dr. Zimmerman continued performing the same type of neck manipulations and the symptoms were not relieved. When she sought treatment from other providers, radiology findings indicated cervical spine instability for which she underwent orthopedic surgery.

Prior to bringing a malpractice action against Dr. Zimmerman, Rosenblit obtained a copy of her medical chart from his office. The medical record indicated that she was not improving and that she was dissatisfied with her condition at her last visit. During the discovery portion of the case, she received another copy of her chart and discovered that it was different from the one that had been previously provided. The new copy of the chart had been altered to create the impression that she had been improving with Dr. Zimmerman's treatment and that she was satisfied. She then added new counts to her complaint to add spoliation and fraudulent concealment of evidence claims.

Dr. Zimmerman explained the discrepancy by stating that he had recopied the chart after being served with the malpractice complaint so as to make it more legible. The court record showed that he had destroyed the original record after recopying. A comparison of the two charts, however, did not indicate alterations consistent with recopying. At his deposition, Dr. Zimmerman testified that he had added new details to make the record more complete.

The trial court separated the malpractice counts from the spoliation and fraudulent concealment counts and conducted individual trials for each. The malpractice trial was conducted first with the jury not knowing about the record alteration.

LOWER COURT'S DECISION: It resulted in a jury verdict in Dr. Zimmerman's favor. When the spoliation and fraudulent concealment trial proceeded before the same jury Rosenblit was awarded compensatory and punitive damages.

COURT'S RATIONALE: On appeal, the court held that Dr. Zimmerman's record alteration was admissible as evidence of Dr. Zimmerman's own perception that the actual records did not support his defense. The court record stated, "A jury could infer from Dr. Zimmerman's behavior that he believed that Rosenblit's medical records would prejudice his position in the litigation" (p. 409). However, because the original chart had been available for the malpractice trial, there was no basis for the fraudulent concealment action against him.

APPEALS COURT'S DECISION: The appeals court also held, however, that the malpractice trial had been unfair to Rosenblit. The jury had awarded a large punitive damages judgment in the spoliation and fraudulent concealment trial. As such, the alteration evidence would have been important enough for the jury to find differently in the malpractice case. Had the jury been aware of Dr. Zimmerman's efforts to conceal his actions, Rosenblit would have fared differently in the malpractice trial. The exclusion of that evidence may have caused an unjust trial. The malpractice judgment in favor of Dr. Zimmerman was reversed and sent back for a new trial.

Important lessons learned from this case are that

corrections, deletions, addendum entries, or alterations must be in accordance with the organizational policies and procedures;
fetal monitoring strips, cardiac monitoring strips, or other diagnostic tests must be preserved with the entire medical record; and
attempts to cover up or falsify a medical record may be more damaging to the defense than the actual clinical error.

DOCUMENTATION SYSTEMS

Historical Perspective

Florence Nightingale, as noted in Chapter 1, was a remarkable leader in so many respects. With regard to documentation systems, for example, she was influential in launching the first such system according to an online history of her accomplishments (Solar Navigator, 2010). In 1857, Queen Victoria invited her to function in the central leadership role in the establishment of the Royal Commission on the Health of the Army. The queen could not appoint Ms. Nightingale to the Royal Commission, since under the custom of British law at the time, only a man could serve as a commissioner. However, Nightingale wrote the commission's 1,000-plus page report and was instrumental in the implementation of its recommendations. The report of the Royal Commission led to a major overhaul of army military care and to the establishment of an Army Medical School and of a comprehensive system of army medical records.

Sectional Documentation

Medical records systems evolved slowly from the implementation of the medical record system Nightingale designed to the mid-20th century.

During that period, the principal documentation system used around the world was sectional documentation, where chart entries were organized by type of individual care provider. Each profession wrote only in its designated section of the patient's medical record. Test results, laboratory reports, consulting opinions, and recommendations were each confined to their unique sections of the chart. Nurses had their section for nursing notes, physicians had their section for doctor's notes, and never did the twain meet.

More than a century later nurses at war were using Nightingale's system of documentation. Below are the recollections of a U.S. Army Nurse in Vietnam, A. Philiben, about the documentation of care for Australian soldier who was a triple amputee with grave infections, who asked her, 40 years later, to "translate for him" what the 1967 notes meant. In response to him, she wrote:

> This was the time that you turned against us. I think you were in the anger stage of the grief (denial, bargaining, anger and acceptance) process. You were very sick . . . and you started taking it out on the nurses.
>
> You remained on the cooling blanket to this point so your fevers were still high. Our head nurse wrote that you were uncooperative. At one point though you demanded 2 blankets and 2 hot water bottles . . . so you must have been cold. Then another nurse wrote that you refused the hot water bottles that you requested. The same nurse wrote "continues to be abusive."
>
> WOW.
>
> The nurses' notes are terrible. We wrote that your stump was irrigated. You only had three, so I'm not sure which one was still troublesome. But whichever one it was it was still draining. (A. Philiben, personal communication, July 28, 2010).

But "Things Have Changed," as that poet philosopher, Bob Dylan, wrote at the turn of the 21st century. New systems emerged that helped the nurse organize thoughts, assessments. and actions became common place throughout the world.

And yet, Dylan's original concept that "The Times They Are a Changin" (Dylan, 1964) has surfaced in health care documentation in 2010 as the new health care reform laws were enacted just as this book was being written. Therefore, this part of the chapter needs to be read with these prospective changes uppermost in mind. In light of the new federal laws discussed in the following sections, it is imperative to consider the features of each documentation system so that in reviewing them the nurse will know which elements to retain and which need to be modified so that documentation systems can conform to the new laws.

Narrative Form Charting

The narrative charting format has played an early and prominent part in the sectional style of entry. Gradually, flow charts, and to a lesser extent check lists, were introduced. The narrative style chart typically contains an initial history, progress notes, care plan, and discharge summary. Events are charted chronologically. Columns are often used to organize the narrative. There can be separate columns for treatments, nursing observations, comments, and other items.

Narrative charting is a straightforward, storytelling format in which the nurse chooses what to document. Entries are made on a blank sheet of paper, or in a vacant few lines or area on a form. It generally lacks a structural format and is often in the progress note segment of the record. This method indicates the client's condition, problems, and complaints, which nursing interventions were used in the care of the patient, and the patient's response to those interventions. The nurse writes in a storyline manner, in sentences, what is judged to be the pertinent information of the shift. Narrative charting can also be used in conjunction with some other flow sheet or checklist.

This type of documentation lends itself well to chronological charting, especially if the entries are made contemporaneously, that is, as the nursing care is provided. The problem is that often the information is recorded without any organizing framework, and, thus, documentation style can vary from practitioner to practitioner. Also risky and problematic in this type of documentation is that recording of events can be overlooked if the nurse fails to write the event down in the "story of the day."

Example Narrative Assessment

As you review the following hypothetical typical narrative assessment presented below, analyze it for completeness and correctness of abbreviations:

07/20/10 1500 hrs. 68-year-old male admitted 7/19/10 for exacerbation CHF. VS T 98.2 F, HR 97, RR 24, BP 140/78. Alert and oriented to person, place, and time. PERRLA. Denies any pain at present. Responds appropriately to verbal stimuli. Speech clear. MAE fully and without impairment, placed on fall precautions due to IV and diuretic therapy. Strength equal and strong in all extremities. Skin warm, dry, and intact. Mucous membranes intact, pink, and moist. Patient has left-upper bridge in place in mouth. Tolerating regular cardiac diet with 2-gram sodium. Patient verbalizes understanding of diet restrictions and is compliant. Respirations even. Breath sounds auscultated to bases with fine rales present at the bases bilaterally. Patient wearing O2 via nasal cannula at 2 liters. Pulse oximeter reading with O2 in place is 97%. Nonproductive cough present. Apical pulse regular rate and rhythm at 97 bpm. Telemetry in place. Nail beds pink with capillary refill >2 seconds. Pedal pulses equal and strong bilaterally. Mild +2 edema noted at ankles bilaterally. No calf tenderness noted on leg. Bowel movement today, soft formed. Uses urinal, urine clear, yellow. IV in place on left forearm, 20-gauge saline lock in place. Dressing intact, with no signs of swelling or infiltration. Patient verbalizes understanding of care plan and CHF education and appears interested in participating in further education. Cardiac care patient teaching booklet given to patient and family for review. Patient willing to review. Side rails up X3, patient ambulating with assistance, bed in low position, and call bell within reach. Instructed to call for any needs and to request assistance before attempting to get up. Patient verbalized understanding. Will continue to monitor. Signed, *Nancy Nurse RN*

In reviewing this narrative, consider the following questions. Was the narrative complete? What standards should be used to assess it? What, if anything, is missing from this narrative? In this narrative form, where there is no standard structure, it may not be apparent if vital information is missing. Were the abbreviations used appropriate?

Advantages and Disadvantages to Narrative Charting

On a positive note, narrative forms are not always bereft of information and they can be all inclusive and accurately reflect the care given during an assigned shift. The narrative forms are flexible, especially for documenting complications, new diagnoses, and other unforeseen occurrences.

The disadvantage of the narrative, however, is noted in a study by Moss, Andison, and Sobko (2007). In that study, inductive content analysis was used to examine the narrative documentation entered in an otherwise structured nursing information system. They found that very little of these narrative entries were used to document nursing care. Rather, the majority of the entries were to provide other health care team members with an overview for care coordination or to document unexpected events. The study showed the need for summary tools for coordination of care across disciplines, thus indicating that narrative charting has its place but is often not comprehensive as a stand alone documentation method.

Nurse leaders and bedside nurses alike have noted that the narrative form is time consuming. Illegibility, improper erasures, or stricken entries stress colleagues and make chart auditing of this system a nightmare. Abnormal data do not stand out. Colleagues are tempted not to read lengthy dissertations and may skip over important information. Because every nuance is not captured, this system is very inefficient and leads to many documentation errors. Left to the discretion of providers with different levels of expertise, the system can result in varying caliber of information gathered. English-as-a-second-language (ESL) writers, which may include traveling nurses or those without good writing skills, pose unique problems in narrative charting. In the hectic environment staff nurses may overlook or fail to remember what to include in a narrative note.

Problem-Oriented Medical Record

The problem-oriented format was the 1960s innovation of Dr. Lawrence Weed. Fifty years later he is professor of medicine emeritus at the University of Vermont's College of Medicine. He is known in health information management as the father of the problem-oriented medical record (POMR) and is still active in technology for the health care world as noted in the following. His innovations included the beginning of the integration of nurses and physicians charting on the same page.

The POMR was developed to assist caregivers in order to think and to better communicate their thoughts and actions and improve efficiency, quality of care, and patient safety. It was refined in the 1970s and then referred to as "SOAP," an acronym for subjective data, objective data, assessment, and plan. SOAPIE is a further refinement. In SOAPIE, I means implementation (nursing actions or interventions) and E is for evaluation. Subsequently, R has been added (SOAPIER) at some facilities and stands for revision. Each letter represents the required information relevant to that particular term.

Example of POMR

The following is a hypothetical example of a SOAPIE note that might be prepared by a staff nurse in a medical unit.

> July 26, 2010, 0900 hours
> S—Subjective—"Nurse, my belly hurts. And my back too. I need my pain med." Family member gave lengthy history of drug and alcohol abuse.
> O—Objective—Called to patient bedside because of complaints of pain. Patient reports pain at the umbilicus, radiating to the back at a level of 9 on a pain scale of 0–10. Last pain medication of Dilaudid 2-mg IV given less than 2 hours ago. Patient requesting more medication. VS T—98.9, HR—102, RR—28, BP—116/78. Pt alternately agitated and lethargic.
> A—Assessment—abdominal pain, not adequately controlled with current pain regime. Acute episode of exacerbation of pain.
> P—Plan—MD Jones called. Order obtained for stat dose of Dilaudid.
> I—Implementation—Patient repositioned and pain medication given.
> E—Evaluation—Patient resting comfortably in bed after medication.
> July 26, 2010, 09:00 hours
> Signed, Norma Nurse, RN
> July 26, 2010, 12:15 hours
> R—Revision—Patient transported for Ultra Sound to diagnose possible abdominal aneurysm.
> Signed, *Norma Nurse, RN*

Recent Changes to the POMR System

The most recent iteration of the POMR system is the APIE, where the acronym stands for assessment, plan, implementation, and evaluation. The object of this approach is to condense patient data into the fewest possible statements by combining subjective and objective data into the assessment section and including nursing actions with the expected outcomes of client care into the plan.

The PIE version stands for problems, intervention, and evaluation of your nursing care. It is made up of a 24-hour flow sheet combined with nursing progress notes. The notes are focused on patient problem statements based on a nursing diagnosis, and each problem is numbered.

Flow Sheets or Graphic Records

Flow sheets or graphic records are used as an easy method to reflect or show a patient's status. They were pioneered by nurse anesthetists in the 1960s and have evolved for uses in many areas of practice and are popular in computerized record systems. Given the current national trend to convert to computer charting, in part driven by the new Federal Health Law (see the following discussion), those who will be helping to design these systems for their facilities or agencies may find graphic records essential since, in graphic records, progress notes highlight data, actions, and responses.

Of particular advantage in acute care settings is that they are helpful for documenting vital signs, medications, intake and output, bowel movements, and other vital functions and observations. Long-term care nurses in a variety of settings use them as well because time parameters can be set to range from minutes to months; thus, these records accommodate to a variety of settings.

For example, intraoperative blood pressure might be recorded every few minutes, whereas in a home setting a weight may be recorded only once a month. In clinics, diabetic data can be tracked at each visit, no matter how frequent or infrequent the visit.

Focus Charting

The focus charting system originated two decades ago to center attention on data, nursing action, and patient response. Focus charting is best used to identify concisely and draw attention to patient problems. It can reflect an acute change in condition, a potential problem, or can be used to document a patient's response to a treatment or procedure. Focus charting reflects one individual issue in patient care and does not combine different issues and responses.

Focus charting systems utilize progress notes, flow charts, history and admission assessments, ongoing assessments, and a care plan. Like flow charts, its progress notes are where data (D), nursing actions (A), and responses (R) are located. In other words, focus charting is often done in progress notes that are displayed as a flow sheet. Of note, because of this feature, it is a computer-friendly approach. It is also a style that facilitates conformity to TJC requirements.

Example of Focus Charting

The usual structure for a focus note is data, action, and response. A hypothetical example of a focus note is as follows:

> July 28, 2010 0900 hours focus nursing note:
> D—Patient received with chemotherapy running via central line. Patient reports feeling nauseated and unable to eat breakfast. Patient with two episodes of emesis with significant retching.
> A—Dr. Procter notified and stat dose of Ondansetron® ordered. Will hold breakfast until patient desires food.
> 10:15 hrs R—Patient verbalized relief of nausea but still unable to eat.
> Signed, *Nancy Nurse, RN*

Charting by Exception

In the 1980s, charting by exception (CBE) made its debut, much to the consternation of those practitioners and lawyers who believed that absent a paper trail, there was no way to rely, to prove, or to have solid evidence that the nurse functioned up to the expected standards of practice. It is a system of documentation in which only significant findings or exceptions to standards or norms of care are recorded or charted.

However, as it has changed and improved, its strengths are now recognized to be many. In this system, there is no need to document routine care. Redundancies and repetitions are eliminated. Abnormal data stand out. Uniform practice is achieved through the use of well-designed assessment and practice standards or guidelines. Trends are tracked through flow charts. The permanent record is updated on an ongoing basis, and nurses at the bedside have flow sheets at hand or on their computer for instant documentation.

The CBE system in its early days played a prominent and problematic role in the *Lama v. Borras* (1994) case discussed below. As now utilized in health care facilities around the country, this computer-friendly system is effective, and legal liability and licensure risks are minimized if nurses are well oriented to its functions and written nursing standards are taught to and used by all staff. The effective system uses interdisciplinary plans of care, an initial database, ongoing flow sheets, and progress notes from all relevant disciplines. The system should contain discharge notes features, nursing care plans based on nursing diagnoses, and should follow the SOAPIE or SOAPIER systems.

At the core of this system is a reliance on nurses to do all appropriate assessments, make all relevant observations accurately, and assure that nursing judgments and actions meet all required practice standards under the circumstances. Enabling such trust to exist in many instances is the use of the flow sheets or charts that use check-off marks to represent care done. Blank spaces raise questions, and, therefore, all spaces should be filled in, even if to contain an explanatory notation. For example, and based on the design of the system, an asterisk (*) in a space can mean that a standard or norm of care was not implemented. An asterisk (*) can also signify that a narrative note has been charted to explain why the standard of care was not met or satisfied. It is imperative that these procedures be defined and communicated so that the system's use is reliable.

To further facilitate this system to function with minimal exposure to civil and criminal liability and practice risks, a CBE system must be designed to conform to all relevant State Nurse Practice Acts and any State Administrative Rules or Health Department Regulations that address the content of medical records. It must also pass muster by any Joint Commission scrutiny. It is wise to incorporate documentation standards set by professional organizations of practitioners, such as those devoted to obstetric, psychiatric, or other nursing specialty.

It cannot be stated strongly enough that the CBE requires much time and effort to educate all nurses on the system. It is an absolute necessity to use it exclusively (the lesson learned from the Lama case below) and to assure that each nurse feels confident that all nurses perform ethically and reliably and do all appropriate assessments on all patients even where there is nothing abnormal to record. Peer trust is essential; otherwise, care not charted could still be interpreted to be care not done. This may cause practice and legal problems as well as staff discontent.

CBE and Disciplinary Matters

It still remains that the CBE format is often criticized, particularly among nurses not accustomed to using it. Deviation from scrupulous use of CBE systems can lead to legal and practice issues on the suspicion that care that was not charted was not done. As described in Chapter 1, Boards of Nursing, some of whom may be lay persons and have members not experienced or knowledgeable of CBE, still have prescribed requirements to uphold state laws. To accomplish their duty, Boards of Nursing and their investigators, following a complaint against a nurse, often use medical records from all types of documentation systems as part of their inquiries. If a CBE system chart is examined and shows that the information they are looking for is not available, investigators can interview colleagues and others to query their memories of what was or was not done.

Consequently, a board may or may not pursue disciplinary action against a nurse on the basis of the outcome of their investigation. If they choose to pursue action against a nurse involving a CBE chart, it may be several years after the event and the nurse will have to rely on the memory of the events in question and convince a board that his or her memories are the most accurate rendition of what happened and explain any gap in charting information. The nurse's credibility is always on the line. Therefore, there are strategies and tactics for defense lawyers to consider, such as the need to present evidence and demonstrate a client's credibility and competency, when cases involve use of CBE.

It becomes clear that a CBE charting system must be well designed to accommodate for care not documented (such as an asterisk in blank spaces to denote a certain reason as provided for in the written nursing standards and preferably somewhere on the form) and used according to facility policy and procedures and all relevant state and federal laws, if it is to protect the nurse in a disciplinary system. A nurse who suspects that a CBE system is malfunctioning should report it with all necessary details, verbally and in writing, to the appropriate administrative person.

CASE EXAMPLE:

CHARTING BY EXCEPTION

Lama v. Borras (1994)

Mr. Lama, the plaintiff, underwent surgical repair by defendant surgeon Dr. Borras, for a herniated disc on May 15, 1986. He developed a postoperative infection while at the defendant hospital. Mr. Lama spent months being treated in the hospital for the infection, after which he brought a negligence suit against the surgeon and the hospital seeking financial compensation for the damages he incurred.

The relevant facts taken directly from the Appeals Court decision are as follows:

On May 17, a nurse's note indicates that the bandage covering [Lama]'s surgical wound was "very bloody," a symptom which, according to expert testimony, indicates the possibility of infection. On May 18, [Lama] was experiencing local pain at the site of the incision, another symptom consistent with an infection. On May 19, the bandage was "soiled again." On the night of May 20, [Lama] began to experience severe discomfort in his back. He passed the night screaming in pain. At some point on May 21, ... an attending physician, diagnosed the problem as ... an infection of the space between discs—and responded by initiating antibiotic treatment.

The Court, and apparently the trial jury, was troubled that a more complete account of [Lama]'s evolving condition was unavailable, it wrote, "because the Hospital instructed nurses to engage in 'charting by exception', a system whereby nurses did not record qualitative observations for each of the day's three shifts, but instead made such notes only when necessary to chronicle important changes in a patient's condition ... " (pp. 475–476)

While plaintiffs made a number of allegations against the Hospital, [the Appeals Court] focused on the allegation that "the failure of the hospital nurses to report on each nursing shift was a cause of the late detection of [the patient's] infection." (pp. 475–476)

The court wrote further:

The Hospital does not contest plaintiff's allegation that a regulation of the Puerto Rico Department of Health, in force in 1986, requires qualitative nurses' notes for each nursing shift. Nor does the Hospital dispute the charge that, during [Lama]'s hospital stay, the nurses attending to [Lama] did not supply the required notes for every shift but instead followed the Hospital's official policy of charting by exception. The sole question, then, is whether there was sufficient evidence for the jury to find that violation of the regulation was a proximate cause of harm to [Lama].

The Hospital questions plaintiff's proof of causation [in that] the Hospital claims that plaintiffs did not prove that the charting by exception policy was a proximate cause of the delayed detection of [plaintiff's] infection.

The Hospital essentially argues that it is uncertain whether the hospital staff observed, but failed to record, any material symptoms that would probably have led an attending physician to investigate the possibility of an infection at an earlier stage. The Hospital notes that, *even under the charting by exception policy,* [Italics added] its nurses regularly recorded such information as the patient's [normal] temperature, vital signs, and any medication given to the patient. Indeed, there is some evidence that [the plaintiff] did not have a fever (one possible sign of infection) before May 21, when [the plaintiff was] diagnosed [with] the infection and began antibiotic treatment.

Nonetheless, *there was evidence from which the jury could have inferred that, as part of the practice of charting by exception, the nurses did not regularly record certain information important to the diagnosis of an infection, such as the changing characteristics of the surgical wound and the patient's complaints of post-operative pain.* [Italics Added] Indeed, one former nurse at the Hospital who attended to [Lama] in 1986 testified that, under the charting by exception policy, she would not report a patient's pain if she either did not administer any medicine or simply gave the patient an aspirin-type medication (as opposed to a narcotic). Further, since there was evidence that [the plaintiff's] hospital records contained some scattered possible signs of infection that, according to [plaintiff's expert witness], deserved further investigation (e.g., an excessively bloody bandage and local pain at the site of the wound), *the jury could have reasonably inferred that intermittent [CBE] charting failed to provide the sort of continuous danger signals that would be the most likely spur to early intervention by a physician.* (Lama v. Borras, 1994pp. 480–481)

COURT'S OPINION: As to the liability of the hospital for its nurse's use of the CBE system of documentation, the court wrote, "It was entirely possible for the jury to conclude that the particular way in which the medical and nursing records were kept constituted evidence of carelessness in monitoring the patient. . . . Perhaps the infection would have been reported and documented earlier" (*Lama v. Borras*, 1994, p. 477).

Professor E. Murphy (2003) commented on this case and cautioned that nurses retain legitimate concern about how credible a jury might find a document in which charting is done automatically or does not contain reference to all nursing assessments. She also notes that the problem with the CBE system may be in its implementation, specifically noting the reasoning in the Lama case that the nurses did not adhere to the CBE but used the narrative style as well. Furthermore, Murphy noted "Any advantage in defending lawsuits provided by traditional systems that require documentation of all nursing activities for the few cases that make it to court must be balanced against time saved and other advantages of CBE (eg, highlighting abnormal trends rather than obscuring them with normal data) to be realized in all cases" (Murphy, 2003, p. 821–823)

Also, it may be argued that the legal defense issues can be addressed through adequate explanations to boards and juries about what the system is and does and how it is properly utilized.

Much space in this chapter has been devoted to CBE. This is due to its potential use as the wave of the future under federal law, particularly due to its design advantages. These include reduction in documentation time, consequent increase in efficiency in use of the nurse's time, visibility of abnormal data with a decrease in the amount of paper used to chart, a computer-friendly format, and features that can be easily accommodated to encompass the best of the other systems.

EMR are quickly becoming the norm, being driven by the new federal health care laws and regulations that are discussed in more detail in the following section. Consequently, many health care providers have begun to reconsider the CBE system.

COMPUTERIZED ELECTRONIC MEDICAL RECORDS

The salient feature of EMRs is that they can include all features of all systems plus the uniqueness of an outcome-based care plan. They have the capacity for progress notes, flow sheets, nursing and other disciplines' care plans, data bases, teaching plans, baseline and ongoing assessments, evaluative statements, and expected and learning outcomes. They are supposed to speed up charting, increase accuracy, and allow retrieval of patient classification information, management reports, and projections for staffing needs.

One way electronic recordkeeping can enhance care and communication across disciplines is through the automatic population of fields. If vital signs are recorded by nursing staff and are then needed by respiratory therapy prior to administering a treatment, the vital signs can automatically be carried over to the appropriate section avoiding redundancy or the possibility of a discrepant record. For legal liability and defense purposes, all of the issues of illegibility and improper erasures or stricken entries are eliminated because there are automatic time and date stamps for each entry.

The program can include system prompts for mandatory data, and if the data are not entered, the computer can send an instant visual or audible notification. Care standards can be tailored for the patient population, from geriatric to neonatal. If data entered are outside the range of standard expectations, various alerts can appear. Different software programs can then require the nurse to perform a range of different actions. Once a patient profile is created and entered into the system, it can be reviewed on each subsequent admission.

Privacy can be addressed through the use of a unique name and password. Under certain appropriate conditions, the computer could request a second signature, such as those involving controlled substances or high-risk medications.

It is clear to see how easily and innocently a fraudulent entry can be put into a record. If a practitioner is logged into a patient record and walks away from his or her data entry station and leaves the record open, another practitioner can then access the patient record and enter information on that patient. The entered information may be correct but is being entered under the previous practitioner's access. The record no longer accurately reflects the care provided to the patient as recorded by the practitioner who is actually logged on. This error is easy to correct and avoid. The safest and most ethical practice and what legal defense lawyers recommend is that users log off a computer terminal when they move away from it. If this is not done and the patient's record is open, it is vulnerable to alteration by another individual and any subsequent documentation will be reflected as made by the provider who left the record open. To succeed in explaining to a trier of fact (judge, jury, Board of Nursing or arbitrator) that the nurse forgot to log off and that he or she did not make the entries is indeed difficult. In such a case, nurses risk having their competency, credibility, and sense of ethics challenged by opposing counsel. And employers may consider the same issues as undesirable, or even a policy violation.

Computerized record systems can also address other issues as follows:

Abbreviations: Most software programs should reject the attempted entry of an abbreviation not on a facility's list of approved abbreviations or that are on the list of unacceptable abbreviations as previously mentioned.
Alterations: As currently designed in most software, it is exceptionally difficult to alter a record that has timed out. Most records remain open during hospitalization but close within hours after discharge.

Error corrections: These are problematic in current software applications. Errors should be corrected as soon as possible because of the timing out feature. Facility policy needs to be followed carefully in all documentation, but especially in this area to avoid injury to patients, and to avoid the appearance of impropriety.

Health Law Reform and EMR

The EMR is the wave of the future and has been renamed the Electronic Health Record (EHR). This was accomplished in The American Recovery and Reinvestment Act of 2009 (ARRA), the Patient Protection and Affordable Care Act of 2010 (ACA or Affordable Care Act; effective March 2010), and the Health Information Technology for Economic and Clinical Health Act (HITECH), with the final rule released on July 13, 2010, by the Center for Medicare and Medicaid Services (CMS). Not all provisions of these acts are immediately in effect or enforceable. However, it is important to know what is required at this time and to prepare for requirements that are effective at a future date.

ARRA and the Affordable Care Act are new laws that are having tremendous significance and influence on systems of documentation and, consequently, on practitioners. After President Obama signed the laws, the rule-making process that creates implementing regulations began and continues as this book goes to press. The laws authorize the Centers for Medicare and Medicaid Services (CMS) to provide incentives to providers for the adoption and "meaningful use" of certified EHR technology, through provisions of HITECH.

"Meaningful use" is the term used to determine whether an eligible party qualifies for incentives under ARRA. The CMS rule includes a definition of meaningful-use criteria in stages, to begin in 2011. Stage 1 criteria include the following:

- Capturing health information electronically in a coded format,
- Using that information to track key clinical conditions,
- Communicating that information for coordination of care, and
- Initiating the reporting of clinical quality measures and public health information.

Under the rules, "eligible professionals" (EPs), eligible hospitals and critical-access hospitals could qualify for monetary incentives for efforts to adopt, implement, or upgrade certified EHR technology for meaningful use, on the basis of two-dozen specific objectives and measures for each care setting, as set out in the following summary. Since the law is voluminous and complicated, this information is provided for general information only, and it is advisable to review the relevant laws with counsel as needed.

Eligibility of the providers:

- Physicians, nurses, and midwife nurses who are not hospital based and whose patient volume is at least 30% attributable to Medicare are eligible for up to maximum 85% of their net allowable technology costs, which is subject to specific annual limits.
- Medicaid incentives will be available only to non–hospital-based clinicians, encompassing dentists, certified nurse midwives, and physician assistants practicing in rural health clinics.
- Medicaid incentives range up to US$65,000 over a 5-year period.
- Acute care hospitals with Medicaid patient volume of 10% or more and children's hospitals with any Medicaid volumes are also eligible.
- Medicaid has not mentioned any penalties for lack of adoption of EHR.
- After obtaining start-up funds, providers who will prove meaningful use can be eligible to receive payments up to US$10,000 annually for an additional 4 years.

The Congressional Budget Office (CBO) estimates that approximately 90% of doctors and 70% of hospitals will be using EHR within the next decade as a result of the American Recovery and Reinvestment Act of 2009 (ARRA).

The HITECH portion of the laws can affect nurses who work in clinics, independent nursing practices, medical offices, and home care, where referrals for care that is medically necessary must originate. The incentive program will provide payments for efforts to adopt, implement, or upgrade certified EHR technology, but they must also demonstrate "meaningful use" of this technology according to the specific objectives. Simply purchasing a certified system is not enough.

The rules will develop standards for all certified EHR systems and require that all systems speak the same language. This will allow the efficient exchange of information among providers and between providers and CMS. At the heart of this concept is the improvement of health care and Medicare and Medicaid fraud and abuse prevention. (See Chapter 3 for more information on this subject.)

The hopes of health care practitioners that are built into and funded in the health care reform laws are that EHRs will help modernize the U.S.

health care and delivery systems, improve quality of care, and reduce associated costs. However, the greatest hurdle may just be resistance to significant change.

D. Blumenthal, MD, in 2009, released the results of a study that points out the then current status of EHRs as the standard in the United States. The study showed only 1.5% of the 300 acute care hospitals studied in the United States had installed EHRs in all major clinical units that performed all of the two-dozen functions considered significant. Such systems incorporated nurses' and doctors' notes, had the capacity to enable the practitioner to order tests, included clinical guidelines to treat conditions relevant to the users' practice areas, and alerted practitioners on possible drug interactions. The funding described above is designed to overcome the historically major impediment of lack of funds for the creation and implementation of EHRs throughout the country's health care system.

Other concerns are that the new laws bring with them other extraordinary challenges such as new threats to patient privacy and opportunities for external intrusions into clinical practice. And nurse educators, ever at the cutting edge, have recognized that nursing school curricula will have to be adapted to prepare future practitioners to use EHRs.

Among the nonfinancial barriers to adoption of EHRs is the time it takes some to enter data and, as Blumenthal suggested, the learning curve for new technology. Some of the biggest issues in health information technology involve sociology and interpersonal dynamics, rather than technology itself. Although computer terminals that crash, main frames that malfunction, and power outages all pose issues for the nurse at the bedside, so does a system that is difficult to accommodate error corrections or perform intuitively the functions that nurses need.

For Medicare and Medicaid beneficiaries, the Health and Human Services Secretary, who oversees CMS, was mandated to encourage use of technology compatible with EHRs. Consequently, ARRA allocated US$59 billion for health care, with approximately US$20 billion designated for EHR adoption. Incentives totaling US$17 billion will be paid as increased Medicare and Medicaid payments. The incentives will start in 2011 and be paid over 5 years to physicians who can show "meaningful use" of an EHR system. Physicians who do not show meaningful use will be penalized in the form of reduced Medicare payments. Hospital-based physicians will not be affected. The main objectives of this package of laws are to lower health care costs, reduce patient care errors, enhance the quality of patient care, and improve access to data through health care information technology. Time will tell whether these objectives are met.

COMPUTERIZED MEDICAL RECORDS IN HOME HEALTH

Home care nurses helped to pioneer computerized records. In 2000, as required by the Budget Reconciliation Act of 1997, CMS instituted a home care documentation system (intended to be computerized but not required). Thus, home health care nurses became familiar with the outcome and assessment information sheet (OASIS). It is the documentation system required under laws that govern home care for Medicare and Medicaid beneficiaries (42 U.S.C. 1395, etc seq., 42 CFR 409 et seq.). It is now usually computerized but can be filled out manually in whole or in part. It utilizes fill-in forms of certain standardized demographic and general information, social and health history, living arrangements, review of systems, and medications and equipment management assessments. In all there are seven-dozen categories of information that can be used to evaluate each home care client.

OASIS is the form utilized during home visits and is complemented by an interdisciplinary plan of care and progress notes, both of which, while in standardized format necessitate a narrative approach. Home care agencies had been allowed an exemption from the precise form in certain narrow circumstances. The new EHR rules will need to be analyzed to determine whether such narrow exemptions will still be granted.

CASE EXAMPLE:

ARBITRATION

In the legal arena some home care nurses' use of the assessment tool and plan and progress notes has demonstrated that errors can lead to reimbursement problems. In one unreported arbitration decision, in which the arbitrator was expected to follow regulations from CMS concerning reimbursement for home care, the home care client was a 30-year-old cerebral palsy patient with numerous physical and mental limitations. He had been a total care patient since the day of his birth and frequently suffered complications.

SUMMARY OF FACTS: Over the years his parents cared for him in their home with the help of visiting nurses, home health aides several days a week, and physical and occupational therapists as appropriate. However, the care checked off by the home health aide as done was frequently not ordered in the plan of care, and, in several instances, when it was ordered it was not checked off as performed. At one point the parents went away for a long weekend, and two aides stayed home alone with the client. The nurse supervisor had visited the client monthly and signed all of the check-off sheets as had the client's mother. As a result there were material discrepancies between services ordered and services provided. The matter was sent to arbitration, and at the hearing no evidence was offered to explain the discrepancies.

DECISION: The arbitrator had to deny reimbursement for the visiting nurse group, and the agency was then faced with the possibility of fraud charges from CMS.

In other home care cases submitted to arbitration, rulings have been against the nursing agencies for several different reasons:

Narrative notes that were illegible;
An assessment tool checked off the patient as being a bedbound client, but the narrative claimed she traveled frequently via plane, train, and drove her own car;
Client's blood sugars described as high in the narrative portion, but the flow sheet showed no record that they anything but within normal limits;
The use of a cane by a quadriplegic was routinely checked off, but in the same section of the assessment form the nurse occasionally checked off that he was bedfast and unable to ambulate or be up in a chair; however, during a 1-year period of documentation there was no indication in any part of the record that he was ever able to walk with or without assistance.

For more on the process of arbitration, see Chapter 10.

AUTOMATED MEDICATION-DISPENSING SYSTEMS

Automated medication dispensing is an expanding technology used to improve safety, provide access, and improve unit operations while providing tracking and recordkeeping capability. There are several brands of these electronic systems that have been in use throughout the United States since the 1980s.

These systems automatically link the facility pharmacy to the point of care. They provide the nursing unit with enhanced recordkeeping capability. With the passive collection of medication administration data, administrators and staff can cull reports and have access to information about trends and usage that prior to automation would be very labor intensive to acquire. The nurse may have bar-coding technology and electronic patient profiling that aids in dispensing medications by confirming the positive identification of patients with the correct medication, dose, time, and route of administration. Bar coding and medication administration can reduce or minimize the possibility for medication administration errors.

Chief among these systems legal protections for the nurse is that they are designed to provide accurate documentation. When medication is removed from the unit, the system creates an automatic computerized record in real time of the information about the medication and when it was pulled from the drawer and passed to the patient. However, that assurance is operable only if the system does not fail. There have been reported failures of these systems by nurse attorneys throughout the country who defend nurses before licensing boards for allegations that their clients took controlled substances for their own use instead of dispensing the medication to the patient.

Another feature of these systems is that many now offer a measure of security and provider identification that is difficult to breach, that is, bio-identification. The legal efficacy of the documentation aspect of these systems is now being tested in the legal arena as this book is being written.

NURSES, DOCUMENTATION, AND COMPLIANCE ISSUES

As noted in Chapter 3, an effective compliance program that includes education can enhance the knowledge of billing personnel, and thus, help to avoid billing errors. Billing errors can result in under- as well as over-billing. Nurses can be at the very legal heart of billing problems.

For example, to be reimbursed for care given to patients in a state's Medicaid program, a health care provider must enter into a contract with the state. Accordingly, the provider is bound by contract to be in compliance with all that state's rules and regulations and those of the federal government, and these rules include billing procedures. It is in this way that compliance and nursing documentation play a distinct role in criminal law matters unrelated to patient care. Consider the following two cases.

CASE EXAMPLES:

NURSES NOTES KEY TO MEDICAID FRAUD CASE

State v. Romero (1990)

In Louisiana, Dr. Romero and his physician-spouse were accused of Medicaid fraud. Both were found guilty on several counts of such fraud. They were sentenced to 5 years hard labor, though the sentences were suspended and both were placed on probation.

The doctors had billed Medicaid for each patient visit made. At trial, the state introduced testimony from the director of nursing at the nursing home involved in the case. She also was the custodian of the documents and, therefore, responsible for the records associated with the facility. She maintained that all pertinent information concerning a patient was contained in these documents and recounted that the nursing staff was instructed and required to document in the [narrative] nurses' notes all pertinent information about a patient, including all doctors' visits and to notify her when a physician visited a patient. The nurses' notes showed that the doctors' visits recorded by the nurse did not match the doctors' billing records.

The director of nursing admitted that she took records home, "thinned them," and returned them to the nursing home for storage (*State v. Romero*, 1990, p. 334). She testified that she regularly culled pages of nurses [narrative] notes, progress notes, physician order sheets, and doctors' orders sheets and other sections from patient charts when the charts became too thick. She placed the culled documents in separate files (the state failed to present these files at trial).

The director of nursing also testified that all staff at the nursing home were instructed to record all doctors' visits to all patients and that she was to be notified at any time of day or night of any such visit.

A licensed practical nurse testified that she never received instructions as to what should be recorded in the nurses' notes. In direct contradiction to the director of nursing's testimony, she also stated that there was neither a procedure nor a requirement to notify the director when a doctor made rounds.

COURT'S DECISION: The Appeals Court found that the nursing notes were "unreliable and untrustworthy" evidence (p. 334). Testimony from the director of nursing and from other nurses at the facility revealed glaring deficiencies in the documents. The physicians' convictions for fraud were upheld.

NURSE CONVICTED FOR FALSIFYING TIME SHEET

State v. McKinney (2008)

A Medicaid fraud conviction was also the fate of Ms. McKinney, a home care nurse, who falsified her time sheet, billed for services that she did not provide, and also billed at a higher rate than permitted by applicable law and regulation. McKinney fraudulently billed the Ohio Medicaid program US$109,000 while she cared for two disabled children.

The lessons learned in these cases is that the nurses documentation and the integrity of the medical record is crucial evidence that can support a provider's claims that he or she did the right thing or can serve as a basis for findings against the provider accused of Medicaid fraud charges.

PRIVACY AND DOCUMENTATION SYSTEMS

The Health Insurance Portability and Accountability Act (HIPAA) of 1996 (P.L.104–191) Title II of HIPAA, known as the Administrative Simplification (AS) provisions, required the establishment of national standards for electronic health care transactions and national identifiers for providers, health insurance plans, and employers. One of the chief objectives of this law is to ensure privacy of health care records. Therefore, nurses must take into account HIPAA requirements when designing a certified EHR under ARRA.

In the recent past, highly publicized incidents of unauthorized viewing of patients medical records have occurred at well-respected health care facilities in the United States. Among the examples, six patient's electronic records were viewed by unauthorized personnel at the UCLA Ronald Reagan Medical Center (Hennessey-Fiske, 2010).

The reported invasions of privacy at the Center involved celebrity patients and included unauthorized access to the records of a famous movie actress who had received long-term treatment. This actress died at the Center on the same day an internationally famous pop star also died there. In the latter instance, records were breached posthumously by workers from disciplines unrelated to the singer's care. The Center was fined US$95,000 by the state of California for the breaches. Two employees involved in the matter were terminated and may ultimately face criminal charges and financial penalties.

The Center reported that privacy law training for employees had been instituted and that new privacy safeguards had been implemented over the past 3 years. A spokesperson for the Center said, "Medical privacy is a fundamental right. . . . Every Californian treated at a hospital should not have to worry about who is viewing their medical information."

Establishing Legal Standards for All Systems of Documentation

It is always a challenge to implement new or changing documentation systems in an organization. An implementation plan must include the means to assure that all users of the system, whether a newly employed nurse or longstanding employee, understand and are able to correctly use the system.

Documentation systems bring with them unique challenges for the traveling nurse. A traveling nurse may be in a different location as often as every few weeks and is exposed to numerous systems around the country. To minimize practice and nursing liability risks, consider a contract term that requires an employment agency to send nurses who are experienced using your particular type of documentation system.

Realistically, this type of nurse (as well as the hiring facility) is completely and wholly dependent on a thorough orientation to the system as an additional way to avoid problems. One very practical solution is to assure that the traveling nurse reviews all relevant policies and procedures on his or her first day or before he or she starts to work, so that he or she has a solid understanding of the documentation system. This process should be carefully documented.

Whereas it is the obligation of the traveling nurse to learn each new system, it is also the obligation of nursing leadership to establish a hiring system that assures that all nurses, including the traveling nurse, are conversant with the facility's policies and practices.

As computerized documentation systems are more widely used, the need to assure that nurses understand their use will also grow. Nursing leaders will be challenged to assure that nurses' use of the systems is consistent and correct. When documentation systems are at issue in court, the burden will be on the users to demonstrate that the system was properly used and performed its functions appropriately.

CONCLUSIONS AND TRENDS

Medical records are legal documents that reflect clinical practice by health care providers. Increasingly, they may be subject to legal review and must withstand the test of reliability—that what is documented is what was intended and that the system used also works as intended. This tendency can be expected to increase particularly under health care reform initiatives.

Federal and state documentation and privacy laws, if violated, may carry heavy consequences for all parties involved so systems must be secure. The challenge of securing computerized systems containing vast amounts of protected health data cannot be underestimated, and the challenges of doing this will have to be met.

Because the widespread use of EHR is rapidly becoming a reality, great care must be used in the design of the system that will best meet practice needs and legal standards. Only the future will tell what the legal ramifications will be for practitioners who fail to document care adequately under the new health care reform laws.

Changes and reform in the health care system nationally places great expectations on the quality of the patient record and nursing documentation. Nursing documentation can serve to support the care and services received, and it is likely that it will be looked to increasingly under federal and state law and regulation for evidence of services provided. Nursing documentation will also serve an increasingly vital role in support of clinical research and in performance improvement.

To the greatest extent possible, nurses must seek accuracy and precision in their documentation. The demands of busy workplaces make this a challenge. Therefore, nurses must be a part of efforts to develop and streamline systems of documentation in order to achieve the best-possible quality in patient-record documentation.

As the move toward EHR continues with a push from health care reform, excellence in nursing documentation will be translated into the electronic world. The success of this effort will depend to a great part on the diligence, quality, and efforts of nurses to achieve the best-possible standard of documentation in health care.

Nurses are advised to know and follow their organizational policies regarding documentation. Nursing notes must also demonstrate that nursing practice was compliant with current, evidence-based practice standards. Nurses perform a critical surveillance role in patient safety. When adverse events occur, the record must indicate that nurses were performing that surveillance role, were monitoring for potential problems, recognized them when they occurred, and timely advised physicians of those concerns.

KEY POINTS

Medical records are legal documents reflecting clinical practice. A patient's medical record may provide the best, or even the only evidence, with which to pursue a malpractice claim against the provider. Similarly, the medical record may be the only defense a health care services provider has against charges of malpractice, negligence, professional misconduct, and criminal deeds.

Medical records must be complete and accurate. Incomplete, missing, altered, or destroyed medical records may give rise to claims of spoliation of evidence, noncompliance with regulatory standards, violation of organizational policies, and departures from the standard of practice.

Any abbreviations, symbols, acronyms, or dose designations must be approved for use by the institution and/or organizational policy. Using unapproved abbreviations may present a patient safety problem as they can be misinterpreted.

Any corrections to documentation in a medical record must be performed in accordance with organizational policies and in a manner that leaves the original entry readable.

The use of numerous and varied systems of nursing documentation pose great challenges for nursing leaders, especially in terms of assuring consistent and correct use of such systems. As documentation systems are computerized, these challenges will increase.

Nursing leaders must be active participants in the design and implementation of documentation systems to assure that they meet professional and legal standards. These activities are likely to require the inclusion of legal and technology experts.

Nursing documentation and the legal world intersect most critically outside the realm of the bedside. In the nursing professional liability area, the nurse leader should understand that patient records-as-evidence is clear: Cases can be won or lost on the sufficiency of documentation by nurses.

Federal and state reimbursement laws have implications for nursing documentation to support the care and services that have been provided. Adequate documentation training for staff should include awareness of the need to conform systems to acceptable nursing documentation practices in compliance with federal and state fraud laws.

■ When documentation systems are at issue in court, the burden will be on the users to demonstrate that the system was properly used and performed its functions appropriately.

REFERENCES

American Recovery and Reinvestment Act of 2009 (ARRA).

Blumenthal, D. (2009). Stimulating the adoption of health information technology. *New England Journal of Medicine, 360,* 1477–1479.

Chace v. Curran, 06-P-1452 (Mass. App. February 25, 2008).

Darling v. Charleston Hospital, 33 Ill.2d 326, 211 N. E. 2d 253 (1965).

Health Information Technology for Economic and Clinical Health Act (HITECH) Act.

Hennessy-Fiske, M. (2010, July 11). *Los Angeles Times.* Retrieved July 22, 2010, from http://www.latimes.com

Institute for Safe Medication Practices. (2010). *Error-prone abbreviations, symbols and dose designations.* Retrieved July 30, 2010, from http://www.ismp.org/Tools/errorproneabbreviations.pdf

Lama v Borras 16 F3d 473 (1st Cir. 1994).

Livingston v. Montgomery, 279 S.W.3d 868 (Tex.App. 5th Cir. 2009).

Masters v. Khuri, 62 Mass. App. Ct. 467 (2004).

Medical Review Panel of Hedda Neville, et al v. Charity Hospital, 984 So. 2nd 170 (La. App. 4th Cir. 2008).

Moss, J., Andison, M., & Sobko, H. (2007). *An analysis of narrative nursing documentation in an otherwise structured intensive care clinical information system.* AMIA Annual Symposium Proceedings (pp. 543–547). Retrieved July 19, 2010, from http://www.ncbi.nlm.nih.gov/pmc/articles/PMC2655835/

Murphy, E. (2003). Charting by exception. *AORN Journal. 78*(5), 821–823.

Patient Protection and Affordable Care Act is contained in H.R. 3590, P.L. 111–148 The reconciliation bill language, which is part of the law, is contained in H.R.4872, P.L. 111–152, effective March 23, 2010.

Philiben, A. (2010, July 28). Online interview.

Ploch v. Hamai, 213 S.W.3d 135 (Mo.App.E.D. 2006).

Rosenblit v. Zimmerman, 166 N.J. 391 (2001).

State v. McKinney, 2008 Ohio 6522 (Ohio App. 2008).

State v. Romero, 559 So.2d 763 (La., 1990).

The Joint Commission. (2010). *The official "Do Not Use" list of abbreviations.* Retrieved July 30, 2010, from http://www.jointcommission.org/patientsafety/donotuselist/

ADDITIONAL READINGS

Clancy, C., Coughlin, J., Baron, R., & Weed, L. (2009). *The future of health informa-tion technology.* The University of the Sciences in Philadelphia Symposium. Retrieved July 24, 2010, from http://www.usp. edu/symposium/.

The Patient Protection and Affordable Care Act of 2010. An overview of the new health care law enacted March, 2010. (n.d.). Retrieved August 31, 2010 from http://www.unitedhealthgroup.com/hrm/Health-Care-Law.pdf

CHAPTER SEVEN

PATIENT RIGHTS AND ETHICAL CONSIDERATIONS

Edie Brous

OBJECTIVES

- Identify the required elements that constitute informed consent.
- Understand the legal obligations of physicians, nurses, and hospitals with respect to informed consent.
- Identify the sources of standards that determine whether the required elements of informed consent have been met.
- Identify areas of exposure to liability for failure to provide adequate informed consent.
- Recognize the major requirements for hospitals and certain health providers under the Patient Self-Determination Act (PSDA).

INTRODUCTION

Liability exposure, regulatory compliance, ethical concerns, and professional responsibilities all make consent an important concept in nursing practice. The fundamental right to determine what will or will not be done to one's person is defined by law and shaped by ethics. A patient's right to accept or refuse treatment is enforced by federal and state law, the Centers for Medicaid and Medicare Services (CMS), The Joint Commission (TJC), and other accrediting bodies, malpractice litigation, and ethical codes.

Nurses in their roles as assessors, teachers, interpreters, and advocates, nurses must understand the complexities of informed consent and their legal and ethical obligations within these contexts.

PATIENT RIGHTS AND ETHICAL CONSIDERATIONS

Informed Consent

Informed consent is not a document; it is a process. The patient is advised of the risks, benefits, alternatives, and costs associated with proposed diagnostic tests or treatments. Only when all the necessary information is imparted and all questions answered is the patient able to make decisions. And only when the patient has made a decision and agreed to a particular intervention may the providers render that treatment. Informed consent does not exist until a fully informed patient is able to make a rational choice about treatment or nontreatment. Informed consent may be defined, therefore, as the process by which a patient is adequately provided all necessary information to participate in health care decisions.

Physician's Duty to Obtain Informed Consent

The legal obligation to obtain informed consent belongs to the *physician*. Generally it is not within nursing's scope of practice to explain risks, benefits, and alternatives to proposed treatment plans. The legal framework of this obligation is changing in light of the practice of advance nurse practitioners and other advance practitioners. Some jurisdictions have recognized this fact and new statutes may now, in some cases, permit the advanced practitioner to obtain informed consent for procedures that they perform. A discussion of this aspect is beyond the scope of this chapter, and the advance practitioner should carefully review the parameters of their practice in this regard. The following cases are illustrative on the point of who bears the duty to provide informed consent.

CASE EXAMPLES:

INFORMED CONSENT

Daniels v. Durham (2005)

SUMMARY OF CASE: An obstetrician performed a "mid-forceps" delivery rather than allowing pushing and a normal vaginal delivery attempt. Assisted by the hospital nurses, he used forceps to rotate the baby 180 degrees to the anterior position and then delivered the baby. Upon delivery, the infant was unresponsive, blue, and not breathing. Subsequent examination revealed she had been born with a cervical spine injury that rendered her paralyzed from the neck down and unable to breathe on her own. She died from the spinal injury, and the parents sued the hospital.

In their suit, the plaintiffs contended that the hospital was liable for its nurses' failure to oppose the doctor's decision to perform a mid-forceps delivery. They claimed the nurses should have refused to assist in the procedure or they should have invoked the hospital chain of command policy. Although the delivery was performed by a private physician, the plaintiffs contended that the nurses breached their duty to obtain informed consent.

The hospital argued that nurses do not have a duty to obtain informed consent. The court agreed and held that the physician has a duty to warn a patient of consequences of a medical procedure. Because the physician was privately retained by the plaintiffs, the duty to inform them of the risks of the procedures was the responsibility of that privately retained physician, not of the hospital or its staff.

COURT'S DECISION: The court held that because nurses do not have a duty to obtain informed consent, the plaintiffs did not have a lack of informed consent or battery claim against the nurses.

Note the similarities in the following case.

Davis v Hoffman (2007)

SUMMARY OF CASE: In this case the plaintiff claimed a hysterectomy was performed without her consent. She sued her surgeon, the hospital, and the nursing staff, alleging that the nurse did not advise her of alternatives to the hysterectomy, did not inform her of possible side effects and risks, and did not inform her that a hysterectomy could be required. As in the *Daniels* matter earlier, the hospital argued that the Doctrine of Informed Consent only applies to physicians, not to hospitals or its nursing staff.

COURT'S DECISION: The court agreed with the hospital's argument and held that nurses do not have a duty to advise patients of risks, benefits, or alternatives. The court stated that the nurse only "witnesses signatures" but does not "obtain consent."

Although it is the physician's legal responsibility to explain risks, benefits, and alternatives to patients, nurses also have obligations regarding consent. Nursing assessments include educational level, language proficiency, level of consciousness, and anxiety. Patients may not express doubts or ask questions of their physicians for a number of reasons. Language or cultural barriers and feelings of intimidation, fear, or embarrassment may prevent patients from honestly communicating doubts or concerns to their physicians. Vision and/or hearing loss may compromise the patient's ability to understand the physician's explanations.

In their health teaching roles, nurses also reinforce and clarify information consistent with the nurse practice act of the states in which they are licensed and the policies of the institutions in which they are employed. The nurse must know who has legal power of consent for minors or patients without capacity, which means the legal authority to consent for oneself and/or ability to comprehend the nature and consequences of giving the consent. In addition, nurses must identify any concerns and conflicts to management and understand that patients have the right to withdraw previously given consent.

The nurse has legal and ethical obligations to advocate for patients in those circumstances. Advising the surgical and/or anesthesia team of the patient's concerns and documenting that communication is essential. If nursing judgment suggests that the patient does not have the ability to understand the risks, benefits, and alternatives regarding the procedure, or that there are remaining issues to be discussed, that information must be communicated to the responsible providers before treatment is rendered. The following case example is illustrative of this point.

CASE EXAMPLE:

Salandy v. Bryk (2008)

SUMMARY OF CASE: This case illustrates the importance of documenting that the surgeon has been informed of the patient's refusal to consent or of continuing doubts or concerns. A Jehovah's Witness signed a "Refusal to Consent to Blood/Blood Component Transfusion" form that stated:

Although my doctor has fully explained to me the nature and purposes of the blood/blood component transfusion, the possible alternatives thereto and the risks and consequences of not proceeding, and I fully understand that such transfusion may be deemed necessary in the opinion of the attending physician or his assistants to preserve life or promote recovery, I nonetheless refuse to consent to the transfusion. (p. 149)

In addition, Salandy signed a surgical consent form that contained the following language:

I also consent to the administration of blood and/or component therapy by transfusion as may be considered necessary [Italics added]. I recognize that there are always risks to life and health associated with blood and/or component transfusions and such risks and alternatives, including the alternative of no blood transfusions, have been fully explained to me. (p. 149)

The consent form also contained a paragraph that stated:

I confirm that I have read and fully understand the reverse side and found it completed prior to signing. I have crossed out any paragraphs above which do not pertain to me. (p. 149)

Nothing was crossed out on the form. The signature on both forms was witnessed by the same resident—a hospital employee—who did not communicate this inconsistency to the surgeon before the patient underwent a knee replacement. The surgeon's standing postoperative orders included auto transfusions that the patient received. She then brought suit for medical malpractice and lack of informed consent against the hospital.

TRIAL COURT'S DECISION: At the trial court level, the surgeon testified that he would not have ordered the autotransfusion if he or the nursing staff had been advised that the patient had signed the "Refusal to Consent to Blood/Blood Component Transfusion" form. An expert witness for the hospital testified that the standard of care for the attending surgeon required him to read the entire chart prior to commencing surgery. The trial court granted the plaintiff's summary judgment motion, meaning that the plaintiff patient asked the court to find the hospital liable for giving the patient a transfusion without her consent, and the court so found. The hospital appealed that lower court decision.

APPELLATE COURT'S DECISION: The appellate court considered the circumstances under which a hospital may be liable for failing to inform a private physician who is about to perform surgery at its facility that his patient has signed a refusal to consent to the transfusion of blood or blood products. In considering relevant case law, the court noted:

In terms of a medical malpractice claim predicated on lack of informed consent, where a private physician attends his or her patient at the facilities of a hospital, it is the duty of the physician, not the hospital, to obtain the patient's informed consent. . . . Moreover, the mere recording or witnessing of consent by a hospital employee is a ministerial task that does not subject the hospital to liability. (p. 152)

The court further stated, "However, the hospital may be liable where it knew or should have known that the private physician using its facilities was acting or would act without the patient's informed consent" (*Salandy v. Bryk, 2008*, p. 152).

The appellate court held that there were issues of fact as to whether the resident placed both the surgical consent form and the "Refusal to Consent to Blood/Blood Component Transfusion" form in the patient's preoperative folder without notifying anyone of the inconsistency and whether in doing so he violated the standards of practice. Because there were issues of fact to be determined, the lower court's granting of the plaintiff's summary judgment motion was reversed and the facts of the case will be established in further proceedings.

Sources of Standards of Informed Consent

Civil Lawsuits

In a lack of informed consent claim, the plaintiff alleges the standard of care was not provided in that he or she was not advised of a complication, outcome, or result that indeed occurred. In addition, the plaintiff claims he or she would not have agreed to the procedure, diagnostic test, or treatment plan had he or she been so advised. The complaint alleges that the provider failed to disclose the risks that could have influenced his or her decision to give or withhold consent.

Common Law

Common law is that law created by lawsuit precedent. Common law standards differ from regulatory (law created by statute or rule) requirements (see discussion of administrative law in Chapter 1). Under the common law, the majority of jurisdictions use a "prudent person" test in determining whether or not a patient was adequately informed. This may be framed as the prudent patient or the prudent physician. When using the prudent patient standard, the court will ask the jury to consider what information a reasonable person of average intelligence would require to make a rational decision and to consider what specific risks, benefits, and alternatives he or she would need to understand before making a medical decision.

When deliberating a particular case, the jury considers whether the patient received enough information to reach a reasoned and thoughtful decision. Was he or she informed of the risks, and was any information withheld that would have influenced his or her decision to give or withhold consent? A prudent person standard would analyze whether enough information was disclosed, including the risks associated with the procedure such that a reasonable person would be enabled to make a rational and intelligent decision to receive or refuse care.

If the patient sustained injury, the court will look to see whether the injury the patient is complaining about was caused by failure to disclose a significant risk. Did the plaintiff have enough information to make a rational and intelligent decision? What information would a reasonably prudent patient under same or similar circumstances have required? In general, the provider will be found liable if the jury concludes that the patient (plaintiff) would not have agreed to the treatment had he or she been adequately advised of the significant risks.

In addition to the prudent patient test, the prudent physician test may also be used. An expert witness may testify as to how a reasonably prudent physician would have advised the patient. Given the patient's mental capacity, what information would a reasonably prudent physician have given a patient in same or similar circumstances? For more information on Expert Witness, see chapter 9.

Regulation and Accreditation

Unlike the generic and objective standard used in lawsuits, regulatory standards require subjective and specific determinations of patient understanding. TJC and the CMS require providers to determine that a particular patient understands the risks, benefits, and alternatives to a proposed treatment or procedure (TJC Standard RI 2.40; 42 CFR § 482.13[b][2]).

Patients have the right to be informed of their health status, to be involved in care planning and treatment, and to request or refuse medically necessary and appropriate treatment. To make these decisions, patients or their representatives must be adequately informed.

To participate in the Medicaid and Medicare programs, hospitals must be in compliance with the CMS Conditions of Participation (CoP). The CoP include specific requirements related to informed consent and address requirements for patient representatives in making care decisions (42 CFR 482.13[b][2]), medical records (42 CFR § 482.24[c][2][v]), and surgical services (42 CFR § 482.51[b][2]).

With the exception of surgical emergencies, CMS requires that informed consent be obtained and the consent form be placed in the patient's medical record prior to surgery (42 CFR 482.24[c][2][v]; 42 CFR 482.51[b][2]). It is important to note that the definition of "surgery" includes any surgical procedure listed in CMS billing codes regardless of whether Medicare actually pays for the procedure. The consent form must include the name of the facility where the procedure is to take place, the specific procedure, the names of the person performing the procedure and administering anesthesia, and a statement that the risks, benefits, and alternatives were discussed. In addition, the patient's signature on the consent form must be dated and timed (42 CFR 482.24[c][2][v]).

Providers should also document that the patient understood and was able to repeat the information. The consent form should include a statement that the form was explained, that questions were answered to the patient's satisfaction, and that there were no blanks on the form at the time it was signed.

A patient may delegate the right to make informed decisions to another person to the extent allowed by individual state law. Hospitals must have specific policies in place regarding, among other things, informed consent, patients' rights, delegation of decision making, refusal of treatment, who can obtain informed consent, which procedures require consent, what constitutes an emergency, and the content of consent forms.

Consent discussions must include a description of the proposed procedure including the type of anesthesia to be used, indications, material risks and benefits, alternatives, probability of the procedure's success, and who will perform the procedure and administer anesthesia. In addition, CMS specifically requires that the discussion include who, other than the surgeon, will be performing important tasks, the level of participation of surgical residents, and the level of supervision by the surgeon (42 CFR 482.24[c][2][v]) (See Chapter 3 for more information).

Areas of Exposure to Claims of Liability

Malpractice and Negligence

Lack of informed consent is a common claim in medical malpractice lawsuits. The claim may be asserted in malpractice cases even when the care itself was in accordance with the standards of practice. This is because failure to obtain consent is, by itself, a legal theory of negligence that allows for the recovery of damages (see Chapter 8).

The most common reason a patient brings a lawsuit for lack of informed consent claim is a treatment complication. The claim is that a patient has suffered from a complication about which he or she was not advised before agreeing to the treatment. The issue in the case is whether or not the patient was advised of the particular complication from which he or she suffered. Because provider and patient memories may differ in this regard, the most valuable defense evidence lies in the provider's documentation.

Licensure

Patients who decide to sue may also file complaints with licensing boards. A complaint with a licensing board is an administrative process that may occur whether or not a lawsuit is filed. Because a complaint has been lodged, the licensing board is obligated to conduct an investigation. The board may ultimately close the matter without taking any disciplinary action, or it may find that the licensed provider has practiced negligently, engaged in professional misconduct, or practiced below acceptable standards. When disciplinary action is taken, providers may be excluded from participation in the Medicare or Medicaid programs and be reported to practitioner data banks. Other consequences for providers, such as nurses, may be an action against the practitioner's license, such as permanent or temporary suspension of license, limits on practice, and other effects (see discussion on powers of Boards of Nursing in Chapter 1).

Criminal

An allegation that a patient received treatment without giving his or her consent can lead to charges of battery. *Battery* is specifically defined by state law, but the term generally refers to unauthorized touching or offensive contact. Unlike negligence, which generally occurs without any ill intent, the criminal offense of battery is an intentional act. Some states allow plaintiffs to assert claims for fraud along with lack of informed consent on the basis that they were misled or given fraudulent information.

Duty to Nonpatient Third Parties

Patients cannot make rational decisions about signing papers, operating machinery, using firearms, or driving motor vehicles unless they are adequately informed that the potential side effects of medications that may be administered or prescribed for them include interference with motor function, and mental clarity, or other functional impairment. Providers may be held responsible for injuries to third parties due to their failure to advise the patient of impairment caused by their medical condition or medication side effects. Some courts have characterized this as a "duty to warn." An example of this would be where a patient takes a medication that causes drowsiness and, as a result, causes an auto accident that injures a third party. The injured third party may have a claim against the prescriber of the medication on the theory that the patient would not have driven the car if he or she had been informed that the medication would make him or her drowsy.

Providers are more likely to be held liable for third-party injuries if the patient's impairment was created by their interventions, that is, if the provider's treatment of the patient created the circumstances by which the patient became impaired. Because it is foreseeable that impaired drivers may injure others, there must be clear documentation that the patient was advised not to drive. The record should also reflect that the patient was lucid when given these instructions and indicated understanding of them.

As with all patient instructions, providers should document the presence of any witnesses to these conversations and obtain the patient's dated and timed signature on written instructions. The patient who has been adequately warned assumes the responsibility of his own actions should those cautions be disregarded.

A recent Massachusetts case illustrates the importance of warning patients about the dangers of driving under the influence of sedating medications.

CASE EXAMPLE:

Coombes v. Florio (2007)

SUMMARY OF CASE: In this case, the mother of a 10-year-old child sued a physician who had prescribed numerous medications to a patient without advising him not to drive. The physician had prescribed Oxycodone, Zaroxolyn, Prednisone, Flomax, Potassium, Paxil, Oxazepam, and Furosemide to a 75-year-old man, who subsequently lost consciousness while driving. The child was standing on the sidewalk when he was struck and killed by the man's car.

LOWER COURT'S DECISION: The lower court granted the physicians motion to dismiss the charges against him, holding that he owed a legal duty only to his patient and not to the public at large.

APPEALS COURT'S DECISION: On appeal, the Supreme Judicial Court of Massachusetts reversed the lower court's dismissal and found the physician liable, holding that a physician owes a duty of reasonable care to everyone foreseeably put at risk by the physician's failure to warn of the side effects of the physician's treatment of a patient, and that considering the number and nature of the drugs prescribed in this case, the age and health of the patient, and an earlier assurance about the ability of the patient to drive, it was foreseeable that the patient would suffer side effects that would impair his driving, and that an accident would result. (p. 184)

Similarly, in the earlier case of *McKenzie v. Hawai'i Permanente Med. Group, Inc.* (2002) the court held that a doctor owed a duty to a person killed in an automobile accident caused by the doctor's patient who was driving after taking medication prescribed for him by the doctor. The court reasoned that a logical reason exists to impose upon physicians, for the benefit of third parties, a duty to advise their patients that a medication may affect the patient's driving ability when such a duty would otherwise be owed to the patient. (*McKenzie v. Hawai'i Permanente Med. Group, Inc.*, 2002, p. 31)

Nurses should carefully and scrupulously document instructions to patients regarding potential impairment from, among other things, medications, seizures, pupil dilation or eye patches, or hypoglycemia. Policies should be clear regarding the length of time a patient must be observed after being medicated, emerging from anesthesia, or receiving conscious sedation.

Reducing Exposure to Liability

Providers obtaining informed consent from patients can reduce their liability exposure by establishing protective relationships with patients.

Informed consent should not be rushed or viewed as an administrative task, nor should it be delegated. The person conducting the informed consent discussion with the patient should be the person who will be performing the procedure. This provider should be fully familiar with the patient's medical history and assess the patient's capacity for understanding what is being discussed.

Patients who feel that they have been active participants in their health care decisions are less likely to bring a claim alleging lack of informed consent. This requires rapport and effective interpersonal communication skills. Whereas other health care professionals may have the patient sign the consent form, the discussion regarding risks, benefits, alternatives, and costs must be conducted by the physician performing the procedure. Lay persons may not understand that undesired outcomes do not necessarily reflect malpractice. The person obtaining informed consent therefore, should discuss the possibility that the procedure may not produce the desired benefit. Documentation should also include a discussion regarding incidental procedures that may be required during the performance of the primary procedure or that the procedure performed or anesthesia type may differ from what was planned if medical judgment indicates.

Sufficient time must be given to patients to read the consent form, discuss its provisions, ask questions, and consider the information. Detailed documentation of the discussion with the patient must include a description of the specific risks, benefits, and alternatives that were discussed and the patient's level of consciousness at the time of the discussion. If other persons are present for the discussion, those witnesses should be identified in the record. Nurses witnessing signatures should also document the patient's level of consciousness at the time the consent was signed.

The patient's response to medications should be documented in the record to avoid claims that consent forms were signed while the patient was distracted from pain or impaired from narcotics. Notation should be made on the consent form of the date and time it was signed. Documentation should include that the patient was given the opportunity to ask questions. Copies of any written materials or diagrams reviewed with the patient should be placed in the chart, and a copy of the consent form should be provided to the patient.

The consent form itself must not contain any statement that is coercive or exculpatory in nature. This means that the language should not include any statement that would appear to pressure a patient into signing or explicitly absolve the physician who is performing the procedure of all responsibility for the outcome. Although it may be important to emphasize that results are individual and not guaranteed, there should be no suggestion that patients are waiving their legal rights when consenting to a procedure. Consent must be given voluntarily and not as a response to feeling pressured. There should be no suggestion that the consent was coerced.

Consent forms should be designed to provide evidence of a complete record of the information provided to the patient. The form may include a checklist of common risks and space for additional risks to be included. The dated, timed, and witnessed consent form should contain language confirming that the form contained no blanks when it was signed, that it was read before being signed, that it was reviewed with the patient, and that questions were answered. It should be written in understandable terms and placed in the patient's medical record prior to the procedure. The consent form must describe the specific procedure the patient is agreeing to undergo, and the provider must stay within the scope of that procedure.

Language barriers must be addressed by using facility-approved interpreters who are identified by last name in the record. In general, it is not a good practice to use family members or nonapproved staff members for interpreting, as there is no assurance that they understand what is being explained and are describing the procedure, risks, benefits, or alternatives properly. Hearing-impaired patients may require the services of a sign-language interpreter.

Anecdotal entries in the medical record may supplement the consent form and address the discussion between the provider and the patient. The consent discussion should be individually tailored to the education and comprehension level of the patient. Understandable lay terms must be used. The provider obtaining consent must determine whether the patient understands what has been discussed and is rationally accepting the risks. The best indication that the patient does understand what has been said is that he or she can repeat the information. Documentation should make it clear and reflect the fact that the patient not only understands or states understanding of the outcomes of the procedure but that he or she can repeat what has been discussed.

Exceptions to Requirement for Informed Consent

Emergency Situations

When treatment delays can result in loss of life, limb, or organ, providers may intervene under the theory of implied consent. Consent is presumed in certain emergency circumstances. State laws vary but the general standard is what a reasonable person would have agreed to in same or similar circumstances. Institutional policies must address provider responsibilities when it is not possible to obtain informed consent prior to urgently needed treatment.

Protocols should address minors and patients without capacity. Documentation should include the provider's clinical impression of why emergency treatment is required, the potential consequences of delay, and what attempts were made to obtain consent from a proxy, which is another designated person who may be in a position to provide consent when the patient cannot. Providers must avoid the appearance of delaying consent discussions for the purpose of claiming urgency as an excuse to perform procedures without consent.

Statutory

Consent may also be presumed in nonemergency situations as determined by state law. Many states allow blood alcohol levels to be obtained from patients being treated for motor-vehicle-accident injuries. The driver is presumed to consent to such testing as a condition for obtaining or maintaining a driver's license in that state. Some states also allow organ and tissue donation in the absence of an express refusal to donate. Public health laws may obviate the need to obtain consent by mandating testing for communicable diseases. Mental health laws may allow for or mandate treatment or admission in the absence of the patient's consent.

Emancipation

Although parental or guardian consent is required for the treatment of minors, state laws recognize "mature minor" or "emancipated minor" doctrines in which consent may be obtained or withheld by the minor directly. The criteria for emancipation is determined at the state level and may include considerations as military service, financial independence, pregnancy, marriage, or high school graduation. Specific state laws address the treatments for which parental consent is not required and generally include reproductive issues, mental health intervention, addiction, and sexually transmitted diseases.

Substituted Judgment

The patient's decision-making capacity is a critical consideration in informed consent. If there is an inability to understand what is being conveyed, it may not be possible to explain the risks, benefits, and alternatives directly to the patient. Mental illness, extreme anxiety, altered levels of consciousness, or intoxication are among the factors that may create the need for an appointed guardian. The courts may become involved in some cases and order treatment or the withdrawal of treatment in the absence of the patient's consent. In cases of diminished capacity, family members may be appointed to act as surrogate decision makers. Providers must document the patient's inability to provide consent. Psychiatric consultations may be indicated to assess the patient's decision-making capacity.

CMS addresses the incapacitated patient by requiring that hospitals consult advanced directives, medical power of attorney, or a patient representative when available. Relevant information must be provided to the patient's representative to assure informed decision making. Once the patient regains capacity, the information is provided directly to him or her (42 CFR § 482.13[b][2]).

Therapeutic Privilege

In rare cases, a provider may avoid disclosing certain risks if in his or her clinical opinion it is determined that information may be detrimental or even endanger the patient. The "therapeutic privilege" does not allow a provider to paternalistically impose his or her opinion as final though, in some cases it may be possible for the provider to make such decisions when it is medically determined that revealing certain risks will destabilize a patient. In narrow circumstances, a clinician may forgo discussion of a particular risk, benefit, or alternative when believing that the information may create emotional or physical injury to the patient. Providers must document the rationale for withholding information and are advised to solicit the input of ethics committees and family members when possible.

RIGHT TO SELF-DETERMINATION

A patient's right to make end-of-life decisions has developed over time and in concert with a number of landmark cases. In 1990 Congress enacted the Patient Self-Determination Act (PSDA) as part of the Omnibus Budget Reconciliation Act of 1990 (PL 101–508). This legislation was intended to "reinforce individuals' constitutional right to determine their final health care" (http://www.libraryindex.com).

Effective December 1, 1991, the PSDA requires all health care providers participating in Medicaid to provide all patients who are 18 years of age or older with the following written information:

* The patient's rights under the law to participate in decisions about his or her medical care, including the right to accept or refuse treatments;
* The patient's right under state law to complete advance directives, which will be documented in his or her medical records; and
* The health care provider's policies honoring these rights.

Providers include hospitals, nursing homes, home health care providers, hospices, and health maintenance organizations (HMOs) but not outpatient-service providers or emergency medical personnel. The PSDA requires health care providers to educate their staff and the community about advance directives. It prohibits hospital personnel from discriminating against patients on the basis of whether they have an advance directive; thus, patients must be informed that having an advance directive is not a prerequisite to receiving care (http://www.libraryindex.com).

Advance directives are documents in which a patient can give instructions about his or her health care and end-of-life choices in a situation where he or she is unable to speak for him or herself. Living wills and medical power of attorney documents are examples of advance directives.

Although providers must make treatment decisions within the patient's advanced directive wishes, it must be carefully explained to patients with existing Do Not Resuscitate (DNR) orders that the team will intervene for correctable surgical or anesthesia problems even though they have DNR status. A distinction must be drawn between resuscitation and treatment of an acute episode.

High-profile cases such as those of Nancy Cruzan (Cruzan, 1988), Karen Ann Quinlan (Quinlan, 1976), and Terri Schiavo (Schiavo, 2005) highlight the conflicts that can occur with end-of-life decisions. Religious, spiritual, and personal value systems play an important role in the choice to continue or discontinue life support. Disagreements abound relative to concepts of privacy, constitutional rights, human dignity, individual versus state interests, guardianship issues, sanctity versus quality of life distinctions, interpretation of living wills and more and are intensely emotional subjects. Organizational ethics committees, Nurse Practice Acts, and the position papers of professional organizations may provide guidance for difficult cases.

Use of Advance Directives

Despite the passage of the PSDA and the high-profile so-called right-to-die cases, the majority of Americans (59%) do not have a living will (Gallup, 2005).

Every state has living-will-type statutes or legislation that provides for the expression of one's right to self-determination. A link to every state's relevant statutes is available at http://www.livingwills-freelegal.org/state-living-will-and-advance-directives-laws.html.

In addition, there are a number of living-will documents that include the forms that one would use to express his or her advance directive wishes. It is important that such a document conforms to the requirements of the relevant laws of the state where a patient undergoes treatment. Many available forms are valid in multiple states.

One excellent document is the "Five Wishes Living Will," a living will form that has been disseminated by a group called "Aging With Dignity" (http://www.livingwills-freelegal.org/Five-Wishes-Living-Will.html).

Five Wishes was originally introduced in 1996 as a Florida-only document, combining a living will and health care power of attorney in addition to addressing matters of comfort care and spirituality. With help from the American Bar Association's Commission on Law and Aging and leading medical experts, a national version of Five Wishes was introduced in 1998. The Five Wishes Living Will meets the legal requirements in 42 states and can be included in the other 9 states along with the state-required http://www.reference.com/browse/Five_Wishes.

CONCLUSIONS AND TRENDS

The right to decide what can be done to one's person is a fundamental right. This right has evolved and been refined over many years and has been codified into the PSDA of 1990. Despite the effort to encourage Americans to execute living wills, the majority of individuals have not done so. Every state has enacted some type of advance-directive legislation.

Nurses have legal duties to patients with regard to informed consent; however, the duty to provide informed consent generally rests with the physician.

Detailed documentation during the process of informed consent and in recording the specifics of the nurses' education of the patient is critical in reducing liability in this area.

As the health care system is reformed and undergoes change, nurses can expect their role and duties to the patients in this area to evolve accordingly.

KEY POINTS

- Informed consent is not a document; it is a process. The patient is advised of the risks, benefits, alternatives, and costs associated with proposed diagnostic tests or treatments.
- The legal obligation to obtain informed consent generally belongs to the *physician*. It is not within nursing's scope of practice to explain risks, benefits, and alternatives to proposed treatment plans.
- There are numerous sources of standards that determine the requirements of informed consent. They include case law, statutory and regulatory law, and CMS and other accreditation bodies.
- Failure to obtain informed consent can expose providers to liability for, among other things, malpractice, battery, and can result in action against one's professional license.
- Physicians can be found to owe a duty to nonpatient third parties where the third party is harmed by the patient who was not informed of the side effects of treatment or medication prescribed by the physicians.

REFERENCES

Aging With Dignity. (n.d.). Retrieved October 19, 2010, from http://www.aging-withdignity.org.

Centers for Medicaid and Medicare Services. (n.d.). *Hospital conditions of participation—informed consent, interpretive guidelines* (Interpretative guidelines 42 CFR § 482.51(b)(2)—surgical services; 42 CFR § 482.13(b)(2)—patient's rights; 42 CFR § 482.24(c)(2)(v)—medical records). Baltimore, MD: Author.

Coombes v. Florio, 450 Mass. 182 (2007).

Cruzan, by Cruzan v. Harmon, 760 S.W.2d 408 (Mo. banc 1988).

Daniels v. Durham, 171 N.C. App. 535 (2005).

Davis v. Hoffman, 591 Pa. 683 (2007).

Gallup. (n.d.). Retrieved October 24, 2010, from http://www.gallup.com/poll/16660/last-wishes-half-americans-written-wills.aspx

In Re Quinlan, 70 N.J. 10 (1976).

Library index. Retrieved October 24, 2010, from http://www.libraryindex.com/ pages/3133/Advance-Directives-PATIENT-SELF-DETERMINATION-ACT. html">Advance Directives–The Patient Self-determination Act</a>

McKenzie v. Hawai'i Permanente Med. Group, In., 98 Haw. 296 (2002).

Reference.com http://www.reference.com/browse/Five_Wishes. Accessed 16 January 2011.

Salandy v. Bryk, 55 A.D.3d 147 (2d Dept 2008).

Schiavo Ex Rel. Schindler v. Schiavo, 404 F.3d 1270 (11th Cir. 2005).

The case of Karen Ann Quinlan. (2001). In *American Decades*. Retrieved October 24, 2010, from http://www.encyclopedia.com/doc/1G2–3468302809.html

The Joint Commission. (n.d.). *The Joint Commission Standard RI 2.40 — informed consent*. Oakbrook Terrace, IL: Author.

APPENDIX

A copy of the Five Wishes Living Will is included in the following pages with the permission of Aging With Dignity. This material is property of Aging With Dignity and is subject to all copyright protections. For additional information, they can be contacted as follows:

Aging With Dignity

http://www.agingwithdignity.org

Phone: (850) 681–2010 ext. 107

P.O. Box 1661, Tallahassee, FL 32302

Five Wishes is Available in 26 Languages

FIVE
WISHES®

MY WISH FOR:

The Person I Want to Make Care Decisions for Me When I Can't **1**

The Kind of Medical Treatment I Want or Don't Want **2**

How Comfortable I Want to Be **3**

How I Want People to Treat Me **4**

What I Want My Loved Ones to Know **5**

print your name

birthdate

SAMPLE

Five Wishes

*T*here are many things in life that are out of our hands. This Five Wishes document gives you a way to control something very important—how you are treated if you get seriously ill. It is an easy-to-complete form that lets you say exactly what you want. Once it is filled out and properly signed it is valid under the laws of most states.*

What Is Five Wishes?

Five Wishes is the first living will that talks about your personal, emotional and spiritual needs as well as your medical wishes. It lets you choose the person you want to make health care decisions for you if you are not able to make them for yourself. Five Wishes lets you say exactly how you wish to be treated if you get seriously ill. It was written with the help of The American Bar Association's Commission on Law and Aging, and the nation's leading experts in end-of-life care. It's also easy to use. All you have to do is check a box, circle a direction, or write a few sentences.

How Five Wishes Can Help You And Your Family

- It lets you talk with your family, friends and doctor about how you want to be treated if you become seriously ill.

- Your family members will not have to guess what you want. It protects them if you become seriously ill, because they won't have to make hard choices without knowing your wishes.

- You can know what your mom, dad, spouse, or friend wants. You can be there for them when they need you most. You will understand what they really want.

How Five Wishes Began

For 12 years, Jim Towey worked closely with Mother Teresa, and, for one year, he lived in a hospice she ran in Washington, DC. Inspired by this first-hand experience, Mr. Towey sought a way for patients and their families to plan ahead and to cope with serious illness. The result is Five Wishes and the response to it has been overwhelming. It has been featured on CNN and NBC's Today Show and in the pages of *Time* and *Money* magazines. Newspapers have called Five Wishes the first "living will with a heart and soul." Today, Five Wishes is available in 23 languages

2

Who Should Use Five Wishes

Five Wishes is for anyone 18 or older — married, single, parents, adult children, and friends. Over 13 million Americans of all ages have already used it. Because it works so well, lawyers, doctors, hospitals and hospices, faith communities, employers, and retiree groups are handing out this document.

Five Wishes States

If you live in the **District of Columbia** or one of the **42 states** listed below, you can use Five Wishes and have the peace of mind to know that it substantially meets your state's requirements under the law:

Alaska	Illinois	Montana	South Carolina
Arizona	Iowa	Nebraska	South Dakota
Arkansas	Kentucky	Nevada	Tennessee
California	Louisiana	New Jersey	Vermont
Colorado	Maine	New Mexico	Virginia
Connecticut	Maryland	New York	Washington
Delaware	Massachusetts	North Carolina	West Virginia
Florida	Michigan	North Dakota	Wisconsin
Georgia	Minnesota	Oklahoma	Wyoming
Hawaii	Mississippi	Pennsylvania	
Idaho	Missouri	Rhode Island	

If your state is not one of the 42 states listed here, Five Wishes does not meet the technical requirements in the statutes of your state. So some doctors in your state may be reluctant to honor Five Wishes. However, many people from states not on this list do complete Five Wishes along with their state's legal form. They find that Five Wishes helps them express all that they want and provides a helpful guide to family members, friends, care givers and doctors. Most doctors and health care professionals know they need to listen to your wishes no matter how you express them.

How Do I Change To Five Wishes?

You may already have a living will or a durable power of attorney for health care. If you want to use Five Wishes instead, all you need to do is fill out and sign a new Five Wishes as directed. As soon as you sign it, it takes away any advance directive you had before. To make sure the right form is used, please do the following:

- Destroy all copies of your old living will or durable power of attorney for health care. Or you can write "revoked" in large letters across the copy you have. Tell your lawyer if he or she helped prepare those old forms for you. *AND*

- Tell your Health Care Agent, family members, and doctor that you have filled out a new Five Wishes. Make sure they know about your new wishes.

3

WISH 1
The Person I Want To Make Health Care Decisions For Me When I Can't Make Them For Myself.

If I am no longer able to make my own health care decisions, this form names the person I choose to make these choices for me. This person will be my Health Care Agent (or other term that may be used in my state, such as proxy, representative, or surrogate). This person will make my health care choices if both of these things happen:

- *My attending or treating doctor finds I am no longer able to make health care choices, AND*
- *Another health care professional agrees that this is true.*

If my state has a different way of finding that I am not able to make health care choices, then my state's way should be followed.

The Person I Choose As My Health Care Agent Is:

First Choice Name _____ Phone _____

Address _____ City/State/Zip _____

If this person is not able or willing to make these choices for me, *OR* is divorced or legally separated from me, *OR* this person has died, then these people are my next choices:

Second Choice Name _____ Third Choice Name _____

Address _____ Address _____

City/State/Zip _____ City/State/Zip _____

Phone _____ Phone _____

Picking The Right Person To Be Your Health Care Agent

Choose someone who knows you very well, cares about you, and who can make difficult decisions. A spouse or family member may not be the best choice because they are too emotionally involved. Sometimes they **are** the best choice. You know best. Choose someone who is able to stand up for you so that your wishes are followed. Also, choose someone who is likely to be nearby so that they can help when you need them. Whether you choose a spouse, family member, or friend as your Health Care Agent, make sure you talk about these wishes and be sure that this person agrees to respect and follow your wishes. Your Health Care Agent should be **at least 18 years or older** (in Colorado, 21 years or older) and should **not** be:

- Your health care provider, including the owner or operator of a health or residential or community care facility serving you.

- An employee or spouse of an employee of your health care provider.

- Serving as an agent or proxy for 10 or more people unless he or she is your spouse or close relative.

4

I understand that my Health Care Agent can make health care decisions for me. I want my Agent to be able to do the following: **(Please cross out anything you don't want your Agent to do that is listed below.)**

- Make choices for me about my medical care or services, like tests, medicine, or surgery. This care or service could be to find out what my health problem is, or how to treat it. It can also include care to keep me alive. If the treatment or care has already started, my Health Care Agent can keep it going or have it stopped.

- Interpret any instructions I have given in this form or given in other discussions, according to my Health Care Agent's understanding of my wishes and values.

- Consent to admission to an assisted living facility, hospital, hospice, or nursing home for me. My Health Care Agent can hire any kind of health care worker I may need to help me or take care of me. My Agent may also fire a health care worker, if needed.

- Make the decision to request, take away or not give medical treatments, including artificially-provided food and water, and any other treatments to keep me alive.

- See and approve release of my medical records and personal files. If I need to sign my name to get any of these files, my Health Care Agent can sign it for me.

- Move me to another state to get the care I need or to carry out my wishes.

- Authorize or refuse to authorize any medication or procedure needed to help with pain.

- Take any legal action needed to carry out my wishes.

- Donate useable organs or tissues of mine as allowed by law.

- Apply for Medicare, Medicaid, or other programs or insurance benefits for me. My Health Care Agent can see my personal files, like bank records, to find out what is needed to fill out these forms.

- Listed below are any changes, additions, or limitations on my Health Care Agent's powers.

_____

_____

_____

_____

_____

_____

If I Change My Mind About Having A Health Care Agent, I Will

- Destroy all copies of this part of the Five Wishes form. *OR*

- Tell someone, such as my doctor or family, that I want to cancel or change my Health Care Agent. *OR*

- Write the word "Revoked" in large letters across the name of each agent whose authority I want to cancel. Sign my name on that page.

WISH 2
My Wish For The Kind Of Medical Treatment
I Want Or Don't Want.

I believe that my life is precious and I deserve to be treated with dignity. When the time comes that I am very sick and am not able to speak for myself, I want the following wishes, and any other directions I have given to my Health Care Agent, to be respected and followed.

What You Should Keep In Mind As My Caregiver

- I do not want to be in pain. I want my doctor to give me enough medicine to relieve my pain, even if that means that I will be drowsy or sleep more than I would otherwise.

- I do not want anything done or omitted by my doctors or nurses with the intention of taking my life.

- I want to be offered food and fluids by mouth, and kept clean and warm.

What "Life-Support Treatment" Means To Me

Life-support treatment means any medical procedure, device or medication to keep me alive. Life-support treatment includes: medical devices put in me to help me breathe; food and water supplied by medical device (tube feeding); cardiopulmonary resuscitation (CPR); major surgery; blood transfusions; dialysis; antibiotics; and anything else meant to keep me alive. If I wish to limit the meaning of life-support treatment because of my religious or personal beliefs, I write this limitation in the space below. I do this to make very clear what I want and under what conditions.

_____

_____

_____

_____

_____

In Case Of An Emergency

If you have a medical emergency and ambulance personnel arrive, they may look to see if you have a **Do Not Resuscitate** form or bracelet. Many states require a person to have a **Do Not Resuscitate** form filled out and signed by a doctor. This form lets ambulance personnel know that you don't want them to use life-support treatment when you are dying. Please check with your doctor to see if you need to have a **Do Not Resuscitate** form filled out.

6

Here is the kind of medical treatment that I want or don't want in the four situations listed below. I want my Health Care Agent, my family, my doctors and other health care providers, my friends and all others to know these directions.

Close to death:

If my doctor and another health care professional both decide that I am likely to die within a short period of time, and life-support treatment would only delay the moment of my death (Choose *one* of the following):

❏   I want to have life-support treatment.

❏   I do not want life-support treatment. If it has been started, I want it stopped.

❏   I want to have life-support treatment if my doctor believes it could help. But I want my doctor to stop giving me life-support treatment if it is not helping my health condition or symptoms.

In A Coma And Not Expected To Wake Up Or Recover:

If my doctor and another health care professional both decide that I am in a coma from which I am not expected to wake up or recover, and I have brain damage, and life-support treatment would only delay the moment of my death (Choose *one* of the following):

❏   I want to have life-support treatment.

❏   I do not want life-support treatment. If it has been started, I want it stopped.

❏   I want to have life-support treatment if my doctor believes it could help. But I want my doctor to stop giving me life-support treatment if it is not helping my health condition or symptoms.

Permanent And Severe Brain Damage And Not Expected To Recover:

If my doctor and another health care professional both decide that I have permanent and severe brain damage, (for example, I can open my eyes, but I can not speak or understand) and I am not expected to get better, and life-support treatment would only delay the moment of my death (Choose *one* of the following):

❏   I want to have life-support treatment.

❏   I do not want life-support treatment. If it has been started, I want it stopped.

❏   I want to have life-support treatment if my doctor believes it could help. But I want my doctor to stop giving me life-support treatment if it is not helping my health condition or symptoms.

In Another Condition Under Which I Do Not Wish To Be Kept Alive:

If there is another condition under which I do not wish to have life-support treatment, I describe it below. In this condition, I believe that the costs and burdens of life-support treatment are too much and not worth the benefits to me. Therefore, in this condition, I do not want life-support treatment. (For example, you may write "end-stage condition." That means that your health has gotten worse. You are not able to take care of yourself in any way, mentally or physically. Life-support treatment will not help you recover. Please leave the space blank if you have no other condition to describe.)

_____

_____

_____

_____

_____

7

*T*he next three wishes deal with my personal, spiritual and emotional wishes. They are important to me. I want to be treated with dignity near the end of my life, so I would like people to do the things written in Wishes 3, 4, and 5 when they can be done. I understand that my family, my doctors and other health care providers, my friends, and others may not be able to do these things or are not required by law to do these things. I do not expect the following wishes to place new or added legal duties on my doctors or other health care providers. I also do not expect these wishes to excuse my doctor or other health care providers from giving me the proper care asked for by law.

WISH 3
My Wish For How Comfortable I Want To Be.
(Please cross out anything that you don't agree with.)

- I do not want to be in pain. I want my doctor to give me enough medicine to relieve my pain, even if that means I will be drowsy or sleep more than I would otherwise.

- If I show signs of depression, nausea, shortness of breath, or hallucinations, I want my care givers to do whatever they can to help me.

- I wish to have a cool moist cloth put on my head if I have a fever.

- I want my lips and mouth kept moist to stop dryness.

- I wish to have warm baths often. I wish to be kept fresh and clean at all times.

- I wish to be massaged with warm oils as often as I can be.

- I wish to have my favorite music played when possible until my time of death.

- I wish to have personal care like shaving, nail clipping, hair brushing, and teeth brushing, as long as they do not cause me pain or discomfort.

- I wish to have religious readings and well-loved poems read aloud when I am near death.

- I wish to know about options for hospice care to provide medical, emotional and spiritual care for me and my loved ones.

WISH 4
My Wish For How I Want People To Treat Me.
(Please cross out anything that you don't agree with.)

- I wish to have people with me when possible. I want someone to be with me when it seems that death may come at any time.

- I wish to have my hand held and to be talked to when possible, even if I don't seem to respond to the voice or touch of others.

- I wish to have others by my side praying for me when possible.

- I wish to have the members of my faith community told that I am sick and asked to pray for me and visit me.

- I wish to be cared for with kindness and cheerfulness, and not sadness.

- I wish to have pictures of my loved ones in my room, near my bed.

- If I am not able to control my bowel or bladder functions, I wish for my clothes and bed linens to be kept clean, and for them to be changed as soon as they can be if they have been soiled.

- I want to die in my home, if that can be done.

8

WISH 5

My Wish For What I Want My Loved Ones To Know.

(Please cross out anything that you don't agree with.)

- I wish to have my family and friends know that I love them.

- I wish to be forgiven for the times I have hurt my family, friends, and others.

- I wish to have my family, friends and others know that I forgive them for when they may have hurt me in my life.

- I wish for my family and friends to know that I do not fear death itself. I think it is not the end, but a new beginning for me.

- I wish for all of my family members to make peace with each other before my death, if they can.

- I wish for my family and friends to think about what I was like before I became seriously ill. I want them to remember me in this way after my death.

- I wish for my family and friends and caregivers to respect my wishes even if they don't agree with them.

- I wish for my family and friends to look at my dying as a time of personal growth for everyone, including me. This will help me live a meaningful life in my final days.

- I wish for my family and friends to get counseling if they have trouble with my death. I want memories of my life to give them joy and not sorrow.

- After my death, I would like my body to be (circle one): buried   or   cremated.

- My body or remains should be put in the following location_____.

- The following person knows my funeral wishes: _____.

If anyone asks how I want to be remembered, please say the following about me:

_____
_____
_____

If there is to be a memorial service for me, I wish for this service to include the following
(list music, songs, readings or other specific requests that you have):

_____
_____
_____

(Please use the space below for any other wishes. For example, you may want to donate any or all parts of your body when you die. You may also wish to designate a charity to receive memorial contributions. Please attach a separate sheet of paper if you need more space.)

_____
_____
_____

9

Signing The Five Wishes Form

Please make sure you sign your Five Wishes form in the presence of the two witnesses.

I, _____, ask that my family, my doctors, and other health care providers, my friends, and all others, follow my wishes as communicated by my Health Care Agent (if I have one and he or she is available), or as otherwise expressed in this form. This form becomes valid when I am unable to make decisions or speak for myself. If any part of this form cannot be legally followed, I ask that all other parts of this form be followed. I also revoke any health care advance directives I have made before.

Signature:_____

Address:_____

Phone:_____ Date:_____

Witness Statement · (2 witnesses needed):

I, the witness, declare that the person who signed or acknowledged this form (hereafter "person") is personally known to me, that he/she signed or acknowledged this [Health Care Agent and/or Living Will form(s)] in my presence, and that he/she appears to be of sound mind and under no duress, fraud, or undue influence.

I also declare that I am over 18 years of age and am NOT:

- The individual appointed as (agent/proxy/ surrogate/patient advocate/representative) by this document or his/her successor,
- The person's health care provider, including owner or operator of a health, long-term care, or other residential or community care facility serving the person,
- An employee of the person's health care provider,

- Financially responsible for the person's health care,
- An employee of a life or health insurance provider for the person,
- Related to the person by blood, marriage, or adoption, and,
- To the best of my knowledge, a creditor of the person or entitled to any part of his/her estate under a will or codicil, by operation of law.

(Some states may have fewer rules about who may be a witness. Unless you know your state's rules, please follow the above.)

Signature of Witness #1	Signature of Witness #2
Printed Name of Witness	Printed Name of Witness
Address	Address
Phone	Phone

Notarization · Only required for residents of Missouri, North Carolina, South Carolina and West Virginia

- If you live in Missouri, only your signature should be notarized.

- If you live in North Carolina, South Carolina or West Virginia, you should have your signature, and the signatures of your witnesses, notarized.

STATE OF_____   COUNTY OF_____

On this _____ day of _____, 20_____, the said _____,

_____, and _____, known to me (or satisfactorily proven) to be the person named in the foregoing instrument and witnesses, respectively, personally appeared before me, a Notary Public, within and for the State and County aforesaid, and acknowledged that they freely and voluntarily executed the same for the purposes stated therein.

My Commission Expires: _____

Notary Public

What To Do After You Complete Five Wishes

- Make sure you sign and witness the form just the way it says in the directions. Then your Five Wishes will be legal and valid.

- Talk about your wishes with your health care agent, family members and others who care about you. Give them copies of your completed Five Wishes.

- Keep the original copy you signed in a special place in your home. Do NOT put it in a safe deposit box. Keep it nearby so that someone can find it when you need it.

- Fill out the wallet card below. Carry it with you. That way people will know where you keep your Five Wishes.

- Talk to your doctor during your next office visit. Give your doctor a copy of your Five Wishes. Make sure it is put in your medical record. Be sure your doctor understands your wishes and is willing to follow them. Ask him or her to tell other doctors who treat you to honor them.

- If you are admitted to a hospital or nursing home, take a copy of your Five Wishes with you. Ask that it be put in your medical record.

- I have given the following people copies of my completed Five Wishes:

  _____
  _____
  _____

Residents of Wisconsin must attach the Wisconsin notice statement to Five Wishes.
More information and the notice statement are available at www.agingwithdignity.org or 1-888-594-7437.

Residents of Institutions In California, Connecticut, Delaware, Georgia, New York, North Dakota, South Carolina, and Vermont Must Follow Special Witnessing Rules.

If you live in certain institutions (a nursing home, other licensed long term care facility, a home for the mentally retarded or developmentally disabled, or a mental health institution) in one of the states listed above, you may have to follow special "witnessing requirements" for your Five Wishes to be valid. For further information, please contact a social worker or patient advocate at your institution.

Five Wishes is meant to help you plan for the future. It is not meant to give you legal advice. It does not try to answer all questions about anything that could come up. Every person is different, and every situation is different. Laws change from time to time. If you have a specific question or problem, talk to a medical or legal professional for advice.

Five Wishes Wallet Card

Important Notice to Medical Personnel: I have a Five Wishes Advance Directive.	My primary care physician is:
_____ Signature	_____ Name
Please consult this document and/or my Health Care Agent in an emergency. My Agent is:	_____ Address City/State/Zip _____ Phone
_____ Name	My document is located at:
_____ Address City/State/Zip	_____ _____
_____ Phone	_____ _____

Cut Out Card, Fold and Laminate for Safekeeping

11

Here's What People Are Saying About Five Wishes:

"It will be a year since my mother passed on. We knew what she wanted because she had the Five Wishes living will. When it came down to the end, my brother and I had no questions on what we needed to do. We had peace of mind."

Cheryl K.
Longwood, Florida

"I must say I love your Five Wishes. It's clear, easy to understand, and doesn't dwell on the concrete issues of medical care, but on the issues of real importance—human care. I used it for myself and my husband."

Susan W.
Flagstaff, Arizona

"I don't want my children to have to make the decisions I am having to make for my mother. I never knew that there were so many medical options to be considered. Thank you for such a sensitive and caring form. I can simply fill it out and have it on file for my children."

Diana W.
Hanover, Illinois

To Order:

Call (888) 5-WISHES to purchase more copies of Five Wishes, the Five Wishes DVD, or Next Steps guides. Ask about the "Family Package" that includes 10 Five Wishes, 2 Next Steps guides and 1 DVD at a savings of more than 50%. For more information visit Aging with Dignity's website, or call for details.

(888) 5-WISHES or (888) 594-7437
www.agingwithdignity.org

Aging
with Dignity

P.O. Box 1661
Tallahassee, Florida 32302-1661

Chapter Eight

Nursing Malpractice/Negligence and Liability

Shellie Karno

OBJECTIVES

- Identify the principles of nursing malpractice/negligence.
- Describe the four elements of a nursing malpractice claim.
- Describe the defenses to a nursing malpractice action.
- Define the standard of care.
- Identify the patterns of malpractice cases.
- Describe "never events."

INTRODUCTION

Historically, nurses were not named as individual parties in medical malpractice actions. This immunity was based on the concept that nurses were not professionals and, therefore, not responsible for their actions. As nursing developed, many factors contributed to the growth and accountability of the profession.

One factor was the law, specifically Tort Law. Tort Law is defined as a legal wrong committed upon person or property (*Black's Law Dictionary*, 2004). Negligence, assault and battery, invasion of privacy, and misrepresentation and fraud are types of Tort Law. Early Tort Law ignored nursing, until the profession began to establish itself as a discipline in the mid-20th century.

Nurses in the U.S. Civil Service obtained professional-status classification. Professional associations representing various specialties in nursing practice were founded. Role responsibilities of nurses were expanded, and advanced practice nursing acts were enacted. Since nurses have been recognized for their ability to be autonomous and independent, nurses have been held accountable and responsible for their actions. The development of nursing as a health care profession established the foundation for the legal requirements of nursing responsibility, accountability, and liability.

PRINCIPLES OF NURSING MALPRACTICE

Negligence

Negligence is defined as the failure to exercise the standard of care that a reasonably prudent person would exercise in the same or similar circumstances (*Black's Law Dictionary*, 2004). When negligence is alleged, the conduct complained of is compared with what an ordinary, reasonable, and prudent person would have done in the same situation.

Negligent conduct can occur by acts of commission or omission. Negligent conduct can be alleged when a person commits an act that a reasonably prudent person would not do; this type of conduct is negligence by commission. Negligent conduct can also be alleged when a person fails to act when a duty exists; this type of conduct is negligence by omission. For example, if a nurse failed to give a patient a dose of Lanoxin at the prescribed time it would be an omission. All omissions do not necessarily rise to the level of negligence as further explained in this chapter.

Professional Negligence

Professional negligence is negligence related to the conduct of professionals, such as nurses, physicians, lawyers, or financial advisors, which falls below a professional standard of care (*Black's Law Dictionary*, 2004) The terms "professional negligence" and "malpractice" are used interchangeably. Professionals' possess specialized learning and expertise and are relied on to provide their knowledge and skill. The law requires that the conduct of such professionals meet the applicable standard of care for that professional group. For example, when allegations of negligence are directed at a nurse, the nurse's conduct is compared to that of a reasonably qualified nurse in the same or similar circumstances.

Negligence Per Se

Negligence per se, or negligence as a matter of law, is found where the individual violates a duty imposed by law or statute. Where a law imposes a specific duty to protect the safety of others, the failure to perform that duty is negligence per se (*Chambers v. St. Mary's School*, 1998).

For example, a nurse would be negligent per se if she or he practiced beyond the scope of the state Nurse Practice Act. However, a finding of negligence per se only subjects the defendant to possible liability; it does not establish liability (*Searcy v. Brown*, 1980). Establishing negligence per se is to establish only the first two elements of negligence: duty and breach of duty.

Proof of a violation of a statute alone does not give rise to a presumption of proximate cause. Establishing liability requires proof that the violation of the statute caused injuries to the plaintiff and the plaintiff's subsequent damages (*Slade v. Smith's Management Corp.*, 1991). The plaintiff still must show that such negligence was a proximate cause of the injury or damages sustained. In the example of negligence per se whereby a nurse practices beyond the scope of a Nurse Practice Act, a plaintiff would still have to prove that the nurse's violation of the Nurse Practice Act proximately caused plaintiff's injuries and damages.

Proximate Cause

Proximate cause is defined as a cause that is considered in law to result in liability (*Black's Law Dictionary*, 2004). It is an act or omission that results in a legal consequence, allowing liability to be imposed.

In other words, a proximate cause is a cause that directly produces an event and without which the event would not have occurred. Proximate cause is also termed a "direct cause," or "legal cause," or "cause in fact." As a practical matter, legal responsibility for an act or omission *must* be limited to those causes that are so closely connected with the result and of such significance that the law is justified in imposing liability. This limitation of legal responsibility for the consequences of conduct prevents the imposition of infinite liability for wrongful acts and sets the boundary of liability for the consequences of an act or omission.

Res Ipsa Loquitur

The doctrine of *res ipsa loquitur* is grounded in the logic of ordinary human experience and permits a jury, on the basis of experience or common knowledge, to infer negligence from the mere occurrence of the injury itself (*Howie v. Walsh*, 2005).

Res ipsa loquitur is a Latin term and literally means, "the thing speaks for itself" (*Lanza v. Poretti*, 1982). It is a rule of evidence that allows for an inference of defendant's negligence based on the circumstances of the injury. The inference is not automatic, and the plaintiff must present circumstantial evidence that allows the inference to be made.

The circumstantial elements that must be proven in a *res ipsa loquitur* case are (a) the injury would not have occurred under ordinary circumstances without negligence, (b) the plaintiff was under the exclusive control of defendant, and (c) the plaintiff did not contribute to cause the injury (Am. Jur. 2d, 2008).

Where a proposition is a matter of common knowledge, expert testimony is not required to establish the proposition as an element for applicability of the *res ipsa loquitur* doctrine (*Heastie v. Roberts*, 2007; *Methodist Hospitals, Inc. v. Johnson*, 2006).

The impact of this doctrine on the rules of evidence varies by jurisdiction. In some jurisdictions, it shifts the burden of proof to the defendant. In other jurisdictions, *res ipsa loquitur* strengthens the inference of negligence that may be drawn by the jury. Some courts hold that the better rule is to allow expert testimony to assist the parties in establishing or rebutting the inference of negligence under a theory of *res ipsa loquitur* (*Seavers v. Methodist Medical Center of Oak Ridge*, 1999).

Examples of malpractice cases where the doctrine of *res ipsa loquitur* was allowed by the court include foreign bodies left in a patient after surgery or a wrongful pregnancy after a bilateral tubal ligation.

Burden of Proof

In a claim for professional negligence, the party bringing the malpractice claim is the plaintiff, and the party being sued for negligence is the defendant (*Black's Law Dictionary*, 2004). The burden of proof refers to the obligation of one party to prove the truth of the allegations or charges (*Black's Law Dictionary*, 2004). In both civil and criminal law, the party bringing the lawsuit bears the burden of proving the allegations. More specifically, in malpractice claims, the plaintiff or plaintiffs are obligated to establish the truth of the operative facts of the case. Whether the plaintiffs have satisfied this burden is not an issue of fact for the jury. It is an issue of law that is determined by the judge.

The term "burden of proof" is applied to two distinct but related concepts: the burden of production and the burden of persuasion. The burden of production tells a court which party must come forward with evidence to support a particular proposition. The burden of persuasion describes the obligation to introduce evidence sufficient to persuade the jury that a particular proposition is true.

Standard of Care

The standard of care is a legal concept and has been judicially defined by the courts as the exercise of the same degree of knowledge, skill, and ability as an ordinarily careful professional would exercise under similar circumstances (*Seavers v. Methodist Medical Center of Oak Ridge*, 1999). A nurse's professional conduct must meet the standard of care for nurses. The standard of care requires a nurse to use the level of care that a reasonably prudent nurse would provide under the same or similar circumstances. The conduct is measured against a similarly educated and experienced nurse with ordinary skill, judgment, and intelligence.

The standard is not set at the level of the most highly skilled nurse and not set at the level of an average practitioner. Nurses who perform at a below-average level may nonetheless be competent and qualified to practice their profession (Am. Jur. 3d). The level of conduct required by the standard of care is the ordinary performance of duties, and not optimal, ideal, or average performance.

It is important to note that the standard of care is not a static measure; it is constantly changing to incorporate scientific and technological advances. In a malpractice action, nurses are held to the standard of care that existed at the time care was delivered. The nurse's conduct will be measured by the standard of care in effect at the time of the alleged malpractice. The relevant standard of care is the standard that existed at the time of the alleged negligence.

The standard of care for today may likely differ from the standard of care learned in nursing school and also from the standard of care current at the time the lawsuit is filed. Case studies illustrating the standards of care for nursing practice will be discussed further on in this chapter.

Expert Witness

In a malpractice action, the plaintiff has the burden of proving that the standard of care was not met and the nurse acted in a negligent manner. The plaintiff can utilize several sources to establish the standard of care.

The use of expert witness testimony is common, and many states require the testimony of a nurse expert to establish nursing negligence.

Historically, a physician could testify regarding the standard of care for nursing in a malpractice case. However, most courts have determined that only a professional within the same practice area could act as an expert witness regarding the standard of care for that profession (*Sullivan v. Edward Hospital*, 2004). Expert witness testimony will be discussed in more detail in Chapter 9.

Liability

Liability is defined as "the quality or state of being legally obligated or responsible" (*Black's Law Dictionary*, 2004). There are many types of liability relevant to the area of professional negligence.

Joint and several liability means that two or more parties are responsible together and individually (*Black's Law Dictionary*, 2004). The plaintiff can sue and recover from both wrongdoers or from either wrongdoer. If a plaintiff pursues both wrongdoers, he does not receive double compensation.

For example, in a malpractice claim, a plaintiff can claim damages from a physician and a hospital, or several physicians and several hospitals. The amount of damages remains the same, regardless of the number of wrongdoers.

Strict liability is liability without fault (*Black's Law Dictionary*, 2004). This concept is applied by the courts in product liability cases where the manufacturer is liable for all defective or hazardous products that threaten personal safety.

Personal liability is the responsibility for payment of an obligation with the personal assets of the responsible party (*Black's Law Dictionary*, 2004).

Vicarious liability is the imposition of liability on one person for the actionable conduct of another, based solely on a relationship between the two persons (*Black's Law Dictionary*, 2004). *Respondeat superior* is based on this indirect or imputed legal responsibility for acts of another.

Respondeat Superior

Respondeat superior is a Latin term literally translated as "let the master speak." The term infers that the master is responsible for the acts of the servant (*Black's Law Dictionary*, 2004). It is a legal theory based on the vicarious liability of the employer for the negligent acts of employees.

The employer's liability for the negligent conduct of employees will only attach when the conduct occurred during the employment relationship and the employee's conduct was within the employee's scope of employment. For example, a nurse volunteering at a church-sponsored health fair is not acting within the scope of her hospital employment. Therefore, the nurse's employer would not be responsible for his or her negligent acts under the theory of *respondeat superior*.

A lawsuit alleging negligence of a nurse employed by a hospital can name the hospital as a defendant or can name the nurse as a defendant or can name both the hospital and the nurse as defendants.

Identification of the employer can be an issue for nurses who are employed by nurse registries or agencies. Nurses may also be employed by physician groups or employed in other practice arrangements. The nurse should review the written agreement with the agency, registry, or practice group and clarify the responsibility for employment and malpractice coverage.

FOUR ELEMENTS OF NEGLIGENCE

The plaintiff has the burden of proving the nurse's negligence. Four essential elements must be proven by the plaintiff for the case to go forward.

Duty

The plaintiff's attorney must prove that a duty existed between the nurse and the patient. Once the nurse patient relationship is established, the nurse has a legal duty to provide the standard of nursing care. The nurse is obligated to use the degree of skill, knowledge, and care offered by a similarly educated nurse.

The relationship that creates the duty of care may arise in several ways. Assignment of the patient in a hospital setting creates a duty, as does a request by a patient for assistance. A nurse's observation of non-standard care delivered by another health care provider also creates an affirmative duty of the nurse to advocate on behalf of the patient's best interests. The nurse's duty to advocate will be discussed in this chapter under the failure to follow the chain of command.

Breach

The plaintiff's attorney must next prove that the nurse breached the duty to provide the standard of care. This breach or failure to provide the standard of care constitutes professional negligence. The plaintiff must prove that the nurse's conduct fell below the appropriate standard of care.

Proof of professional negligence can be established by the use of expert testimony, internal standards such as job descriptions, policy and procedure manuals, or external standards such as nursing association guidelines, Joint Commission standards, or the state Nurse Practice Act.

Proximate Cause

Causation of injury is the third element required to prove a nurse's professional negligence. The plaintiff must prove that the failure to provide the standard of care is the proximate cause or "cause in fact" of the injury.

Even if the plaintiff can prove the nurse's professional negligence, the nurse will not be liable unless the plaintiff can convince the judge or jury that the nurse's negligence caused the alleged injury. In other words, the plaintiff must show that the injury would not have occurred but for the nurse's negligence.

The standard of proving causation in a malpractice case is that the judge or jury must find it more probable than not that the cause of the injury was attributable to the nurse's negligence than to any other cause.

Damages

Lastly, the plaintiff must prove that he or she was injured and sustained damages. Damages entitle the plaintiff to seek compensation for injuries. Compensable damages include physical, emotional, and financial injury.

Depending on the jurisdiction the case was filed in, a plaintiff may seek compensation for medical expenses, pain and suffering, disfigurement, loss of enjoyment of life, and future earnings.

Table 8.1 Four Elements of Negligence

Duty: Once the nurse patient relationship is established, the nurse has a legal duty to provide the standard of nursing care.

Breach: The plaintiff's attorney must next prove that the nurse breached the duty to provide the standard of care.

Proximate Cause: The plaintiff must prove that the failure to provide the standard of care is the proximate cause or "cause in fact" of the injury.

Damages: The plaintiff must prove that he or she was injured and sustained damages. Damages entitle the plaintiff to seek compensation for injuries.

PATTERNS OF MALPRACTICE CLAIMS AND CASE EXAMPLES

Medication Error

Medication errors cause at least one death every day and injure approximately 1.3 million people annually in the United States (U.S. Food and Drug Administration Center for Drug Evaluation and Research, 2004).

The National Coordinating Council for Medication Error and Prevention (NCC MERP) has approved the following as its working definition of medication error: "Any preventable event that may cause or lead to inappropriate medication use or patient harm, while the medication is in the control of the healthcare professional, patient, or consumer" (NCC MERP, 2009). Errors can occur at any stage of practice, for example, prescribing, repackaging, transcribing, dispensing, administering, or monitoring. Common types of errors involve similar product names, abbreviations, labeling, and packaging by the manufacturer, miscalculation of dose, physician ordering errors, and omission errors (Academy of Managed Care Pharmacy, 2009). Since many errors are caused by system failure rather than human error, patient safety research and initiatives have encouraged a systems approach to address the frequency of medication errors. Health care institutions and the pharmaceutical industry have adopted a variety of systems methods aimed at the reduction of medication error.

CASE EXAMPLE:

MEDICATION ERROR

Harris County Hospital District v. Estrada (1993)

SUMMARY OF FACTS: Carolina Gonzalez, a 73-year-old woman, received her routine care at the West End Medical Clinic. She presented to the clinic with complaints and symptoms of an infection. She was examined by Dr. John Bradberry, a Baylor College of Medicine resident physician. She was given a prescription for Bactrim, notwithstanding a documented history of allergy to sulfa drugs. Mrs. Gonzalez suffered a severe allergic reaction and expired 16 days later.

NURSING ALLEGATIONS:

- Failure to review medical record documentation for history of allergies.
- Failure to maintain appropriate documentation of history.
- Failure to provide adequate discharge instructions regarding adverse reactions to medication.

COURT PROCEEDINGS: Before filing the lawsuit, the Gonzalez family settled with Bradberry and Baylor College of Medicine. The family subsequently sued the clinic for the nursing allegations.

The plaintiff's nursing expert testified that it was the discharge nurse's independent duty to compare the prescription with the patient's medical record for contraindications, such as allergies, and to bring any inconsistencies to the attention of the physician.

In addition, the nurse expert testified that the discharge nurse also has a duty to instruct the patient on the symptoms of an adverse reaction and what to do in the event of a reaction. The nurse expert further testified that the sole proximate cause of the inappropriate prescription and death was the negligent record keeping by the clinic's nursing staff.

A second nurse expert testified that the clinic nursing staff had a duty to review the prescription with the plaintiff, provide discharge instructions, and advise the plaintiff to seek immediate medical attention in the event of a drug reaction. Evidence was presented showing that a drug reaction can be reversed if treated quickly.

The examining physician testified that he relied on the clinic's computer print out that showed Gonzalez had no allergies. The computer printout and patient record is given to a physician upon examination of a patient.

The computer sheet is a summary of the medical data contained in the patient record prepared by the medical records clerk. The nurse failed to review the patient record or verbally confirm any allergy history with the patient. The jury determined that the nurse's failure to meet the standard of care for documentation requirements and

> discharge instructions was a proximate cause of the allergic reaction and subsequent death.
>
> COURT'S DECISION: The jury returned a guilty verdict against the nurse and awarded damages to the Gonzalez family.

This case illustrates the importance of an independent review of the record by the nurse and the risk involved in depending on physicians, computers, or clerks for critical clinical data. This case also illustrates the importance of discharge instructions and patient teaching, as this preventable death could have been avoided had the nurse spent time talking to the patient or caretaker regarding allergies, possible drug reactions, and appropriate interventions.

Failure to Follow Policies and Procedures

Patient care procedures and hospital policies provide guidelines for current and accepted practice. The development of procedures and policies is influenced by accreditation standards, state and federal legislation, court decisions, patient care rights, clinical research, outcome data, and scientific evidence.

Compliance with policies and procedures when providing nursing care helps to assure consistency with the standard of care. Practicing procedure-based nursing care can prevent injury to patients.

Policies and procedures are related, though they have distinct definitions. A policy is the institutional expectation of staff members and reflects the philosophy of the entity. However, a policy does not obviate the need for individual judgment or negate the nurse's accountability for decision making.

A procedure is a step-by-step description of what to do in a given situation. Examples include a specific protocol for medication administration, notification procedures for adverse events, or department-specific patient monitoring requirements.

Although policies and procedures are helpful in establishing consistent standards of practice, they are also helpful to the plaintiff's attorney in proving the elements of negligence. Plaintiff's attorneys routinely request hospital policies and procedures during the discovery stage of trial. A nurse's failure to adhere to the policy can be construed as a deviation from the standard of care and used as proof of the nurse's negligence.

However, policies and procedures function as a shield *and* sword. Defense attorneys also examine policies and procedures. Compliance with treatment procedures serves as evidence of adherence to the standard of care and can convince a jury that the nurse was not negligent.

The following case involves a patient care protocol for medication administration that was violated.

CASE EXAMPLE:

NURSES LIABLE FOR FAILURE TO FOLLOW POLICIES, PROCEDURES, AND TREATMENT PROTOCOL

Bentiveniga v. St Francis Hospital (2004)

SUMMARY OF FACTS: This 34-year-old plaintiff was 9 months pregnant when she presented to the hospital with complaints of a severe headache. She had a known prenatal history of malignant hypertension. She was admitted to the labor and delivery unit and assessed by an experienced obstetric nurse.

Upon examination by a second-year resident, she was diagnosed with severe preeclampsia. Laboratory testing revealed a type of preeclampsia involving hemolysis, elevated liver function, and low platelets.

The hospital's treatment protocol for preeclampsia required the administration of Labetalol (an antihypertensive) at 10-minute intervals in increasing doses of 10, 20, 40, and 80 mg until blood pressure stabilization is reached. The nurse administered 3 doses of 10 mg of Labetalol, resulting in stabilization of the plaintiff's blood pressure.

Labor was induced, and the plaintiff's blood pressure became elevated. The plaintiff became unresponsive. The fetus was delivered by cesarean delivery. The plaintiff suffered a brain hemorrhage and was placed on ventilatory support. A decision was made to disconnect the ventilator, and the plaintiff expired 3 days after delivery. Nursing malpractice was alleged.

NURSING ALLEGATIONS:

- Failure to follow hospital policy.
- Failure to administer medications as per policy.

COURT PROCEEDINGS: At trial, the hospital presented a physician expert who testified that the plaintiff's preeclampsia was so severe she likely would not have survived even with additional antihypertensive medication as provided for in the policy. The hospital presented a proximate-cause defense, stating that the plaintiff's attorney had failed to prove that the plaintiff would have survived but for the nurse's failure to administer additional Labetalol.

The plaintiff's expert stated that the nurse's failure to comply with the protocol was the proximate cause, or cause in fact, of the death.

Both parties also presented nurse experts who testified regarding the standard of care for nurses in complying with a treatment protocol.

COURT'S DECISION: The jury returned a verdict in the amount of US$22 million in favor of the plaintiff.

This case is very significant, and not exclusively due to the high jury verdict. The jury sent a very strong message to the nurse regarding her breach of duty to the plaintiff.

The jury seemingly disregarded the issue of whether the nurse's conduct proximately caused the death. The jury was focused on the treatment protocol and found the nurse liable.

The plaintiff's attorney presented a medical expert who testified that additional medication administered in quicker sequence would have improved the outcome. Yet the proximate cause element was overshadowed by the jury's expectation regarding the nurse's responsibility for compliance with protocol.

Written treatment procedures are necessary tools for communicating and standardizing care. However, procedure manuals also present liability exposure for the institution; therefore, it is imperative that the policies are practical, up to date, and familiar to nursing staff.

Failure to Notify Physician and Document

Communication between members of the health care team is essential for the provision of quality patient care. As members of the health care team, nurses have a duty to exercise their professional judgment and determine the need to advise other members of the team of significant clinical patient data.

The ability to correctly identify significant clinical data that must be communicated is a standard of care. Failure to comply with the standard of care requiring identification of significant clinical data and reporting the information to the appropriate health care team member can result in the exclusive liability of the nurse.

Patient history and complaints, changes in a patient's condition, laboratory or radiology results, and disagreement between health care team members, are examples of clinical data that require notification.

The method of notification depends on the urgency of the situation. Documentation in the medical record may suffice for communicating routine aspects of care. Where a nurse determines that immediate intervention is warranted, placing a phone call and documenting the call is insufficient notification. Duty requires that significant data are actually communicated and the team member responded to as the patient's condition requires.

Where a nurse determines that the response is inadequate, the nurse is further obligated to follow the chain of command and notify another health care team member or administrator (see the upcoming discussion in this chapter on issues related to chain of command and the discussion on documentation in Chapter 6).

CASE EXAMPLE:

NURSES FAILURE TO DOCUMENT AND REPORT CRITICAL CLINICAL INFORMATION VIOLATES NURSING STANDARD OF CARE

Ramsey v. Physicians Memorial Hospital (1977)

SUMMARY OF FACTS: Parents brought this lawsuit on behalf of their two male infants aged 1 and 2 years, respectively. The family lived in a rural area in the state of Maryland. The mother had found and removed two ticks from her 1-year-old son. Several days later, she noticed a rash on both minors that started on their heads and chests and was accompanied by fever. Both minors were brought to the emergency department of Physicians Memorial Hospital by their parents.

The mother reported to the emergency department nurse that she had found and removed ticks from the younger son. The nurse did not relay this history to the examining physician, Dr. Del La Paz, nor did she document the history in the record. Dr. Del La Paz made a diagnosis of measles and discharged the minors.

Two days later, the rash had spread to both minors' extremities, and their fever persisted. The minors were brought back to the emergency department where another physician, Dr. Azer, examined them.

He consulted with the family pediatrician and recommended that the pediatrician evaluate the children. The pediatrician examined both minors and made a tentative diagnosis of measles.

Four days later, their conditions worsened, and the mother was unable to reach the primary care pediatrician. The next day, the 2-year-old was found dead. The 1-year-old was taken to and examined at a different facility. Two ticks were found, and he was diagnosed and treated successfully for Rocky Mountain Spotted Fever. The autopsy on the 2-year-old showed he died of Rocky Mountain Spotted Fever. Nursing malpractice was alleged.

NURSING ALLEGATIONS:

- Failure to notify physician of significant clinical data.
- Failure to document significant clinical data.

COURT PROCEEDINGS: At trial, medical experts for both parties testified that the diagnosis of Rocky Mountain Spotted Fever is difficult. Rocky Mountain Spotted Fever is relatively rare and is caused by the bite of an infected tick. There are several differential diagnoses to be considered, including measles, based on common symptoms such as rash and fever. Lack of knowledge of the tick history severely compromised the ability to make the correct diagnosis.

A tentative diagnosis of measles was viable, as the minors had not been vaccinated against the measles, and it would be common to find two brothers exhibiting symptoms of measles at the same time. In contrast, Rocky Mountain Spotted Fever is not contagious and simultaneous infection is unusual.

COURT'S DECISION: The jury found in favor of the parents, and against the hospital, but exonerated the first emergency department physician, Dr. Del La Paz. The court found the evidence supported the jury's determination that the failure of the nurse to notify Dr. Del La Paz of the patient history constituted a violation of the standard of care. The court further stated that the nurse's failure was a contributing proximate cause of the death of one child and the serious illness of the other child.

This case illustrates the importance of communicating clinical data, including patient history and presenting complaint. Any unusual or out-of-the-ordinary event in a patient's history has potential impact on a patient's well-being.

The jury easily found Dr. Del La Paz as *not guilty,* given the fact that the nurse failed to report the tick history. The court held that the evidence failed to make a submissable case as to the negligence of the physician.

Liability for the death of one minor, and liability for the serious illness of the second minor was attributed solely to the nurse. Although the nurse was not individually named as a defendant in this lawsuit, the hospital was named. The court relied on the theory of *respondeat superior* in finding the nurse liable for her negligent conduct. The standard of care required the nurse to report the tick history to the physician and to document the history. Having failed to verbally report the tick history to the first physician, written documentation of the history in the patient record would have alerted Dr. Del La Paz and would have alerted the second emergency department physician or the pediatrician.

This case is interesting from both a clinical and legal perspective. The case illustrates the importance of communicating clinical data, including patient history and presenting complaint. The published case does not report on the nurse's testimony so it is unclear whether the nurse inadvertently forgot to report and document the tick history or believed the history was not clinically significant.

The lesson to be learned remains the same: Any unusual or out-of-the-ordinary event in a patient's history has potential impact on a patient's well-being and must be reported and documented.

Legally speaking, the case is interesting from an evidentiary standpoint and is problematic because a physician testified with regard to the nursing standard of care. This case was tried in 1977, and most states now require experts to be qualified within the same field of study as that of the professional under scrutiny.

Failure to Follow the Chain of Command

Nurses are patient advocates. The American Nurses Association articulates the principle of patient advocacy in its Code of Ethics. "As an advocate for the patient, the nurse must be alert to and take appropriate action regarding any instances of incompetent, unethical, illegal, or impaired practice by any member of the health care team" (American Nurses Association, 2001, p. 14).

Hospitals and other health care organizations provide health care team members with a policy or hierarchy for addressing concerns about a team member's conduct that jeopardizes the patient's well-being. The ability of the nurse to intervene in a positive manner when confronting questionable provider practice requires good communication skills, assertiveness, knowledge about conflict resolution, and the chain-of-command process.

Yet successful dispute resolution cannot occur in a vacuum. It is predicated on a culture of patient safety and nurse empowerment by those in leadership positions.

Confronting questionable conduct and invoking the chain of command are associated with some degree of trepidation and fear by nurses and other health care professionals (Joint Commission on Accreditation of Healthcare Organizations, 2002). A recent study revealed that 85% to 95% of the 1,700 respondents (nurses, physicians, and administrators) were unable to speak up when observing colleagues acting incompetently, fail to follow clinical guidelines, and make mistakes. The obstacles to reporting questionable performance cited by the study respondents included fear of retaliation, negative impact on future work relationships, lack of time or opportunity to address the issue, and a failure to perceive confronting unsafe patient care as one's job or duty (American Association of Critical-Care Nurses, 2005).

The nurse has a duty to serve as patient advocate and confront practices inconsistent with quality care. Leadership support for the role of patient advocate is essential for a chain-of-command process that is functional 24 hours a day and 7 days a week. Orientation and continuing education of health care team members to the facility's chain of command policy, conflict resolution training, and communication skills are key to promoting safe quality care and preventing patient injury.

CASE EXAMPLE:

NURSES MUST INVOKE CHAIN OF COMMAND AND INTERVENE ON BEHALF OF PATIENT

Barragan. v. Antonia Watrobka, CNM (2004)

SUMMARY OF FACTS: Nicole Martinez was 18 years old with a due date of May 6, 2003. Her prenatal care was provided by a midwifery service at an urban university hospital. Her prenatal course was complicated by multiple infections, for which she was hospitalized in November 2002, January 2003, and March 2003. She was positive for Group B beta strep.

On April 18, 2003, she presented to the hospital with complaints of contractions. Upon examination it was determined she was not in active labor. Electronic fetal monitoring demonstrated a reassuring fetal heart rate. She was discharged home, but she returned to the hospital 8 hours later with ruptured membranes and in active labor.

She was admitted under the care of the midwifery service, despite a practice agreement between the hospital and midwifery service requiring obstetric management for patients with suspected chorioamnionitis. The fetal heart rate was tachycardic, and the midwife ordered penicillin.

As labor progressed, the external fetal monitoring tracing was intermittent, and the labor and delivery nurse requested internal monitoring of the fetal heart rate. The midwife denied the request on the basis of her belief that the fetus was being adequately monitored. The labor and delivery nurse brought the disagreement to the attention of the charge nurse, but no change in management resulted.

Maternal fever developed, and the baby was delivered shortly thereafter. Apgar scores were low, and the infant required intubation. The baby was diagnosed with spastic quadriplegia and cerebral palsy, and severe physical and language delays. She cannot stand, sit, walk, or roll over and is fed with a gastrostomy tube. Nursing malpractice was alleged.

NURSING ALLEGATIONS:

- Failure to follow the chain of command.
- Failure to notify obstetric attending physician.
- Failure to comply with policy requiring physician management of high-risk conditions.
- Practicing beyond the scope of a nurse practice agreement.

COURT PROCEEDINGS: Prior to trial, the hospital settled this case for US$9 million. Nurse Midwife Watrobka, Labor & Delivery Nurse Torres, and Charge Nurse Kim, were all hospital employees. Despite some positive expert reviews of the case, defense counsel determined a settlement was in the best interest of the defendants in light of the severity of the injury and the cost of damages.

Plaintiff's nursing experts were critical of all three nurses involved in the care. Midwife Watrobka was criticized for several aspects of her clinical care. She was also criticized for her failure to refer the care of this high-risk patient to the obstetric service, pursuant to her written agreement with the hospital and consistent with hospital policy.

Nurse Torres was criticized for her failure to invoke the chain of command when the midwife declined to initiate internal fetal monitoring. Despite Nurse Torres' notification of Charge Nurse Kim regarding her disagreement with the midwife's plan of care, Torres was criticized for her failure to pursue further reporting when the charge nurse did not intervene. Nurse Torres was also criticized for her failure to contact the obstetric attending physician regarding her assessment of inadequate monitoring.

Plaintiff's nursing experts were also critical of Nurse Kim for her failure to intervene on behalf of the patient and work toward a resolution of the conflict. Nurse Kim was also criticized for her failure to contact the attending obstetrician.

The nurse's duty to invoke the chain of command was breached by three levels of nurses: an advanced practice nurse, a supervisory nurse, and a staff nurse.

Midwife Watrobka, an advanced practice nurse, would not concede that chorioamnionitis required transfer of patient care to an obstetrician. State law required an advanced practice nurse to maintain a practice agreement with a physician or group of physicians. The collaborative agreement mandated transfer of high-risk patients to the obstetric service, and the agreement specified suspected chorioamnionitis as a high-risk factor.

Breach of a practice agreement can give rise to investigation and discipline by the state nursing board. Yet the hospital defendants testified that transfer was not the actual practice on the unit and had ceased to be the practice for several years. Yet the practice agreement was not updated, nor was the hospital policy.

As we learned in the case of *Bentiveniga v. St Francis Hospital*, juries are unforgiving of failures to comply with written policies, procedures, and agreements. When drafting or reviewing policies and procedures, you can be certain that these documents will be used as evidence in a malpractice trial. It is imperative that written documents are realistic and are consistently reviewed and updated.

Labor & Delivery Nurse Torres stated that she followed the chain of command by notifying the charge nurse and documenting her notification in the medical record. Notification of a supervisor regarding inconsistencies in patient care is only the first step in meeting the nursing duty of following the chain of command. Documentation of that first step to "cover yourself" does not promote quality care for the patient or release the nurse from liability.

The standard of care for meeting the obligation of following the chain of command requires pursuing and continuing up the organizational reporting structure. Nurses should be empowered and supported by hospital administration and medical staff to meet the chain-of-command standard of nursing care.

DEFENSES TO ALLEGATIONS OF MALPRACTICE

The legal system provides a process for defending against allegations of malpractice (see Chapter 9). Several defense strategies, if successful, can result in a verdict of *not guilty* for defendants.

Of course, the best defense against allegations of nursing negligence is to practice within the standard of care. A proactive approach to assure nonnegligent practice is utilization of risk management principles when delivering patient care (see Chapter 5).

Statute of Limitations

The law provides time periods within which a claim must be filed. This period is known as the Statute of Limitations.

A defense of Statute of Limitations can be asserted for claims filed outside the period prescribed by law (*Black's Law Dictionary*, 2004). Claims filed outside the period prescribed by law are dismissed on the basis of the defense that the Statute of Limitations has expired. These statutes are state specific. In some states, the statute of limitations for negligence claims is 2 years from the date of injury.

Certain jurisdictions extend the statute of limitations, for example, to 4 years, by the enactment of a discovery rule. The discovery rule provides a specified period wherein the plaintiff, using reasonable diligence, should have discovered the injury.

A minor or disabled person, as defined by law, may be provided with a longer period to file a claim. A statute of repose may be adopted to limit the statute of limitations. This statute places an outermost limit on the period within which a claim can be filed. The purpose of the statute of repose is to mitigate infinite liability of defendants.

Plaintiff's Failure to Prove the Elements of Negligence

At trial, a plaintiff must prove all four of the elements of negligence that were described previously in this chapter. The four elements are duty, breach of duty, proximate cause, and damages. However, the inability to prove each element does not prevent the case from being filed, and costs of litigation will be incurred while establishing this defense. Moreover, litigation practice is an imperfect process. Even when a plaintiff fails to prove his case, a trial can still result in a verdict in favor of the defendants.

One example of a favorable verdict for the plaintiff in the absence of proof of the essential elements of negligence involves missing or altered medical records. Certain jurisdictions have enacted rules requiring a judge to instruct the jury that missing or altered medical records are to be construed *against* the defendants and in favor of plaintiff's case.

Another example of a favorable verdict for a plaintiff in the absence of proof of negligence is a claim involving a sympathetic plaintiff with a severe injury. A weak expert who did not present well at trial or a defendant who came across as arrogant or unknowledgeable can influence a jury's verdict. Plaintiff experts and defense experts vary in their opinions on proximate cause, resulting in a battle of the experts. The verdict of a jury of lay people may make their determination based on the deposition of the expert with a stronger resume or the expert with better speaking skills.

Lastly, a defendant can make the decision to settle a lawsuit, even though the facts and expert opinions of the case do not support the allegations of malpractice. This may occur for business reasons, public relations reasons, or to avoid the cost of defense or a runaway jury verdict.

Plaintiff's Contributory or Comparative Negligence

The contributory negligence defense states that the plaintiff's own conduct contributed to the injuries he or she sustained and that the conduct was below the standard the plaintiff needed to uphold for his or her own protection (*Black's Law Dictionary*, 2004). Depending on the jurisdiction, if the plaintiff is negligent, he or she is barred from recovering damages from the defendant.

This defense views both parties as being at fault. Because the plaintiff did not act with reasonable care, he or she cannot be enriched by his or her own negligence. Since the contributory negligence defense prevents an injured plaintiff from receiving any compensation, some jurisdictions have modified the defense to account for the comparative value of each party's negligence.

Comparative negligence apportions the negligence of each party and reconciles the amount of recovery accordingly (*Black's Law Dictionary*, 2004). For example, if the damages award is US$100,000.00, and the plaintiff is found to be 25% negligent, the plaintiff would recover US$75,000.00.

Certain jurisdictions have established a threshold limit for comparative negligence, called "modified comparative negligence." Under a modified comparative negligence defense, the plaintiff is barred from receiving any damages if he or she is more than 50% negligent.

Immunity

Immunity exempts an individual or entity from liability under certain circumstances. In the past, the doctrine of charitable immunity protected nonprofit hospitals from lawsuits, and the doctrine of sovereign immunity protected government health care delivery systems from lawsuits. This immunity was either based on Common Law or specifically provided for by statute.

Currently, however, few states maintain charitable or sovereign immunity statutes. Both nonprofit hospitals and government hospitals are routine defendants in professional liability claims.

Moreover, statutory immunity provisions do not prevent a suit from being filed. Rather, an immunity provision provides the basis for dismissal of a lawsuit, if the judge determines that immunity applies. In addition, immunity is not absolute. If the alleged professional negligence is found to be willful, reckless, or grossly negligent, immunity protections would not apply.

Good Samaritan Statutes

Despite the erosion of the charitable and sovereign immunity doctrines, immunity from lawsuits still exists for health care providers under state-specific Good Samaritan statutes. Since a nurse is under no legal duty to render assistance unless there is a nurse–patient relationship, each state has enacted Good Samaritan laws to encourage health care professionals to stop and render assistance at the scene of an accident or disaster. The individual provisions of Good Samaritan laws vary greatly from state to state. The laws generally provide immunity from liability for negligent acts or omissions when rendering care in an accident, in an emergency, or under other specified circumstances.

States vary in their statutory construction of the protections of the Good Samaritan Act, and in the circumstances that constitute an emergency. Many states apply Good Samaritan immunity to hospital staff that provides emergency care to patients in the hospital who were not under their personal care. In Illinois for example, courts have used the act to immunize doctors in the context of an emergency situation arising within a hospital (*Henslee v. Provena Hospitals*, 2005). The basis for the immunity is the absence of a preexisting patient relationship that gives rise to a duty.

Good Samaritan statutes are also predicated on the requirement that the emergency care is provided in good faith and without fee. Courts have scrutinized whether the intent to provide medical services without a fee was made in good faith or whether the decision not to bill for services was made pursuant to a bad outcome or in anticipation of litigation (*Hernandez v. Alexian Brothers Health System*, 2008). It is important to stay current with the development of case law in your state regarding Good Samaritan immunity.

MEDICAL ERROR, NEVER EVENTS, AND NURSING LIABILITY

Medical Error

In 1999, the Institute of Medicine released a report entitled *To Err Is Human: Building a Safer Health System*. Medical error is defined as "any mistake, inadvertent occurrence, or unintended event or unintended outcome in the delivery of health care, which may or may not result in patient injury." (Liang & Small, 2003, p. 222).

The report stated that iatrogenic injuries caused by medical error are a leading cause of morbidity and mortality in the United States. The report estimated that as many as 98,000 people die each year as a result of hospital errors. Costs associated with medical errors were estimated at anywhere from US$17 billion to US$29 billion.

In a follow-up study, the National Quality Forum, a patient advocacy group, issued its report, *Serious Reportable Events in Healthcare*, in 2002. With a focus on health care quality measures, the report identified 27 adverse events that are serious and preventable, which was later expanded to 28 adverse events. The identification of these adverse events laid the foundation for the classification of hospital-acquired conditions (or "HACs") as "never events."

Never Events

The federal government responded to these and other reports by authorizing the Center for Medicare and Medicaid Services (CMS) to adjust Medicare payments to hospitals to encourage the prevention of HACs (The Leapfrog Group, 2007)

CMS issued final regulations implementing a policy for which a patient may not be classified into a higher-paying diagnostic-related group (DRG) if a reasonably preventable complication in care occurs. For discharges occurring on or after October 1, 2008, hospitals will not receive additional payment for cases in which one of the selected conditions was not present on admission; that is, the claim would be paid as though the HAC, the secondary diagnosis, were not present (Social Security Act, Section 1886, 42 U.S.C. 1395ww[d][4]).

The new rule renders the selected HAC nonreimbursable by Medicare. The conditions selected by the Secretary of Health and Human Services for nonreimbursement had to meet certain criteria. The criteria include that the condition (a) being reasonably preventable through the application of evidence-based guidelines, (b) be designated as a major complication, and (c) be of high cost or high volume. (CMS, 2009). From the list of 28 serious adverse events, 11 HAC's ,or never events, were identified for which no reimbursement will be provided. These never events are as follows:

- Postsurgery retention of foreign object
- Air embolism
- Blood incompatibility
- Decubitus ulcer (Stages 3 and 4)
- Falls and trauma
- Catheter-associated urinary tract infection
- Vascular catheter-associated infection
- Mediastinitis postcoronary artery bypass graft

- Surgical-site infection for specified procedures
- Extreme manifestations of poor glycemic control
- Postoperative DVT/pulmonary embolism related to hip or knee procedures

Table 8.2 shows data published by the CMS listing the 11 HACs, the number of cases of each condition that occurred in fiscal year 2007, and the cost of treatment for the condition per hospital stay.

Nursing Liability for Never Events

The new rules are billing and reimbursement rules and do not define the standard of care for treatment. However, the aforementioned HACs represent conditions that commonly appear in lawsuits alleging professional negligence.

Is the occurrence of a never event proof of negligence? A plaintiff might argue that allegations related to any of the 11 HACs constitute negligence per se. Or the plaintiff might argue that the occurrence of a HAC constitutes *res ipsa loquitur* (see discussion in this chapter on negligence per se and *res ipsa loquitur*). Will the plaintiff still be required to demonstrate that the nurse did not meet the standard of care?

Table 8.2 Frequency and Cost of Hospital-Acquired Conditions

Hospital-Acquired Condition	Number of Cases	Cost/Hospital Stay
Foreign object retained after surgery	750	$63,631
Air embolism	57	$71,636
Blood incompatibility	24	$50,455
Pressure ulcer stages III and IV	257,412	$43,180
Falls and trauma	193,566	$33,894
Catheter-associated urinary tract infection	12,185	$44,043
Vascular catheter-associated infection	29,536	$103,027
Mediastinitis after CABG	69	$299,237
Surgical site infection	269 37 (total 306)	$148,172 233,614 (total 381,786)
Manifestations of poor glycemic control	11,469 3,248 212 (total 14,929)	42,974 35,215 36,581 (total 114,770)

Source: Based on data from Fiscal Year 2007.

The CMS rules do not change the legal analyses of negligence per se and *res ipsa loquitur*. A plaintiff's assertion that a never event should never occur and that the existence of a HAC is proof in and of itself of negligence can be effectively countered by competent defense counsel.

CMS reimbursement rules are irrelevant in a malpractice claim and should not be admissible in a civil trial as evidence of negligence. A statute that describes reimbursement policies cannot support a claim of malpractice, as it does not provide evidence of a deviation from a standard of care or establish violation of a statute.

CMS's rate of reimbursement to a defendant health care provider for care related to a complication is irrelevant to the issues that are resolved by the finder of fact in a malpractice claim. Evidence that the provider was refused reimbursement is inadmissible. How a collateral source, like CMS or any other payer, handled a medical bill, is inadmissible as evidence of civil liability. The use of the phrase "never event" in the context of malpractice litigation is misleading and nondescriptive. The term is prejudicial in clinical situations where there is medical evidence that the condition can occur even when a patient receives appropriate care. In point of fact, CMS generally does not use the term "never event" to describe conditions covered by the new rule. Rather, they are referred to as Serious Reportable Events, and the HAC's for purposes of CMS payment issues are drawn from the list of Serious Reportable Events.

HACs are medically complex and may be caused by a number of factors unrelated to negligence. CMS's reimbursement rules are irrelevant to subsequent malpractice litigation brought after the fact by a plaintiff. The rules do not prove what the standard of care is, whether the nurse deviated from the standard, whether an alleged deviation proximately caused harm, or what the damages are.

CMS rules do provide a new coding process whereby the hospital can indicate whether the condition was present on admission, so that reimbursement will be provided for treatment associated with that condition. The conditions can occur even when patients receive appropriate care.

The impact of CMS's recent reimbursement policies on malpractice litigation is a matter of speculation at this point. However, the impact of the reimbursement rules on a hospital's bottom line is clear. Going forward, Medicare, Medicaid, and private insurance companies will deny reimbursement to hospitals for costs related to HACs.

In addition, Medicare Law also requires CMS to reduce payments to hospitals that don't successfully report quality measures. The intent of CMS's reimbursement rules is to provide a powerful new incentive to improve patient care. A realignment of incentives that rewards proactive measures aimed at preventing HACs, and denies reimbursement for complications, meets the goal of encouraging safety and reducing never events (see Chapter 3).

The American Hospital Association (AHA) has taken a proactive approach and sent an advisory letter to its 5,000 member hospitals, health systems, and other health care organizations (AHA, 2009).

The AHA states that America's hospitals are committed to delivering safe care and hospitals work hard to implement preventive systems that provide the best care possible. The letter further states that upon the occurrence of an adverse event, hospitals have undertaken strategies to support the injured patient and family. Many hospitals have developed policies for addressing billing issues related to preventable adverse events.

The AHA has adopted a set of principles that provide guidance on when a hospital should forego payment from patients, insurers, and employers for the costs associated with a serious event that occurred to a patient during the course of care. The AHA recommended that its member hospitals review their no-charge policies and consider implementing changes consistent with CMS's reimbursement rules.

PREVENTION

Although there is no absolute method for avoiding lawsuits, preventive measures can be undertaken that may preclude allegations of professional negligence against the nurse. These measures help create a set of preventive principles that can guide everyday practice within a proactive framework that focuses awareness of professional negligence.

Adherence to Standards of Care

The law does not require the nurse to protect patients against every foreseeable harm. The law requires the nurse to practice in accordance with what other reasonably qualified nurses would do in the same situation.

Practicing within established standards of care sounds so simple. Yet it requires that the nurse be knowledgeable regarding the conduct required by those standards. Participation in continuing education courses can be accomplished by attending in-service education offered by an employer. Continuing education can also be obtained at an outside conference offered by a professional group. Both options help assure that the nurse's level of knowledge is consistent with the current standard of care.

Evaluation of skills through checklists or performance evaluations serve to maintain and improve technical skills. This is especially important in light of the burgeoning technology of the health care industry. The standard of care is an evolution; it progresses and changes at a dynamic rate. Maintaining skills and knowledge of new treatments, new technology, and new equipment is vital to nursing practice. Updating one's skill set and knowledge base to keep up with new or established advances can also be accomplished through journal articles and professional organization publications. Assuring that nursing practice adheres to the standard of care can best be accomplished by utilizing each available opportunity for education and training.

Job Orientation

Another vital preventive principle for limiting exposure to allegations of professional negligence is adequate orientation to a new job. This is true regardless of the nurse's previous training or experience. Although it may seem obvious that a recently graduated nurse requires extensive orientation, so too does the experienced nurse who is assuming a new position.

Whereas certain nursing skills may transfer across specialties, an experienced nurse will require orientation to become acclimated to a new clinical environment. Transition to a new facility or a new unit within the same facility, or to a new specialty, requires orientation to procedures, equipment, documentation forms, unit staff, caseload, chain of command, and a variety of other tools necessary to provide safe patient care.

Orientation checklists are useful for both the new employee and for management. An orientation checklist delineates performance expectations and provides documentation that the expectations have been met. Communication by the new hire regarding learning needs is key to a successful orientation process. No question should be left unasked, and nurses undergoing orientation should be encouraged and empowered to identify skills that need further development.

Job Descriptions

Closely related to the preventive principle of job orientation is the matter of job descriptions. A job description articulates the qualifications of the position and defines patient care responsibilities. When seeking a new position, it is imperative that the nurse request and carefully review the information provided in the job description. Acceptance of a position requires the nurse to perform his or her role within the parameters of the job description.

Compliance with a job description supports the nurse on several playing fields. First and foremost, compliance with a job description helps assure patient safety. Second, professional conduct and clinical practice that is consistent with a job description can be utilized by the nurse in a positive manner at the time of his or her performance evaluation. Lastly, conformity with a job description is important from a liability perspective.

In the event of a lawsuit alleging nursing negligence, the job description may be introduced into evidence. The nurse's conformity with the job description can be proof that the nurse's conduct complied with the standard of care. On the other hand, the plaintiff can also use the job description to demonstrate that the nurse's conduct was not supported by the job description and the nurse failed to meet the standard of care.

Policies, Procedures, and Protocols

Following patient care policies, procedures and protocols is the best defense against allegations of nursing negligence. Patient care manuals are the mothers of all reference materials, and a nurse should visit them often. Be certain that patient care procedures will be scrutinized by the attorneys for both the plaintiff and the defendants. Whether the written procedure manual will support a plaintiff's case was decided by the nurse on the day of the alleged injury. Whether the policies, procedures, and protocols help defend the nurse's conduct is exclusively under the control of that nurse. Implementation of patient care policies, procedures, and protocols will support and defend the care provided. Deviation in nursing practice from the responsibility and technique delineated in patient care manuals is tantamount to admitting liability. As discussed previously in this chapter, the case example of *Bentiveniga v. St. Francis Hospital* illustrates the liability associated with the failure to follow policies and procedures.

Patient care manuals are instrumental in providing nonnegligent care and further promote patient safety and quality care. Because these documents are based on current, accepted practice, adherence to patient care procedures helps the nurse avoid omissions in care that could result in injury to a patient. The development of policies, procedures, and protocols is influenced by many factors, including nursing and medical literature, scientific research, federal and state legislation, including the CMS's Conditions of Participation and local departments of public health, accreditation standards, patient care rights, and court decisions. Patient care manuals should be updated on a regular basis to incorporate advancements in care, new technologies and equipment, expanded scopes of nursing practice, and recent legislation.

CONCLUSIONS AND TRENDS

As nurses gain professional recognition and autonomy, they will continue to be held accountable for their actions. They are confronted with increased challenges in the workplace as the health care delivery system continues to make sweeping changes.

It is important to note that in a medical malpractice or negligence action, nurses are held to the standard of care that existed at the time the action occurred. Even though the standard of care for nursing practice is constantly changing to incorporate the scientific and technological advances or medicine, nurses need to be knowledgeable of the current standards of nursing practice in order to deliver safe patient care.

Nurses play a vital role in the health care delivery system as they deliver care and advocate for their patients.

KEY POINTS

- Negligence is defined as the failure to exercise the standard of care that a reasonably prudent person would exercise in the same or similar circumstances (*Black's Law Dictionary*, 2004).
- Negligent conduct can occur by acts of commission or omission. Negligent conduct can be alleged when a person commits an act that a reasonably prudent person would not do; this type of conduct is negligence by commission.
- Negligent conduct can also be alleged when a person fails to act when a duty exists; this type of conduct is negligence by omission.
- The standard of care is a legal concept and has been judicially defined by the courts as the exercise of the same degree of knowledge, skill, and ability as an ordinarily careful professional would exercise under similar circumstances (*Seavers v. Methodist Medical Center of Oak Ridge*, 1999).

⬜ There are four essential elements of negligence: duty, breach of duty, causation (proximate or direct), and damages.

⬜ For the plaintiff to prevail in a negligence lawsuit, he or she must prove all four elements of negligence.

REFERENCES

Academy of Managed Care Pharmacy. (2009). *Concepts in managed care pharmacy series*. Retrieved January 13, 2009, from www.amcp.org/amcp.ark

American Association of Critical-Care Nurse and Vital Smarts. (2005). *Silence kills: The seven crucial conversations for heathcare*. Aliso Viejo, CA: Author.

American Hospital Association. (2008). *Implementing a no-charge policy for serious, adverse events*. Retrieved January 26, 2009, from www.aha.org/aha/advisory/2008/080212-quality-adv

American Nurses Association. (2001). *Code of ethics for nurses with interpretive statements*, p. 14. Washington, DC: Author.

40A AM. JUR. 2D Hospitals and Asylums § 1194 (2008).

31 Am. Jur. 3d *Proof of Facts* 203, § 3

Barragan, Mia, a Minor, by and through her parents and next friends, Nicole Martinez and Saul Barragan, and Nicole Martinez ans Saul Barragan, Individually, v. Antonia Watrobka, Mirella Torres, Radhika Ailawadi, Arlene Wallace, and Lauren Kim, Circuit Court of Cook County, Illinois, 2004 L 002958.

Black's Law Dictionary (8th ed.). (2004). Tort. Retrieved January 23, 2009, from http://west.thomson.com/home

Centers for Medicare and Medicaid Services. (2009). *Hospital acquired conditions overview*. Retrieved January 20, 2009, from www.cms.hhs.gov/HospAcqCond

Chambers v. St. Mary's School, 82 Ohio St. 3d 563, 697 N.E. 2d 198, 127 Ed. Law Rep. 997 (1998).

Estate of Rachelle Bentiveniga, Deceased v. St. Francis Hospital of Evanston, Circuit Court of Cook County, Illinois, 2004 L 007673.

Harris County Hospital District v Joe Estrada et al., 872 S.W. 2nd 759 (1996).

Heastie v. Roberts, 226 Ill. 2d 515, 315 Ill. Dec. 735, 877 N.E.2d 1064 (2007); Methodist Hospitals, Inc. v. Johnson, 856 N.E. 2d 718 (Ind. Ct. App. 2006).

Henslee v. Provena Hospitals, 373 F.Supp.2d 802 (N.D.Ill. 2005).

Hernandez v. Alexian Brothers Health System (Ill. App. 1 Dist., 2008).

Howie v. Walsh, 2005 WL 464847(N.C. Ct. App. 2005).

Institute of Medicine. (1999, November). *To err is human: Building a safer health system*. Washington, DC: Author.

Joint Commission on Accreditation of Healthcare Organizations. (2002). Root causes: A failure to communicate: Identifying and overcoming communication barriers. *Joint Commission Perspective on Patient Saf*ety, 2(9), 4–5.

Lanza v. Poretti, 537 F. Supp. 777 (1982). 10 FED. R. EVID. Serv. 1104.

Liang, B. A. & Small, S.D. (2003). Communicating about care: Addressing federal-state issues in peer review and mediation to promote patient safety. *Houston J. Health L. Policy*, Vol 3. pp. 219–264.

National Coordinating Council for Medication Error Reporting and Prevention. (2009). *What is a medication error*. Retrieved January 21, 2009, from http:www.nccmerp.org/about MedErrors.html

National Quality Forum. (2002). *Serious reportable events in healthcare*. Washington, DC: Author.

Ramsey, John Jr. et al., v. Physicians Memorial Hospital, Inc., 36 Md. App. 32, 373 A.2d 26 (1977).

Searcy v. Brown 607 S.W. 2d 937 (Tex. Civ. App. Houston [1st Dist.] (1980).

Seavers v. Methodist Medical Center of Oak Ridge 9 S.W. 3d 86 (Tenn. 1999).

Slade v. Smith's Management Corp. 119 Idaho 482, 808 P.2d 401 (1991).

Social Security Act Section 1886 (d) (4); (42 U.S.C. 1395ww(d)(4).

Sullivan, Juanita, Individually and as Special Administrator of the Estate of Burns Sullivan, Deceased, v. Edward Hospital, et al., 209 Ill.2d 100, 806 N.E. 2d 645, 282 Ill. Dec. 348 (2004).

The Leapfrog Group. (2007). *Leapfrog Group Hospital survey*. Washington, DC: Author.

U.S. Food and Drug Administration Center for Drug Evaluation and Research. (2004, February). *Medication errors*. Washington, DC: Author.

ADDITIONAL READINGS

Brent, N. J. (2007). *Nurses and the law: A guide to principles and application*. Philadelphia: W. B. Saunders.

Finkelman, A. (1986). *Policies and procedures for psychiatric nursing*. Rockville, MD: Aspen.

Meyers, K., & Fergusson, P. (1988). *Nurse at risk*. Des Moines, IA: HealthPro.

Chapter Nine

Anatomy of Civil and Criminal Trials

Paula DiMeo Grant and Neil J. Reardon

OBJECTIVES

- Become familiar with the process and procedures of a civil trial.
- Understand the burdens of proof required in a court of law.
- Define discovery and identify discovery methods.
- Describe the process of jury selection.
- Define the role of the expert nurse witness.
- Describe function of the jury and deliberations.
- Define the crimes of a misdemeanor and a felony.
- Describe Miranda rights.
- Understand the implications of a charge of "Driving While Under the Influence" (DWI/DUI) of drugs or alcohol, and professional licensing.

INTRODUCTION

Throughout this textbook you have read the decisions of various cases brought in federal and state courts in this country. Before a lawsuit is filed in a court of law, counsel must conduct an analysis of the issues and applicable laws to determine the appropriate court to bring the action. The statute of limitations is examined to see if in fact the action is time barred by the statute.

This chapter will illustrate the judicial process and procedure for bringing civil and criminal actions. The burden of proof for these actions, as well as the parties responsible for the burden, will be reviewed. The importance of discovery and admissible evidence are also described. Jury selection, role of the judiciary, and the role of the expert witness will be discussed. In many instances, nurse leaders, because of their educational background and expertise, serve in the important role of expert witness to assist counsel, judges, and juries in the analysis and explanation of medi-colegal issues. Case examples will be used to illustrate salient points.

ANATOMY OF A CIVIL TRIAL

Pretrial Phase

Preliminary Steps to a Civil Trial

Sandra Day O'Connor, former associate justice of the Supreme Court of the United States, said it best:

> The courts of this country should not be the place where the resolu-tion of disputes begins. They should be the places where disputes end—after alternative methods of resolving disputes have been considered and tried. The courts of various jurisdictions have been called the "courts of last resort." (American Bar Association [ABA], 1991).

Unfortunately, the courts of this country are, in fact, where the res-olution of many disputes begins. Civil trials are costly, time consuming and can add an emotional toll. In federal courts, a civil trial is a right afforded by the U.S. Constitution, Amendment Seven that states:

> In suits at common law, where the value in controversy shall exceed twenty dollars, the right of trial by jury shall be preserved, and no fact tried by a jury, shall be otherwise reexamined in any court of the United States, than according to the rules of common law.

State courts also offer a similar right to a civil trial that is found in the state's constitution. Plaintiffs and defendants can relinquish the right to a trial by jury. And a bench trial (judge without a jury) is also used in certain cases, such as a family or child custody matter and some probate matters.

Plaintiff Versus Defendant: Filing the Complaint

A lawsuit begins with the plaintiff filing a complaint in the appropriate court of law. A complaint is a legal document or formal statement referred to as a pleading naming the parties to the action and the allegations of wrongdoing set forth in counts stating that the law has been violated. In a civil case, the plaintiff is the party instituting the action against the defendant who may be an individual and/or a corporation. For example, in a medical malpractice case, it is the "Injured Party versus Physician, Nurse and/or Hospital." When there is a wrongful death action based on allegations of medical malpractice, it is the decedent's estate and administrator or executor of the estate who bring the action.

Subsequently, after the filing of the complaint in a court of law, the defendant(s) will be served the complaint with a court order, or a subpoena, a legal writ mandating the defendant(s) to appear in court. The defendant(s) must respond within the specified time frame by filing an answer to the complaint or by filing a counterclaim (claim in opposition) against the plaintiff. In the event the defendant does not respond in a timely manner, a default judgment may be entered against the defendant.

Depending on the circumstances, lawsuits may be instituted in state or federal courts. It is one of the decisions made by counsel before filing the suit. A court will have no authority to decide a case unless it has jurisdiction over the person or property involved. To have jurisdiction, "a court must have authority over the subject matter of the case and the court must be able to exercise control over the defendant, or the property involved must be located in the area under the court's control" (ABA, n.d., p. 1).

Burden of Proof

In a civil case, the plaintiff has the burden of proof and the standard is the preponderance of evidence or, in some cases, by clear and convincing evidence. The burden of proof is the requirement to prove or disprove a disputed fact. To prevail, the plaintiff must prove the allegations in the complaint by more convincing evidence than that provided by the defendant. This is accomplished by the presentation of testimony and evidence through the discovery process and at trial. The criminal burden of proof is a stricter standard and will be discussed later in this chapter.

Evidence

Generally, evidence will be admissible in a court of law provided that it is relevant and not hearsay. Hearsay is a statement made by a witness in court that is not first hand and is offered in evidence to prove the truth of the matter asserted. Hearsay is not admissible in a court of law.

Evidence may be used by the parties to prove or refute the allegations made or the facts presented. The presentation of evidence takes two basic forms: (1) testimony, and/or (2) documentary, which are reports that require authentication and is discussed more fully in this chapter. According to *Black's Law Dictionary*, "Evidence is something including testimony, documents and tangible objects that tends to prove or disprove the existence of an alleged fact" (2010, p. 498). The admissibility of evidence is governed by the rules of evidence of the court and are strictly followed.

Medical Malpractice: Certificates of Merit

Prior to filing a medical malpractice action, the attorney may be required to obtain a certificate of merit from a physician who provides information indicating that the case is legitimate. Most states require these certificates to prevent frivolous suits from being filed (Widman, 2009). For example, in the state of Maryland, to bring a malpractice action against a physician, the physician providing the certificate of merit must include the following three elements:

1. Where the doctor is licensed to practice medicine;
2. An opinion written with a reasonable degree of probability that the treating doctor departed from the applicable standard of care in treating the plaintiff and whether there was damage from the breach of the appropriate standard of care; and
3. That the doctor does not devote annually more than 20% of the doctor's professional activities that directly involve testimony in personal injury claims (Miller, 2006). The requirements for certificates of merit regarding these claims vary from state to state.

Discovery Process

The discovery process is an important part of the pretrial phase of a lawsuit. It allows the parties to learn the details about the case, and also provides a formal mechanism for the parties to exchange information regarding the evidence and witnesses to the matter at hand. It is designed to prevent surprises at trial. Discovery clarifies and defines the issues presented and identifies the witnesses to be called at trial and the purpose of their testimony. It is accomplished through the use of interrogatories, depositions of the parties and witnesses, production of documents, and requests for admissions. The Federal Rules of Civil Procedure 26–37 provide the mechanisms for discovery as well as state court rules of procedure.

Interrogatories and production of documents. Interrogatories are a series of questions served by the plaintiff to the defendant and served by the defendant to the plaintiff. They are to be answered in writing and signed under oath. Requests for production of documents and requests for admissions may accompany the interrogatories. Requests for production of documents are used to further clarify a procedure or question at issue. They may consist of certain records, documents, and tangible objects and are considered evidence. Interrogatories provide the parties with vital information regarding the case in preparation for depositions and trial. Below is a sample interrogatory to a physician or a nurse defendant:

> Sample: Interrogatory Number 1:
> Set forth in detail your full name, address, educational background, licenses, and certifications and dates obtained.
> Answer: Interrogatory Number 1:
> See attached curriculum vitae.

Depositions. Depositions provide another significant mechanism for discovery, and are conducted by opposing counsel. They enable the parties to learn the facts and issues of the case in a face-to-face setting. A deposition is an out-of-court testimony, given under oath, by a person (parties or witnesses) for settlement purposes or to be used at trial. The testimony is recorded by a court reporter or videotaped. Testimony given at a deposition can be used to impeach or discredit a witness for inconsistent statements at trial. Depositions are also useful tools for assessing the demeanor and the ability of the deponent (person being deposed) to answer questions. It also gives opposing counsel a chance to meet in person if they have not already done so. The following table presents tips that will help to prepare for a deposition.

Exhibit 9.1 Deposition Tips

1. Preparation is the key.
2. Thorough review of all pertinent documents.
3. Be familiar with the process.
4. Understand the question.
5. Just answer the questions asked.
6. Answers should be as succinct as possible.
7. Tell the truth.
8. Be courteous.
9. Speak clearly; depositions are recorded or videotaped.

Motions

Motions are requests made by either party to the judge to make a legal ruling. Common pretrial motions include a Motion to Discover and a Motion to Dismiss and are explained below.

A Motion to Discover is used when one party seeks to gain information from the adverse party and is unable to do so in the regular course of interrogatories or production of documents.

A Motion to Dismiss is when one party asks the court to dismiss the lawsuit because the case lacks a legally sound basis or is lacking of a prima facie case.

A prima facie case is defined by *Black's Law Dictionary* (2010) as 1. "The establishment of a legally required rebuttable presumption. 2. A party's production of enough evidence to allow a fact-trier to infer the fact at issue and rule in the party's favor" (p. 1028).

Motion for Summary Judgment

A motion for a summary judgment is when one party asks the court for judgment on the merits before the trial when there is no dispute about the facts and only a question of law remains (ABA, "Steps in Trial," n.d.). In American jurisprudence, questions of law are for the court to determine and questions of facts are in the purview of the jury upon hearing the evidence.

During litigation, it may be the belief of a party that the depositions and other discovery methods demonstrate that there are no genuine issues of material fact that a jury needs to consider for a verdict to be rendered. Thus, summary judgment is the mechanism used as described below.

CASE EXAMPLE:

Hoard v. Roper Hospital, Inc., et al. (S.C. 2010)

Issue: Whether or not it was proper to reverse a summary judgment motion granted by the Lower Court to defendant radiologist?

SUMMARY OF FACTS: This tragic case involved a newborn who suffered from brain damage and paralysis as a result of alleged negligence of four defendants following the insertion of a umbilical vein catheter (UVC), which apparently was malpositioned and caused injuries. All defendants, except the radiologist, entered into a settlement agreement with the plaintiff.

The radiologist's motion for summary judgment was based on the fact that his alleged failures did not cause the catastrophic outcome. Thus, the radiologist argued that without the requisite element of causation, there could not be medical negligence. The attorneys for the radiologist further argued that the treating physician had reviewed the X-rays himself and made an independent decision not to reposition the UVC. Therefore, culpability, if any, simply rested with the treating physician.

COURT'S DECISIONS: The Lower Court agreed and granted the defendant radiologist's motion for summary judgment. The case was appealed to an intermediate court (the next highest court) that reversed the decision of the trial court. Upon appeal to the Supreme Court of South Carolina, the summary judgment in favor of the radiologist was reinstated (Brenner & Bal, 2010).

Whereas this case represents an example of when a summary judgment motion was appropriate, summary judgment motions are granted, as a matter of law, when there is no genuine issue of material fact. They are granted with great care and careful analysis as it precludes the plaintiff's case from going forward to trial.

Expert Witnesses

Expert witnesses play a vital role in civil malpractice actions. They assist the judge and jury to understand scientific evidence and the appropriate standard of care. Depending on the circumstances, they may be consulting witnesses who do not testify at trial. In the alternative, they may be witnesses testifying at trial.

It is likely that expert witnesses will be deposed by opposing counsel during the pretrial phase. Expert witnesses testifying at trial should be aware that any testimony given during the deposition, or any opinion letter written, may be used to impeach or discredit them in the event of inconsistent statements. Diligent preparation for the deposition is necessary. Complete knowledge of the facts and the expert witness's expertise will contribute to his or her credibility both during the deposition and at trial. Professional nurses qualify as expert witnesses; the qualifications are later discussed.

Role of the expert nurse witness. Educational preparation, state laws, and court decisions have helped shape the progress professional nurses have made to gain autonomy and accountability, thus paving the way for them to depose as expert nurse witnesses. The decision to serve as an expert nurse witness rests solely with the nurse. Before accepting an assignment as an expert nurse witness, the nurse should have a clear understanding of the case, the expectations of counsel, and have completed a conflicts of interest check, indicating that there are no factors present that would impair his or her objectivity.

Upon acceptance of an assignment as an expert nurse witness, it is prudent for the nurse to have a signed agreement with the attorney or law firm outlining the terms and conditions including the responsibilities, the time-frame for completion, and the compensation for services rendered. The nature of the case and the number of parties will dictate the number of hours anticipated. Most experts are hired in the capacity of independent contractors. For details on the independent contractor status, see Chapter 4.

Nursing negligence/malpractice and the nurse expert. An in-depth analysis of nursing negligence/malpractice was covered in Chapter 8 of this book. As a review, and in the context of the expert nurse witness, the underlying question in every nursing negligence or malpractice action is whether or not the nurse's action, either an omission or commission, deviated from the standard of care. If a deviation occurred, did that deviation proximately cause harm or injury to the patient? In proving nursing negligence or malpractice, the following elements, in question format, must be present and answered in the affirmative:

1. Did the nurse owe a duty to the patient?
2. Did the nurse breach that duty by an act or omission?
3. Did the breach of duty proximately cause injury or damage to the patient?
4. Did the patient suffer a loss or damages as a result of the above?

The expert nurse witness begins the case evaluation and opinion formation by analyzing those questions.

Case evaluation and opinion formulation. Before an expert nurse witness can give an opinion as to whether or not the standard of care was breached, it is crucial to evaluate the case by reviewing all the medical records, including nurses' notes, physicians' notes and orders, laboratory reports, radiology reports, and other pertinent documents. Establishing a time-line of events can prove useful. Additional resources, such as Nurse Practice Act, Code for Nurses, standards of nursing practice, facility policies and procedures, nursing textbooks, journals, and licensing regulations are helpful in formulating opinions. An important caveat to keep in mind is that the standard of care to be examined is the one in effect at the time the injury occurred. Depending on the jurisdiction, a nurse expert may be required to substantiate his or her opinion a written, signed statement.

Completion of Discovery: Pretrial Settlement

Upon completion of discovery, the parties may enter into settlement negotiations or mediation. Most courts require pretrial settlement conferences to encourage settlement. It is reported that the vast majority of cases are settled before trial (Canary, 1991).

In some jurisdictions, there is mandatory mediation required by the court. For example, since the early 1990s, the District of Columbia Superior Court mandates mediation in civil cases, including medical malpractice after discovery has been completed and before trial. The program has a panel of experienced attorney/mediators who are, based on their expertise, assigned to mediate medical malpractice cases. The mediation program has been successful and it is well received by parties and attorneys. Mediation empowers the parties to control the outcome of the case. In the event that the case does not settle at mediation, the parties proceed to trial. For more information on negotiation and mediation see Chapter 10.

Once the pretrial phase has been completed, if the case is not dismissed or settled, it will proceed to trial. Counsel will have spent many hours in preparation. The theory or legal justification and theme or story line has been developed. Jury selection begins.

Trial Phase

Qualifications of Expert Witnesses

The qualifications of expert witnesses are described by Federal Rule of Civil of Civil Procedure, Rule 702, which states:

> If scientific, technical or other specialized knowledge will assist the trier of fact to understand the evidence or determine a fact in issue, a witness qualified as an expert by knowledge, skill, experience, training or education may testify thereto in the form of an opinion or otherwise.

The qualifications of the nurse to serve as an expert in a court of law are determined by the judge. Although courts have increasingly looked to the nursing profession in addressing issues pertaining to nursing malpractice, in the past it was the physician who testified as to the standard of nursing care, and in some jurisdictions that practice remains.

CASE EXAMPLES:

Haney v. Alexander (N.C. App. 1984)

Issue: Whether or not it was appropriate for a physician to testify as to the standard of nursing care in a wrongful death action?

COURT'S DECISION: In Haney, the Appellate Court in North Carolina addressed the issue of a physician testifying as to the standard of nursing care. It ruled that the lower court acted within its discretion by allowing a cardiologist and family practitioner to testify regarding a nurse's duty to "completely" monitor the vital signs such as blood pressure and to notify the physician of the patient's deteriorating condition that ultimately led to his death. The court found that in the context of basic nursing duties the plaintiff's medical witness demonstrated sufficient knowledge of the relevant standard of care to be deemed an expert witness.

This practice is changing as exemplified by the following case example.

Sullivan v. Edward Hospital et al. (IL. S. Ct., 2004).

Issue: Whether or not a board certified internist was competent to testify as to the standard of care of a nurse in a malpractice action?

SUMMARY OF FACTS: The facts of this case reveal that a 74-year-old male was admitted to the hospital for a urinary tract infection. He had a history of suffering a stroke and was partially paralyzed. It was reported that though he could not speak, he was able to understand. During the evening shift, he attempted to get out of bed and became agitated. The evening nurse notified his treating physician and requested a posey restraint. Instead, the physician ordered a sedative which was administered. Although he was monitored, he fell out of bed, struck his head, and sustained a head injury as a result. (He expired in 1999 from an unrelated event.)

In 1998, this case was filed against the treating physician and the hospital. The complaint alleged that the hospital, through the nurse, and the physician failed to monitor, medicate, and restrain the plaintiff. Damages were sought for negligence. At trial, the plaintiff called a board certified internist to testify as to the applicable standard of nursing care. The physician expert testified as to his extensive experience working with doctors and nurses in the area of patient fall protection.

His testimony included a deviation of the standards of nursing care in three areas: (1) the nurse failed to notify her supervisor that the patient was a fall risk, (2) the nurse's failure to provide an alternative to the posey restraint, and (3) the nurse's failure to properly communicate the patient's condition to the physician (The American Association of Nurse Attorneys [TAANA], 2007).

LOWER COURT'S DECISION: The Trial Court entered a directed verdict for the hospital because the plaintiff's only medical expert was ruled incompetent to testify as to the standard of care for the nursing profession. A directed verdict is a ruling made by the trial judge that takes the case from the jury because the evidence will permit only one reasonable verdict (*Black's Law Dictionary*, 2010). There was a jury verdict in favor of the defendant physician.

APPELLATE COURT'S DECISION: The Appellate Court affirmed the decision as did the Supreme Court of Illinois. TAANA submitted an Amicus Brief (friend of the court) on behalf of the defendant, and the Supreme Court in its ruling cited the TAANA brief.

For your information, the *Sullivan* case is reproduced in its entirety in the Appendix. The Sullivan decision is an extremely important one for nurses. Its positive impact on the profession of nursing will have lasting effects.

The Trial Phase

Jury Selection

Serving as a juror in a trial can be a rewarding and challenging experience. Potential jurors are assembled by the courts using the names of licensed drivers and registered voters. In civil cases, there is a variation in the number of jurors impaneled (selected and sworn-in) depending on the community. In high-profile cases, attorneys may engage the services of trial consultants in the selection of the jury.

The following rule specifies number of jurors and polling procedures that apply in a trial. Polling procedures are used at the time a jury announces its verdict.

Rule 46 of Federal Rules of Civil Procedure states: Number of Jurors, Verdict: Polling:

(a) Number of Jurors. A jury must begin with a least 6 and no more than 12 members, and each juror must participate in the verdict unless excused under Rule 47 (c).

(b) Verdict: Unless the parties stipulate otherwise, the verdict must be unanimous and must be returned by a jury of at least 6 members.

(c) Polling: After a verdict is returned but before the jury is discharged, the court must on a party's request, or may on its own, poll the jurors individually. If the poll reveals a lack of unanimity or a lack of assent by the number of jurors that the parties stipulated to, the court may direct the jury to deliberate further or may order a new trial. (LII, 2010)

Voir Dire

Prospective jurors are screened to prevent bias on the jury. This process is called *voir dire*. According to *Black's Law Dictionary* (2010), *voir dire* is "a preliminary examination of a prospective juror by a judge or lawyer to decide whether the prospect is qualified and suitable to serve on a jury."

A *voir dire* consists of a series of questions asked to potential jurors by the judge or attorney to assist counsel in the jury selection process.

If the potential juror answers questions that show that he or she cannot be impartial, the potential juror will be excused for cause. There is no limit to the number of jurors who may be challenged and dismissed for cause, which also includes dismissal based on unfavorable background information. On the other hand, there is a limitation on excusing jurors because they do not meet the attorney's jury profile for the case. This is called peremptory challenges, and there are strict limits set on the number or peremptory challenges that can be made (Canary, 1991).

Jury Selection Questionnaire

In some instances, a prospective juror may be asked to complete a questionnaire as was done in the following case, in re Benedictin Products Liability Litigation, and reported in the *BNA Civil Trial Manual* (1987). The questionnaire had 46 questions consisting of name, address, date of birth, whether married or single, and the categories of employment, education, family information, as well as information about the juror's knowledge of, and feelings about, the case. The questions were probing, and the following instructions accompanied the questionnaire.

Potential juror questionnaire instructions.

- You may become a juror in the trial of the Benedictin litigation. The attached questions require answers. They will assist the selection of a jury to hear this case.
- Please answer all of the questions to the best of your ability. Do not ask for help.
- We need you to answer honestly so that we may select a fair and impartial jury. Do not assume that any of your answers will qualify or disqualify you from serving on this jury.
- Please print your answers clearly in black ink.
- If you cannot answer a question because you do not understand it or do not know the answer, please write in "Do Not Understand" or "Do Not Know" in the space provided for your answer. If you want to explain your answer and there is not enough room to do this in the space provided for the answer, please write in the margin next to the questions.
- Beginning now please do not watch any TV program, listen to any radio programs or read any articles concerning Benedictin, or discuss it with anyone unless you are excused from jury duty in this case.
- Please do not attempt to learn anything about Benedictin. Your cooperation and help is very much appreciated (Reproduced with permission

from *BNA Civil Trial Manual*, pp. 71:212–213. Copyright 1986 by The Bureau of National Affairs, Inc. (800-372-1033)http://www.bna.com).

The Ohio jury chosen in the Benedictin case returned a verdict for the drug manufacturer based on its findings that the antinausea drug Benedictin did not cause birth defects in the children of women who used the drug during pregnancy (*BNA Civil Trial Manual*, 1986).

Trial Begins With Opening Statements

Once the jury is impaneled, a trial begins with an opening statement by counsel for the plaintiff. The purpose of the opening statement is to tell the jury what the case is about and how counsel plans to present testimony and evidence to the jury. It should not be argumentative. It gives counsel an opportunity to tell the plaintiff's side of the story. The jury is instructed not to consider the opening statements as evidence. Following the plaintiff's opening statement, defendant's counsel gives the defendant's version of the case in an opening statement. Counsel for both plaintiff and defendant can be creative in his or her approach to opening statements as they want to capture the jury's attention. The following is an example of a plaintiff's attorney presenting the first paragraph of an opening statement.

Example: beginning of an opening statement by plaintiff's counsel.

Ladies and Gentleman of the jury, you will probably all agree that nurses change lives. Well, on December 31, 2000, a nurse's life was changed when she sustained an injury to her back while caring for a combative patient. And her life was changed on New Year's Eve.

The beginning of this opening statement established a theme that "nurses change lives," but in this instance went on to say that a nurse's life was changed—and it was changed on New Year's Eve, usually a time for celebration. The attorney would go on to explain how and why the nurse's life was changed.

Selecting the key phrase is a method used by trial attorneys to develop a theme throughout the case. What counsel wants to do in this instance is to create a lasting image in the minds of jurors. It should not be an exaggeration of the facts. Charts and diagrams may also be used in opening statements as long as they are not prejudicial. The opening statement should create enough interest to maintain the jurors' undivided attention throughout the trial.

The goal of plaintiff's counsel is to portray his or her client's injuries, whether physical, emotional, or financial, in a way that makes the jurors want to help. At the same time, the actions of the defendant will probably be depicted as wrong irrespective of whether it was deliberate or negligent. On the other hand, defense counsel will more than likely downplay the plaintiff's injuries and make the occurrence appear unfortunate and perhaps the fault of someone else or the plaintiff (*BNA Civil Trial Manual*, 1986).

In addition, defense counsel can remind the jury that opening statements are not to be considered evidence. This means that it cannot be considered as evidence for purposes of arriving at a verdict. Following opening statements by plaintiff and defendant counsel, the examination of the witnesses begins. The order of calling witnesses will be determined by counsel.

Presentation of Evidence by the Plaintiff

The plaintiff begins by calling witnesses and presenting evidence to the jury to prove the allegations in the complaint by a preponderance of the evidence. Evidence may include testimony, documents, and reports as long as they have relevance. The rules of evidence as established by the courts are strictly followed, and the judge will rule on the admissibility of evidence if objected to by counsel. In nursing malpractice cases, expert nurse witnesses may be utilized by both plaintiff and defendant to prove or disprove nursing malpractice.

Expert Nurse Witnesses at Trial

The nurses' educational background, knowledge, skill, expertise, and training enable them to serve as expert witnesses and provide testimony in a court of law. The qualification of the nurse to serve as an expert in a court is determined by the judge following direct examination. Once the nurse is qualified as an expert, the credibility of the nurse expert is determined by the jury.

Direct Examination

Qualifying the nurse to be an expert is accomplished by the attorney who hired the expert and consists of asking a series of questions at trial by direct examination. Counsel will ask the nurse expert to state the following:

1. Please state your name and address for the court.
2. What is your educational background?

3. What professional licenses do you hold?
4. What certifications do you have?
5. What is your nursing experience?
6. Where are you employed and what is your title?
7. Do you hold any nursing leadership positions?
8. Have you published any nursing articles?
9. Have you received any nursing awards?

The nurse is then proffered or put forth to the court as an expert. The above questions lay the foundation for the judge to accept the expert. After acceptance, the attorney will ask the expert for an opinion regarding the specifics of the case and the basis of the opinion. Open-ended questions are used during direct examination to provide an opportunity for the expert to explain his or her findings to the jury. If the expert submitted a written report, that may also be used in trial. Exhibits may also be used to enhance testimony. Leading questions on direct examination are prohibited. Leading questions are those that call for a yes or no answer and actually suggest an answer.

Example of a Leading Question

Question: Isn't it true that the patient was found on the floor next to the bed because he did not have a posey restraint?"

At this juncture, the opposing counsel would object and the judge would probably sustain the objection, which means the witness should not answer the question. If the judge overrules the objection, the witness may answer. The witness, while testifying, needs to be cognizant of objections because the judge's response to the objection may determine whether or not he or she is required to answer the question.

Introduction of Exhibits

Exhibits are considered documentary evidence. They include, but are not limited to, expert reports, they include, among other things, medical reports, opinions, documents, X-rays, photographs, and public records.

Exhibits need to be authenticated and should not be inflammatory. Evidence may be considered inflammatory if it produces anger, bias, or similar emotional response. If photographs are used, they should show an accurate depiction of the subject and be free from distortions. Exhibits may be introduced into evidence and referred to by the expert nurse witness.

Upon completion of direct examination by "friendly counsel," the expert will likely be cross-examined by opposing counsel.

Cross-Examination

The purposes of cross-examination are (a) to elicit favorable testimony to enhance the position of the other side, and (b) to discredit or impeach the witness. It is during cross-examination of a witness that deposition testimony may be used to impeach, or discredit, the witness. Therefore, prior to trial, an in-depth review of the deposition testimony minimizes impeachment for inconsistent statements. On cross-examination, unlike on direct examination, leading questions are permissible. As stated previously, leading questions usually call for a yes or no answer. On cross-examination, the questioning of the witness only includes the information and testimony elicited on direct examination. The discovery or introduction of new information is not allowed during cross-examination.

Redirect and recross examinations. Depending on the circumstances it may be necessary for plaintiff's counsel to redirect the witness followed by recross-examination by the defense. After the plaintiff's witnesses have been called and examined the plaintiff will rest its case. Counsel will tell the judge, "Plaintiff rests." That is the signal to the defense to make either make a motion for a directed verdict or present its evidence to the jury.

Directed Verdict Motion

At the close of the plaintiff's case, the defendant may make a motion for a directed verdict by arguing that the plaintiff did not meet its burden of proof by the preponderance of the evidence. If a motion is made and the judge grants the motion, defendant prevails. If the judge does not grant the motion, the defense presents its case (ABA, 2010).

Presentation of Evidence by the Defendant

The presentation of evidence by the defendant will follow in the same manner as plaintiff's presentation of the evidence. The defense will call witnesses, including expert witnesses, to refute the plaintiff's case. The plaintiff will then have an opportunity to cross-examine defendant's witnesses. After the defendant rests its case, the plaintiff will have an opportunity to rebut the evidence. Following the conclusion of the presentation of evidence by both sides, closing arguments will be made.

Closing Arguments

Closing arguments provide an opportunity for counsel to go before the jury and give a summary of the case. This is where the art of persuasion plays an important role. Counsel wants the jury to believe that the burden of proof was met and that the jury should return a verdict for his or her client.

Just as in the opening statement, a theme is also developed for the closing. Universal themes such as the value of human life, justice, and community safety seem to have jury appeal from a plaintiff's perspective. The summation should cover the highlights of the case telling the jury what to focus on during deliberations (*BNA Civil Trial Manual*, 1986). Some trial experts believe that the closing arguments should be more like a conversation with the jury, keeping the jury interested. There are times when the jury instructions that are given by the judge are incorporated into the closing argument. It gives the jury a preview of what is to follow the closing arguments and what they need to focus on in deliberations.

Some may recall the closing argument in a criminal case when counsel said to the jury, "If the glove does not fit, you must acquit." This is the last chance that counsel will have to connect with the jury. Closing argument is where the style and personalities of counsel come into play as some are more flamboyant than others. Generally speaking, counsel has free reign to be creative in persuading the jury to return a verdict in favor of his or her client. Upon completion of the closing arguments, the case is ready for jury instructions.

Jury Instructions: Jury Deliberations and Verdict

Jury instructions are given to the jury by the judge. The jury is instructed on the law of the case. The judge reviews the rules of the court with the jury. The judge also decides what, if any, exhibits the jurors are allowed to take into the jury room. A jury foreman or presiding juror is selected and announces the verdict at the conclusion of deliberations, or asks for clarification during deliberations if necessary. The judge may use a verdict form to assist the jurors with the application of the law to the facts.

Sample verdict form. The following is a Sample Verdict Form used in a negligence action by The Honorable Charles R. Richey, Judge, U.S. District Court for the District of Columbia (Reproduced with permission from *BNA Civil Trial Manual*, pp. 111:209 © 1985 by the Bureau of National Affairs, Inc. (800-372-1033) http://www.bna.com.)).

1. Do you find that plaintiff has proven by a preponderance of evidence that defendant was negligent? Yes_____ No_____ If answer

is Yes, proceed to Question 2. If your answer is No your job is complete. Have your foreperson sign this statement at the bottom of the page indicated below.

2. Do you find that plaintiff has proven by a preponderance of the evidence that defendant's negligence was the proximate cause of plaintiff's alleged injuries? Yes_____ No_____ If your answer to Question 2 is Yes proceed to Question 3. If your answer is No, your job is complete. Have your foreperson sign this statement at the bottom of the page indicated below.

3. Do you find that the defendant has proved by a preponderance of evidence that the plaintiff assumed the risk of the accident and resulting injuries to the plaintiff? Yes_____ No_____ If your answer to Question 3 is Yes, your job is complete. Have your foreperson sign at the places indicated below. If your answer to Question 3 is No, then proceed to Question 4.

4. Do you find that the defendant has proved by a preponderance of the evidence that the plaintiff was contributorily negligent as defined in the Court's Instructions on the law? Yes_____ No _____

5. If your answers to Questions 1 and 2 are Yes, and your answers to Questions 3 and 4 are No, then you shall answer the following question:

What damages did the plaintiff prove by a preponderance of the evidence were the proximate cause of defendant's negligence?

AMOUNT OF DAMAGES $_____

A verdict form of this nature walks the jury through the elements of negligence and the applicable law in that jurisdiction. Jury verdict forms are useful tools, especially in complex matters. They provide a road map for the jury to follow to its final conclusion, which may not be an easy journey. Following the conclusion of jury deliberations, the jurors enter the courtroom and are seated. The suspense is over as the foreperson reads the jury's verdict. The jurors are polled, and the trial is officially over.

POSTTRIAL PHASE

Posttrial Motions and Appeals

Depending on the circumstances, posttrial motions may be filed for various reasons. For example, a motion may be made to have the judge reduce the amount of damages awarded to a plaintiff. The party who lost may also file an appeal with a higher court as illustrated in the case examples.

Even after a party is successful at the trial level, the case may not be over for many years.

ANATOMY OF A CRIMINAL TRIAL

The Criminal Process

The People Versus the Defendant

A crime is a wrong against the public good and creates the situation where the people, the government, or the state is making an allegation against an accused otherwise known as the defendant. The state is usually seeking the imposition of a fine or imprisonment, and the process is punitive in nature rather than remedial as in a civil case, for example, *Duval v. Duval* (1974).

The lawyers who represent the state are known as the prosecutors. Most states have adopted statutes through the legislature defining crimes, and these laws define the nature and extent of punishment that can be imposed. There are basically two classifications of crimes: felonies and misdemeanors. Felonies are serious offenses for which the maximum penalty is greater than 1 year of imprisonment. Felonies are such crimes as murder, assault where there is injury, theft where the dollar amount is over a certain threshold, or rape, burglary, and other serious violations of the law.

Misdemeanors are less serious offenses where the maximum punishment is not in excess of 1-year imprisonment. Misdemeanors would include such crimes as simple assault, shoplifting, driving while intoxicated, disorderly conduct, and resisting arrest.

Investigation

Crimes in most states are initially investigated by police officers whose actions are limited by local statutes and the state and federal constitutions. The particular federal constitutional provisions that are enumerated in the bill of rights include the following amendments and apply to all criminal prosecutions.

> FOURTH AMENDMENT—the right of the people to be secure in their persons, houses, papers, and effects, against unreasonable searches and seizures . . . and no warrants shall issue, but upon probable cause, supported by oath or affirmation, and particularly describing the place to be searched, and the persons or things to be seized.

FIFTH AMENDMENT—the right against double jeopardy, nor shall any person be compelled in any criminal case to be a witness against himself, nor be deprived of life, liberty or property without due process of law.

SIXTH AMENDMENT—guarantees the right in all criminal prosecutions . . . to a speedy public trial by an impartial jury, the right to confront adverse witness(es) and to have the assistance of counsel.

EIGHTH AMENDMENT—prohibits excessive bails, fines and cruel and unusual punishment.

How Criminal Charges Are Brought

Criminal charges are brought against the accused in one of three ways:

1. Indictment, voted by a grand jury;
2. The filing of information by the prosecuting attorney; or
3. By a police officer's citation for minor traffic violations, or this process may also be used for certain misdemeanors or other minor criminal matters (ABA, 2010).

The charge must contain the time, date, and location of the alleged criminal act, as well as details of the crime.

The Arrest: Miranda Rights

After the accused has been arrested and taken into police custody, but before interrogation takes place, they must be given Miranda rights that include the following: (a) that any information they give to police may be used against them in a court of law, (b) they have the right to remain silent, (c) they may consult with an attorney before and during questioning, and (d) they may have a court-appointed attorney in the event they are unable to afford to hire one (*Miranda v. Arizona*, 1966). The Miranda rule is an area of the law that is hotly contested in the criminal area.

Pretrial Procedures

Arraignment

The charge(s) of the accused are read by a judge, clerk or magistrate in what is known as the arraignment. The penalties that the charge(s) carry if found guilty is also read along with the defendants' right to trial and right to counsel. At this juncture, the defendant will enter a plea of guilty or not guilty or nolo contendere (also known as no contest). If the defendant pleads no contest, an admission of guilt is not made.

Bail

Bail is determined by the judge. Bail is the amount of cash or bond that is paid to the court to release the defendant and ensure his or her return to court. The amount of bail set is determined by the court based on factors that include the risk of defendant fleeing, the type of crime committed, the danger posed by the defendant, and the safety of the community. The more serious the crime, the greater will be the bail. For lesser crimes, there may be times that a criminal defendant is released without posting bail.

Plea Bargaining

Plea bargaining is the negotiation process between the prosecutor and the lawyer representing the criminal defendant. Once an agreement is reached, the prosecutor will make recommendations to the judge. The judge may or may not accept the plea agreement. Plea bargaining remains a popular method used to resolve criminal cases. It saves time and expense, and it may avoid a harsher prison term. If there is no plea bargain, the case will proceed to trial.

The Criminal Trial

Trial Before a Judge

A person accused of a misdemeanor that is punishable by jail for up to 1 year has a right to a trial by jury that is guaranteed by the federal and most state constitutions in all but petty offenses (*Baldwin v. New York*, 1970). In these cases, the trial proceeds before a judge who decides guilt or innocence on the basis of evidence.

Trial Before a Jury

The selection of a jury is conducted much in the same manner as discussed in the civil trials. When a person is accused of a felony, a crime that is punishable by more than a year in jail, trial by jury is an important and cherished constitutional right.

The right to trial by jury is constitutionally required only for "serious" offenses. An offense is always "serious" if the potential punishment for the crime is greater than 6 months imprisonment. The U.S. Supreme

Court decided "that the right to trial by jury in most criminal cases is so fundamental that it constitutes an element of due process that the state is obligated to provide . . . " (AJS, 2009, p. 2).

A jury trial commences when the jury, usually 12 persons, is sworn, and the charge is read by the clerk. The procedure at trial is for both the prosecution and the defense lawyers to make opening statements followed by the presentation of evidence.

Burden of Proof and Presentation of Evidence

The presentation of evidence is crucial. In order for the criminal defendant to be convicted of a crime, the prosecution as the burden of proof to prove all the allegations made against the defendant beyond a reasonable doubt. In general, evidence presented takes two forms, direct and circumstantial, as described in the following:

1. Direct evidence generally includes eye witnesses' accounts of a crime, a confession, or a weapon such as a "smoking gun."
2. Circumstantial evidence suggests facts by implication or inference; physical evidence, such as blood-stained clothing, suggests criminal activity.

Dna evidence has advanced and is used as a powerful tool when introduced as evidence at a criminal trial. It is used to convict the guilty and exonerate the innocent. Forensic nurses are most familiar with this area of the law. All evidence introduced in criminal trials is governed by the rules of evidence and the rules of criminal procedure as adopted by the court. These rules are strictly adhered to. The judge will make rulings on the admissibility of evidence on the basis of objections made by the lawyers. At the end of the case, the lawyer for the state or the people and the lawyer for the defendant make closing arguments.

The jury is instructed on the relevant law by the judge. The jury then deliberates and is sometimes sequestered depending on the case. Following deliberations, the jury returns a verdict of guilty or not guilty by a unanimous decision. In the event there is a "hung jury," that is a jury that is unable to reach a verdict, the case may be dismissed or there may be a new trial. The criminal defendant who is convicted of a crime has a right to appeal.

Special Situations

Driving While Intoxicated: A Charge of DWI/DUI

Driving while intoxicated, otherwise known by the acronym DWI/DUI, is an area of law that has become specialized for lawyers, and the penalties have become much more severe in recent years. The people accused and those ultimately convicted of DWI/DUI encompass a broad cross-sector of society, including all social, economic, and age categories.

A charge of DWI/DUI against a nurse can have dire consequences associated with a nursing license, even though one can argue that it does not substantially relate to the qualifications and functions of duties of a registered nurse (*Sturges v. Board of Registered Nursing, Department of Consumer Affairs, State of California*, 2010).

To be convicted of DWI/DUI, the state or government must prove, beyond a reasonable doubt, that the individual was operating a motor vehicle on a public way while impaired by alcohol or drugs or any combination thereof. Most states have placed DWI in the criminal area, so a conviction creates a criminal record. There are penalties, including loss of driver's license, fines, fees, jail time, mandatory alcohol awareness programs, increase in insurance obligations, and lastly, the requirement to have an interlock device installed in your automobile that tests your blood alcohol level prior to and while driving.

Usually the most litigated issue in a DWI/DUI case is impairment. Impairment in most states has been defined if a person's ability to operate a vehicle is impaired to any degree. Most states have a legal limit under per se laws of .08 blood alcohol contact. A per se law in such a case means that if a driver is found to have a blood alcohol level of .08, then in the eyes of the law they are guilty of DUI/DWI, and no additional proof of impairment is needed to convict them of the offense. This measurement can be taken from someone's breath, urine, or blood sample. If someone exceeds the legal limit he or she is presumed to be impaired and, therefore, unfit to drive an automobile. Another way for the state to prove impairment is erratic operation of the automobile and the police officer's or other witnesses' observation of the accused. The police officer, after making a stop for suspected DWI/DUI, administers a series of field sobriety tests that are recognized by the National Highway Traffic Safety Administration.

Such tests include the walk and turn tests, standing balance tests, and other such similar tests that measure a person's mental and physical agility. The field sobriety tests focuses on the abilities needed for safe driving and include balance, coordination, and information processing.

Most states have an implied consent law that means that if a person is arrested for DWI, his or her consent is implied in regards to the taking of a breath, urine, or blood sample, even though the person does not actually give consent. The theory is that if one is exercising the privilege to drive an automobile, he or she impliedly consents to the test. If a driver refuses the test there are penalties for such refusal, which can include loss of license. In some cases if there is serious injury or death the state may be able to procure a blood sample without the permission of the accused.

DWI is a serious social problem with increased penalties that have been passed by state legislatures every year. One night of poor judgment can have disastrous consequences for an ordinary citizen and for the licensed professional nurse who would then be classified as a criminal defendant. Most people are not aware of the severity of the penalties unless a conviction happens to them or someone else close to them. There is little or no tolerance for someone who drives with alcohol in his or her system. It is important to remember that the standard for impairment is when a person is under the influence of a controlled drug or intoxicating liquor if he or she has taken into his or her system a sufficient quantity of said drug or liquor so that his or her ability to operate a vehicle is impaired to any degree (*Slate v. Slater*, 1969).

Criminal Background Checks for Nursing Licensure

Most states now require a criminal background check to obtain a nursing license. Therefore, an arrest and conviction for a DUI/DWI any crime may have serious consequences for all nurses, including prospective nurses. Many educational institutions also require criminal background checks for admissions into nursing programs, especially for clinical rotations in health care facilities. In order to address criminal actions regarding drug abuse and/or DUI/DWI. some boards of nursing have implemented voluntary rehabilitation programs in order to avoid or minimize harsh penalties affecting licensure.

CONCLUSIONS AND TRENDS

The system of American jurisprudence provides individuals with certain rights. Those rights include the right to confront witnesses and have both civil and criminal matters brought to trial for resolution.

In civil cases such as malpractice, if the plaintiff is successful, the resolution usually provides for monetary damages. Criminal cases, however, involve the protection of society and enforcing codes of behavior in accordance with the law that may result in penalties and/or incarceration if the defendant is found guilty.

The courthouse experience can be intimidating if one is unfamiliar with the process. A visit to a courthouse during the presentation a case can provide an invaluable experience for nurses.

As Health Care Law continues to evolve and the practice of nursing expands the expert nurse witness will continue to play an integral role both in and out of the courthouse. The current trend whereby the nurse, rather than the physician, testifies as to the standard of nursing care in nursing malpractice cases will continue.

Since patient safety is paramount, criminal background checks of nurses are now required in most states to obtain a nursing license. Moreover, nursing educational institutions also require a criminal background check as part of the admissions process. Nursing boards continue to examine the development and implementation of programs for nurses with substance abuse problems.

It is important that nurses understand court proceedings and legal mandates to effectively participate in the legal process.

KEY POINTS

- A civil lawsuit begins with the plaintiff filing a complaint in the appropriate court of law. A complaint is a pleading that names the parties to the action and the allegations of wrongdoing.
- A court will have no authority to decide a case unless it has jurisdiction over the person or property involved.
- Prior to filing a medical malpractice action against a physician, an attorney may be required to obtain a certificate of merit that the case is legitimate.
- The discovery process includes interrogatories, production of documents, and deposition testimony. Its purpose is to learn the facts and issues of the case for settlement purposes or for trial. Discovery also prevents surprise at trial and may be used to discredit witnesses.
- Evidence includes testimony, documents, and tangible objects that tend to prove or disprove the existence of an alleged fact (*Black's Law Dictionary*, 2010).
- Professional nurses qualify to serve as witnesses in nursing malpractice/ negligence claims.
- The standard for proving civil cases is preponderance of the evidence or by clear and convincing evidence. The standard for proving criminal cases is beyond a reasonable doubt.

- Crimes fall into two major categories: misdemeanors and felonies.
- Most states require criminal background checks for nurses when obtaining professional nursing licenses. Therefore, any arrests or convictions may have severe consequences for nurses.
- "Driving while intoxicated," otherwise known as DWI or DUI, encompasses a broad cross-sector of society, including all social, economic, and age categories.
- Plea bargaining is the negotiation process between the prosecution and the lawyer representing the criminal defendant.
- When a criminal defendant is arrested and taken into police custody, before interrogation Miranda Rights must be given.

REFERENCES

American Bar Association. (1991). *Court and community: Partners in justice.* Washington, DC: Author.

American Bar Association. (n.d.). *Steps in a trial: Bringing the charge.* Retrieved November 13, 2010, from http://www.abanet.org/publiced/courts/bringingcharg.html

American Bar Association. (n.d.). *Steps in a trial: Jurisdiction and venue*, p. 1. Retrieved September 25, 2010, from http://www.abanet.org/publiced/courts/jurisdiction.html

American Bar Association. (n.d.). *Steps in a trial: Motions.* Retrieved September 27, 2010, from http://www.abanet.org/puliced/courts/motions.html

American Judicature Society. (2009). *Juries in depth: Right to a jury trial*, p. 2. Retrieved September 29, 2010, from http://www.ajs.org/jc/juries/jc_right_overview.asp

Baldwin v. New York, 399 U.S. 66 (1970).

Black's law dictionary (9th ed.). (2010). St. Paul, MN: West Group.

BNA civil trial manual. (1986). Jury selection: Juror profiles and screen theories (Section 71:212, No. 29, pp. 12–13). Washington, DC: Bureau of National Affairs.

BNA civil trial manual. (1985). Jury deliberations and verdict: Verdict forms and interrogatories (Section 111:209, No. 4 , p. 11.

Brenner, H., & Bal, S. (2010). *Summary judgment in medical malpractice: The case of Hoard v. Roper Hospital.* Retrieved October 1, 2001, from http:view.aspxrid=64870

Canary, J. (1991). *Understanding the courts.* Chicago: American Bar Association.

Duval v. Duval, 114 NH 422 (1974).

Federal rules of civil procedure. (2009). Retrieved October 28, 2010, from http://wwwlawcornell-edu/rules/frcp

Haney v. Alexander, 323 SE 2d 430 (N.C. Ct. App. 1984).

LII/Legal Information Institute. (n.d.). *Federal rules of civil procedure, rule 48.* Retrieved October 25, 2010, from http: /www.law.cornell.edu/rules/frcp/rule48.htm

Miller, R. V. (2006). *Medical malpractice cases in Maryland: What a Maryland malpractice lawyer must do before filing suit*, p. 2. Retrieved September 25, 2010, from http://www.marylandinjurylawyerblog.com/2006/08/medical_malpractice_cases_in m_1.ht . . .

Miranda v. Arizona, 384 U.S. 436 (1966).

State v. Slater, 109 NH 279 (1969).

Sturges v. Board of Registered Nursing, Department of Consumer Affairs, State of California, No. CPF-09–510060, Superior Ct, CA (2010).

Sullivan v. Edwards, 806 NE 645 (Il. S.Ct. 2004). www.il.us/courtopinions/supremecourt/2004

The American Association of Nurse Attorneys. (2007, June 26). *TAANA position: Expert testimony in nursing malpractice actions* (pp. 1–11). Retrieved April 14, 2001, from http://associationdatabase.com/aws/TAANA/pt/sd/news_article/3453/_parent/layout_detail . . . .

Widman, A. (n.d.). *Certificates of merit and medical malpractice: What's at stake for states.* Retrieved September 10, 2010, from http://centerjd.org

APPENDIX

Docket No. 95409-Agenda 9-November 2003

*JUANITA SULLIVAN, Indiv. and as Special Adm'r of the Estate of Burns Sullivan, Deceased, Appellant, v. EDWARD HOSPITAL et al., **Appellees***

Opinion Filed February 5, 2004

JUSTICE FREEMAN delivered the opinion of the court:

Plaintiff, Juanita Sullivan, individually and as special administrator of the estate of Burns Sullivan (Burns), brought a medical malpractice action in the circuit court of Du Page County. Plaintiff named as defendants Edward Hospital (the hospital) and Dr. Amelia Conte-Russian. Plaintiff claimed that the hospital, through one of its nurses, and Dr. Conte-Russian were negligent in the care and treatment of Burns. The trial court entered a directed verdict for the hospital after plaintiff's only medical expert was ruled incompetent to testify as to the standard of care for the nursing profession. The trial court subsequently entered judgment on a jury verdict in favor of Dr. Conte-Russian.

The appellate court affirmed. 335 Ill. App. 3d 265. We allowed plaintiff's petition for leave to appeal (177 Ill. 2d R. 315(a)), and now affirm the appellate court.

BACKGROUND

The record reveals the following pertinent facts. In March 1995, Burns suffered a second stroke, which resulted in partial paralysis to his right side, impairing his ability to walk independently. Also as a result of the stroke, Burns could not speak, but could understand others and respond with physical gestures. Since March 1995, Dr. Conte-Russian, a general internist, had been Burns' regular treating physician.

On November 1, 1997, Burns, then 74 years old, was admitted to the hospital for treatment of a urinary tract infection. While at the hospital, Dr. Conte-Russian was Burns' primary care physician. The hospital categorized a patient's risk of falling between two levels. A patient who has no impairments of any kind is characterized as a level I fall risk. A patient who has any physical or mental impairments that increase the risk of falling is characterized as level II. Because of Burns' history of partial paralysis, he was characterized as level II.

On the evening of November 2, 1997, nurse Carrie Lewis was Burns' primary nurse. Burns had been in his bed, equipped with four side rails, all of which were raised. Between 7 P.M. and 9:30 P.M., nurse Lewis went into Burns' room and found Burns attempting to get out of bed through the side rails. After each of the first two occurrences, nurse Lewis found Burns to be alert, oriented, and able to understand her instructions to stay in bed. After the third occasion, Burns still appeared alert and oriented. However, nurse Lewis became concerned because of Burns' failure to follow instructions and because Burns now appeared to be agitated. Nurse Lewis was concerned that Burns might again attempt to get out of bed and that he could fall if he did so.

Based on these concerns, nurse Lewis telephoned Dr. Conte-Russian at approximately 9:30 P.M. and asked the doctor to order a "posey vest" to restrain Burns to his bed. A posey vest is used to restrain a patient by placing the vest on the patient and then tying the vest straps to the bed. Dr. Conte-Russian advised nurse Lewis that a posey vest might result in Burns becoming even more agitated. Rather than using a physical restraint, Dr. Conte-Russian ordered the administration of the drug Ativan to calm Burns and help him sleep. Dr. Conte-Russian prescribed a very small dosage and left it to nurse Lewis' discretion to administer more Ativan if needed.

At approximately 10 P.M., nurse Lewis administered to Burns one milligram of Ativan, which was expected to last for at least two hours. Between 10 P.M. and midnight, nurse Lewis and a nurse's aide checked on Burns approximately every half hour. By 10:30 P.M. Burns was asleep; he was sleeping at each half-hour check. At approximately 12:05 A.M., a nurse's aide walked past Burns' room and looked inside; Burns appeared to be sleeping. At 12:10 A.M., a monitor technician heard a noise in the area of Burns' room and so informed nurse Lewis. Upon receiving this report, nurse Lewis ran to Burns' room and found him on the floor with his head bleeding from a cut above his left eye. Apparently, Burns had attempted to get up from his bed and walk; however, he fell and struck his head on the hospital room floor. As a result of the fall, Burns developed a subdural hematoma, for which he received treatment. At the request of his family, Burns was subsequently transferred to another hospital.

On November 6, 1998, plaintiff and Burns filed a two-count complaint against the hospital and Dr. Conte-Russian. The complaint alleged that the hospital, through nurse Lewis, and Dr. Conte-Russian, failed to properly monitor, medicate, or restrain Burns. In count I, Burns sought damages for injuries proximately caused by defendants' negligence. In count II, plaintiff sought damages for loss of consortium. In September 1999, Burns died of a third stroke, which was unrelated to plaintiff's allegations of negligence. On December 28, 1999, Burns' death was formally reported to the trial court; plaintiff was appointed special administrator of Burns' estate and substituted as the sole plaintiff.

At trial, plaintiff attempted to establish the hospital's liability vicariously through the actions of nurse Lewis. Plaintiff called Dr. William Barnhart to testify as her medical expert. Dr. Barnhart is a board-certified physician specializing in internal medicine and has substantial experience in observing and working with physicians and nurses in the area of patient fall protection. Plaintiff intended for Dr. Barnhart to testify to the applicable standards of care for physicians and nurses, and the failure of both Dr. Conte-Russian and nurse Lewis to meet their respective standards of care.

Dr. Barnhart testified as to the standard of care for a licensed nurse and the instances in which nurse Lewis deviated from the standard of care. According to Dr. Barnhart, one such instance included nurse Lewis' failure to properly communicate Burns' condition to Dr. Conte-Russian during their phone conversation. The trial court found that plaintiff did not properly disclose Dr. Barnhart's opinion on this issue during pretrial discovery, in violation of Supreme Court Rule 213(g) (177 Ill. 2d R. 213(g)). Therefore, the trial court struck the testimony relating to nurse Lewis' communications with Dr. Conte-Russian.

According to Dr. Barnhart, nurse Lewis deviated from the standard of care for a licensed nurse also by her failure to adhere to proper nursing procedures in the care and treatment of a patient. Dr. Barnhart opined that nurse Lewis, after having failed to receive Dr. Conte-Russian's approval to use a posey vest on Burns, should have gone up the nursing chain of command to pursue her concerns that Burns would attempt to get out of bed; that she should have provided for an alternative to the posey vest to protect against the risk of a fall; and that nurse Lewis should have had a sitter in Burns' room, or should have moved Burns' bed to an area where Burns could have received constant supervision. At the close of plaintiff's case, the trial court struck this testimony on the grounds that a physician is incompetent to testify to the standard of care placed upon a licensed nurse.

Dr. Barnhart was plaintiff's only medical expert as to the standard of care for the nursing profession. After the trial court ruled that Dr. Barnhart was incompetent to testify as to that standard, the court granted the hospital's motion for a directed verdict. Thereafter, the jury returned a verdict in favor of Dr. Conte-Russian and the trial court entered judgment thereon. The appellate court affirmed. 335 Ill. App. 3d 265.

This court allowed plaintiff's petition for leave to appeal. 177 Ill. 2d R. 315(a). We subsequently granted the Illinois Trial Lawyers Association leave to submit an *amicus curiae* brief in support of plaintiff. We also granted the American Association of Nurse Attorneys leave to submit an *amicus curiae* brief in support of the hospital. 155 Ill. 2d R. 345. We will refer to additional pertinent facts as they relate to the issues plaintiff raises before this court.

ANALYSIS

I. Dr. Barnhart's Testimony

Plaintiff contends that the trial court erred in striking, as a discovery sanction, Dr. Barnhart's testimony relating to nurse Lewis' communications with Dr. Conte-Russian. Plaintiff also contends that the trial court erred in striking Dr. Barnhart's testimony relating to the standard of care for the nursing profession and, consequently, entering a directed verdict in favor of the hospital.

A. Discovery Violation

During pretrial discovery, plaintiff submitted a disclosure pursuant to Supreme Court Rule 213 (177 Ill. 2d R. 213), which disclosed the names and addresses of plaintiff's witnesses and "the subject of their testimony."

This disclosure included Dr. Barnhart's name and address, and the following description of his anticipated testimony:

It is anticipated that Dr. Barnhart will testify that it is his opinion that Dr. Conte[-]Russian and Edward Hospital deviated from the accepted standards of medical care by disregarding Mr. Burns Sullivan's status as a level II fall risk suffered from cognitive impairment and inability to understand directions and was found trying to climb out of bed on three prior occasions even though he suffered from Hemi-paralysis. He will testify that Dr. Conte-Russian and the Edward Hospital staff should have restrained Mr. Sullivan in bed so that he could not get out. Further, he will testify that the attempt to sedate Mr. Sullivan by issuing medication as opposed to restraints was not properly performed. He will also testify that it is his opinion that Mr. Sullivan was not properly monitored during sedation despite his inability to understand direction and physical impairments. He will also testify that in his opinion Mr. Burns Sullivan's injuries were sustained as a result of medical negligence.

Dr. Barnhart will testify that in his opinion, Dr. Conte-Russian, after having been advised of Mr. Sullivan's three prior attempts to get out of bed and remove his IV[,] should have ordered restraints for Mr. Sullivan. He will testify that in his opinion Dr. Conte-Russian and the Edward Hospital medical staff should have ordered restraints for Mr. Sullivan. That in his opinion, Dr. Conte-Russian and the Edward Hospital medical staff should have monitored Mr. Sullivan more frequently after the decision not to use restraints was made. That as a result of Dr. Conte-Russian's decision not to properly restrain Mr. Sullivan, he fell out of bed and sustained brain injury including a subdural hematoma.

At trial, Dr. Barnhart's testimony reflected this disclosure. However, he also testified that one instance where nurse Lewis deviated from the standard of care for professional nurses was her failure to adequately communicate Burns' condition to Dr. Conte-Russian during their phone conversation.

At the close of Dr. Barnhart's testimony, the hospital moved to strike that portion of his testimony relating to nurse Lewis' communication of Burns' condition to Dr. Conte-Russian. Plaintiff conceded that Dr. Barnhart's specific opinion regarding nurse Lewis' failure to adequately communicate with Dr. Conte-Russian was not included in plaintiff's Rule 213 disclosure. The trial court granted the hospital's motion to strike this testimony.

This cause was tried prior to the amendment of Rule 213 effective July 1, 2002, so we will refer to its preamendment version. Supreme Court Rule 213(g) requires that, upon written interrogatory, a party *must* disclose the subject matter, conclusions, opinions, qualifications, and all reports of a witness who will offer any opinion testimony. 177 Ill. 2d R. 213(g). Further, Supreme Court Rule 213(i) imposes on each party a continuing duty to inform the opponent of new or additional information whenever such information becomes known to the party. 177 Ill. 2d R. 213(i). The Rule 213 disclosure requirements are mandatory and subject to strict compliance by the parties. *See f v. Ingalls Memorial Hospital*, 311 Ill. App. 3d 7, 21 (1999); *Warrender v. Millsop*, 304 Ill. App. 3d 260, 265 (1999). The admission of evidence pursuant to Rule 213 is within the sound discretion of the trial court, and the court's ruling will not be disturbed absent an abuse of that discretion. *Susnis v. Radfar*, 317 Ill. App. 3d 817, 828 (2000); *See f*, 311 Ill. App. 3d at 22.

As noted, plaintiff concedes that Dr. Barnhart's specific opinion regarding nurse Lewis' failure to adequately communicate Burns' condition to Dr. Conte-Russian was not included in plaintiff's Rule 213 disclosure. However, plaintiff argues that the "gist" of Dr. Barnhart's trial testimony regarding nurse Lewis" telephone conversation with Dr. Conte-Russian was an "elaboration" or a "logical corollary" of, or "effectively" implicated, plaintiff's Rule 213 disclosure.

The trial court did not accept this argument, and neither do we. As the trial court reasoned, "you have to drop down to specifics." Rule 213 permits litigants to rely on the disclosed opinions of opposing experts and to construct their trial strategy accordingly. *Firstar Bank of Illinois v. Peirce*, 306 Ill. App. 3d 525, 532 (1999). The supreme court rules represent this court's best efforts to manage the complex and important process of discovery. One of the purposes of Rule 213 is to avoid surprise. 177 Ill. 2d R. 213(g), Committee Comments. To allow either side to ignore Rule 213's plain language defeats its purpose and encourages tactical gamesmanship. *Department of Transportation v. Crull*, 294 Ill. App. 3d 531, 537 (1998). Our appellate court has stated:

> Rule 213 establishes more exacting standards regarding disclosure than did Supreme Court Rule 220 ***, which formerly governed expert witnesses. Trial courts should be more reluctant under Rule 213 than they were under former Rule 220 (1) to permit the parties to deviate from the strict disclosure requirements, or (2) not to impose severe sanctions when such deviations occur. Indeed, we believe one of the reasons for new Rule 213 was the need to require

stricter adherence to disclosure requirements. *Susnis*, 317 Ill. App. 3d at 828–29, quoting *Crull*, 294 Ill. App. 3d at 538–39.

We agree. Given this stricter standard of compliance, we hold that the trial court did not abuse its discretion in finding that plaintiff violated Rule 213(g). See *Susnis*, 317 Ill. App. 3d at 829.

Plaintiff further argues that even if Dr. Barnhart's testimony constituted a discovery violation, the extreme remedy of striking the testimony constituted an abuse of the trial court's discretion. We disagree. "Where a party fails to comply with the provisions of Rule 213, a court should not hesitate sanctioning the party, as Rule 213 demands strict compliance." *Peirce*, 306 Ill. App. 3d at 533, quoting *Warrender*, 304 Ill. App. 3d at 268. In determining whether the exclusion of a witness is a proper sanction for nondisclosure, a court must consider the following factors: (1) the surprise to the adverse party; (2) the prejudicial effect of the testimony; (3) the nature of the testimony; (4) the diligence of the adverse party; (5) the timely objection to the testimony; and (6) the good faith of the party calling the witness. The decision whether or not to impose sanctions lies within the sound discretion of the trial court, and that decision will not be reversed absent an abuse of discretion. *Warrender*, 304 Ill. App. 3d at 268; *Ashpole v. Brunswick Bowling & Billiards Corp.*, 297 Ill. App. 3d 725, 727 (1998).

The record shows that, regarding the first factor, the hospital was clearly surprised by Dr. Barnhart's testimony. Plaintiff concedes that the Rule 213(g) disclosure did not contain the opinion to which Dr. Barnhart testified. Further, nowhere in his deposition does Dr. Barnhart suggest or imply that nurse Lewis failed to communicate appropriately with Dr. Conte-Russian and that this failure proximately caused Burns' fall.

Regarding the second and third factors, the nature of the testimony and its prejudicial effect are manifest. Dr. Barnhart testified regarding an instance of how the hospital deviated from the standard of care for nurses. This was a theory of negligence of which the hospital should have been informed. Regarding the fourth through the sixth factors, the record shows that the hospital was diligent in sending its Rule 213 interrogatories to plaintiff; that the hospital timely objected to the contested testimony; and that this lapse in an otherwise detailed summary of Dr. Barnhart's anticipated testimony does not indicate good faith.

The purpose behind Rule 213 is to avoid surprise and to discourage tactical gamesmanship. "Rule 213 brings to a trial a degree of certainty and predictability that furthers the administration of justice. The rule should be enforced by trial judges." *Peirce*, 306 Ill. App. 3d at 536. We cannot say that the trial court abused its discretion in striking this portion of Dr. Barnhart's testimony. See *Susnis*, 317 Ill. App. 3d at 829 (finding no abuse of discretion when trial court bars expert physician testimony after party fails to make Rule 213 disclosure of testimony regarding the relevant standard of care).

B. Nursing Standard of Care

Plaintiff also contends that the trial court erred in striking Dr. Barnhart's testimony relating to the standard of care for the nursing profession and, consequently, entering a directed verdict in favor of the hospital. "In directing a verdict, the trial court determines *as a matter of law* that there are no evidentiary facts out of which the jury may construe the necessary fact essential to recovery" (Emphasis added) *Jones v. O'Young*, 154 Ill. 2d 39, 47 (1992). Accordingly, our review is *de novo*.

This court has explained the requirement of expert medical testimony in a medical malpractice action as follows:

> In a negligence medical malpractice case, the burden is on the plaintiff to prove the following elements of a cause of action: the proper standard of care against which the defendant physician's conduct is measured; an unskilled or negligent failure to comply with the applicable standard; and a resulting injury proximately caused by the physician's want of skill or care. [Citations.] Unless the physician's negligence is so grossly apparent or the treatment so common as to be within the everyday knowledge of a layperson, expert medical testimony is required to establish the standard of care and the defendant physician's deviation from that standard. *Purtill v. Hess*, 111 Ill. 2d 229, 241–42 (1986)

Accord *Dolan v. Galluzzo*, 77 Ill. 2d 279, 282 (1979).

In this case, the trial court ruled that Dr. Barnhart was incompetent to testify as to the standard of care for the nursing profession and nurse Lewis' deviations therefrom. The appellate court upheld the trial court's ruling. 335 Ill. App. 3d at 269–72. In *Jones*, 154 Ill. 2d at 43, this court summarized the test of an expert physician's competency to testify:

> In *Purtill v. Hess* (1986), 111 Ill. 2d 229, this court articulated the requirements necessary to demonstrate an expert physician's qualifications and competency to testify. First, the physician must be a

licensed member of the school of medicine about which he proposes to testify. (*Purtill*, 111 Ill. 2d at 242–43, citing *Dolan v. Galluzzo* (1979), 77 Ill. 2d 279.) Second, "the expert witness must show that he is familiar with the methods, procedures, and treatments ordinarily observed by other physicians, in either the defendant physician's community or a similar community." (*Purtill*, 111 Ill. 2d at 243.) Once the foundational requirements have been met, the trial court has the discretion to determine whether a physician is qualified and competent to state his opinion as an expert regarding the standard of care. *Purtill*, 111 Ill. 2d at 243.

If the expert physician fails to satisfy either of these foundational requirements, "the trial court must disallow the expert's testimony." *Jones*, 154 Ill. 2d at 44.

Dolan established the first requirement, that is, that a health care expert witness must be a licensed member of the school of medicine about which the expert proposes to testify. *Dolan* explained that there are different systems or schools of medicine with varying tenets and practices, and that testing the care and skill of a practitioner of one school of medicine by the opinion of a practitioner of another school would result in inequities. The practitioner of a particular school of medicine is entitled to have his or her conduct tested by the standards of that school. *Dolan*, 77 Ill. 2d at 283 (and authorities cited therein).

This court in *Dolan* further observed:

Illinois statutes [citations] provide for the regulation of practitioners of medicine and surgery, physical therapy, nursing, pharmacy, dental surgery, podiatry, optometry, etc. This is a clear expression by the legislature of public policy to recognize and regulate various schools of medicine. The various acts regulating the health professions [citations] provide for different training, and regulate the treatment each profession may offer. *** We simply are not disposed to provide for what, in effect, may result in a higher standard of care when the legislature, by recognizing various schools of medicine, has not done so. To do so would not only be unfair ***, but it would also assume that science and medicine have achieved a universal standard of treatment of disease or injury. Such is not the case. In its wisdom, the legislature has recognized a fundamental tenet of contemporary life: no one person, group or school has yet succeeded in abstracting a universal medical method from the many changing methods used in science and medicine. *Dolan*, 77 Ill. 2d at 284.

Accordingly, the *Dolan* court held that "in order to testify as an expert on the standard of care in a given school of medicine, the witness must be licensed therein." *Dolan*, 77 Ill. 2d at 285.

Plaintiff argues that Illinois law no longer holds that a health professional expert witness must always be a licensed member of the school of medicine about which the expert proposes to testify. In support of her argument, plaintiff cites the following from *Jones*:

> By hearing evidence on the expert's qualifications and comparing the medical problem and the type of treatment in the case to the experience and background of the expert, the trial court can evaluate whether the witness has demonstrated a sufficient familiarity with the standard of care practiced in the case. The foundational requirements provide the trial court with the information necessary to determine whether an expert has expertise in dealing with the plaintiff's medical problem and treatment. *Whether the expert is qualified to testify is not dependent on whether he is a member of the same specialty or subspecialty as the defendant but, rather, whether the allegations of negligence concern matters within his knowledge and observation.* (Emphasis added.) *Jones*, 154 Ill. 2d at 43.

Based on the italicized sentence, plaintiff argues that *Jones* "retreats from any rigid, formalistic rule" that a health professional expert witness must be a licensed member of the school of medicine about which the expert proposes to testify.

We cannot accept this argument. *Jones* clearly reaffirms this court's decision in *Purtill* describing *two* foundational requirements: that the health care expert witness must be a licensed member of the school of medicine about which the expert proposes to testify; and that the expert must be familiar with the methods, procedures, and treatments ordinarily observed by other health care providers in either the defendant's community or a similar community. Indeed, the very next sentences in *Jones* following the italicized sentence upon which plaintiff relies state: "If the plaintiff fails to satisfy either of the foundational requirements of *Purtill*, the trial court must disallow the expert's testimony (*Purtill*, 111 Ill. 2d at 244.). The requirements are a threshold beneath which the plaintiff cannot fall without failing to sustain the allegations of his complaint." *Jones*, 154 Ill. 2d at 44. It is only *after* determining that both foundational requirements are satisfied that the court proceeds to evaluate whether the allegations of negligence concern matters within the expert's knowledge and observation. Instead of retreating from the license requirement, *Jones* clearly reaffirms that a plaintiff must satisfy both requirements. *Jones*, 154 Ill. 2d at 44, citing *Purtill*, 111 Ill. 2d at 244.

Plaintiff similarly points to language in *Gill v. Foster*, 157 Ill. 2d 304 (1993), in arguing that Dr. Barnhart's lack of licensure in the nursing profession should have gone only to the weight of his testimony and not its admissibility. Plaintiff misreads *Gill*. In that case, the trial court barred the plaintiff's expert, a licensed general surgeon, from testifying that the defendant, a licensed radiologist, deviated from the standard of care. *Gill*, 157 Ill. 2d at 315–16. The plaintiff in *Gill* argued that his expert was licensed to practice medicine in all of its branches and, therefore, the expert's testimony should have been admitted, with his qualifications going to the weight of his opinion. This court agreed with the plaintiff; however, only after finding that the plaintiff had satisfied the licensing requirement. *Gill*, 157 Ill. 2d at 317. We cited to *Purtill* for its three-step analysis: the two foundational requirements of licensure and familiarity, and the discretionary requirement of competency. *Gill*, 157 Ill. 2d at 316–17. When this court ruled that the plaintiff's expert could testify, it was in the context of the trial court's discretion to determine whether the physician was qualified and competent to state his opinion regarding the standard of care. *Gill*, 157 Ill. 2d at 317. This court was not discussing whether the plaintiff's expert satisfied the licensing requirement. Far from overruling *Dolan* and its progeny, *Gill* expressly upheld *Purtill*'s three-step analysis. Clearly, *Gill* and *Jones* do not stand for the proposition that this court has disregarded, or should disregard, the licensing requirement first established in *Dolan*.

Plaintiff next contends that the appellate court failed to consider section 2–622 of the Code of Civil Procedure (735 ILCS 5/2–622 (West 2000)), enacted in 1985, subsequent to *Dolan*. Section 2–622 provides that in any medical malpractice action, the plaintiff's attorney must attach to the complaint an affidavit stating that the plaintiff has consulted with a health professional in whose opinion there is a "reasonable and meritorious cause" for the filing of the action. The plaintiff must file a written report, attached to the affidavit, prepared by that health professional indicating the basis for his determination. The section specifically provides:

> If the affidavit is filed as to a defendant who is a physician licensed to treat human ailments without the use of drugs or medicines and without operative surgery, a dentist, a podiatrist, or a psychologist, or a naprapath, the written report must be from a health professional licensed in the same profession, with the same class of license, as the defendant. For affidavits filed as to all other defendants, the written report must be from a physician licensed to practice medicine in all its branches. 735 ILCS 5/2–622(a)(1) (West 2000).

Plaintiff asserts that section 2–622 evinces a legislative intent that physicians are competent to testify about the standard of care for the nursing profession.

We cannot accept this contention. The written health professional report required by section 2–622(a)(1) is a pleading requirement designed to reduce the number of frivolous medical malpractice lawsuits at an early stage before litigation expenses mount. *DeLuna v. St. Elizabeth's Hospital*, 147 Ill. 2d 57, 65 (1992). The health professional's report establishes only that the plaintiff has a meritorious claim and, therefore, reasonable grounds for pursuing the action. The requirements of section 2–622 do not rise to the level of substantive elements of a claim for medical malpractice. *Gulley v. Noy*, 316 Ill. App. 3d 861, 864 (2000); *Mueller v. North Suburban Clinic, Ltd.*, 299 Ill. App. 3d 568, 573 (1998). The report constitutes only a threshold opinion, based on a health professional's overview of the case. The health professional's report constitutes only "an advisory opinion." *McAlister v. Schick*, 147 Ill. 2d 84, 93 (1992). Because the purpose of section 2–622 is to eliminate frivolous lawsuits at the pleading stage, the statute has no bearing on the type of evidence relied upon at trial. *Lyons v. Hasbro Industries, Inc.*, 156 Ill. App. 3d 649, 655 (1987). Further, the fact that *Jones* and *Gill*, which clearly uphold *Dolan*'s license requirement, were decided subsequent to the enactment of section 2–622 belies any tension between the statute and this court's precedent.

Plaintiff next cites *Wingo v. Rockford Memorial Hospital*, 292 Ill. App. 3d 896 (1997), in support of her argument against the requirement that a health care expert witness must be licensed in the school of medicine of which the expert proposes to testify. Plaintiff contends that if *Wingo* is applied to this case, Dr. Barnhart should be allowed to testify to the standard of care applicable to nurse Lewis.

In *Wingo*, three physician expert witnesses testified that a nurse deviated from the applicable nursing standard of care by failing to properly communicate the condition of a patient to the treating physician. The physicians opined that the nurse's deviation from the standard of care resulted in a baby being born with brain damage. *Wingo*, 292 Ill. App. 3d at 903–04.

The court in *Wingo* distinguished that case from this court's precedent and held that the license requirement of *Dolan* did not apply:

> We find that the facts of the instant case do not fit within the license requirement of *Dolan* or *Jones*. Those cases indicate that the reason for the rule is to prevent a higher standard of care being imposed upon the defendant and to ensure that the testifying expert has expertise in dealing with the patient's medical problem and treatment and that

the allegations of negligence are within the expert's knowledge and observation. Those concerns have not been sacrificed here. In the instant case, the allegations of negligence against nurse Welden did not concern a nursing procedure but, rather, related to what a nurse is required to communicate to a physician about what transpired since the physician last saw the patient. As such the allegations of negligence do not concern an area of medicine about which there would be a different standard between physician and another school of medicine. Furthermore, it was established that the allegations of negligence were well within the testifying doctors' knowledge and experience. We believe that a physician should be entitled to testify about what he or she is entitled to rely upon in the area of communication from a nurse in the context of an obstetrical team rendering care to a patient in a hospital. *Wingo*, 292 Ill. App. 3d at 906.

Accordingly, the court held that no error occurred in allowing the physicians to testify as to the applicable nursing standard of care in that case. *Wingo*, 292 Ill. App. 3d at 906.

The appellate court in this case correctly reasoned that *Wingo* does not apply. In this case, the trial court struck Dr. Barnhart's testimony regarding nurse Lewis' communication with Dr. Conte-Russian as a sanction for violating Rule 213(g). Thus, the precise factual scenario of *Wingo* is not present. Dr. Barnhart's remaining opinion testimony related to nursing procedures. 335 Ill. App. 3d at 271. In distinguishing *Wingo* from this case, the appellate court did not discuss the merits of *Wingo*, and neither do we. The present case falls squarely within the license requirement of *Dolan* and its progeny.

Accordingly, what remains for us is to apply *Dolan*'s license requirement for health care expert witnesses to the remainder of Dr. Barnhart's testimony. As noted, Dr. Barnhart testified that nurse Lewis failed to adhere to proper nursing procedures. He opined that nurse Lewis should have pursued her concerns that Burns was a fall risk by going up the nursing chain of command; that she should have provided for an alternative to the posey vest; and that she should have provided for constant supervision.

We agree with the trial and appellate courts that, based on *Dolan*, Dr. Barnhart was not competent to testify regarding the standard of care for the nursing profession and nurse Lewis' deviations therefrom. *Dolan* specifically included the nursing profession in discussing its rationale for the license requirement. This court acknowledged that the legislature established nursing as a unique school of medicine. *Dolan*, 77 Ill. 2d at 284. Further, the dissent in *Dolan* lends support to the conclusion that

Dolan's licensing requirement includes the nursing profession. The dissent stated: "Under [this] holding a physician would be unable to testify to nursing standards of care even though nurses operated under [the physician's] supervision or to testify to standards for midwives, and this because the physician was not licensed as a nurse or a midwife." *Dolan*, 77 Ill. 2d at 286 (Ward, J., dissenting, joined by Goldenhersh, C.J.). Clearly, this exact issue was contemplated by this court in *Dolan*, which unequivocally required that a health care expert witness must be a licensed member of the school of medicine about which the expert testifies.

We note that *amicus* Illinois Trial Lawyers Association expressly agrees with the *Dolan* dissent and contends that the license requirement should not be a threshold test. The Trial Lawyers Association posits: "There is nothing which a nurse can do which a doctor cannot do." To be sure, this supposition is generally accepted. *Amicus* American Association of Nurse Attorneys (AANA) concedes that in many jurisdictions physicians have been allowed to testify as to the nursing standard of care. See, *e.g.*, *Paris v. Kreitz*, 75 N.C. App. 365, 380, 331 S.E.2d 234, 245 (1985) (noting that "physicians are clearly acceptable experts with regard to *** nurses"); *Goff v. Doctors General Hospital*, 166 Cal. App. 2d 314, 319–20, 333 P.2d 29, 33 (1958) (reasoning that "surely, a qualified doctor would know what was standard procedure for nurses to follow").

However, the proposition that "[t]here is nothing which a nurse can do which a doctor cannot do" presumes a universal standard of treatment among physicians and nurses. *Dolan* expressly rejected this assumption. *Dolan*, 77 Ill. 2d at 284 (rejecting the assumption "that science and medicine have achieved a universal standard of treatment of disease or injury"). AANA persuasively reasons:

A physician, who is not a nurse, is no more qualified to offer expert, opinion testimony as to the standard of care for nurses than a nurse would be to offer an opinion as to the physician standard of care. *** Certainly, nurses are not permitted to offer expert testimony against a physician based on their observances of physicians or their familiarity with the procedures involved. An operating room nurse, who stands shoulder to shoulder with surgeons every day, would not be permitted to testify as to the standard of care of a surgeon. An endoscopy nurse would not be permitted to testify as to the standard of care of a gastroenterologist performing a Colonoscopy. A labor and delivery nurse would not be permitted to offer expert, opinion testimony as to the standard of care for an obstetrician or even a midwife. Nor would a nurse be permitted to testify that, in her experience, when she calls a physician, he/she usually responds in a certain manner. Such testimony would be, essentially, expert testimony as to the standard of medical care.

Scholars share this reasoning:

Physicians often have no first-hand knowledge of nursing practice except for observations made in patient care settings. The physician rarely, if ever, teaches in a nursing program nor is a physician responsible for content in nursing texts. In many situations, a physician would not be familiar with the standard of care or with nursing policies and procedures which govern the standard of care. Therefore, a physician's opinions would not be admissible in jurisdictions which hold the expert must be familiar with the standard of care in order to testify as an expert. An example of a common situation which gives rise to allegations of nursing negligence occurs when a nurse fails to follow the institutional 'chain of command' in reporting a patient condition to a physician who subsequently refuses to attend to the patient condition. It is unlikely that a physician would be familiar with the policy and procedure involved in handling such a situation. It is as illogical for physicians to testify on nursing standard of care as it would be for nurses to testify about medical malpractice. E. Beyer & P. Popp, *Nursing Standard of Care in Medical Malpractice Litigation: The Role of the Nurse Expert Witness*, 23 J. Health & Hosp. L. 363, 365 (1990).

This scholarly insight has spread to litigators:

Testimony from a physician about the standard of care may be subject to objection because the physician is not a nurse and does not have direct knowledge of nursing standards of care. A physician's statement that he or she often observes nurses and therefore knows what they do may be inadequate. P. Sweeney, *Proving Nursing Negligence*, 27 Trial 34, 36 (May 1991).

Beyond scholars and litigators, courts have begun to accept this reasoning.

In some jurisdictions, "the physician is no longer permitted to testify about the nursing standard of care since the physician is not a nurse and does not possess direct knowledge of nursing standards." F. Cavico & N. Cavico, *The Nursing Profession in the 1990s: Negligence and Malpractice Liability*, 43 Clev. St. L. Rev. 557, 578 (1995); see *Dolan v. Jaeger*, 285 A.D.2d 844, 846, 727 N.Y.S.2d 784, 786–87 (2001) (upholding trial court's dismissal of nursing malpractice action where physician anesthesiologist was only expert to testify as to nurse's standard of care); *Vassey v. Burch*, 45 N.C. App. 222, 226, 262 S.E.2d 865, 867 ("Although the affidavit of [the physician] may be sufficient to establish the accepted standard of medical care for a doctor in his office, it does not establish the standard of care for a nurse in a hospital"), *rev'd on other grounds*, 301 N.C. 68, 269 S.E.2d 137 (1980). According to one scholar:

> These cases represent a growing recognition on the part of courts that nursing, as a profession, has moved beyond its former dependence on the physician, and into a realm where it must and can legally account for its own professional practices. In doing so, the experts who provide the testimony, and the literature from which their opinions are derived, come from the nursing profession. C. Kehoe, *Contemporary Nursing Roles and Legal Accountability: The Challenge of Nursing Malpractice for the Law Librarian*, 79 Law Libr. J. 419, 428–29 (1987).

Based on this reasoning, AANA argues that Dr. Barnhart should not be permitted to offer expert testimony against nurse Lewis based on his observation of nurses.

We agree. By enacting the Nursing and Advanced Practice Nursing Act (225 ILCS 65/5–1 *et seq.* (West 2000)), the legislature has set forth a unique licensing and regulatory scheme for the nursing profession. As AANA observes, under the nursing act, a person with a medical degree, who is licensed to practice medicine, would not meet the qualification for licensure as a registered nurse, nor would that person be competent to sit for the nursing license examination, unless that person completed an accredited program in nursing. See 225 ILCS 65/5–1 *et seq.* (West 2000). The appellate court in this case correctly reasoned:

> Dr. Barnhart is not a licensed member of the nursing profession. To allow the doctor to testify as to the standard of care applicable to the nursing profession implicates the risks raised by *Dolan*, namely, the imposition of a higher standard of care and the muddling and mixing of various tenets and practices unique to each profession. 335 Ill. App. 3d at 272.

We uphold the trial court's ruling on the competency of Dr. Barnhart to testify as to the standard of care for the nursing profession. We expressly reaffirm the license requirement of *Dolan* and its progeny and decline plaintiff's invitation to deviate therefrom.

As a consequence of ruling that Dr. Barnhart was not competent to testify as to the standard of care for the nursing profession, the trial court entered a directed verdict in favor of the hospital. A directed verdict will be upheld where "all of the evidence, when viewed in its aspect most favorable to the opponent, so overwhelmingly favors movant that no contrary verdict based on that evidence could ever stand." *Pedrick v. Peoria & Eastern R.R. Co.*, 37 Ill. 2d 494, 510 (1967). A directed verdict in favor of a defendant is appropriate when the plaintiff has not established a *prima facie* case. A plaintiff must present at least some evidence on every essential element of the cause of action or the defendant is entitled to judgment in his or her favor as a matter of law. *Nastasi v. United Mine Workers of American Union Hospital*, 209 Ill. App. 3d 830, 837 (1991). If the plaintiff fails to produce a required element of proof in support of her cause of action, then no cause is presented for the jury's consideration and the entry of a directed verdict for the defendant is proper. *Mayer v. Baisier*, 147 Ill. App. 3d 150, 155 (1986); see 3A Nichols Illinois Civil Practice §62:9 (rev. 2003).

In this case, plaintiff was required, and failed, to establish the applicable standard of care through the testimony of a medical expert. The only evidence plaintiff offered on this issue was the testimony of Dr. Barnhart, which the trial court properly struck. Therefore, plaintiff failed to establish a *prima facie* case of medical malpractice against the hospital through the acts of nurse Lewis. The trial court correctly determined as a matter of law that there was no evidentiary basis out of which the jury could have construed the necessary facts essential to recovery. See *Jones*, 154 Ill. 2d at 47. We uphold the trial court's directed verdict in favor of the hospital.

II. Jury Instruction on Proximate Cause

Plaintiff next contends that the trial court committed reversible error by giving the jury the long-form proximate cause instruction from Illinois Pattern Jury Instructions, Civil, No. 12.05 (2000). According to plaintiff, the evidence did not show another party to be the sole proximate cause of Burns' injuries.

We need not address this contention, as it is waived. Supreme Court Rule 315(b)(3) requires a petition for leave to appeal to contain "a statement of the points relied upon for reversal of the judgment of the Appellate Court." 177 Ill. 2d R. 315(b)(3). Rule 315(b)(5) requires the petition to contain "a short argument *** stating *** why the decision of the Appellate Court should be reversed or modified." 177 Ill. 2d R. 315(b)(5). In this case, the "points relied upon for reversal" and "argument" sections of plaintiff's petition for leave to appeal focused exclusively on the issue of the competency of Dr. Barnhart to testify as to the standard of care for the nursing profession.

Plaintiff concedes that she did not raise this issue in the petition for leave to appeal. However, in a footnote in her brief, plaintiff claims that *Caveney v. Bower*, 207 Ill. 2d 82 (2003), allows her to assert this issue. We disagree. In *Caveney*, the appellant *did* raise the contested issue in the petition for leave to appeal (*Caveney*, 207 Ill. 2d at 86–87), but here, plaintiff did not. It is quite established that issues not presented in the petition for leave to appeal are not properly before this court and are deemed waived. *In re A.W.J.*, 197 Ill. 2d 492, 499 (2001) (and cases cited therein); *Rodgers v. St. Mary's Hospital*, 149 Ill. 2d 302, 313 (1992).

However, plaintiff invokes an exception to the waiver rule. Certainly, it is within our discretion to address the merits of an issue not properly raised in an appellant's petition for leave to appeal. *Deal v. Byford*, 127 Ill. 2d 192, 200–01 (1989). This court has explained that:

> the waiver rule is a principle of administrative convenience, an admonition to the parties; it is not a jurisdictional requirement or any limitation upon the jurisdiction of a reviewing court. In this regard, this court has recognized that a reviewing court may, in furtherance of its responsibility to provide a just result and to maintain a sound and uniform body of precedent, override considerations of waiver that stem from the adversarial nature of our system. *Dillon v. Evanston Hospital*, 199 Ill. 2d 483, 504–05 (2002).

Accord *People v. Ward*, 113 Ill. 2d 516, 523 (1986), citing 87 Ill. 2d R. 366(a)(5).

In this case, we see no reason to override plaintiff's waiver of this issue. The appellate court fully considered the question of whether the long-form proximate cause instruction was properly given to the jury. 335 Ill. App. 3d at 273–74. We therefore conclude that further review of this issue is unnecessary. See *A.W.J.*, 197 Ill. 2d at 500; *Ward*, 113 Ill. 2d at 523.

CONCLUSION

For the foregoing reasons, the judgment of the appellate court is affirmed.

Affirmed.

JUSTICE RARICK, concurring in part and dissenting in part:

> I concur with the majority's holding that the trial court did not abuse its discretion in finding that plaintiff violated Supreme Court

Rule 213(g) (177 Ill. 2d R. 213(g)), and in striking this portion of Dr. Barnhart's testimony. However, I cannot agree with the majority's conclusion that Dr. Barnhart was not competent to testify to the standard of care applicable to the nursing profession in this case.

The majority holds that this case "falls squarely within the license requirement of *Dolan* [*v. Galluzzo*, 77 Ill. 2d 279 (1979)]" (slip op. at 14), and rejects plaintiff's reliance on *Wingo v. Rockford Memorial Hospital*, 292 Ill. App. 3d 896 (1997), which set forth an exception whereby physicians may testify regarding "what a nurse is required to communicate to a physician." *Wingo*, 292 Ill. App. 3d at 906. While the majority finds that "the precise factual scenario of *Wingo*" (slip op. at 14) is not present in the instant case, I believe that any factual distinctions are insignificant where the rationale behind the *Wingo* decision fully applies.

While declining to address the merits of *Wingo*, the majority notes *Wingo*'s holding that the reason for the license requirement of *Dolan* is to "prevent a higher standard of care being imposed upon the defendant and to ensure the testifying expert has expertise in dealing with the patient's medical problem and treatment and that the allegations of negligence are within the expert's knowledge and observation." Slip op. at 14, quoting *Wingo*, 292 Ill. App. 3d at 906. The majority also acknowledges that Dr. Barnhart has "substantial experience in observing and working with *physicians and nurses* in the area of patient fall protection." (Emphasis added.) Slip op. at 3. Therefore here, as in *Wingo*, the concerns expressed in *Dolan* are not at issue because the record establishes that Dr. Barnhart's particular expertise encompasses the proper standard of care for *both* physicians and nurses pertaining to patient fall protection. Thus, I would adopt the reasoning of *Wingo* which holds that the license requirements of *Dolan* do not apply where the allegations of negligence "do not concern an area of medicine about which there would be a different standard between physician and another school of medicine." *Wingo*, 292 Ill. App. 3d at 906.

For the foregoing reasons, I would hold that the circuit court erred in granting a directed verdict for the hospital because Dr. Barnhart was competent to testify as to nurse Lewis' deviations from the proper procedures in the area of patient fall protection. The judgments of the appellate and circuit courts should be reversed in part. Accordingly, I respectfully dissent.[1]

---

1. See Sullivan v. Edwards, 806 NE 645 (Il. S.Ct. 2004). www.il.us/courtopinions/supremecourt/2004.

CHAPTER TEN

DISPUTE RESOLUTION FOR NURSES

Donna-Marie Boulay and Paula DiMeo Grant

OBJECTIVES

- Appreciate the use of dispute resolution processes for nursing practice.
- Understand the basic principles of negotiation as used in health care.
- Learn when and how to use mediation.
- Understand the basics of the arbitration process.
- Define the mediation process.
- Describe the role of the mediator.
- Identify conflict management styles.
- Describe the differences between mediation and litigation.
- Define bioethics mediation.

INTRODUCTION

Virtually all of human kind lives and works in a world that longs for peace, a place where disputes either never happen or end with ease. In reality, disputes between people always have happened, and they will continue to happen. Resolution of disputes takes much care, often great energy, determination, and appropriate skill. If disputes are not prevented or if they are left unresolved they can fester and poison human relations.

For nurses, there are known ways to minimize disputes that occur in the work place, and methods to resolve them when they do happen. A familiar method is negotiation.

Negotiation relies heavily on the tools and skills of communication. Nurses are knowledgeable and experienced in communication. Thus, nurses need only to sharpen and focus such tools to improve their ability to manage conflict.

This chapter focuses on three time-tested tools that nurses can use to prevent and manage disputes either on their own or with help. They are negotiation, mediation, and arbitration.

Definitions of Negotiation, Mediation, and Arbitration

Black's Law Dictionary (1979) defines negotiation, mediation, and arbitration as follows:

1. "Negotiation is process of submission and consideration of offers until acceptable offer is made and accepted" (p. 934).
2. "Mediation is the act of a third person in intermediating between two contending parties . . ."; "Settlement of a dispute by action of intermediary (neutral party)" (p. 885).
3. Arbitration is "the reference of a dispute to an impartial (third) person chosen by the parties to the dispute who agree in advance to abide by the arbitrator's award issued after a hearing at which both parties have an opportunity to be heard" (p. 96).

METHODS OF RESOLVING DISPUTES

Negotiation

Negotiation is the tool most of us use to solve and to prevent interpersonal problems and other disputes. It is a tool frequently used in all aspects and stages of life, from cradle to grave. For example, as we maneuver through congested commuter traffic we negotiate with numerous other drivers to prevent accidents. If one driver breaks a rule of the road or behaves erratically, the "negotiations" fall apart, and accidents or disputes may arise.

Negotiation in the health care world is commonplace. It is routine to negotiate with patients, patients' families, coworkers, peers, collaborators, colleagues, employers, supervisors, and those supervised. Nurses in management find themselves negotiating with regulators, other upper-level executives, trustees, suppliers, vendors, and sometimes unions. Bedside nurses often need to negotiate care plans with inpatients, residents, home care clients, families, and colleagues. Negotiations are routine with employees concerning staffing plans. For nurses managing the business operations of health care, there are negotiations with vendors and contractors. And for nurse practitioners, there are negotiations and collaborative agreements with physicians and other health care providers.

Some people are better bargainers than others. Experienced negotiators tell us that the more we negotiate, the more confidence we gain. As our successes multiply and as we put into use the principles of negotiations that professionals use our self-confidence builds and our anxieties about negotiating lessen. However, even the most accomplished negotiators know what it is like to have negotiations fail. But, if negotiations do fail there are ways to resolve matters that are quick, relatively inexpensive and which can promote civility in relationships.

For nurses in the workplace, negotiation is a varied and complex process and presents intellectual and emotional challenges. Therefore, this chapter includes guidance on how to build confidence when negotiating—by sharpening skills and thus minimizing the stress often associated with negotiation.

Exhibit 10.1 Negotiation Principles

1. Be prepared
2. Know your needs
3. Set goals
4. Recognize all issues
5. Identify options
6. Choose best solution
7. Determine initial position
8. Decide bottom line
9. Determine fallback position
10. Know what the other person wants
11. Work for a win/win solution
12. Watch your words
13. Bargain in good faith
14. Stay Alert
15. Get it in writing

Principles of Negotiation

As noted, a sense of confidence is at the heart of a successful negotiator. In the same way that confidence is needed to drive through commuter traffic, confidence will help to obtain favorable terms in an employment or vendor contract or to function well with a colleague, employee, or supervisor.

The 15 principles of negotiation set out below are essential to any negotiation process, and using them to improve negotiation skills helps build confidence. They are particularly useful in the complex world of nursing practice. Nurses can make them work to help with negotiating most anything with confidence. Using these principles will build confidence in the most challenging situations, even for inexperienced negotiators. Consistent use of these principles will reap benefits in your workplace. They can be used to maintain good relationships with colleagues and to achieve the deal or terms desired with suppliers and contractors. Nurses who design care plans can use them to increase the quality of communication with patients and consequently improve patient involvement. The principles are:

1. *Be prepared:* Negotiation should be delayed or postponed if preparation is not complete. If negotiations must take place despite less than optimal preparation, then one should carefully weigh the consequences of possibly not achieving the desired outcome. In other words, the parties must understand and be prepared for the consequences of not being adequately prepared.
2. *Know your needs:* The parties should fully and with precision know the needed outcome of the negotiation. The question becomes what does each party really need to get from the negotiation, and why is that outcome needed? This knowledge allows consideration of all aspects of the situation and can encourage more creative thinking. Fisher and Ury of Harvard, popularized this interest-based approach to negotiating in the 1980s.
3. *Set goals:* Prepare a detailed, written list of desired outcomes of the negotiation and arrange them by priority. Beside each goal, write an explanation of the reasons why that goal is desired.
4. *Recognize all issues:* Prepare a written list describing all aspects of the goals. For example, if the negotiation is related to buying a computer for a nurse consulting practice, some issues that would be listed for discussion might include software capacity, affordability, and service. Be as specific as possible about each point identified. It is very important to the success of the negotiation to be able to articulate to yourself and others the reasons for the desired outcomes.
5. *Identify options:* In other words, identify outcome options that would be acceptable if you are not able to get the first desired outcome in the negotiating session. Carefully articulate and prioritize the options.

Understand why the alternate options are acceptable. Precise knowledge of alternate options before the negotiation begins helps achieve flexibility in the process. Flexibility is an advantage for a negotiator in that the ramifications of alternate outcomes are known in advance, permitting the negotiator and parties to evaluate the alternate options intelligently as the negotiation progresses.

6. *Choose best solution:* The options explored in principle 5 should be evaluated to determine the best solution if the first-choice solution cannot be reached. This enables the negotiation to proceed to conclusion even if the first-choice outcome is not achievable.

7. *Determine initial position:* If the parties have identified their needs and the reasons for their desired outcomes, they are less likely to have a rigid, single, nonflexible position. The initial position (or demand or offer) should be realistic.

8. *Decide bottom line:* The bottom line is what professional negotiators use to refer to the very least the parties will agree to. It means the absolute minimum. For example, if one is negotiating an employment contract, the bottom line might consist of a minimum salary demand, necessary benefits, bonus requirements, or child care opportunities. The bottom line contains all critical features that are unique and essential to the situation.

    It is best to know the bottom line before the start of negotiations, so that the negotiation can be completed with dignity. If a party cannot get all that they want, but can achieve the bottom line, then the negotiation can conclude with an acceptable outcome.

    The essence of the bottom line is that point where a party can choose to walk away from the negotiation. Therefore, it is an extremely important question that must be known in the preparatory stage.

9. *Determine fallback position:* The fallback position is somewhere above the bottom line and somewhere below the opening option or demand. This permits the parties to strategize how they will present their demands so that they are most likely to be successful in achieving their goals. It promotes the presentation of realistic demands.

10. *Know what the other person wants:* This is one of the hardest principles. Once the party prepares for each of the above nine points, they should do the same for the person(s) with whom they will negotiate. The analysis may not be perfect, but it will come close enough to level the playing field so that you can negotiate from a position of strength. This sounds like an awesome chore, but it is done all the time. For example, parents guess at their children's wants, develop a pretty good sense of their needs, and can predict their responses. So

do friends, significant others, neighbors, and colleagues make educated guesses about what other people need and want.

11. *Work for a win/win solution:* This does not mean that each side gets everything they want. But it does mean that they adjust their thinking to aim for an agreement or a solution that everyone will accept. Win/win means that each side wants to win, but not at the expense of the other party losing. To be most successful, this attitude requires that the other person has the same attitude and the same goal at the outset of negotiations. Achieving this balance, this fairness, in the negotiation process is an important consideration for good workplace relationships. People who feel good about negotiating with you will want to work with or do business with you. Be aware that what happens in a negotiation is important for all parties' reputation and the respect of the person(s) with whom they are negotiating.

12. *Watch your words:* Be careful with speech and behavior. This applies before, during, and after the negotiation. Everyone should be aware of what he or she says, when he or she says it and to whom, all of which can influence the chance of arriving at an agreement that all will keep. Pay attention to everyone's body language. Compare what a person is saying out loud to what his or her body language is saying.

13. *Bargain in good faith:* This is an ethical as well as a practical principal and, of course, helps to preserve a good reputation. Good faith encompasses honesty, decency, and integrity. Those who are perceived to negotiate in good faith are more likely to get concessions than those who do not. People who negotiate in good faith are less likely to have negotiations and agreements fall apart.

14. *Stay alert:* Be on the lookout for the negotiator who does not play fair. If one party is a collaborative type of negotiator, a win/win type, and the other person is not, then that person could sabotage the negotiations or take advantage of the situation. A satisfactory outcome is less likely. The parties should let their judgment about what is fair behavior be their guide. If each party is alert to unfairness, it can be dealt with effectively.

15. *Get it in writing:* Most workplace negotiations do not end with a formal written agreement, signed by all the parties. The next best thing is to take careful notes of what was agreed t, and send a simple note to the other party listing the agreed-upon terms, such as "Thank you for agreeing to work Thanksgiving for me, and I will work Christmas for you."

Use of the 15 negotiation principles will help overcome fears that one cannot negotiate well or will not be able to get what they need. Use the steps as a guide to practice negotiating several things. Use them to develop an effective style, and to build confidence. In addition, there are hundreds of books and courses on how to negotiate. These can be evaluated and explored in more depth as needed.

There are many reasons why negotiations fail and agreements fall apart. Not all people are equally skilled at negotiating, and not all people want to negotiate. Negotiation, though an excellent tool, requires people of good will and determination, objectivity, and skills on par with those people they are negotiating with. Some individuals want to win only at the other person's expense instead of collaborating, so that all parties win. Commonly, in a civilized workplace, negotiations are fair, routine, and successful. Sometimes they meet with varying levels of success as measured by goals accomplished and an atmosphere conducive to fostering efficiency. When negotiations fail to achieve agreement, mediation is available. The following exhibit identifies four basic points that can help achieve success in negotiations.

Exhibit 10.2 Negotiation: 4 Basic Points

1. People: Separate the people from the problem
2. Interests: Focus on interests, not positions
3. Options: Generate a variety of possibilities before deciding what to do.
4. Insist that the result be based on some objective standard.

Source: Fisher and Ury, 1983 p. 11.

Mediation

Mediation is facilitated negotiation, a process for use when negotiating on your own fails to prevent or resolve issues or disputes. It is the next tool in line, after negotiation, in the resolution process.

The concept of mediation is one of voluntariness and empowering parties to fashion their own remedies to settle the dispute. As a result of its cost-effectiveness and ability to sustain or enhance interpersonal relationships, mediation is a desirable process for resolving disputes in health care. Because of collective bargaining agreements, nurses may be familiar with labor mediation. Certainly, mediation is an alternative to the costs, both financial and personal, of trial or litigation. And it is often used in nonlitigation settings such as the workplace. The mediation process will be reviewed later in this chapter.

Types of Mediation

There are three basic types or approaches to mediation:

1. Facilitative
2. Evaluative
3. Transformative

The approach used depends on the parties, the nature of the dispute, and the mediator's skills. When selecting a mediator, his or her skill in these approaches should be assessed.

Facilitative mediation. This approach is based on the belief that with the assistance of a neutral person whom the parties trust, people can work through and resolve their own disputes. In a facilitative mediation, the mediator controls the process, such as setting the ground rules for how to resolve the problem. The mediator asks questions to identify the rationale behind the demands of each party, what they need in fact, and the issues of the disagreement. The mediator then assists the disputants to look at solutions that benefit both parties. The goal is to assist all disputants to understand how they can succeed in reaching an agreement.

Evaluative mediation. Evaluative mediation is an approach used in lawsuits when the outcome is purely monetary. It can be used in professional liability and employment cases. However, as apologies and other techniques are becoming increasingly part of the resolution of professional liability cases, the evaluative approach may not be as helpful. It has become most helpful when a case has gone beyond the apology stage (successful or not) and monetary damages remain an obstacle to solution. The mediator then might need to meet with the lawyers to evaluate with them the strengths and weakness of each side of the case. Evaluative mediation remains an important approach for contract disputes and when lawyers need objective outside input to assist their client in seeking a realistic outcome.

Transformative mediation. This approach is based on the premise that parties should take control of how they manage conflict. Transformative mediators try to change the nature of the parties' conflict interaction by

- helping them appreciate each other's viewpoints ("recognition") and
- strengthening their ability to handle conflict in a productive manner ("empowerment").

In this approach, the mediator may intervene in the conversation between the parties to call attention to moments of recognition and empowerment. Ground rules are set only if the parties agree to set them. At the same time, the mediator does not direct the parties to topics or issues. Instead, the mediator follows the parties' conversation and helps them to talk about what they think is important. The transformative mediator does not offer an opinion on the strengths or weaknesses of the parties' cases. The mediator does not suggest solutions. This approach is used quite successfully in large corporations for disputes between staff and management. Reaching agreements is less important here because in transformative mediation the skills acquired by the parties to resolve disputes on their own are a basic goal of the approach.

The Three Mediation Types: Similarities

The three types of mediation share similarities.

- The parties choose a neutral person, a mediator, who is not involved in the dispute.
- The parties choose someone all parties trust, and who they believe will keep discussions confidential until they are ready to tell the other side.
- The mediator can be responsible for facilitating the mediation process, such as scheduling, location for mediation session or sessions, guiding the flow of all communication between the disputants and managing the negotiations. Because the mediator is only the facilitator, negotiation skills are critical for disputants involved in mediation. The skilled mediator asks questions to elicit information about each party's needs and goals and looks for initial positions and other key factors, thus giving advantage to the party who has had time to prepare well.
- The parties meet with the mediator. Disputes involving high-tech matters are often conducted online, in chat rooms, or using other technological communication techniques. Nevertheless, the process is essentially the same.
- Once each party and the mediator understand that an agreement has been reached to settle the dispute, the mediator commits to writing the agreement for signing by the disputants. The written agreement includes details about each party's agreed-upon activities and timelines.

Advantages to Mediation

The key advantages of mediation are summarized as follows:

- In the workplace, if coworkers cannot reach agreement among themselves, a mediator can help. They can listen in private to the disputants' comments about one another and then help them to negotiate a solution that all can live with. In this way, everyone can save face and, more important, go forward and work together peacefully.
- Mediation is popular because it is highly effective. Research in Hennepin County District Court in Minnesota in 2005 showed that 85% of all disputes that were mediated found resolution.
- It is affordable and cost-efficient.
- It is not as time consuming as other dispute resolution processes such as litigation.
- It promotes cordial relationships.
- The disputants choose the person to mediate their dispute. This means the disputants must reach their first agreement unaided. Most times they choose mediators that all of the disputants trust. Many health care workplace disputes do not need outside, professional mediators. However, if there is the need for a mediator from outside the facility or agency, engage one who is properly trained and is affordable. It is not recommended to choose one who offers to work for a percentage of the outcome. This is unethical under most mediator codes of ethics, such as the rules of the American Arbitration Association. Of course, the parties involved can agree to divide up the mediator's fees in whatever way they choose. Ethical considerations are reviewed later in this chapter.
- Mediation is confidential. It is private. There is no public record. The parties agree to keep everything confidential and the laws of most states uphold that benefit.
- Relationships are preserved. Patients, residents, home care clients, professional partnerships, vendor and supplier contracts, colleagues, and other relationships that are important can be preserved and strengthened through the use of mediation.
- The parties maintain control. In mediation, the parties make the decisions. There is no Judge, no jury, no outside "decider" or "trier of fact" of any kind who dictates the resolution. In a sense, the parties are empowered to resolve matters without the interference of anyone else. They can say to the mediator what they want to and what they need to. The mediator can be expected to facilitate discussions between the parties with an eye to sustaining civility at all times.

- A win/win outcome can be achieved. Although in a typical mediation neither party may be completely satisfied, the parties usually recognize the value of each other's position and the agreement reached. Thus, the disputants will gain closure and certainty. If done correctly, there are no losers in mediation.
- Parties are empowered to solve their disputes, put past bad feelings aside, and move forward.

Although mediation is an excellent process, it can fail. Mediations are usually voluntary, unless mandated by the court or statute as later discussed. No participant in the mediation process is required to agree to the terms of a mediated agreement that they have worked long and hard to negotiate. However, mediated agreements challenged in court are more likely than not to be upheld. Not everyone is well suited to participate in mediation, but most people appreciate that is beneficial to resolve disputes as quickly and as efficiently as possible.

Avoiding Problems in Negotiation and Mediation

Being prepared is the best way to avoid or minimize problems. The parties should know what they want to accomplish, their strengths and weaknesses, what they can live with, and perhaps most important, what they can live without. Try to understand what the other person wants to accomplish, including strengths and weaknesses, and what the other person can live with and without.

Above all, know whether the other person is willing to collaborate to obtain agreement or whether that person will try to win at any expense. If a party cannot be trusted to collaborate honestly and fairly to reach agreement, consider another person to help in working through the negotiations. If this is not possible, a negotiated agreement may not be achievable, or the help of a third party, a mediator, may be needed.

If all parties choose mediation and reasons then arise to convince you that the other person will behave unfairly or dishonestly, it is highly unlikely that mediation will succeed. If such problems are discovered after the process has started and the mediator cannot prevent or solve such problems, then mediating the dispute is unlikely to result in an agreement that all disputants accept as win/win. At that point, the solution is clear: End the negotiations or mediation and obtain the help of an arbiter to resolve the matter.

Arbitration

When negotiation or mediation fails, there still may be a nonlitigation solution to a dispute because the disputants may seek someone other than themselves or a mediator to make decisions. This type of dispute resolution is arbitration. In the workplace, nurses are probably most familiar with the process of arbitration as a result of employment contracts in facilities that are unionized.

As a dispute resolution tool, arbitration is an effective "last step" in the grievance process prior to litigation. And though arbitration is less expensive than litigation, it can be more expensive than mediation.

Ordinarily, using arbitration is necessary if mandated by contract and only if negotiations followed by mediation fail or the parties simply cannot or will not participate in either process. Arbitration is the next formal step in the dispute resolution process after negotiation and mediation.

Arbitration Principles

The process of arbitration is almost like a court trial; each side is usually represented by a lawyer, there are prearbitration hearing conferences, before a hearing each side can ask for written documentation or types of evidence from the other side, and then a hearing is held. The hearing looks like and has the feel of a real trial, except that it is usually shorter and the arbitrator is ethically bound to allow in all evidence, some of which would not be allowed in a court proceeding. However, the arbitrator can consider such evidence with the weight of acceptability that he or she thinks is most appropriate.

The arbitrator has the authority to make a decision as a judge or jury would. The arbitration process can be costly in development of paperwork and preparation. Unlike mediation, disputants cannot control the outcome. Each party will try to persuade an arbitrator to see things their way. A major advantage that arbitration has over litigation is that the parties can outline the parameters that the decision will include.

Arbitration has significant differences from a public trial. To begin, it is a private process. A court reporter is usually not present. There is no requirement to be in a courtroom. The formal courtroom rules of evidence do not apply. In arbitration, the parties have an expanded opportunity to tell their side.

Arbitration is usually less expensive than a trial because there are no endless rounds of depositions, interrogatories, and pretrial hearings.

It does not take as long a period of time from the start of arbitration until the arbitrator's award is handed down.

The parties usually agree that the arbitrator's decision is final. If the parties have chosen binding arbitration, only rarely is there a right to appeal to a higher court. The parties choose the arbitrator. In a court proceeding the parties usually do not have the right to choose who their judge will be. An arbitrator, to be acceptable to both parties, should be neutral and trusted by all the disputants. Organizations such as the American Arbitration Association are equipped to supply a list of arbitrators from which to choose and to administer the process for the disputants.

When Litigation is Needed

Litigation is the correct process to use for constitutional issues and for the resolution of complex legal questions and remedies that an arbitrator lacks the power to award. Litigation is expensive and time consuming and requires significant time commitment.

Consequently, nurses will usually find it preferable to prevent disputes and if they do arise, to find ways of solving problems. If that fails, the next best step is to consider mediation. Should both of those steps fail to resolve the issues, consider having someone make that decision in an arbitration proceeding. Remember that arbitration, if used, is usually an end process. Appeals to a court of law are rarely allowed.

The following are examples of when each of the three processes was used:

Negotiation

A and Z worked on the same unit and each wanted to take off for the Thanksgiving holiday. Both said the supervisor, no longer with the facility, had told each of them that they could have it off. The current supervisor said the staffing was short because of an early flu outbreak and the unit could not afford to have either of them take the time off. In talking, A said her family was coming over in the morning for a mid-afternoon meal. Z said he was going to his friends for dinner. Z said he could work the day shift for A if she would work the evening for him. The new supervisor agreed because staffing needs were met and he wanted to build good relationships with his staff. Thus, resolution was achieved.

Mediation

In a culturally diverse rehabilitation facility, some of the residents played their musical selections loudly. Other residents objected to the style of music as well and played their own culturally appropriate music loudly. All music blasted simultaneously from boom boxes. Neither group was fluent in the others' language and anger ruled the unit. The staff, unhappy with the noise and fluent in all relevant languages, tried numerous peacemaking overtures, and made and tried to enforce rules, but the atmosphere deteriorated.

An outside mediator, with outside interpreters, was hired by the facility. The mediator listened separately to each of the two groups of residents and staff in three separate meetings and learned about activities and the specifics of the unit functioning. The mediator pointed out several possible solutions, such as consolidating the schedules for each groups' individual therapies off the unit and freeing up a space of time for each group to play their music. Each group thought it was a great idea to have time to themselves and expressed willingness to change their scheduled therapy (if all the members of the other group would) to accommodate the opportunity to play their music without hassle.

The mediator met with the various therapy departments and asked whether they might consider enabling this solution by accommodating different scheduling needs for each of the residents. They agreed it was a feasible thing to do.

The mediator then asked whether the staff would meet with each group to explain how the loud sound interfered with the care they were rendering to each member of the group. They agreed. There was a meeting of the minds, and all of the groups signed a paper saying they would keep their part of the bargain.

Following their agreement, each of the groups went to their new therapy schedules and on the unit played their music within acceptable decibel levels for the duration of their various stays.

Arbitration

A state agency fired a nurse. She then filed a complaint with the state's Civil Rights agency. She alleged her employer discriminated against her because of her obesity by enforcing against her, but not others, time-at-work policies.

The state encouraged the parties to negotiate a solution to the matter. Negotiations were unsuccessful. Mediation was tried, but the state said their civil service rules would not permit the solutions the nurse proposed, such as reinstating her and transferring her to another department. The nurse rejected an amount of money equal to 3 months of her salary and payment of her attorney's fee that the state offered to settle the matter. Consequently, the state invoked its right to arbitrate.

The only evidence the nurse presented was her own testimony that she believed she was treated differently than were other employees for time off. The state presented time cards showing others had clocked in and out on time, but that the nurse took unauthorized time off in addition to sick leave and vacation to which she was not entitled and that she took several hours–long lunch breaks.

The state submitted documentation from the nurse's personnel file that she was counseled to change that behavior and that not changing it would result in a termination proceeding.

The arbitrator, one of the authors in this book, ruled in favor of the state agency. This arbitration, as the vast majority of all arbitrations are, was completely private. The parties had no legal reason to appeal the outcome to a court and no ruling was published.

Case Example:

Children's Hospital Inc v. Minnesota Nurses Association (1978)

In one of the rare published arbitration rulings, the arbitrators' ruling was appealed to a court. In this matter, two head nurses in a hospital were removed from their ICU positions and the positions were eliminated. The nurses and hospital worked under a collective bargaining agreement reached by the Hospital and the Nurses' Association. The association took the matter to arbitration, pursuant to the collective bargaining agreement and the arbitrators ruled in favor of the nurses, ruling that they and their positions should be reinstated. The hospital appealed to a trial court claiming that the arbitrators exceeded their powers by interpreting the collective bargaining agreement between the parties to find that the hospital's elimination of two head-nurse positions violated that agreement.

COURTS' DECISIONS: The Lower Court agreed with the nurses and then the hospital appealed to the state's Supreme Court. The state Supreme Court held that because the plain language of the collective bargaining agreement made any dispute arising out of the interpretation of or adherence to the terms and provisions of the agreement clearly subject to arbitration, that the arbitrators did not exceed their powers. Then, in a rare rebuke of the defending hospital, the court wrote that disagreement with the merits of an arbitration decision is not a ground for vacating the decision of an award.

THE MEDIATOR

Role of the Mediator

As previously discussed, a mediator is an individual who is trained to assist the parties in a dispute to resolve their differences. The mediator, unlike a judge or arbitrator, has no decision-making authority. A mediator facilitates the mediation process by assisting the parties to reach a mutually satisfying resolution while maintaining respect for one another and an understanding of each other's differences. The mediator assists the parties to increase awareness of each other's needs and is often referred to as the agent of reality. During the mediation process, the role of the mediator also includes identifying the common threads of the dispute and clarification of the goals and issues at hand, while maintaining open channels of communication.

The mediator is also responsible to conduct the mediation process in a fair and ethical manner while maintaining neutrality and confidentiality. A mediator's life experiences, knowledge, and expertise are important factors to consider when choosing a mediator. In some instances, those experiences can enhance the process. Take for example, former president Jimmy Carter and the Camp David Accords, which is discussed in greater detail below. This is an excellent example of the attributes of a skilled mediator.

An Effective Mediator: President Jimmy Carter

An effective mediator is discussed at length in *When Talk Works: Profiles of Mediators* (Kolb, 1994). According to Kolb, "to understand Carter's approach to mediation, one must first understand that historic 1978 meeting of Egypt's Anwar Sadat, Israel's Menachem Begin and President Jimmy Carter, the mediator" (Kolb, 1994, p. 376).

The mediation process began on September 4, 1978, with the Egyptian and Israeli teams arriving at Camp David with Jimmy Carter as the mediator. In preparation for mediation, Jimmy Carter immersed himself into getting to know everything there was to know about these two diverse leaders. He prepared diligently for mediation. Thus, the mediation process began with Jimmy Carter meeting separately or caucusing with each of these two leaders and encouraging them to be flexible and to think creatively. On the second and third days, because of the ground work laid on the first day, the three men met together in a joint session.

For the remainder of the summit, which lasted for 13 days, Begin and Sadat did not meet together again. They did not get along, and reaching an agreement did not seem likely. When the parties refuse to meet with one another as in this situation, the mediator is confronted with great challenges.

However, President Carter was well equipped to handle this situation. "He negotiated vigorously with each leader separately, focusing on both the general principles and difficult details for possible agreements" (Kolb, 1994, p. 378). He appealed to both men's real desire for peace that was the common thread.

President Carter had both a powerful and personal mediation style. One poignant illustration of how he drew upon many of his experiences happened on the 11th day when an impasse occurred, and he was able to convince Sadat not to leave the summit. He told him that if he left the summit their friendship and mutual trust would be damaged. Sadat did not leave the summit. However, on the last day, another impasse occurred. This time, it was with the Israeli team, who did not like the language regarding Jerusalem in the proposed agreement.

Once again, Jimmy Carter used his personal and persuasive skills as a mediator. Here is what Carter did. He had remembered earlier in the day when Prime Minister Begin requested that he sign photographs for his grandchildren. Anwar Sadat had already signed the photographs. President Carter's secretary suggested that the photographs be personalized with the grandchildren's names. President Carter agreed, and each photograph was personalized with the names of the Prime Minister's grandchildren and signed by President Carter (Kolb, 1994).

As President Carter handed the personalized photographs to the prime minister, emotions flowed. The prime minister thanked President Carter and looked at each photograph separately while repeating the grandchild's name. He told the president a little about each child and especially about the one that seemed to be his favorite. A chord was struck and talks continued.

Following the personal and emotional sessions with these leaders, as well as the ability of President Carter to break the impasses by addressing the difficulties, the historic agreement known as the Camp David Accords was reached on September 17, 1978 (Kolb, 1994).

As evidenced by this remarkable example, there is no doubt that President Carter is a talented and skilled mediator. During negotiations, he drew upon his personal and professional experiences as a world leader, as a friend, and even as a grandfather. He was diligent, persuasive, and tenacious throughout the process. This example illustrates how mediators can bring their personal style and life experiences to the negotiating table to assist the parties in achieving their goals—even in a situation, such as this one at Camp David, where an agreement did not appear likely.

Characteristics of Effective Mediators

The qualities or characteristics of effective mediators include some of the same qualities that make effective nurses. Those characteristics include: neutrality, understanding, patience, good listening skills, good communication skills, creativity, respect for others, good judgment, flexibility, and trustworthiness.

Mediators do not take sides in disputes. Nor do they make decisions for the disputants. Mediators have no ownership in a dispute. It is essential for disputants to realize that. Only the disputants own the dispute and the agreement they work to achieve. Therefore, all decisions are solely in the hands of the disputants. However, in the interest of fairness to all and for efficiency, the mediator may suggest options for scheduling mediation sessions, its location, and points for the disputants to consider as they negotiate a resolution to their dispute.

The nurse may be called upon to be the negotiator between disputants, such as patients or subordinates who need help to get their disputes resolved. In the workplace context, "outside" assistance often refers to a supervisor that all parties agree upon and one who can provide that help in the form of facilitated negotiations. Thus, if the nurse is knowledgeable about negotiating, it is possible for a nurse to facilitate negotiations that are not complex in nature. Complex disputes are those that include large numbers of people; involve personal, nonworkplace issues; are exceptionally time consuming; involve huge sums of money (multimillion dollar matters are traditionally handled by a team of negotiators); and those that the disputants believe need the help of an outside professional mediator.

Professional, effective mediators will have knowledge and training in the mediation process. Subject matter expertise is also helpful, and as noted earlier, neutrality is crucial. If at any time during a mediation the mediator appears not to be maintaining and demonstrating neutrality toward all parties in the dispute, the parties should discuss this with the mediator and achieve satisfaction on this issue before allowing the mediation to continue. It is also important that the mediator be sensitive to strongly held values and have an awareness of cultural, economic and gender differences. At all times, the mediator remains in control of his or her own biases and prejudices and has the ability to focus and be steadfast.

The mediator also needs to be diligent in the preparation for mediation and creative during the process. The mediator should be cognizant of any conflicts of interest that are present or that may arise during the mediation session so that he or she can take the proper action in accordance with ethical codes of responsibility.

Mediator Training

Generally, a basic training course for mediators consists of 40 hours of lecture and role playing. A certificate of completion is given at the end of the course. There are colleges and universities that offer continuing education courses in dispute resolution. In addition, alternative dispute organizations offer seminars and workshops at the beginner and advanced levels. There are court mediation programs that require the trainee to be an experienced attorney; however, there are many non–court-connected programs that have no such requirement. In fact, there are many practicing mediators who are not attorneys. At the present time, there are no licensure requirements for mediators. It is advisable to check whether there are any state or federal statutory requirements that apply to your particular situation.

Many mediators have dual professions and bring a wealth of knowledge and expertise to the mediation process. For example, there are some Legal Nurse Consulting Programs that offer a basic course in dispute resolution. Nurses, by virtue of their training and expertise, are uniquely qualified to mediate health care disputes with proper mediation training. Basic courses in negotiation and mediation can enhance the skills of the nurse in the delivery of health care at any level.

The Common Motivators of Mediation

The following are reasons why mediation is a preferred process in certain disputes. These motivating factors are as follows:

1. *Efficiency:* Mediation is efficient by minimizing expense and by expediting a resolution. It also enables the parties to have a direct exchange in the presence of a third person.

2. *Individual factors:* Mediation allows for control in the decision-making process. Some prefer the informal mediation process versus the formal arbitration or trial process that can be long, protracted, and expensive. Individuals may also fear or dislike the court system and seek fairness outside a court of law. In some instances, a decision rendered by a court of law may be necessary.

3. *Honoring a relationship:* Mediation can minimize the deterioration of a relationship and reduce bitterness and hostility. There may be a desire of one or both for reconciliation. There may also be a desire to honor a business relationship or family/community connection. Mediation provides a safe place to express thoughts and feelings that could not be expressed elsewhere. Moreover, the process preserves mutual good will and respect (Harvard Law School, 2001, pp. 13–14).

Mediation Tools and Principles

To enhance the process of mediation and have a better understanding of the dispute, it is important for the mediator to understand the patterns of controversies. According to Stulberg, there are patterns to controversies even though the atmosphere differs in each dispute. He describes these patterns as the 5 Ps of conflict management: (1) perception, (2) problems, (3) processes, (4) principles, and (5) practices (Stulberg, 1987, p.12).

1. *Perception:* Upon hearing the word *conflict* your perception may include anger, fear, tension, anxiety, frustration, hostility, and distrust. Those responses reflect the negative; rarely do we associate disputes with the positive. One can expect emotional responses.

2. *Problems:* Certain problems are inevitable, and encounters in the following relationships can be ripe for conflict.
   a. Employer–employee
   b. Doctor–patient
   c. Nurse–doctor
   d. Supervisor–subordinate

   In the previous chapters, various conflict situations arose where doctors and nurses were sued by a patients for malpractice, and employers were sued by employees for wrongful discharge. Those examples illustrate how conflicts unresolved end up in a court of law.

3. *Processes:* The processes used to resolve problems range from negotiation between two or more individuals, to mediation, arbitration, and

litigation. On a large scale, legislation may be used to solve problems affecting large groups of people.

4. *Principles:* The principles of justice and fairness should be part of any process chosen to resolve controversies. Confidentiality in the process and trust in the mediator are paramount.

5. *Practices:* Individual power and self-interest may be factors in the process used to resolve the dispute. It is essential that the mediator be cognizant of whether the power is balanced or imbalanced and whether self-interest is an underlying goal that can have a detrimental effect on reaching a mutually satisfying agreement (Stulberg, 1987).

Behavior Assessment in Conflict Situations

One tool designed to assess an individual's behavior in conflict situations is the Thomas–Kilman Conflict Mode Instrument. This tool is premised on the theory that behavior can be described along a continuum of assertiveness (concern for self) and cooperativeness (concern for others) (Walsh, 2000).

This instrument defines the five basic conflict management styles as (1) competition, (2) collaboration, (3) avoidance, (4) accommodation, and (5) compromise.

1. *Competition:* The competitive negotiator is highly assertive and at the same time is simultaneously uncooperative. The goal is to win. This individual may be aggressive in pursuit of his or her goals without regard to the other party's interest. This mode can be useful in emergency situations when decisive action is necessary by the nurse, and there is no time to solicit input from others.

2. *Collaboration:* The collaborative negotiator is not only highly cooperative but also highly assertive in seeking solutions not only to benefit his or her interests but also the interests of the other party. The goal is win/win. This mode can be useful to understand another's perspective, brainstorm solutions, and create a consensus of opinion.

3. *Avoidance:* The negotiator who employs this style as a conflict resolution method uses delay tactics to accomplish goals. By avoiding conflict, the negotiator does not seek to assert his or her or the other party's interest. This mode can be useful in certain situations such as gathering additional information or to defer decision making as a strategy. It

may prove to be useful in volatile situations and if the risk of conflict exceeds potential benefit. This negotiator is considered both uncooperative and unassertive.

4. *Accommodation:* The accommodator is one who negotiates in a very cooperative and unassertive manner. The goal here is to yield. He or she gives deference to the will of others. This method can be useful in situations to defuse emotions or to obtain cooperation from the other side. It can also signal willingness to compromise. Just as there is no one "right" way to mediate, the same holds true for the five conflict management styles; one style is not necessarily better than the others. Most individuals will use one or more of the modes during the mediation process. There may be a natural preference to rely on one mode more than another. Understanding your own preferences will help you recognize whether, in fact, another mode may be more useful in certain situations.

5. *Compromise:* The compromiser is an individual who will seek the middle ground to solve the dispute. This conflict management style seeks to get mutual concessions from the parties. An equitable agreement is the goal (Walsh, 2002).

THE MEDIATION PROCESS

Motivation, by the parties to mediate, is the driving force and the key element for success in the mediation process.

Mediation Preparation

Premediation

For mediation to work effectively, thorough preparation by the parties, attorneys representing the parties and the mediator is vital. It is necessary for the parties to have an understanding of the process of mediation in general and to review the issues to be resolved at mediation.

As discussed earlier in this chapter, mediation is structured or facilitated negotiation; therefore, it is important that the parties identify their interests or needs and the relative importance of each. The attorney can assist in that regard. Various options for resolution should be addressed as a framework for discussion. In most situations, and prior to mediation, the mediator will receive a written case summary from each side, outlining the parameters of the dispute.

The summary should also include the issues to be resolved, the demand made, and whether or not there have been any offers of settlement. The mediator prepares for the session by reading the information received and by asking for clarification or additional information in the premediation phone calls that are made to the parties or their counsel. The mediator is also responsible to complete a conflicts of interest check to uphold his or her ethical obligations. In addition, preparation may include a review of the various conflict management styles as previously illustrated. At any given time, during premediation or mediation, those conflict management styles may be operative.

Prior to mediation, fees should be discussed and agreed upon. There may be an agreement or a statement of understanding to be signed by the parties to the mediation.

The Six Stages of Mediation

1. *Mediator's opening statement:* Mediation begins with the mediator's opening statement. It is an opportunity for the mediator to set the stage for the session. The opening statement is an introduction and will include a brief summary of the mediator's background. The mediator also gives an explanation of the mediation process and the mediator's role. In addition, confidentiality of the session is explained along with the timeframe. The goals and guidelines are reviewed.

   Premediation documents, such as a statement of understanding, are signed if necessary. The mediator asks the participants whether they have any questions and then begins the session.

2. *Case presentation by the parties/attorneys:* Following the opening statement by the mediator there is a presentation by the parties and/or their attorneys of what the dispute is about. This stage is also known as the information-gathering stage and is accomplished in a joint session with all parties present. Each side gets an opportunity to give an explanation of how and why the dispute arose. At this juncture, the mediator reframes the information given by the parties to be certain that there is a clear understanding.

   It is especially important that the mediator listens actively and acknowledges what is being said. Equal time should be given to the parties to explain their side of the case.

3. *Issue development and discussion:* The mediator, at this stage, organizes the issues to be resolved and sets the agenda for discussion. The mediator facilitates a discussion of the items raised and identifies the common threads.

4. *Options generated/brainstorming:* The mediator encourages the parties to generate options for resolution. All options are put forth at this stage. The mediator may accomplish this goal by calling a caucus or individual sessions (meeting with each side separately). Any disclosures by each side during a caucus are confidential unless permission is given to the mediator for disclosure to the other side.

5. *Evaluation of options:* The options presented during Stage 4 are evaluated by the parties with the assistance of the mediator. Concessions may be necessary to reach a mutually satisfying agreement. This is the stage that alternatives are discussed and analyzed. These alternatives may be referred to as the following: BATNA (Best Alternative to a Negotiated Agreement) and WATNA (Worst Alternative to a Negotiated Agreement) are discussed. (Fisher, Ury, & Patton, 1991).

6. *Agreement:* The goal of mediation is to reach an agreement that is mutually satisfying to all involved. The terms and conditions of the agreement, if reached, are put in writing and must be signed by the parties. It is necessary for the mediator to determine that the parties understand the agreement and have entered into it freely and without coercion. The agreement is a contract and may be enforceable in a court of law should a breach occur.

If an agreement is not reached, the fact that the parties agreed to meet and issues have been clarified brings them that much closer to resolving the dispute in the future. Depending on the matter and complexity of issues to be resolved, the mediation session can take from 2 to 8 hours, and some may require multiple sessions.

Exhibit 10.3 The Six Stages of Mediation

1. Mediator's opening statement
2. Case presentation by the parties and/or attorneys
3. Issue development and discussion
4. Brainstorming/generating options
5. Evaluation of options
6. Parties reach agreement to settle dispute

ETHICAL CONSIDERATIONS

Although mediators do not adhere to any one approach during the mediation process and are encouraged to rely on their creativity and expertise in tailoring each mediation to meet the needs of the parties, they are responsible to follow ethical guidelines as promulgated by their respective organizations. The American Bar Association, the Board of the Association for Conflict Resolution, and the Executive Committee of the American Arbitration Association approved the 2005 revisions to "The Model Standard of Conduct for Mediators on September 8, 2005" (*Dispute Resolution Magazine*, 2006).

THE MODEL STANDARDS OF CONDUCT FOR MEDIATORS

Standard I: Self-Determination

A. A mediator shall conduct a mediation on the basis of the principle of party self-determination. . . .

Standard II: Impartiality

A. A mediator shall decline a mediation if the mediator cannot conduct it in an impartial manner. . . .

Standard III: Conflicts of Interest

A. A mediator shall avoid a conflict of interest or the appearance of a conflict of interest during and after a mediation. . . .

Standard IV: Competence

A. A mediator shall mediate only when the mediator has the necessary competence to satisfy the reasonable expectations of the parties.

Standard V: Confidentiality

A. A mediator shall maintain the confidentiality of all information obtained by the mediator in mediation unless otherwise agreed to by the parties or required by applicable law.

Standard VI: Quality of Process

A. A mediator shall conduct a mediation in accordance with these standards. . . .

Standard VII: Advertising and Solicitation

A. A mediator shall be truthful and not misleading when advertising. . . .

Standard VIII: Fees and Other Charges

A. A mediator shall provide each party or each party's representative true and complete information about mediation fees. . . .

Standard IX: Advancement of Mediation Practice

A. A mediator should act in a manner that advances the practice of mediation. A mediator promotes this standard by engaging in some or all of the following:
   1. Fostering diversity within the field of mediation.
   2. Striving to make mediation accessible to those who elect to use it, including providing services at a reduced rate or on a pro bono basis as appropriate.
   3. Participating in research when given the opportunity, including obtaining participant feedback when appropriate.

4. Participating in outreach and education efforts to assist the public in developing an improved understanding of, and appreciation for, mediation.
5. Assisting newer mediators through training, mentoring, and networking.... (*Dispute Resolution Magazine*, 2006, pp. 35–38).

There are other ethical guidelines that have been published and adopted by dispute resolution organizations and programs. These ethical standards provide a framework for mediators. Other professionals, such as nurses and attorneys, should also be cognizant of any ethical provisions, canons, or standards promulgated by their professions that may affect their mediation practice.

MODELS OF MEDIATION

Mediation in Health Care

Bioethical Mediation

The use of mediation in bioethical situations is relatively new and has proved to be useful when families and medical and nursing staffs are facing painful ethical dilemmas. According to Dubler and Liebman (2004),

Bioethics is a body of scholarship produced by philosophers, lawyers, medical care providers, and theologians, who in a dialogue over the past few decades have identified shared values that provide the basis for normative principles and rules.... Bioethics also includes the ethical principles of patient autonomy (supporting and facilitating the capable patient's exercise of self-determination); beneficence (promoting the patient's best interest and well-being and protecting the patient from harm); non-maleficence (avoiding doing harm to the patient); and distributive justice (allocating fairly the benefits and the burdens related to health care delivery. (p. 6)

Bioethics is also about legal precedent as established by the courts at both the state and federal levels. Legislation has also played a role in bioethics.

Bioethical mediation provides the parties with a dignified and respectful process for the resolution of ethical dilemmas. According to Noll (2004), bioethical mediation is another example of how positive peacemaking is not only affecting our institutions but also our culture and daily lives.

In the 2004 article titled "Bioethical Mediation: Peacemaking and the End of Life" Noll poignantly describes a bioethical mediation in the folllowing case example.

CASE STUDY:

BIOETHICAL MEDIATION

SUMMARY OF FACTS: Joseph was in the intensive care unit on life support. The prognosis for his recovery was grim, but there was the possibility that final surgery might save him. The likelihood of success was not great considering Joseph's frail condition.

Victoria, his wife of 50 years, wanted the surgery; John, his son, who held a durable power of attorney over medical decisions, did not want the surgery. No one knew how long Joseph would live, and the hospital was concerned about the use of an expensive, scarce (sic) hospital bed. Joseph had instructed that no extraordinary means be used to prolong his life. A conflict evolved between the hospital, Victoria, and John over Joseph's future care.

The hospital staff called a bioethics mediator to intervene, and the mediator consulted with the medical team and the nursing staff to better understand the medical situation. She asked the entire group who would be the most appropriate to represent the hospital and medical team. The medical resident and nurse agreed to participate.

The Mediator met with Victoria and John who were in a nearby waiting area close to Joseph's room. She sat down with them and explained that she was retained by the hospital in situations like this to help people find common ground. She briefly explained the process choice to Victoria and John. They agreed to participate in mediation.

THE MEDIATION PROCESS BEGINS: Victoria began by describing her long marriage to Joseph and her inability to accept his death. Her story was moving and tearful. The mediator gently summarized Victoria's story, creating an empathic connection with her. John spoke next about his love for his father, and his responsibility to carry out his father's wishes under the power of attorney. He hated the responsibility thrust on him and the fact that his obligation to his father conflicted deeply with his own needs and his mother's desires. Again, the mediator summarized John's perspective.

The mediator asked the resident and the nurse to give a summary of the medical situation. The mediator asked for clarification and simplification so Victoria and John could fully understand Joseph's condition. Victoria and John were invited to ask questions to clarify anything they did not understand.

ISSUE IDENTIFICATION: When everyone was satisfied that his or her stories had been told and heard, the mediator asked Victoria and John to identify the interests they needed satisfied to resolve the conflict. As the mediator assisted them in articulating their personal interests, everyone realized that John and Victoria were really aligned. The hospital's interests were expressed clearly by the resident and the nurse. First and foremost was Joseph's care.

OUTCOME: After further discussion, the tearful decision was made to remove Joseph from life support and provide him comfort and palliative care. Joseph passed on later that night (Noll, 2004, p. 1).

Session summary: You will note how the mediator was skillful in connecting with all parties involved in this ethical dilemma. In addition, the mediator summarized the perspectives of the parties. This technique is important as it is vital that the mediator understands issues at hand as seen from various perspectives. This mediator showed a deep concern for all parties and an understanding of the issues at hand. The mediator exhibited many of the qualities discussed previously in this chapter.

Mediation took place in a joint session with all parties present at all times, unlike the mediation conducted by Jimmy Carter in the previous example of a mediation. Here, mother and son were able to articulate their stories and express their feelings in an open manner with all participants present. There was no animosity, and they were also able to discuss their individual perspectives and their mutual love for a husband and a father. In addition, they were able to hear the medical resident and nurse describe the medical situation of their loved one and that Joseph's care was paramount. It is certain that the information given brought comfort to family making this heart-wrenching decision. Ethical principles were also taken into consideration by the parties to this mediation. Patient autonomy was maintained while supporting the shared values of the patient and family.

The mediator asked for clarification and simplifications so that the family could fully comprehend the medical condition. The family was also invited to ask questions to clarify anything that they did not understand. In the final analysis, John and his mother were in agreement in removing Joseph from life support and providing him comfort with palliative care. This difficult decision was made after all parties were heard and understood. And all questions were answered. The mediation session, as described by Noll, was conducted in a very professional manner by a highly skilled mediator. Active listening and good communication skills were employed very effectively in this example.

Rush Model of Mediation

Another example of a successful mediation program in a health care setting has become known as the "Rush Model." In 1995, Rush University Medical Center in Chicago instituted mediation instead of litigation in medical malpractice actions and formed a co-mediator program, which brings both the plaintiff and defendant bars together, to mediate medical malpractice cases. A panel of experienced attorneys form the key element to this successful program. The plaintiff chooses the co-mediators to mediate the case. Co-mediators include an experienced plaintiff attorney, one who represents the injured party and an experienced defense attorney, one who defends the health care provider and/or institution sued. The co-mediator program or "Rush Model" has proved to be a success in encouraging plaintiffs and their counsel to participate in mediation (Blatt, Brown, & Lerac, 2009).

Mediation in the Medicare Program

In September 2003, the Centers for Medicare and Medicaid Services (CMS) introduced mediation to the Medicare program nationwide. Only complaints that do not exhibit significant clinical quality of care concerns are considered for mediation. It is reported that physicians and patients who participated in mediation during the pilot study reported satisfaction with the process and outcome and achieved a sense of closure.

Approximately 80% of Medicare beneficiary complaints are related to misunderstandings, lack of communication, or the patient's perception of treatment. Cases such as these have the potential of forming the basis of malpractice actions. In this mediation, nurses are often used as a comediator assisting the mediator to better understand the health care issues to be resolved. Other individuals with health care backgrounds may also be used as comediators. The mediation session, in this setting, usually takes 2 to 4 hours (IPRO & CMS, 2003).

Medical Malpractice Mediation: A Court Setting

The Superior Court of the District of Columbia, Multi-Door Resolution Program mandates mediation before a medical malpractice case is submitted to the trier of fact (judge or jury) for resolution. This court-connected mediation program has been in effect since 1991, and it has proved to be successful in bringing many cases to closure before trial. In this model, suit is filed and discovery must be completed prior to mediation. Prior to mediation, the attorneys representing the parties are required to complete a confidential settlement statement (CSS) for mediation. The CSS summarizes the case and outlines the positions of the parties. The mediator receives a copy of the CSS from plaintiff's counsel and defendant's counsel prior to mediation. Any questions pertaining to the CSS are clarified during the premediation phone calls made to counsel by the mediator.

All parties to the action are required to attend the mediation session that lasts approximately 2 hours. In addition, the person with settlement authority is also required to attend the session. There are times when more than one session is necessary to bring the case to resolution. Since mediation in this setting is court mandated, there are requirements and formalities that may not exist in other settings. While parties in this mediation model are required to attend the mediation, they are not required to reach a settlement in the matter mediated. This is important as the essence of mediation is that it is a voluntary process.

There are distinct differences in the process of mediation and litigation. Table. 10.1 indicates some of the significant differences between mediation and litigation.

In comparing mediation to litigation, it becomes increasingly clear that, in many instances, mediation better serves the parties in resolving their dispute in a confidential and efficient manner without the publicity and expense of a long, and protracted trial. The programs described

Table 10.1 Mediation and Litigation: The Differences

Mediation	Litigation
Parties control outcome	Judge or jury control outcome
Settlement only with party approval; mediator does not decide	Final or binding decision by judge or jury
Mediator guides discussion; exchange of information is voluntary	Judge and jury hear only evidence allowed by rules of procedure and discovery is required
Process is informal	Process is formal, parties testify under oath
Process is private and confidential	Process is open to the public and recorded by a stenographer
Settlement agreement can be based on views, opinions, and needs of the individuals	Decision based on facts, evidence, and the law
Looks forward, allows parties to have closure, and move on	Losing party may appeal and the closure may not happen for years
Allows for continued relationships	May result in mistrust or animosity
Low cost	Costly
May involve a single session of several hours	Can take years for pre-trial, trial, and possible appeals

Source: From Mediate Don't Litigate: Your Co-op/Condo Residential Dispute, *reprinted with permission of the New York City Bar Association.*

in this chapter further illustrate that mediation is becoming a popular mechanism to resolve disputes. The following describes recent trends in the utilization of mediation other health related situations.

Conflict Management Standard in Health Care Settings

The Joint Commission (TJC) issued a new leadership standard titled "Conflict Management Standard, LD.01.03.01," which became effective January 2009. It is expected to explore the expanded use of mediation to manage conflict in the health care setting. The overall standard states: "The governing body is ultimately accountable for the safety and quality of care, treatment and services." The elements of performance for this new standard includes the development of a code of conduct that defines behaviors that are acceptable, inappropriate, and/or disruptive. In addition, the standard also calls for the development and implementation of a process to manage disruptive or inappropriate behaviors. (Bovio, 2009).

Vermont: Mediation in Workers' Compensation Claims

As of August 31, 2009, the state of Vermont requires mediation in workers' compensation matters. Most of the individuals been named to its mediator panel, are attorneys with experience in the area of workers' compensation. The goal of the program is to address the workers' compensation claim at an early stage, with the hope of reaching a resolution in a fair and efficient manner (21 VSA, Section 663a).

Elder Mediation

Elder mediation in the areas of probate, guardianship, and family caregiving offers the opportunity for creative problem solving and the possibility of avoiding costly, time-consuming disagreements that can "tear a family apart," according to Susan Curcio, a Florida Certified Family Mediator. She notes that the state of North Carolina has implemented a mediation program in guardianship matters (Curcio, 2009).

CONCLUSIONS AND TRENDS

It is important to remember that no matter what the setting is or which method of dispute resolution is utilized—negotiation, mediation, or arbitration—preparation is vital.

Negotiation and mediation enable the parties to be empowered by fashioning their own remedies to settle the dispute. Arbitration, on the other hand, has an arbitrator render a decision based on the facts and evidence presented at a hearing.

It is, however, important for all parties involved to review what is the best-case scenario and what is the worst-case scenario to a negotiated agreement, while being mindful of what the likely outcome will be. Trends indicate that there will be an increased use of these methods to resolve health care disputes as described in the above examples. Nurse leaders are uniquely qualified to be significant contributors in the processes of dispute resolution.

KEY POINTS

Negotiation relies heavily on the tools and skills of communication. Nurses are learned and experienced in communication. Thus, nurses need only to sharpen and focus these tools to improve their expertise to manage conflict.

The concept of mediation is one of voluntariness and empowering the parties to fashion their own remedies to settle disputes.

A mediator is an individual trained to assist the parties in a dispute to resolve their differences. A mediator is not a decision maker. A mediator maintains open channels of communication throughout the mediation process.

Arbitration, as a dispute resolution tool, is effective as the last step in the grievance process if the parties are unable to reach an agreement.

The process of arbitration is similar to a court trial: Each side is usually represented by a lawyer, there are prearbitration hearing conferences, evidence may be asked for by each side and submitted, and a hearing is held before an arbitrator who then makes a decision regarding the outcome.

Litigation is expensive, time consuming and requires significant time commitment.s

REFERENCES

American Arbitration Association, American Bar Association's Section of Dispute Resolution, & Association for Conflict Resolution (2006). The model standards of conduct for mediators: September 2005. *Dispute Resolution Magazine*, 33–38.

Black's law dictionary (5th ed.). (1979). St. Paul, MN: West Publishing.

Blatt, R., Brown, M., & Lerner, J. (n.d.). Co-*mediation: A success story at Chicago's Rush Medical Center*. Retrieved June 20, 2010, from http://www.adrsystems. com/news/co-mediation.pdf

Bovio, H. H. (2009). Mediation in healthcare. *Mediate.com Newsletter*. Retrieved July 1, 2009, from htpp://www.mediate.com./articles/bovioH1,cfm?nl=218

Children's Hospital, Inc. v. Minnesota Nurses Association, 265 N.W.2d 649 (1978).

Curcio, S. (2009). *Elder mediation matters: Probate, guardianship and family caregiving*. Retrieved January 10, 2010, from http://www.mediate.com/search. cfm

Dubler, N. V., & Liebman, C. B. (2004). *Bioethics mediation: A guide to shaping shared solutions*. New York: United Hospital Fund.

Employers' Liability and Workers' Compensation, 21 VSA, Section 663 (a) (2009).

Fisher, R., & Ury, W. (1981). *Getting to yes: Negotiating agreement without giving in.* Boston: Houghton Mifflin.

Fisher, R., Ury, W., & Patton, B. (1991). *Getting to yes* (2nd ed.). New York: Penguin Books.

IPRO & Centers for Medicare & Medicaid Services. (2003). *Mediation dialogue.* Washington, DC: Author.

Harvard Law School. (2001). *Proceedings from Program of Instruction for Lawyers (PIL): Advanced mediation workshop.* Boston: Author.

Kolb, D. M. & Associates. (1994). Jimmy Carter: The power of moral suasion in international mediation. In D. M. Kolb (Ed.), *When talk works* (pp. 375–393). San Francisco: Jossey-Bass.

New York City Bar Association. (n.d.). *Mediate don't litigate your co-op condo residential dispute* [Brochure]. New York: Author

Noll, D. E. (2004). Bioethical mediation: Peacemaking and end of life conflicts. *Mediate.com Newsletter.* Retrieved July 1, 2009, from htpp:www.Mediate.com/articles/noll13cfm

Stulberg, J. B. (1987). *Taking charge: Managing conflict.* Washington, DC: Heath and Company.

Walsh, M. C. (2002). Measures of psychological preferences. *JAMS, The Resolution Experts, 33*–35.

ADDITIONAL READINGS

Brand, N. (n.d.). *ADR: How to get through your first mediation and what to expect.* Retrieved August 17, 2009, from http://www.cdc.gov/od/adr/1stmed.htm

IPRO—Medicare Mediation Program. (n.d.). Retrieved September 12, 2009, from http://www.ipro.org/index/medicare-mediation-program

Spector, R. A. (2000). Mediation in medical liability litigation. *Journal Louisiana Medical Society, 152,* 429–435.

Thomas, K. W., & Kilman, R. H. (2001). *Thomas–kilman conflict mode: Profile and interpretive report.* Palo Alto, CA: Xicom (Subsidiary of Consulting Psychologists Press, Inc.).

"Ask the Nurse Attorney"

As nurse attorneys, we get asked a lot of questions! Interestingly, a number of the questions are inquiries that we have heard before.

This section poses some of these frequently asked questions, and our nurse attorney contributors have provided answers. The purpose of the answers is to offer general guidance—NOT to offer specific legal advice. Therefore, these questions and responses do not constitute legal advice. The responses should not be relied upon to handle any particular legal situation or dilemma.

Where a nurse has a specific legal situation to address, competent legal representation should be retained so that the lawyer can fully review the specific facts and applicable law and regulation before issuing responses or advice.

However, we believe that nurses will find these questions and answers useful, and a good starting place for analyzing issues and matters that occur with regularity!

Thanks to our contributors for their excellent responses!

The Editors

"ASK THE NURSE ATTORNEY"

Dear Nurse Attorney,

I am a registered nurse employed by a hospital, and I was told that if I get sued the hospital provides insurance for me. I was talking with some of my nurse colleagues, and there are differences of opinion about carrying our own malpractice insurance. What do you advise? Should I still carry my own malpractice insurance?

Signed,
Concerned Nurse

Dear Concerned Nurse,

Yes, I strongly advise that you should maintain your own professional liability insurance policy. Because hospitals have vicarious liability for their employees, hospital policies are in place to protect the *hospital*, not the *employee*. Although your interests as an employee and the hospital's interests as the employer are generally not in conflict, the hospital policy still leaves many gaps in your coverage and can leave you vulnerable as a licensed professional. Should you be accused of functioning outside your scope of employment, or in violation of your hospital's policies and procedures, the hospital may not be liable for your actions. In such cases, you are considered to be on a "frolic and detour" and your interests may be adverse to those of your employer's. Remember that the hospital lawyer must do what is in the best interests of the client. *You* are not the client. The *hospital* is the client.

Your employer's policy does not cover you for suits that arise from events occurring outside the workplace because your actions in those events were not within the course of your employment nor intended to promote the interests of your employer. Employer policies do not cover you for licensure protection, should a complaint be made against you to the board of nursing. Your own professional liability policy provides a measure of protection for those actions by allowing you to be represented by counsel during the investigation and disciplinary process.

Employer policies also do not cover you for indemnity claims. Should a physician (or your employer) be found liable in a suit for an adverse event to which you contributed, there could be an action against you to recover those losses. Your hospital policy will not cover you for those claims.

Finally, it is important to know if your hospital has a claims made or occurrence policy. Here is the difference. A "claims made policy" provides coverage only if both: the incident giving rise to the claim occurs during the period of the policy and the claim is filed during the coverage period of the policy. An "occurrence policy" covers incidents arising during the coverage period, regardless of when the claim is reported. Therefore, with a "claims made" policy, you may not be covered once you terminate your employment. In such cases you would need "tail coverage" which covers incidents that are reported after the policy coverage period.

For all these reasons and more, The American Association of Nurse Attorneys strongly advises nurses to maintain professional liability coverage regardless of employer policies.

Signed,
Edie Brous, RN, MS, MPH, Esquire
New York, NY

"ASK THE NURSE ATTORNEY"

Dear Nurse Attorney,

Many years ago, I served as an in court expert witness and would like to serve again. Since it has been a long time, I wonder what I need to focus on in order to be well prepared to serve as an expert witness again. What are the areas of concern I should be aware of?

Signed,
Nurse Expert

Dear Nurse Expert,

While testifying in a legal proceeding as a nurse expert is both professionally challenging and financially rewarding, there are several issues you should consider before undertaking this endeavor.

As an initial consideration, you will be required to satisfy the court's standards regarding the qualifications of an expert. Most courts require an expert to be experienced with the standard of nursing care, procedures and treatments relevant to the allegations against the nurse defendant. The standard also requires that an expert witness has devoted a majority of work time to clinical practice, teaching, or research in relation to the type of treatment that gave rise to the plaintiff's complaints. While some jurisdictions have not articulated these standards in their court rules, your value as an expert and your credibility with a jury, requires that your area of nursing practice match the clinical practice area of the nurse defendant.

Another consideration relates to any publications you may have authored. Expect that the opposing attorney will have read your publications, and that he or she will question you regarding your writings. They will look for inconsistencies between your testimony and publication, and will question you about them. Inconsistencies, of course, can be addressed based on differing circumstances, nursing judgment, or subsequent studies, but you need to be prepared for this.

This also applies to any previous deposition testimony you provided either as an expert, a defendant, or as a witness. Expect that the opposing attorney has read your prior deposition transcripts, and will be looking for inconsistencies in your statements and writings.

Finally, make sure your cumulative expert work is balanced between serving as an expert on behalf of the plaintiff and serving as an expert on behalf of the defendant. This approach will obviate any allegations of your bias as an expert, and will enhance your credibility as an expert.

Signed,
Shellie Karno, RN, BS, JD
Chicago, IL

"ASK THE NURSE ATTORNEY"

Dear Nurse Attorney,

I am a nurse administrator, and I recently received a subpoena to appear for a deposition in a medical malpractice action. It seems that the hospital is being sued in regard to a case that occurred three years ago. I apparently was on duty at the time of the incident. This has never happened to me before. What do I do?

Signed,
Subpoenaed Nurse

Dear Subpoenaed Nurse,

There are a number of steps you need to take, but it is important to stay calm and collected as you work through this process.

To start, you should immediately contact the general counsel or risk manager at the hospital, tell them about the subpoena and ask that an attorney be assigned to represent you. Usually, this is the same attorney that is representing the hospital in the case, unless a conflict of interest should arise (a conflict of interest might be where the attorney or you have an interest or association that prevents objective representation on your behalf). In the case of a conflict of interest, they should assign a different attorney to represent you.

Do **not** review the record associated with the matter in question by yourself; do not discuss the case with anyone and do not carry out any inquiry or investigation on your own. Any record review of inquiries should be specifically under the direction of your attorney. To do otherwise is to risk that activities you carry out on your own will be "discoverable"—that is, subject to inquiry or production by the opposing party. When you do only what the attorney representing you tells you to do, your activities are then considered to be within the attorney client privilege or work product doctrine. This helps to protect them from scrutiny by the opposing side.

In addition, never alter the record in any way, and never destroy any documents. Modification or destruction or any documents associated with a case lends suspicion that there is an attempt to conceal facts. Don't let that happen in your case.

You will likely be summoned to a deposition, which is taking testimony under oath. Depositions require preparation, so you should be prepared to meet with your attorney and to have ample time to review the documents of the case, as well as what you will provide as testimony. Be sure to do this enough in advance of the deposition so you are not rushed or feeling pressured on the day of the deposition.

If for any reason you are not comfortable or satisfied with the legal representation provided to you, advise your hospital's general counsel or risk manager, and ask that your risk manager be involved in your preparation if possible. Some malpractice counsel may not have a nursing background, and the risk manager may be able to bridge the communication gap.

If your employer refuses to provide an attorney for you, or you feel that your employer's counsel is not acting in your best interests, retain your own counsel to represent you at your deposition. If you have your own malpractice insurance, you can request that an attorney be assigned. At any rate, you should have legal representation at the deposition. While you may not be named as a defendant in the lawsuit at the time of the deposition, there is always a possibility that you could be added as a defendant later. Therefore, you must have legal counsel to assist you in representing your interests.

The bottom line is: have sound legal advice; request the support and assistance of your risk manager if you desire this; allow adequate time to prepare and above all, just tell the truth! The protections of the law are there for you as well as for the opposing side!

Signed,
Pamela D. Miller, RN, BSN, JD, CPHRM
Bridgeport, CT

"ASK THE NURSE ATTORNEY"

Dear Nurse Attorney,

I am a registered nurse and received a letter from the Board of Nursing that they are investigating a complaint that was filed against me. I cannot imagine what the complaint could be, but it has me unnerved. What should I do? What are my rights?

Signed,
Nurse Under Board Review

Dear Nurse Under Board Review,

First, you are right to seek advice after receiving this letter. You should never ignore such a letter, and the first step you should take is to contact an attorney right away for assistance. Most Boards of Nursing allow legal representation, and you do not want to deal with this alone.

There is usually a deadline for responding to the Board. If you are near or past the deadline, acknowledge receipt of the letter and request an extension of time in which to respond. Your attorney may assist you with this first step. Your attorney will also take steps to preserve your right to have a hearing; this is crucial in order to avoid a determination on the matter without the opportunity to a fair and impartial hearing.

Avoid having any "off the record" discussions about this matter. Once you have consulted with counsel, you will work with him or her to respond in a way that addresses only the merits of the complaint.

If you are employed, your organization may provide legal representation for you. This may depend on the nature of the matter. If it involves any aspect of your employment, you would want to advise your employer. In addition, some malpractice carriers provide a specific amount of money for reimbursement for defense in administrative proceedings, so if you have your own malpractice policy, please inquire. Note that this is an administrative proceeding involving the Board of Nursing (as compared to a suit involving a court action). However, testimony given may be admissible later in a malpractice suit.

If you have any documents relevant to the matter, you should take care to preserve them, and of course, do not destroy or alter any records. Do not discuss the merits or any aspects of the complaint with anyone or perform any research unless directed to do so by counsel.

Finally, in choosing an attorney, one that has a successful track record before the Board of Nursing is a good choice.

Signed,
Pamela D. Miller, RN, BSN, JD, CPHRM
Bridgeport, CT

"ASK THE NURSE ATTORNEY"

Dear Nurse Attorney,

I am a registered nurse concerned about my delegation responsibilities. Can I be sued if a patient sustains an injury caused by the person I delegated the responsibility to?

Signed,
Delegating Nurse

Dear Delegating Nurse,

Yes, it is possible to be sued if you delegate responsibilities to another person and a patient is injured as a result. This is also known as supervisor liability. Even if you are not a supervisor per se, that is a member of management, your assignment to another person, whether an RN, LPN or nurse's aide, should be made thoughtfully.

When assigning a task to another, be aware of his or her training and experience, and availability to complete the task. Assignments must be made within the scope of practice for the individual. For example, don't ask another RN to do something that really should be addressed by a physician, or a more experienced nurse or Licensed Independent Professional (LIP).

Also, when assigning duties to a nursing assistant, be careful to keep the task within his or her scope of practice. A delegating nurse could be held liable for assigning the assessment of an unstable patient to a lesser qualified individual, or even to another experienced RN who is unable to carry out the assignment due to work overload.

Many states have specific provisions for delegation in their nurse practice act. Familiarize yourself with the scope of practice laws in your state for all disciplines that you delegate to, and review case examples from your state Board. Work with your organization to understand and define how delegation is safely carried out.

The Joint Statement on Delegation, issued in 2005 by the ANA and the National Council of State Boards of Nursing is a helpful resource. The Joint Statement advises that the nursing process itself cannot be delegated. In addition, it recommends that the nurse take into consideration the condition of the patient, the competence of the individual and the degree of supervision required. Five rights of delegation are defined: the right task, under the right circumstances, to the right person, with the right direction and communication, and under the right supervision and evaluation. As always, your State Board of Nursing will define scope of practice and delegation, and the State's interpretation is controlling.

Signed,
Pamela D. Miller, RN, BSN, JD, CPHRM
Bridgeport, CT

"ASK THE NURSE ATTORNEY"

Dear Nurse Attorney

I am a professional nurse and I want to start my own home health business. Since I have no experience with starting a business, what are the basic steps I should consider to do this correctly?

Signed,
Nurse Entrepreneur

Dear Nurse Entrepreneur,

Preparation, **painstaking preparation,** is the key to starting up a business. The following is an outline of basic steps only. Advanced steps will become clear as you work your way through the basics.

1. Assess your skills. Do you have management experience? Do you have the mindset to be an entrepreneur? Are you willing to discover what you do not know and then to learn what you must?
2. Write out your personal goals.
3. Determine your business goals. Identify possible partners, if appropriate.
4. Assess your time management needs to meet the needs of each of your obligations. Schedule time to plan. Control how you use your time.
5. Plan in detail. Articulate your mission. Determine the marketability of a home care agency in the area you want to serve.
6. Research your competition and analyze the data you uncover.
7. Develop a business plan that includes your research, time lines and the type of business entity. For example, many home care agencies are non-profits. Others are for-profit in those states that allow health care to be delivered by for-profits.
   a. Choose a business name.
   b. Decide on a location for your office in the area you will be serving.
   c. Decide what equipment you need.
   d. Prepare a budget.
8. There are many relevant publications in libraries, bookstores and online that cover all of these subjects. Plan to spend time reviewing and taking notes on all the relevant, current and reliable material you can. Beware there are many sources of information that may not be tailored to your needs or your State or to Federal requirements.
9. Work with an accountant familiar with Federal Laws and your State's Medicaid laws to set up an accounting system that carefully conforms to them. Determine your tax year, business deductions, compensation methods and local, state and federal tax requirements.
10. A lawyer is essential to assist in this process, and can help with all local and state business licenses, registrations and in conforming your operations to complex Medicare and Medicaid requirements. Choose an attorney familiar with nursing practice who will be available for consultation as you grow.

11. Decide the size of the agency, how many employees you will hire, and what expertise you will need to provide services. Evaluate the options for financing your business.
12. Establish your code of ethics and business philosophy.
13. Ask others who have started their own enterprises what it took and what it takes to survive and thrive.

Good luck in your entrepreneurial effort. Do remember: the investment you make now in careful planning and engaging experts at this stage will pay off later in avoidance of unanticipated problems. I wish you success!

Signed,
Donna-Marie Boulay, RN, JD, MANM
Roseville, MN

Glossary

AARA: American Recovery and Reinvestment Act of 2009.

Abuse (Corporate Compliance Definition): A practice (usually a pattern of errors) that results in financial loss to the Medicare or Medicaid program.

ACA: Affordable Care Act of 2010.

Action: A legal dispute between two parties that is taken to court for a resolution.

ADA: Americans with Disabilities Act, which was designed to ensure that the disabled had full access to the American employment market. It was enacted in 1992.

ADEA: Age Discrimination in Employment Act prohibits discrimination based upon age; it protects persons age 40 and older. It was enacted in 1967.

Administrative Law: Body of laws formulated by state and federal agencies.

Administrative Procedure Act: Rules and regulations followed by administrative agencies to conduct investigations and fair hearings.

Admissible Evidence: Evidence that can be admitted in a court of law. If there are questions of admissibility, the judge determines if the evidence can be admitted.

Advance Directives: Documents in which you give instructions about your health care when you are in a situation in which you are unable to speak for yourself. Living wills and medical power of attorney documents are examples of advance directives.

Adverse Event: An injury caused by medical management rather than by the underlying disease or condition of the patient, or an event that involves the patient but does not result in actual injury to the patient.

Allegation: In legal pleading, an assertion of fact.

Amicus Brief: Also known as a "Friend of the Court Brief," it is a document filed in support of a party's position that gives an analysis and rationale for the support thereof.

Answer: Responses made by the Defendant or Respondent to the allegations made in a legal complaint.

Antikickback Statute: The federal antikickback statute, 42 U.S.C. § 1320a-7b(b), prohibits individuals or entities from knowingly and willfully offering, paying, soliciting or receiving remuneration to induce referrals of items or services covered by Medicare, Medicaid or any other federally funded program (except the Federal Employees Health Benefits Program).

APIE: Assessment, Plan, Implementation and Evaluation; the object of this documentation approach is to condense patient data.

Apparent Agency: Also referred to as Ostensible Agency, is the condition that arises, for example, where the patient believes that a physician is acting under the authority of the hospital (in this case called the principal) when that authority has not in reality been granted through a relationship such as employment.

Appeal: When a losing party takes the case to a higher court for review.

Appellant: The party who appeals the decision to a higher court.

Arbitration: "The reference of a dispute to an impartial (third) person chosen by the parties to the dispute who agree in advance to abide by the arbitrator's award issued after a hearing at which both parties have an opportunity to be heard" (Black's Law Dictionary, 1979, p. 96).

Arbitrator: A trained individual who has the authority to control the arbitration proceeding, and make a determination of the outcome.

Arraignment: The first appearance of a criminal defendant in court to hear the charges and to enter a plea.

Automated Medication Dispensing Systems: First introduced in the 1980's, these systems automatically link the facility pharmacy to the point of care, and provide the nursing unit with enhanced record keeping capability.

Bail: Money in the form or cash or bond paid to the court by the defendant to secure release from custody and to ensure appearance in court at a later date. Failure to appear will be a forfeit of bond or cash.

Bill of Rights for RNs: A statement of professional rights in the workplace adopted by ANA in 2001; it can serve to form the basis for organizational policies and procedures in the workplace.

Bioethics Mediation: The use of mediation to assist healthcare providers, patients, family members, and others in the resolution of ethical dilemmas.

Bio-Identification: Identification based on Biometrics, meaning identification based on biological characteristics such as, among other things, unique fingerprints, analysis of the capillary vessels located at the back of the eye iris, and the analysis of the colored ring that surrounds the eye.

Blood Alcohol Level: It is the legal limit of the concentration of alcohol in the bloodstream. The measurement can be taken from one's breath, urine, or blood sample.

Bloodborne Pathogens: "Infectious materials in blood that can cause disease in humans, including hepatitis B and C and human immunodeficiency virus, or HIV" (OSHA, 2010).

Bloodborne Pathogens Standard: Mandates the employer to have a written plan incorporating the requirements for workplace safety and education regarding bloodborne pathogens as established by the Occupational Safety and Health Administration.

Bona Fide: Something authentic and genuine that is carried out in good faith without deception or fraud.

Breach of Contract: When one or more of the terms and/or conditions of a contract have been breached or violated by the party or parties to the agreement.

Burden of Proof: Obligation of one party to prove the truth of the allegations. In a civil matter, the burden of proof is on the plaintiff to prove that the allegations made by a preponderance of the evidence. In a criminal matter, the government or state must prove that the defendant is guilty beyond a reasonable doubt.

Capacity (Legal): The legal right and/or mental and intellectual fitness to perform some act, such as enter into a contract or consent to a medical procedure.

CBE: Charting by Exception. Introduced in the 1980's, with this system there is no need to document routine care. Only significant findings or exceptions to standards or norms of care are recorded or charted.

CBO: Congressional Budget Office.

Certificates of Merit: In medical malpractice actions, some states require a certificate of merit from an expert that the case is legitimate.

Certiorari: [Law Latin "to be more fully informed"] The U.S. Supreme Court uses certiorari to review most of the cases that it decides to hear (Black's Law Dictionary , 9th ed., Abridged, 2010).

Charitable Immunity: An immunity from civil liability and particularly as regards negligent torts, that is granted to a charitable or nonprofit organization. The legal doctrine of charitable immunity holds that a charitable organization is not liable under tort law (http://definitions.uslegal.com).

Civil Law: The branch of law that pertains to rights and duties of individuals in non-criminal matters such as malpractice and breach of contract claims.

Claim: In the legal and insurance world, a claim is a written demand for payment. Malpractice claims may begin with a letter from a patient, or on behalf of a patient, by an executor of an estate, family member or attorney. Claims may also be initiated by the formal filing of a lawsuit.

CMS: Centers for Medicare and Medicaid Services.

Collaborative Agreement: Employment agreements between physicians and nurse practitioners outlining terms and conditions for delivery of health care services. In some states it is mandated by law.

Collective Bargaining Agreement: An agreement between an employer and a union outlining the terms and conditions of employment for employees covered by the agreement for a specified period of time.

Common Law: The system of jurisprudence which originated in England and was later applied in the United States. It is law based on judicial precedent.

Complaint: Legal pleading with allegations made by Plaintiff or Complainant.

Complainant: Individual making a complaint to the Board of Nursing or other administrative body.

Compliance: Conformance with requirements of laws, policies, procedures and conduct.

Comprehensive Error Rate Testing: A program established by CMS that measures the error rate for certain claims submitted to Medicare for reimbursement.

Conditions of Participation: Minimum health and safety standards that organizations must meet in order to begin and continue participating in the Medicare and Medicaid programs.

Conflict of Interest: A situation whereby a person in a position of trust has self interests or relationships that do or have the potential to interfere with their ability to make fair and impartial decisions.

Consent Agreement: A voluntary agreement entered into by the parties to a disciplinary action.

Consideration: In order for a valid employment contract to exist there must be consideration, or payment for services. Consideration is one of the elements necessary to establish a contract.

Contract for Employment: A valid employment contract consists of three basic elements: an offer, acceptance and consideration. It outlines terms and conditions of employment between employer and employee.

Corporate Compliance Program: An organization wide program composed of a code of conduct and written policies, internal monitoring and auditing standards, employee training, feedback mechanisms and other features, all designed to prevent and detect violations of governmental laws, regulations and policies.

Corporate Integrity Agreement: A detailed and restrictive agreement, usually lasting 4 to 5 years, imposed on providers by the Office of the Inspector General (OIG) when serious misconduct is discovered through an audit or self-disclosure.

Corporation: A corporation is defined as a legal entity or structure created under the authority of the laws of a state, consisting of a person or group of persons who become shareholders. The entity's existence is considered separate and distinct from that of its members.

Court Reporter: An individual who records testimony of witnesses verbatim in a court of law or at a legal proceeding and transcribes and gives a written report.

Covenant of Good Faith and Fair Dealing: In some states it is an exception to the Employment-At-Will-Doctrine. This legal concept is based on the assumption that employers will treat employees fairly and in good faith in the workplace.

Criminal Law: A wrong committed against person or property with intent: misdemeanors (lesser crimes) and felonies (higher crimes). These crimes may impose fines and/or prison sentences.

Cross-Examination: Questioning of a witness by opposing counsel following direct examination at trial or other proceeding.

Current Procedural Terminology: A code set that describes medical, surgical, and diagnostic services in order to provide uniform information about medical services and procedures.

Cy Pres Doctrine: From French, meaning "as close as possible." When a gift is made by will or trust (usually for charitable or educational purposes), and the named recipient of the gift does not exist, has dissolved, or no longer conducts the activity for which the gift is made, then the estate or trustee must make the gift to an organization which comes closest to fulfilling the purpose of the gift (http://legal-dictionary.thefreedictionary.com).

Declaratory Judgment: Court decisions establishing rights of parties or expressing opinions of the court; a ruling by a court that explains or further interprets a question or point of law in order to resolve an uncertainty.

Defamation: Harming the reputation of another by writing called libel, or spoken words called slander. These actions are sometimes included in wrongful termination cases.

Defendant: The person or entity against whom a lawsuit if filed.

Delegation: In the employment setting, the assignment of a nursing task by a registered nurse to another, such as a qualified and properly trained nursing assistant; one who is supervised by the registered nurse who delegated the responsibility.

Deposition: Testimony of a witness that is taken under oath and recorded, or videotaped to be used for settlement purposes or at trial.

Designated Health Service: Those health services published annually by CMS to which the physician self-referral (Stark) prohibition applies.

Direct Examination: Questions asked to a witness by the attorney of the party who called the witness at a trial or other proceeding.

Directed Verdict: When evidence dictates only one outcome and the trial judge makes a determination to decide the case instead of the jury.

Discovery: A process that provides mechanisms for parties to exchange information and evidence about the case that proves or disproves allegations made; it includes interrogatories, production of documents and depositions of witnesses.

Disparate Impact: When a practice or standard that is not intended to be discriminatory nonetheless disproportionately affects individuals having a disability or belonging to a particular group based on their age, ethnicity, race or sex.

Disputants: The named parties to a dispute.

Dissolution: The end of the legal existence of an entity.

DMEPOS: An acronym for "Durable Medical Equipment, Prosthetics, Orthotics and Supplies," typically referred to as DME or durable medical equipment.

Doctrine of Corporate Liability: This Doctrine imposes liability on hospitals for the negligence of physicians and other health practitioners, particularly where these persons are not employees.

DUI or DWI: Operating a motor vehicle while intoxicated or under the influence of drugs. Most states have placed this charge in the criminal area of the law.

EHR: Electronic Health Record. Essentially has the same meaning as EMR (Electronic Medical Record), but EHR is viewed as the favored term to use when describing or discussion electronic record systems.

Employment-At-Will-Doctrine: The right of an employer to terminate an employee for good reason, bad reason or no reason at all in the absence of a contract or law stating otherwise.

EMR: Electronic Medical Record.

EMTALA: The Emergency Medical Treatment and Labor Act (EMTALA) passed in 1986 by the U.S. federal government. This act requires any hospital that accepts payments from Medicare to provide care to any patient who arrives in its emergency department for treatment, regardless of the patient's citizenship, legal status in the United States or ability to pay for the services. EMTALA applies to ambulance and hospital care.

Evidence: All means by which an alleged matter of fact is established or disproved. Evidence may include testimony of witnesses, introduction of documents, records, exhibits, etc.

Exclusion (Medicare or OIG): A penalty that prohibits certain individuals and entities from participation in any Federal health care program.

Exculpatory Evidence: Evidence that tends to exonerate or absolve of wrongdoing, clear from liability, blame or guilt.

Exhaustion of Remedies: A rule in administrative law and procedure that requires an aggrieved party to pursue all administrative remedies before filing a lawsuit in a civil court in order to resolve the disagreement. When all other available remedies are exhausted, then a party usually can proceed to file a law suit.

Expert Witness: An individual with specialized knowledge and skills that can assist the trier of fact to understand scientific or technical issues at trial or at another proceeding. Professional nurses qualify as expert witnesses.

False Claims Act: The primary federal statute that defines how the government can determine if a person may be held responsible or may have liability for making a false claim. Used in connection with corporate compliance, refers to improper submission of claims for Medicare or Medicaid services.

Felony: A serious crime; the accused is usually incarcerated for one or more years or can even receive the death penalty.

FHR: Fetal Heart Rate.

Fiduciary Duties: A fiduciary duty is an obligation to act in the best interest of another party. For instance, a corporation's board member has a fiduciary duty to the shareholders, a trustee has a fiduciary duty to the trust's beneficiaries, and an attorney has a fiduciary duty to a client (http://definitions.uslegal.com).

Fifth Amendment: The constitutional amendment that protects an individual from self-incrimination in a criminal matter.

FMLA: Family and Medical Leave Act provides an unpaid leave of absence up to twelve weeks to certain employees experiencing various family emergencies. It was enacted in 1993.

Focus Charting: Systems utilizing progress notes, flow charts, history and admission assessments, and a care plan.

Fraud: It is an intentional deception or misrepresentation with the intention of receiving some unauthorized benefit.

Grand Jury: A group of individuals who are chosen to decide whether or not the evidence is strong enough to indict a suspect for a specific crime.

Health and Human Services (HHS): The United States federal department that administers all federal programs dealing with health and welfare.

Health Care Finance Administration HCFA: The part of the U.S. Department of Health and Human Services (HHS) that is responsible for administering Medicare and and the federal portion of Medicaid. It is now referred to as the Centers for Medicare and Medicaid Services (CMS).

Health Care Risk Management: "... clinical and administrative activities undertaken to identify, evaluate, and reduce the risk of injury to patients, staff, and visitors, and the risk of loss to the organization itself" (Carroll, 2006).

Health Insurance Portability and Accountability Act (HIPAA): A law enacted by Congress in 1996, which in addition to other things, contains provisions within the Act that address the security and privacy of health data.

Hearsay Rule: Evidence of a statement which is made other than by the witness testifying at a hearing or trial offered to prove the truth of the matter asserted. Generally, this evidence is inadmissible.

HIPAA: Health Insurance Portability and Accountability Act of 1996.

HITECH: Health Information Technology for Economic and Clinical Health Act. The final rule was released on July 13, 2010 by CMS.

Hospital-Acquired Condition: A condition acquired by a patient while hospitalized that was not present on admission.

Human Rights Act: Laws enacted by state legislatures prohibiting various forms of discrimination.

Hung Jury: A jury that is unable to reach a verdict.

Impasse: When negotiating parties have reached a standstill or are deadlocked.

Implied Contract: An exception to the Employment-At-Will-Doctrine; a contract that is implied by actions or verbal assurances by employers and relied upon by employees.

Incident Reporting: An "early warning system intended to identify risk situations or adverse events in a timely manner to trigger prompt investigation from a claims management perspective as well as corrective action to prevent similar future events" (Carroll, Volume 1, 2006, p. 552).

Incorporation: The process by which a corporation is created and becomes a legal entity distinct from its owners.

Indemnity: The method by which companies will attempt to alleviate the concerns of officers and directors regarding their personal exposure to liability and thus their financial well-being by protecting them from personal loss.

Independent Contractor: " . . . one who is entrusted to undertake a specific project but who is left free to do the assigned work and to choose the method for accomplishing it" (Black's Law Dictionary, 2010, p. 659).

Injunction: Court order to stop an act from occurring or to stop an act from continuing under certain circumstances.

Issue: A point or dispute between two or more parties.

JNOV: Judgment non obstante veredicto; notwithstanding the verdict by the jury; it is when the judge enters the verdict for the other party, thus overturning the verdict.

Joint and Several Liability: A form of liability whereby when two or more people are found liable for damages, the winning plaintiff may collect the entire judgment from any one of the parties, or from any and all of the parties in various amounts until the judgment is paid in full.

Joint Commission (The): The Joint Commission is an independent, not-for-profit organization that evaluates and accredits health care organizations and programs.

Judgment: A determination of the rights of parties; a decision rendered at the end of a hearing or trial.

Just Cause: Clauses in employment contracts or Employment Manuals that state an employee may not be terminated except for just cause or good cause.

Justicability: Requirement that a matter present a case or controversy to be decided by a court of law.

Liability: The quality or state of being legally obligated or responsible.

Limited Liability Company: A flexible business structure that blends characteristics of partnerships and corporations.

Litigation: The process of deciding the outcome of a dispute in court or through the administrative process.

MAE: Mobility Assistive Equipment. Function based, focusing on the person's ability to safely accomplish mobility-related activities of daily living in the home, such as toileting, grooming, and eating with and without the use of MAE.

Mediation: A voluntary process; the " . . . settlement of a dispute by action of an intermediary (neutral party)" (Black's Law Dictionary, 1979, p. 885). There are three types of mediation: 1. Facilitative, 2. Evaluative and 3. Transformative.

Mediator: A trained individual who is responsible for facilitating the mediation process. The mediator has no decision making power.

Medical Screening Exam: An examination provided to a person presenting at an emergency facility. Per EMTALA requirements, the examination must be adequate to determine whether or not an emergency condition exists or whether the person is in active labor.

Medicare: A federal health insurance program for persons who are 65 years of age or older; or are entitled to Social Security or Railroad Retirement disability cash benefits for at least 24 months; or have end stage renal disease (ESRD); or are in a category of certain otherwise non-covered aged persons who elect to pay a premium for Medicare coverage.

Medicare Conditions of Participation: See Conditions of Participation

Medicare Modernization Act: A law of the United States enacted in 2003 that produced significant revamping of the Medicare program.

Misdemeanor: A lesser crime than that of a felony; it may be punishable by fines and other penalties or confinement for a short period of time.

Miranda Warning: The requirement that a suspect in police custody, before interrogation takes place, must be informed of the right to remain silent, the right to have a lawyer present during questioning or to have one appointed if the suspect is unable to afford one.

Mistrial: A trial that ends without a verdict.

Motions: Requests made by either party during the course of a lawsuit which asks the court for a ruling or a decision.

Mutual Assent: Meeting of the minds between two parties to a contract. In the employment setting it is a mutual understanding of the terms and conditions of employment before entering into a contract.

Narrative Form Charting: This system of charting consists of an initial patient history, progress notes, care plan and discharge summary. It is straightforward with the nurse writing in a story-like manner for each shift. This type of charting can also be used in conjunction with flow sheets or check lists.

Negligence: The failure to exercise the standard of care that a reasonably prudent person would exercise in the same or similar circumstances.

Negligence Per Se: Negligence established by violation of a duty imposed by law or statute.

Negotiation: "Is the process of submission and consideration of offers until an acceptable offer is made and accepted" (Black's Law Dictionary, 1979, p. 964).

Never Events: An error in medical care that is identifiable, preventable and serious in its consequences for patients. Also referred to as Serious Reportable Event.

NLRA: National Labor Relations Act passed by Congress which provides employees with the right to engage in collective bargaining activities.

NLRB: National Labor Relations Board is the federal agency responsible for enforcement of the NLRA.

Not for Profit or Nonprofit: An organization incorporated under state laws and approved by both the state's Secretary of State and its taxing authority as operating for educational, charitable, social, religious, civic or humanitarian purposes.

Nursing Jurisprudence: Laws pertaining to the practice of nursing.

OASIS: Outcome and Assessment Information Sheet. It is the documentation system required under the laws which govern home care for Medicare and Medicaid beneficiaries.

Objections: Made by opposing counsel during a proceeding or trial to exclude certain testimony or evidence from being admitted; a trial judge will sustain or overrule the objection.

Office of the Inspector General (OIG): Agency within the Department of Health and Human Services (HHS), that was established in 1976 to identify and eliminate fraud, abuse and waste in HHS programs, and to promote efficient and economic departmental operations.

Operation Restore Trust: A multidistrict, multi-government agency initiative launched in 1995 to focus on ferreting out fraud and abuse in the Medicare system.

OSHA: Occupational Safety and Health Administration is the agency that establishes and enforces health standards and workplace safety measures enforcing the provisions of the OSH Act.

OSH Act: Occupational Safety and Health Act was enacted by Congress in 1970 which requires employers to provide their employees with working conditions that are free from known dangers.

Ostensible Agency: Also referred to as Apparent Agency, is the condition that arises where the patient believes that a physician is acting under the authority of the hospital (in this case called the principal) when that authority has not in reality been granted through a relationship such as employment.

Parens Patriae: Government acting to protect the general welfare of its citizens.

PEA: Pulseless Electrical Activity.

Peer Review: Peer review is a process used for checking the work performed by one's equals (peers) to ensure it meets specific criteria.

PERRLA: Acronym for *p*upils *e*qual, *r*ound, *r*eact to *l*ight, *a*ccommodation. While performing an assessment of the eyes, one evaluates the size and shape of the pupils, their reaction to light, and their ability to accommodate.

Per se Law: A per se law in the context of DUI/DWI means that if a driver is found to have a blood alcohol level of .08, then in the eyes of the law they are guilty of DUI/DWI, and no additional proof of impairment is needed to convict then of the offense.

Petitioner: Party presenting a petition to a court or administrative body for action to be taken against the respondent.

PIE: Problems, Intervention, and Evaluation of nursing care. It is composed of a 24-hour flow sheet combined with nursing progress notes.

Plaintiff: A person or entity who brings an action in a court of law.

Plea: In a criminal matter, defendant's declaration of guilty or not guilty, or no contest.

Plea Bargain: Negotiations between the accused party and the prosecutor for a resolution of the case.

POMR: Problem Oriented Medical Record. First introduced in the 1960s to assist caregivers to think and to better communicate thoughts and actions; to improve efficiency, quality of care and patient safety. It was the beginning of the integration of nurses and physicians charting on the same page.

Preponderance of the Evidence: In civil cases a general standard of proof, where the evidence presented is "more probable than not."

Present on Admission: A condition that is present at the time an order for inpatient admission occurs.

Prima Facie Case: "The establishment of a legally required rebuttable presumption or a party's production of enough evidence to allow the fact-trier to infer the fact at issue and rule in the party's favor" (Black's Law Dictionary, 2010, p. 1028).

Professional Corporation: A corporation formed for the purpose of conducting a profession which requires a license to practice, including nurses, attorneys, physicians, dentists, certified public accountants, architects, and real estate brokers.

Professional Negligence: Negligence related to the conduct of professionals, such as nurses, physicians, lawyers, or financial advisors that falls below a certain standard.

Progressive Discipline: A method used by employers to discipline employees for infractions which may progressively lead to termination. It is a common provision found in collective bargaining agreements.

Prosecuting Attorney: Also known as the district attorney; the attorney responsible for bringing charges against criminal defendants. A public official appointed or elected.

Proximate Cause: A cause that is legally sufficient to result in liability.

Public Defender: An attorney who represents indigent criminal defendants and is appointed and paid by the state or government.

Punitive Damages: Damages awarded over and above actual damages for conduct that is egregious and willful; to punish the wrongdoer and deter such conduct.

Reasonable Accommodation: Any modification or adjustment to a job or the work environment that will enable a qualified applicant or employee with a disability to participate in the application process or to perform essential job functions. Reasonable accommodation also includes adjustments to assure that a qualified individual with a disability has rights and privileges in employment equal to those of employees without disabilities. (Department of Justice)

Registered Agent or Office: The person or business designated to receive notice when the corporation or company is a party in a legal action such as a lawsuit.

Res Ipsa Loquitur: The doctrine providing that the mere occurrence of injury raises an inference of negligence.

Respondeat Superior: The vicarious liability of the employer for the negligent acts of employees.

Respondent: Party answering the allegations brought in a complaint or pleading; or party against whom an appeal is made.

Right to Sue Letter: Issued by the Equal Employment Opportunity Commission (EEOC), allowing claimant to proceed to filing suit in a court of law based on a discriminatory action which falls under the purview of that Agency.

Root Cause Analysis: A process for identifying the basic or causal factors that underlies variation in performance, including the occurrence or possible occurrence of a Sentinel Event.

Safe Harbor: A safe harbor is a provision of a statute or a regulation that reduces or eliminates liability under the law, so long as an agreement or an arrangement meets the requirements of the safe harbor.

Sanction: That part of a law that imposes a penalty for its violation.

Sentinel Event: Defined by The Joint Commission as an unexpected occurrence involving death or serious physical injury, or the risk thereof.

Serious Reportable Events: An error in medical care that is identifiable, Never Event.

Sexual Discrimination: Discriminatory conduct, usually in the context of employment that excludes one sex for the benefit of the other.

Sexual Harassment: "(1973) A type of employment discrimination consisting in verbal or physical abuse of a sexual nature" (Black's Law Dictionary, 2010).

Shareholder: One who holds shares of stock in a corporation.

SOAP: Subjective, Objective, Assessment and Plan. A charting system used with POMR.

SOAPIE: Same as SOAP; with Intervention and Evaluation of care provided.

SOAPIER: Same as SOAPIE; some facilities have added R which stands for Revision.

Specified Term Employee: An employee hired for a specified period of time or fixed term.

Spoliation of Evidence: The intentional or negligent withholding, hiding, alteration or destruction of evidence relevant to a legal proceeding.

Standard of Care: The exercise of the same degree of knowledge, skill, and ability as an ordinarily careful professional would exercise under similar circumstances.

Standing: Requirement that person bringing an action has the right to bring such matters before the Court.

Stare Decisis: Case law that is upheld or followed by courts unless there is justification to decide otherwise.

Stark Act: The Stark law, often referred to as the anti-referral law, governs physician self referral for Medicare and Medicaid patients.

Statute of Frauds: A legal doctrine that requires certain contracts to be in writing signed by the parties. In the employment context, it is a contract that cannot be performed within a year.

Statute of Limitations: A time limitation within which a suit may be brought for an alleged wrong doing. Statutes of limitation vary depending upon the location of the lawsuit and the type of suit.

Subpoena: A document issued by an attorney in a particular case, a court or other authority such as a notary or licensing agency, compelling the appearance of a witness to give testimony at a judicial proceeding.

Subpoena duces tecum (with documents): A Subpoena that requires that you bring certain documents with you that are in your possession.

Summary Judgment Motion: The moving party (party requesting the motion) asks the judge to rule in their favor because there is no genuine issue of material fact.

Summons: A legal document informing the individual that an action has been taken against them and their rights thereof.

Thomas-Kilman Conflict Mode Instrument: A tool designed to assess an individual's behavior in conflict situations. The instrument defines five basic conflict management styles ranging from competitive to compromising.

Trier of Fact: The person who determines the facts in a legal proceeding, such as judge, jury, Board of Nursing, or arbitrator.

Venue: The appropriate place for a lawsuit to take place based upon certain factors which gave rise to the lawsuit or the location of the parties.

Voir Dire: ("Pronounced *vwahr deer* also *vor deer* or *vor dir*") "to speak the truth . . . A preliminary examination of a prospective juror by a judge or lawyer to decide whether the prospect is qualified and suitable to serve on a jury" (Black's, Law Dictionary, 2010, p. 1350).

Whistleblower or Qui Tam: An action under a statute that can be brought by an informer. In certain Qui Tam actions, a portion of the penalties, fines, awards can be awarded the whistleblower.

Workers' Compensation Laws: State statutory laws governing benefits and compensation for workplace injuries sustained by employees that arise out of or during employment. It is usually the exclusive remedy for employees when injured on the job.

INDEX